NINETEENTH-CENTURY
FRENCH SONG

NINETEENTH-CENTURY
FRENCH SONG

Fauré, Chausson, Duparc, and Debussy

BARBARA MEISTER

Indiana University Press   Bloomington & London

To my children

This book was brought to publication with the assistance
of a grant from the Andrew W. Mellon Foundation.

Library of Congress Cataloging in Publication Data

Meister, Barbara, 1932–
Nineteenth-century French song.

Bibliography: p.
Includes index of 1st lines.
1. Songs, French—History and criticism. 2. Fauré,
Gabriel Urbain, 1845–1924. Songs. 3. Chausson,
Ernest, 1855–1899. Songs. 4. Duparc, Henri, 1848–1933.
Songs. 5. Debussy, Claude, 1862–1918. Songs.
I. Title.
ML2827.M36   784'.3061   79-2171
ISBN 0-253-34075-6   1 2 3 4 5 84 83 82 81 80

In the great blue desert
We walk with God!
We walk with God!

Seule   Poem by Théophile Gautier
Alone   OPUS 3/1

Dans un baiser l'onde au rivage
Dit ses douleurs!
Pour consoler la fleur sauvage
L'aube à des pleurs.
Le vent du soir conte sa plainte
Aux vieux cyprès,
La tourterelle au térébinthe
Ses longs regrets.

Aux flots dormants quand tout repose,
Hors la douleur
La lune parle et dit la cause
De sa pâleur,
Ton dôme blanc,
Sainte Sophie
Parle au ciel bleu,
Et tout rêveur, le ciel confie
Son rêve à Dieu!

Arbre ou tombeau, colombe ou rose,
Onde ou rocher
Tout, ici-bas, a quelque chose
Pour s'épancher...
Moi je suis seule et rien au monde
Ne me répond!
Rien que ta voix morne et profonde,
Sombre Hellespont!

This is the first of Fauré's early songs in which hints of the composer's musical genius are to be found. Its minor modality automatically makes it sound more sophisticated (G minor is the key for high voice), as does the choice of a far more evocative text than those chosen for the first four songs.

The piano begins with tonic octaves, which might or might not be tolling bells, answered by short, gloomy phrases in the bass. The first phrase of the melodic line contains two important characteristic devices: the half-step rise and fall on "*au ri*vage," which creates a dissonance with the accompanying octave, and the cadence under "Dit ses douleurs!" which resolves first to an unexpected major VI chord (the standard false or deceptive cadence) and then to the minor I. This entire phrase is repeated up a third (on Bb) for the next lines. The half-

step rise and fall is part of the third melodic phrase, but here the harmony is consonant. The false-then-true cadence ends the final melodic segment. The same music is used for all three verses, but, since each segment is short and effective, one does not feel that the song is unduly repetitious.

> In a kiss the wave to the shore
> Tells of its sadness!
> To console the wild flower
> The dawn has some tears.
> The evening wind tells its woe
> To the old cypress,
> The turtle-dove to the turpentine tree
> Its long regrets,
> To the sleeping seas when all rest,
> Beyond sadness
> The moon speaks and tells the reason
> For its pallor,
> Its dome white,
> Saint Sophie
> Speaks to the blue sky,
> And, always the dreamer, the sky confides
> Its dream to God.
> Tree or tomb, dove or rose,
> Wave or rock,
> Everything here on earth has something
> To which to open its heart . . .
> I, I am alone and nothing in the world
> Responds to me,
> Nothing but the mournful and deep voice of the Hellespont!

Sérénade Toscane
Tuscan Serenade

Poem by Romain Bussine

OPUS 3/2

> O toi que berce un rêve enchanteur,
> Tu dors tranquille en ton lit solitaire,
> Eveille-toi, regarde le chanteur,
> Esclave de tes yeux, dans la nuit claire!
> Eveille-toi, mon âme, ma pensée,
> Entends ma voix par la brise emportée,
> Entends ma voix chanter!
> Entends ma voix pleurer, dans la rosée!
> Sous ta fenêtre en vain ma voix expire,
> Et chaque nuit je redis mon martyre,
> Sans autre abri que la voûte étoilée,
> Le vent brise ma voix et la nuit est glacée;
> Mon chant s'éteint en un accent suprême,
> Ma lèvre tremble en murmurant, je t'aime,
> Je ne peux plus chanter!

Ah! daigne te montrer! daigne apparaître!
Si j'étais sur que tu ne veux paraître
Je m'en irais, pour t'oublier, demander au sommeil
De me bercer jusqu'au matin vermeil,
De me bercer jusqu'à ne plus t'aimer!

Two of the most beautiful of Fauré's early songs "Sérénade Toscane" and "Après un Rêve," are settings of Italian poems translated into French by Romain Bussine (1821–1899), a singer and cofounder with Camille Saint-Saëns of the Société Nationale de Musique.

The "Serenade," the earlier of the two pieces, is the first of Fauré's songs in which the piano has an important melodic line. This melody, most often an echo of the singer's line, is skillfully used by the composer to modulate from one key to the next, and to provide structural unity when the voice has varying material.

There is another advance in this song, in that Fauré, instead of repeating the same music for all three sections, gives us a new melodic line for the final four lines of poetry.

The brief piano introduction establishes the tonic chord (C minor for high voice) and the gently rocking 9/8 rhythm. The loved one so wistfully petitioned might be asleep in a cradle, a hammock, or a gondola. The chords are strummed as though on a lute or guitar.

The voice enters with an octave interval:

O you whom an enchanting dream cradles,
You sleep tranquilly in your solitary bed,
Awaken, look at the singer,
Slave to your eyes, in the clear night!
Awaken, my soul, my thought,
Hear my voice carried by the breeze,
Hear my voice sing!
Hear my voice cry, in the rosy light!

As the poet begs his beloved to listen to him, he becomes more and more impassioned. The climactic *forte* is on the phrase with the highest note, "Entends ma voix chanter!" after which the less forceful "Entends ma voix pleurer" seems quite plaintive.

The second verse begins a little louder than the first:

Under your window my voice in vain expires,
And each night I repeat my martyrdom,
With no shelter other than the starry skies,
The wind breaks my voice and the night is icy;
My song is extinguished in a last tone,
My lips tremble while murmuring "I love you,"
I can sing no more!
Ah! deign to show yourself! deign to appear!

This time the climactic line is a despairing one—"Je ne peux plus chanter!" While its setting is identical to that in verse one, the deeper intensity of the words must be projected by the singer.

The final section is somewhat slower and a little more resigned:

If I were certain that you should never wish to appear
I would go away, in order to forget you, to demand of sleep
To cradle me until morning's golden light,
To cradle me until I no longer love you!

Once again the climax of the section is on the high A ("ou*blier*"), but it is a much subdued climax. During the last nine measures of the song the accompaniment has some interesting details: the V^7 over the tonic in the ninth measure before the end, the III^+ two bars later, the tonic major and III minor which follow, and—most effective—the raised seconds in measures four, three, and two before the final major close.

La Chanson du pêcheur (Lamento)   Poem by
Song of the Fisherman—Lament   Théophile Gautier
                                                      OPUS 4/1

Ma belle amie est morte,
Je pleurerai toujours!
Sous la tombe elle emporte
Mon âme et mes amours.
Dans le ciel sans m'attendre,
Elle s'en retourna,
L'ange qui l'emmena
Ne voulut pas me prendre.
Que mon sort est amer!
Ah! sans amour sans amour
S'en aller sur la mer!

La blanche créature
Est couchée au cercueil,
Comme dans la nature
Tout me paraît en deuil!
La colombe oubliée
Pleure et songe à l'absent.
Mon âme pleure et sent
Qu'elle est dépareillée!
Que mon sort est amer!
Ah! sans amour sans amour
S'en aller sur la mer!

Sur moi la nuit immense
Plane comme un lincuel,

Je chante ma romance
Que le ciel entend seul!
Ah! comme elle était belle, et combien je l'aimais!
Je n'aimerai jamais
Une femme autant qu'elle!
Que mon sort est amer!
Ah! sans amour sans amour
S'en aller sur la mer!

This little lament, while of the utmost simplicity, is really quite touching. Both words and music convey the grief of the fisherman, who is so sad and lonely on the vast sea, without his love.

After the piano's A minor arpeggio (in high voice) which concludes first on a VI chord (false cadence) and then resolves to the tonic, the singer has an unaccompanied *recitativo*. This pattern continues until bar eight, where the piano's triplet figure becomes a steady accompaniment.

Each of these *recitativo* lines has in its last few notes accidentals by which we are moved to the next key. The harmonic motion, which accelerates from every other bar to every bar under the *recitativos*, continues at a still greater pace after bar eight, and it is not until the end of the first verse ("S'en aller sur la mer!") that we return to the tonic. This motion, of course, lends interest and provides musical tension.

The words begin poignantly:

My beautiful love is dead,
I shall cry forever!
Into the grave she carries
My soul and my love.

It is here that the pace begins to quicken.

To heaven without waiting for me
She returned

Now the accompaniment goes into full swing:

The angel who led her away
Didn't want to take me

The sad refrain is supported by constantly shifting arpeggiated chords, many of which are diminished to provide facile modulation:

How bitter is my fate!
Ah! without love, without love
To wander on the sea!

The emotional high point of this section is found in the refrain, on the second "sans amour." The soft final line is woeful indeed, and the

minor scale and figure in the piano part reflect the mood with artless purity.

With the exception of the last line, the second verse has the same musical material as the first. The words are, of course, different:

> The white creature
> Is couched on the bier,
> How in nature
> Everything seems to me in mourning!
> The forgotten dove
> Cries and thinks of the absent one.
> My soul cries and feels
> That it is incomplete!

> Refrain

To lead us into the new material of the final section, Fauré takes us past the tonic under "S'en aller" to further modulations. This additional harmonic motion conveys the ever-increasing agitation and intensity expressed in the words:

> Upon me the vast night
> Hovers like a shroud,
> I sing my story
> Which only the sky hears!
> Oh how beautiful she was,
> And how I loved her!

Under this last line a *crescendo* has begun, leading to the passionate outcry—the most powerful moment in the song—which follows:

> I shall never love
> A woman as I loved her!

For the final repeat of the refrain, Fauré has found his way back to the harmonic setting of its other two statements, and the song finally ends on the tonic.

Lydia   Poem by Leconte de Lisle
                                                          OPUS 4/2

> Lydia sur tes roses joues
> Et sur ton col frais et si blanc,
> Roule étincelant
> L'or fluide que tu dénoues;
> Le jour qui luit est le meilleur,
> Oublions l'éternelle tombe,

Laisse tes baisers, tes baisers de colombe
Chanter sur ta lèvre en fleur, sur ta lèvre en fleur.

Un lys caché répand sans cesse
Une odeur divine en ton sein:
Les délices comme un essaim
Sortent de toi, jeune déesse.
Je t'aime et meurs, ô mes amours,
Mon âme en baisers m'est ravie!
O Lydia, rends-moi la vie,
Que je puisse mourir, mourir toujours!

This song contains a charming musical pun which is much easier to recognize in its original key (F major): if you play an octave from F to F using only white notes (no Bb) you have the so-called Lydian mode; in the fourth and fifth measures of the song Fauré raises the Bb to B♮, thus putting the song in that mode temporarily. Of course, ancient modes, like the modern major and minor, depend on their intervals, not their actual pitch, for their identity, so the pun is just as valid in the version for high voice (G major—here the necessary alteration is the C♯).

There are other antique touches throughout the song. Under "Laisse tes basiers," for instance, we have the progression D minor–C major (or E minor–D major in the transposition for high voice) for the flavor of olden days; the frequent use of simple four-part harmony adds to the effect.

The use of an antique mode and style is entirely suitable for a setting of a poem by Leconte de Lisle, for this poet, leader of the so-called Parnasse (a group of young poets who rejected the excesses of Romanticism and wanted a return to the purity and formalism of ancient Greece), looked back to the great Hellenistic Era for inspiration.

In this "gather-ye-rose-buds-while-ye-may" poem, he is somewhat less detached than is his wont, but the tight rhyme scheme (*abba, cddc, effe, ghhg*) is quite typical:

Lydia on your rosy cheeks
And on your neck so cool and white,
Rolls sparkling
The fluid gold that you give forth;
The day that is shining is the best,
Let us forget the eternal tomb,
Let your kisses, your dovelike kisses,
Sing on your blossoming lips, on your blossoming lips.

The music for the second verse is identical to that of the first:

A hidden lily ceaselessly exudes
A divine scent in your bosom;

Delights like a swarm
Emanate from you, young goddess.
I love you and die, oh my love,
My soul is carried away in kisses!
Oh Lydia, give me life
That I might die, die forever!

Chant d'automne   Poem by Charles Baudelaire
Song of Autumn   OPUS 5/1

Bientôt nous plongerons dans les froides ténèbres
Adieu, vive clarté de nos étés trop courts!
J'entends déjà tomber, avec un choc funèbre,
Le bois retentissant sur le pavé des cours.
J'écoute en fremissant chaque bûche qui tombe:
L'échafaud qu'on bâtit n'a pas d'écho plus sourd.
Mon esprit est pareil à la tour qui succombe
Sous les coups du bélier infatigable et lourd;
Il me semble, bercé par ce choc monotone
Qu'on cloue en grande hâte un cercueil quelque part!
Pour qui? c'etait hier l'été, voici l'automne!
Ce bruit mystérieux sonne comme un départ!
J'aime, de vos longs yeux la lumière verdâtre,
Douce beauté! mais aujourd'hui tout m'est amer
Et rien, ni votre amour, ni le boudoir, ni l'âtre,
Ne me vaut le soleil rayonnant sur la mer!

The extended piano prelude to this song is full of foreboding. The
tonic C minor octaves solemnly toll the passing hours as the rising
and falling figure, with its rhythmic hesitation, leads to a fading minor
arpeggio. After an ominous silence the octaves and figuration begin
again, but the arpeggio now leads to a dramatic diminished chord and
an intensification of the rising and falling triplet scheme. These triplets
fade into the rather bleak accompanying figure on the dominant, but
still in minor (the key for high voice is C minor).

The voice begins quietly:

Soon we shall plunge into the cold shadows

There is a big *crescendo* to a *forte* at "Adieu."

Farewell lively brightness of our too short summers!

The melodic line rises and falls dynamically, as it does in pitch. Surprisingly enough, however, the harmonic resolution under "trop
courts!" is to a consoling Bb major. The predominantly major modality
continues for the next seven bars, although the words are far from
cheerful:

I hear fall already, with a funereal blow,
The wood resounding on the pavement of the courtyards.

We now return to a predominantly minor modality:

Shuddering, I listen to each falling log;
The scaffold one builds has no more muffled an echo.

Singer and accompaniment are at full strength here, and the
piano part becomes more and more dramatic; but a diminuendo sets
in almost immediately. In fact, the dynamics for this entire section veer
rapidly from one extreme to another.

My spirit is like the tower, which succumbs
Under the indefatigable and heavy blows of the battering-ram;
It seems to me, rocked by the monotonous blows,
That someone in great haste nails a coffin somewhere!
For whom? . . .

After the G major arpeggio in the piano part, the song becomes
sweet and gentle:

. . . it was summer yesterday, here it is autumn!
The mysterious sound rings like a farewell!

The final section of this long, rambling song is so different from
the rest that it warrants an introduction of its own. The tempo is a bit
slower and the dynamic level quite subdued throughout. The piano
begins with a three-note melodic phrase (F, E, D for high voice), which
is given twice to two different harmonic accompaniments. The singer
echoes this melody, which later returns for piano alone, for singer and
piano in unison, and for singer alone. The supporting harmonies are
remarkably varied and the singer alters the rhythm, but the melody is
always easily identifiable. The words are sad but gentle:

I love the greenish light of your long eyes,
Sweet beauty! but today everything is bitter to me
And nothing, neither your love, nor the boudoir, nor the hearth,
Is worth to me the sun shining on the sea!

The entire final section has had C major as its tonal center. This
change to the parallel major adds to the meandering, loosely knit character of the song.

Rêve d'amour   Poem by Victor Hugo
Dream of Love   OPUS 5/2

S'il est un charmant gazon
Que le ciel arrose,

Où naisse en toute saison
Quelque fleur éclose,
Où l'on cueille à pleine main.
Lys, chevre-feuille et jasmin,
J'en veux faire le chemin
Où ton pied se pose.

S'il est un sein bien aimant,
Dont l'honneur dispose,
Dont le tendre dévouement
N'ait rien de morose,
Si toujours ce noble sein
Bat pour un digne dessein,
J'en veux faire le coussin
Où ton front se pose.

S'il est un rêve d'amour
Parfumé de rose,
Où l'on trouve chaque jour
Quelque douce chose,
Un rêve que Dieu bénit,
Où l'âme à l'âme s'unit,
Oh! J'en veux faire le nid
Où ton coeur se pose.

The poems of Victor Hugo seem to inspire in Fauré a gentle and simple musical response, for, with the exception of the piano introduction, this song is almost as naive and uncomplicated as Fauré's first three published songs, all of which use texts by Hugo.

The format of the song is a common one: an eight-bar piano introduction and sixteen-measure verse which are repeated in their entirety, a second repeat of the piano solo and first eight bars after the vocal entry, with new material for the closing eight bars of the verse, and a final repeat of the piano solo as a postlude. This tight structural unity is in marked contrast to the preceding song, which wanders freely from section to section. The sentiments of the poem are well suited to this type of treatment, as is the rhyme scheme: *abab, cccb, abab, cccb, dbdb, eeeb*. Note that of the twenty-four lines, nine end with the "ose" sound. Hugo was a born rhymer who was able to extemporize for hours in poetic form, so it was no problem for him to find countless words with the same final sound.

The opening bars of the introduction have a nice touch, typical of Fauré's maturing harmonic style: the first measure seems to be a G^7 which should lead to C (this analysis is based on the key for high voice, F major) but instead leads to the tonic. There is, however, no feeling of resolution on the second measure, which leads to further modulation (D minor^7–G minor, A^7–B♭), and it is not until the real V^7–I in measures 7–8 that we are certain of our tonal center.

Nous vivons sur l'abîme,
Au sein de l'infini,
Des flots rasant la cime,
Dans le grand désert bleu
Nous marchons avec Dieu!
Nous marchons avec Dieu!

Here we have another example of Fauré's youthful efforts in the song form. Once again the same music is used for each of the three verses of the poem despite the wistfulness of the words in the middle verse. The piano figure is rhythmically uniform from beginning to end; it is obvious that the accompaniment—and it is never more than sheer accompaniment—is supposed to suggest the ocean's waves.

The simplicity of the harmonic scheme is indicated by the pedal instruction: one pedal for each measure. Some harmonic interest is created by the use of the tonic (F major for high voice) as a pedal point for several measures and by the double-stemmed bass notes in the measures that follow.

The melodic line is equally naive, beginning with the tonic triad and ending with the tonic scale. The climax in verses one and three is the result of the successive climbs to C, D, Eb, E♮ and finally F on the words "argent," "la Sonde," "brûlé," "gelé," and "Jusqu'au pôle gelé" in verse one and their counterparts in verse three. In deference to the different mood in verse two, instead of a climax at this point there is a *rallentando*.

On the water blue and deep,
We go traveling
Circling the world
In a silvery wake,
From the islands of the Sonde,
From the Indies with their burning skies,
To the frozen pole,
To the frozen pole.

We think of the land
We constantly flee,
Of our old mother,
Of our young loves.
But the light waves
With their sweet refrain,
Lull our chagrin,
Lull our chagrin.

Sublime existence,
Rocked by our nest,
We live on the abyss,
In the bosom of the infinite
Of the billows scraping the peaks,

truncated final verse. Its harmonies are simple, with only the augmented chord in measure three (not counting the introduction) to give a
slight Gallic flavor. The melodic line flows along pleasantly with no
competition from the completely subordinate piano part.

Alone, together, enraptured, singing,
How in love they are;
How they reap the spring that God sows,
What sparkling laughter in these shadows,
Once filled with pale faces and somber hearts.
They are newly married,
They send each other charming various cries
Of joy, fresh echoes intermingled in the trembling wind,
Gaiety to which the dark convent adds zest,
Alone, together, enraptured, singing,
How in love they are;
How they reap the spring that God sows,
What sparkling laughter in these shadows,
They pluck the jasmins on the stones
Where the Abbess joined her hands in prayer,
They seek each other, chase each other
One feels dawning love grow in the night
Of the old cloister.
They go on, billing and cooing, they adore one another
They embrace at every moment, then again
Under the columns, the arches, the marbles:
It is the story of birds in the trees.

Les Matelots   Poem by Théophile Gautier
The Sailors   OPUS 2/2

Sur l'eau bleue et profonde,
Nous allons voyageant,
Environnant le monde
D'un sillage d'argent,
Des îles de la Sonde,
De l'Inde au ciel brûlé,
Jusqu'au pôle gelé,
Jusqu'au pôle gelé!

Nous pensons à la terre
Que nous fuyons toujours,
A notre vieille mère,
A nos jeunes amours.
Mais la vague légère
Avec son doux refrain,
Endort notre chagrin,
Endort notre chagrin!

Existence sublime,
Bercés par notre nid,

at the age of twenty-five, studying briefly with Massenet, but left to become a private student of César Franck. Since he was killed in a bicycling accident in 1899, his life span as a composer was tragically short. His best known works are his songs, *Poème* for violin and orchestra, *Concerto* for violin, piano, and string quartet, and *Chanson Perpetuelle* for voice and orchestra.

Henri Duparc (1848–1933)

Duparc, another student of César Franck, also came to music relatively late in life. His penchant for extreme self-criticism led him to destroy almost everything he wrote, including some compositions that were highly valued by Franck and other composers of eminence. Virtually all that remains of his *oeuvre* are two orchestral works (a symphonic poem, *Lenore,* and *Aux Etoiles,* an orchestral nocturne), a vocal duet ("La Fuite"), and the songs. In 1885 a strange mental collapse left him incapable of further work. He left Paris and went to Switzerland where for the next forty-eight years he lived a reclusive and nonmusical life.

Claude Debussy (1862–1918)

The most important of the composers in our discussion is, of course, Claude Debussy. His background was that of the comfortable bourgeois, and although his family was not particularly musical, they in no way objected to his pursuit of his musical goals. He had the normal training at the Paris Conservatoire, finally receiving its highest accolade, the Grand Prix de Rome.

Like Fauré, he led a quiet life devoted to his family and his work. He preferred the company of artists and writers to that of musicians and had considerable literary talent himself (see the songs for which he wrote his own poems: "De Grève," "De Rêve," "De Fleurs," "De Soir," and "Noël des Enfants qui n'ont plus de maisons"). He wrote lively, witty musical criticism, and appreciated the subtle poetry of Verlaine, Baudelaire, and Mallarmé.

His most important works include the opera *Pelléas et Mélisande,* the orchestral *Nocturnes, La Mer, Prélude à l'après-midi d'un faune* and *Images* (of which *Iberia* is a section), and the String Quartet. He brought a whole new vocabulary to solo piano literature, and his *Préludes, Images, Children's Corner, Pour le Piano, Estampes,* and *Arabesques* have become staples of the repertoire.

Gabriel Fauré

Le Papillon et la fleur   Poem by Victor Hugo
The Butterfly and the Flower   OPUS 1/1

La pauvre fleur disait au papillon céleste:
Ne fuis pas! . . .
Vois comme nos destins sont différents, je reste
Tu t'en vas!
Pourtant nous nous aimons, nous vivons sans les hommes,
Et loin d'eux!
Et nous nous ressemblons et l'on dit que nous sommes
Fleurs tous deux!

Mais hélas, l'air t'emporte et la terre m'enchaine,
Sort cruel!
Je voudrais embaumer ton vol de mon haleine,
Dans le ciel!
Mais non, tu vas trop loin, parmi des fleurs sans nombre,
Vous fuyez!
Et moi je reste seule à voir tourner mon ombre
A mes pieds!

Tu fuis, puis tu reviens, puis tu t'en vas encore
Luire ailleurs!
Aussi me trouves-tu toujours à chaque aurore
Tout en pleurs!
Ah! pour que notre amour coule des jours fidèles,
O mon roi!
Prends comme moi racine ou donne-moi des ailes
Comme à toi!

This first published work by Fauré is little more than a salon piece.
Its arch text by Victor Hugo is set to a banal um-pah-pah accompaniment with piano interludes of equally limited imagination. Nowhere
does one find the inimitable touch of the master Fauré was to become.
One need only compare the opening bars of the piano introduction,
which are obviously meant to suggest the free-flying butterfly, to the

first section of Robert Schumann's piano piece "Papillons," which happens to be in the same key and is also an early work (Opus II), to see how ordinary the Fauré portrayal is.

Analysis of the basically I–IV°–V–I harmonies seems unnecessary, and the composer has clearly indicated where the expressive moments are. One must avoid a coy delivery of the words since they already veer too strongly in that direction.

The poor flower said to the celestial butterfly:
Don't fly away! . . .
See how our destinies are different, I stay
You go away!
Yet we love one another, we live without men,
And far from them!
And we look alike and it is said that
We are both flowers!

But alas, the air carries you away and the earth chains me,
Cruel fate!
I should like to perfume your flight with my breath
In the sky!
But no, you go too far, among countless flowers,
You fly!
And I remain alone watching my shadow turn
At my feet!

You fly, but you return, then you go again
To shine elsewhere!
Thus you always find me at each dawn
All in tears.
Ah! that our love might flow in faithful days,
O my king!
Take root like me or give me wings
Like you!

Mai   Poem by Victor Hugo
May   OPUS 1/2

Puisque Mai tout en fleurs dans les prés nous réclame,
Viens, ne te lasse pas de mêler à ton âme
La campagne, les bois, les ombrages charmants,
Les larges clairs de lune au bord des flots dormants;
Le sentier qui finit où le chemin commence
Et, l'air et le printemps, et l'horizon immense,
L'horizon que ce monde attache humble et joyeux,
Comme une lèvre au bas de la robe des cieux.

Viens, et que le regard des pudiques étoiles,
Qui tombe sur la terre à travers tant de voiles
Que l'arbre pénétré de parfums et de chants,

Que le souffle embrasé de midi dans les champs;
Et l'ombre et le soleil, et l'onde, et la verdure,
Et le rayonnement de toute la nature
Fassent épanouir comme une double fleur,
La beauté sur ton front et l'amour dans ton coeur!

While far from strikingly original, this second published song of Fauré's is much less cloying than its predecessor. This is partly attributable to the more direct, less "cute" text chosen for this piece.

It is clear that Fauré has not yet found his unique harmonic style, but, despite the ordinary V^7–I cadences, there are pleasant harmonic touches in many places. At no point does the piano emerge from its role as mild-mannered accompanist to the gentle, uncomplicated vocal line.

We begin with a two-bar introduction in which the G major tonality (original key) is established. The singer enters:

Since May, all in bloom in the fields, calls us,
Come, don't tarry in intermingling in your soul
The countryside, the woods, the charming shadows,
The great moonlights at the banks of sleeping waters;

At this point the harmonies become richer and more complex: we have G minor to Bb major, then G minor to a diminished chord with a major third, then F to an augmented F and a false cadence to E minor. The words up to this cadence have been:

The path which ends where the road begins
And the air and the springtime, and the immense horizon,

A *crescendo* builds to a small climax at "le printemps" on the augmented chord, but a *decrescendo* and *rallentando* pull us back for the E minor measure. A new and more important *crescendo* builds to a *forte* on "Comme une lèvre," where we have the highest note of the piece.

The horizon which this world presses, humble and joyous,
Like a lip at the bottom of the robes of the skies.

Another *rallentando* and *decrescendo* now bring us back to the original key, and the entire song is sung again to new words:

Come, and let the glance of the bashful stars,
Which falls on earth through so many veils,
Let the tree impregnated with perfumes and songs,
Let the breeze embraced by noon in the fields;
And the shadow and the sun, and the wave, and the greenness,
And the glow of all nature
Cause to bloom like a double flower,
The beauty of your face and the love in your heart.

In this second verse the words form a verbal *stretto,* as example piles upon example of nature's wonders. This makes the climax at "La beauté sur ton front" even more convincing than its counterpart in the first verse.

Note: In the edition of Fauré songs published by Edward B. Marks Music Corporation there is a misprint in measure 22: the D♮ should be a D♭, as it is in the comparable place in the recapitulation.

Dans les ruines d'une abbaye   Poem by Victor Hugo
In the Ruins of an Abbey   OPUS 2/1

Seuls, tous deux, ravis, chantants, comme on s'aime;
Comme on cueille le printemps que Dieu sème,
Quels rires étincelants dans ces ombres,
Jadis pleines de fronts blancs, de coeurs sombres.
On est tout frais mariés,
On s'envoie, les charmants cris variés
De la joie frais échos mêlés au vent qui frissonne,
Gaîté que le noir couvent assaisonne,
Seuls tous deux ravis, chantants, comme on s'aime,
Comme on cueille le printemps que Dieu sème,
Quels rires étincelants dans ces ombres,
Jadis pleines de fronts blancs, de coeurs sombres.
On effeuille des jasmins sur la pierre
Où l'abbesse joint les mains en prière,
On se cherche, on se poursuit
On sent croître ton aube amour dans la nuit
Du vieux cloître.
On s'en va se becquetant, on s'adore.
On s'embrasse à chaque instant, puis encore,
Sous les piliers, les arceaux, et les marbres:
C'est l'histoire des oiseaux dans les arbres.

Since the twenty songs which constitute Fauré's Op. 1 through 8 all appeared before the composer's twentieth birthday (1865), it is not surprising that most of them are somewhat derivative efforts which do not display the unique style Fauré was to develop later.

It is interesting that several of these early songs are settings of poems by Victor Hugo (1802–1885), probably the most famous nineteenth-century Romantic poet in all France. Hugo's output was enormous and embraced many styles. At his best he was a powerful and dramatic writer, at his worst a facile versifier who sinks almost to the level of doggerel.

The structure of this song is dictated by the poem—thirty-two measures for verse one (after the two-bar introduction) repeated *in toto* for verse two, with the first sixteen bars repeated once again for the

Dreyfus in particular and the Jews in general, and the latter ready to come to Dreyfus' defense. Other controversies over Church-State relations, income tax, Labor's right to strike, alliance with England, fear of German might, and so forth raged as political and social unrest continued to characterize French society right up to the outbreak of World War I.

We have saved for last the musical influences on the composers to be studied. First we must note a powerful negative influence: having already produced many of his masterpieces by the year 1857, Richard Wagner was at that time at work on *Tristan and Isolde*. By and large the French composers rejected his aesthetic with its huge orchestra, extended forms, grandiose concepts and superhuman pretensions. Debussy even parodied the love-music of Tristan in his "Golliwog's Cake-Walk."

The most immediate positive influence on our composers was the Belgian César Franck (1822–1890), whose extensive use of chromaticism and augmented chords and intervals became a trademark of French music. Before Franck we have Hector Berlioz (1803–1869) and Charles Gounod (1818–1893), whose *Faust* appeared in 1858. Through these composers we can trace the particularly Gallic flavor that finds expression in the sensuous yet delicate art songs of Fauré, Duparc, Chausson and Debussy.

Gabriel Fauré (1845–1924)

Gabriel Fauré was born in 1845. His musical gifts were recognized when he was quite young and he was sent to study in Paris. While still at L'École Niedermeyer he met Saint-Saëns, who introduced him to the works of Liszt and Wagner. By the time he was twenty years old he had published twenty songs and three *Songs without Words* for piano.

After graduating from L'École Niedermeyer, Fauré worked as an organist. He served in the army during the Franco-Prussian War and later return to Paris to teach in L'École Niedermeyer. He lived a quiet life, marked by the success of some of his works (in particular the *Requiem*) and the failure of others. When not quite sixty years of age he began to grow deaf, and by 1920 he was forced to resign his position as Director of the Conservatoire. Despite this handicap several of his important chamber works date from 1920 to 1924.

Ernest Chausson (1855–1899)

Chausson is one of the few composers of note to have begun the serious study of music as an adult. He entered the Paris Conservatoire

the insistence on painting exactly what they saw rather than what they were expected to see, and the nondidactic, nonmoralistic detachment so characteristic of all the arts of this period.

Although the artists of this time were essentially nonpolitical, no picture of the era would be complete without a brief word on its social and political background. It is easiest to begin at the end, for the period is brought to an abrupt close by the beginning of World War I. Chausson died at the age of forty-four in 1899; although Duparc lived until 1933 he had ceased to compose long before 1914; Debussy's creative powers were drained by his illness and the trauma of war, and his death came in 1918. Only Fauré continued to work after our cutoff date, but after 1910 there is a marked decline in the strength and originality of his songs.

Since the earliest works in our study—Fauré's first twenty songs— were published in 1865, we shall use this date as our historical beginning. At that precise moment the Second Empire, the reestablishment under Louis-Napoléon (or Napoléon III, as he was called) of his uncle Napoléon I's Empire, was in its liberal phase. Responding to pressure, the Emperor had begun to move towards parliamentary government at home and less aggressive attitudes abroad. Nevertheless the bourgeoisie was still agitating for a Republican form of government. In 1867 the misguided attempt to set up a French-controlled Empire in Mexico failed, and the unfortunate Emperor Maximilian was executed. The weakness of Napoléon III's financial and military position was made apparent by his inability to defend or avenge Maximilian, and the war with Prussia and subsequent downfall of the Second Empire soon followed (1870–1871).

The Franco-Prussian war was a complete disaster for France. Paris was under siege for four months and there was no real government to direct the armies or negotiate effectively with the powerful Bismarck. Out of the turmoil eventually there emerged a Constitution (1875), a Republic, and finally peace. Too many political issues had been left unresolved for there to be real stability, however, and as various factions fought among themselves General Boulanger, the archetypical man-on-a-white-horse, rose to prominence advocating a war of revenge against Prussia (1886). The military dictatorship he wanted was narrowly avoided, and the threat rallied moderate Republicans to new efforts at genuine stability.

The next severely disruptive political issue in this era was the Dreyfus case, in which a Jewish army officer was falsely accused of selling information to the Germans. Emile Zola's famous *J'accuse* was the literary response to this crisis, which almost resulted in civil war. Conservatives and Liberals were polarized, with the former against

Sully-Prudhomme, and others—all share this aesthetic to a large degree.

From time to time the composers under discussion chose older texts for their songs. Many of Fauré's early songs are settings of Romantic poems by Victor Hugo; for one song he used a quatrain from *Le Bourgeois Gentilhomme* by the 17th century playwright Molière; Debussy went back to the pre-Classic poems of François Villon, Charles d'Orléans, and Tristan l'Hermite; Duparc used a translation of an elegy by Thomas Moore for his song "Elégie"; and Chausson set Maurice Bouchor's translations from Shakespeare to music.

In one instance the influence of an artist on a poet must be noted. Verlaine's entire collection *Les Fêtes Galantes* from which Fauré chose three, and Debussy eight poems as texts (including the early songs "Mandolines" and "Pantomime") was inspired by an exhibit of the paintings of Watteau. Indeed, Debussy liked one of these poems—"Clair de lune"—so well that he wrote two songs to it!

Other nonliterary events often loomed important in the genesis of these songs. The paintings of Whistler, first seen in Paris in that fateful year 1857, captivated the imaginations of Baudelaire and, much later, Debussy. Javanese and other exotic music inspired Debussy to experiment with pentatonic and other non-European scales and figures. By the turn of the century elements of Afro-American jazz rhythms had begun to find their way to France via New Orleans, and one hears the barest hints of this flavor in some of Debussy's later songs.

With Paris the center of creative life, there was constant cross-fertilization among the artistic, literary and musical circles. In 1863, a date as significant for painting as 1857 is for literature, the so-called *Salon des Refusés,* Salon of the Rejected Ones, exhibited paintings turned away by the Royal Academy, including three masterpieces by Manet. The most controversial of these works was *Le Déjeuner sur l'Herbe,* which shows two fully clothed men picnicking in a park with two women, one nude, the other scantily dressed. Certainly nudes were no novelty in painting; what was new and scandalous was the moral detachment, the lack of historical or allegorical disguise, the freedom from judgmental platitudes. This is, of course, the attitude of the Symbolist poets and, by association, the composers who used their poems as texts for art songs.

After Manet we may list the dozen or so painters who left the studio to paint *en plein air,* their backgrounds and subjects alike saturated with sunlight. Known in general as Impressionists, they include some of the most familiar figures in the art world: Monet, Dégas, Cézanne, Renoir, Seurat, Morisot, Sisley, Pissarro, Van Gogh, and Gauguin. In these painters we find the pantheistic response to nature,

INTRODUCTION

In 1857 two major literary events occurred in Paris: the much awaited publication of Gustave Flaubert's novel *Madame Bovary* and the somewhat startling appearance of Charles Baudelaire's collection of poetry, *Les Fleurs du Mal*. These two works presaged the era which many consider to have been France's artistic prime, the period of the Symbolist poets, Impressionist painters, and the composers whose songs are the subject of this book—Gabriel Fauré (1845–1924), Henri Duparc (1848–1933), Ernest Chausson (1855–1899), and Claude Debussy (1862–1918).

Since the writer of songs must deal with words as well as music, the literary climate of a period is one of the basic factors in its song style. That this climate was influenced by—nay, overwhelmed by—the two seminal works mentioned above is undeniable. Both Flaubert and Baudelaire rejected the Romantic idea of Art-at-the-service-of-social-good in favor of the purity of Art-for-art's sake; both aimed for scientific precision in the expression of the most ephemeral poetic experience; both strove for an objective, detached portrayal of the most intimate personal thoughts and feelings. This aesthetic differs considerably from the spontaneous, subjective effusions of the Romantics.

Throughout the masterpieces of Flaubert and Baudelaire, one feels the "climate of delicate universal analogy"[1] that permeates and characterizes Symbolism, with its "capacity to disperse the soul gently over nature"[2] and its concept of the "correspondence" of all things. The poets whose works are most frequently used as texts for the songs discussed in this study—Paul Verlaine, Théophile Gautier, Leconte de Lisle, Théodore de Banville, Armand Silvestre, Villiers de l'Isle Adam,

1. Cohn, Robert Greer, *The Writer's Way in France* (Philadelphia: University of Pennsylvania Press, 1960), p. 208.
2. Ibid., p. 206.

emphasizing the meaning of the original words rather than their meter. No attempt has been made to provide singable or rhymed translations. In a large number of cases the texts have not previously been translated.

The accompaniment of each song has been analyzed harmonically, not as an exercise in analysis but to point out to the accompanist special effects in the piano part, moments of particular beauty or power. Since most of these songs are a genuine partnership between singer and pianist, the care with which the latter approaches his part is crucial to the success of the performance.

While part of this literature is often heard in song recitals, many of the finest songs are completely overlooked in favor of the dozen or so best-known pieces. A case in point is Fauré's ten-song cycle *La Chanson d'Eve,* which, despite its high artistic level, is scarcely known at this time. This is undoubtedly due to the fact that it is not included in any of the collections, nor does the French edition in which it is available provide English texts. Enterprising recitalists will find herein some very interesting program ideas!

To help singers whose knowledge of the French language is less than complete, the author has discussed peculiarities of pronunciation and unusual derivations of words where pertinent to the understanding of a song. Where a poem has historical significance, when it is associated with an important event in the life of the poet, any piece of information that might enhance understanding and interpretation has been included.

PREFACE

In no area of the art song does one find a more felicitous union of words and music than in the two hundred or so *mélodies* of Fauré, Chausson, Duparc, and Debussy. These four composers brought to the magnificent poetry of their contemporaries, Verlaine, Gautier, Baudelaire, Mallarmé, Leconte de Lisle, and others, the delicacy, sensitivity, and voluptuousness that characterize French music of this era from 1865 to 1914.

This book is a comprehensive study of the entire body of songs for solo voice and piano accompaniment by these four composers. From the tentative efforts of Fauré's Opus 1/1, through his masterful middle years to the waning powers of his Opus 118, each of his ninety-seven songs is explored. The meager, but marvelous output of Duparc, the thirty-four songs of Chausson, and the fifty-six *mélodies* of Debussy—every example of this remarkable repertoire is described, analyzed, and assessed.

It is the author's intention to have included in this study every published song for solo voice and piano by each of the four composers. In some instances, publishers have included in their collections songs originally composed for voice and orchestra. Unless these adaptations work exceptionally well, it has been decided to eliminate them from this discussion on the grounds that, with the enormous genuine repertoire at our disposal, it seems foolish to program less effective piano reductions. Hence, *Chanson Perpetuelle* by Chausson, Lia's Air or Azael's Air from *L'Enfant prodigue* by Debussy, or the excerpts from Fauré's *Shylock*, which appear in various collections for solo voice and piano, will not be found.

The purpose of this undertaking is to increase performers' and listeners' understanding and appreciation of this literature. With this object in mind the author has given her own translations for each text,

| Les Mirages | 160 | L'Horizon Chimérique | 171 |
| C'est la Paix! | 169 | | |

Ernest Chausson

Nanny	178	La Caravane	202
Le Charme	179	Les Morts	204
Les Papillons	180	Le Temps des lilas	206
La Dernière feuille	182	Serres chaudes	208
Sérénade italienne	183	Les Heures	219
Hébé	184	Ballade	220
Le Colibri	186	Les Couronnes	223
Nocturne	188	Chanson de Clown	224
Amour d'antan	189	Chanson d'amour	226
Printemps triste	190	Chanson d'Ophélie	228
Nos souvenirs	192	La Chanson bien douce	230
Apaisement	194	Le Chevalier Malheur	232
Sérénade	196	Cantique à l'épouse	234
L'Aveu	198	Dans la forêt du charms et de	
La Cigale	200	l'enchantement	236

Henri Duparc

Chanson triste	239	Sérénade florentine	256
Romance de Mignon	241	Le Manoir de Rosamonde	257
Sérénade	243	Testament	259
Soupir	245	Phidylé	261
Le Galop	247	Lamento	264
L'Invitation au voyage	249	Elégie	266
La Vague et la cloche	252	La Vie antérieure	268
Extase	255	Au pays où se fait la guerre	270

Claude Debussy

Nuit d'étoiles	274	Ariettes oubliées	307
Beau soir	276	Deux Romances	322
Fleur des blés	277	Les Angélus	326
Mandoline	279	Dans le jardin	327
Pantomime	281	La Mer est plus belle	330
Clair de lune	283	Le Son du cor s'afflige	332
Pierrot	284	L'Echelonnement des haies	335
Apparition	285	Fêtes galantes I	337
Zéphyr	287	Proses lyriques	342
Rondeau	288	Chansons de Bilitis	355
La Belle au bois dormant	290	Fêtes galantes II	363
Voici que le printemps	292	Trois chansons de France	370
Paysage sentimental	294	Le Promenoir des deux amants	376
Le Balcon	296	Trois Ballades de François Villon	379
Harmonie du soir	299	Trois Chansons de Mallarmé, 1913	389
Le Jet d'eau	301	Noël des enfants qui n'ont plus	
Recueillement	303	de maisons	395
La Mort des amants	305		

Bibliography 399   Index of First Lines 400

Contents

Preface vii   Introduction ix

Gabriel Fauré

Le Papillon et la fleur	1	Le Pays des rêves	59
Mai	2	Les Roses d'Ispahan	62
Dans les ruines d'une abbaye	4	Noël	64
Les Matelots	5	Nocturne	66
Seule	7	Les Présents	67
Sérénade Toscane	8	Clair de lune	69
La Chanson du pêcheur	10	Larmes	70
Lydia	12	Au cimetière	72
Chant d'automne	14	Spleen	75
Rêve d'amour	15	La Rose	77
L'Absent	18	Mandoline	79
Aubade	20	En sourdine	81
Tristesse	21	Green	83
Sylvie	23	A Clymène	85
Après un rêve	25	C'est l'extase	87
Hymne	27	En prière	89
Barcarolle	29	*La Bonne Chanson*	91
Au bord de l'eau	30	Sérénade	108
La Rançon	32	Le Parfum impérissable	109
Ici-bas !	34	Arpège	111
Nell	35	Prison	113
Le Voyageur	37	Soir	116
Automne	39	Dans la forêt de Septembre	117
Pòeme d'un jour	41	La Fleur qui va sur l'eau	120
Les Berceaux	45	Accompagnement	123
Notre amour	47	Le plus doux chemin	126
Le Secret	49	Le Ramier	127
Chanson d'amour	51	Le Don silencieux	129
La Fée aux chansons	53	Chanson	130
Aurore	55	*La Chanson d'Eve*	132
Fleur jetée	57	*Le Jardin Clos*	149

As though in compensation for the harmonic complexity of the piano's solo, the melodic line is strictly held to F major for the first eight bars. In the second half of the verse (under "main" and "feuille"), augmented chords lead to a modulation to G minor, but we are immediately brought back to the tonic by a good old-fashioned V–I in the last line.

The words for the first verse are:

If there is a charming lawn
Which the sky moistens,
Where in each season is born
Some flower that blooms,
Where one gathers freely
Lilies, honey-suckle and jasmin,
I would make of it the path
On which your foot treads.

Verse two:

If there is a very loving breast
Disposed to honor,
Whose tender devotion
Has nothing of the morose,
If always this noble breast
Beats with worthy design,
I would make of it the cushion
On which your forehead rests.

Verse three:

If there is a dream of love
Perfumed with roses,
In which one finds each day
Some sweet thing,
A dream that God blesses,
Where soul to soul is united,
Oh! I would make of it the nest
In which your heart rests.

The dynamics in the first two verses are subdued and almost monochromatic. In the third verse the tempo is slower, and more dynamic emphasis is given to the rising and falling melodic line. The last eight bars of the melody, with their wider leaps and expressive chromaticisms, are far more intense than the comparable places in the first two sections; nevertheless the dynamic range is still modest.

L'Absent   Poem by Victor Hugo

The Absent One   OPUS 5/3

Sentiers où l'herbe se balance,
Vallons, côteaux, bois chevelus,
Pourquoi ce deuil et ce silence?
"Celui qui venait ne vient plus!"

Pourquoi personne à ta fenêtre?
Et pourquoi ton jardin sans fleurs?
O maison où donc est ton maître?
"Je ne sais pas! il est ailleurs."

Chien, veille au logis!
"Pourquoi faire? La maison est vide, à present!"
Enfant qui pleures-tu? "Mon père!"
Femme, qui pleures-tu? "L'absent!"

Où donc est-il allé? "Dans l'ombre!"
Flots qui gémissez sur l'écueil,
D'où venez-vous? "Du bagne sombre!"
Et qu'apportez-vous? "Un cercueil!"

The quiet dignity of this song gives it considerable strength and sets it apart from the eleven early songs by Fauré already discussed. This is partly due to the poem, which has more philosophical overtones than most because it deals with the death of a whole human being, not just a one-dimensional "lover."

The piano begins quietly with a march-like series of Ab–G chords. The main key (for high voice) is C minor, but the opening bars focus on Ab and it is not until measure seven, under "chevel*us*," that the C minor tonality is made clear. Over this continuing rhythmic figure the voice enters:

Paths where the grass sways,
Valleys, hillsides, mossy trees,
Why this mourning and this silence?

After its gentle entrance, the voice begins a *crescendo*. When the vocal line breaks off after the question, the *crescendo* is continued to a *forte* by the piano. There is a sudden *piano* for the sad answer to the question (the instruction comes later for the piano, but obviously the accompaniment must accommodate itself to the singer's dynamics here)—

"He who came here comes no more!"

This line is delivered on only two notes. The near monotone and sudden quiet create a dirgelike effect. The brief piano interlude which follows moves us up a fourth to a new tonal center, where the accompanying figure and melodic phrase of the opening section are repeated for the first two lines:

> Why is there no one at your window?
> And why is your garden without flowers?

For the next line,

> O house, where then is your master?

Fauré brings us back to C minor, but not for long, for constant modulation brings us to E♭, the relative major, for the plaintive "Je ne sais pas!"

> I do not know! he is elsewhere."

The next section is less inspired harmonically, with a simple triplet figure supporting the melody in broken major chords:

> Dog! guard the home!
> "For what reason?
> The house is empty now!"

A nice enharmonic change (C♯–D♭ in the bass) leads to a G♭ tonal center for the beginning of the next quatrain:

> Child, for whom do you weep?
> "My father."
> Wife, for whom do you weep?
> "The absent one!"

Startling momentary dissonances created by suspensions (E♭♭ against D♭ under the first "pleures" and two measures later, in the accompaniment, E♭ against D under the second "pleures") emphasize the grief behind these simple words. This is a foretaste of the harsher, actual dissonances in the following section (see in particular the measure sixteen bars before the end). The emotional high points of the song are contained in the above lines, as the child and widow give their brief answers.

The piano interlude which follows is a stormy outburst, which finally settles on C minor as the central key. There is one fiery dissonance (D against E♭), and plenty of unleashed passion before the dynamics gradually become subdued and the return to the original introductory passage is accomplished.

> Where then has he gone?
> "Into the darkness."
> Billows which shudder against the reefs,
> From where do you come?

"From the dark dungeons!"
And what do you bring?
"A coffin."

This entire last section aims for a big dramatic effect. Emphasis on the descending line of the whole notes in the bass (from "D'où venez-vous?") helps create the desired intensity, as do the sombre chords and weighty silences. A full V^7–I cadence completes the song: Fauré had not as yet abandoned this closing formula.

Aubade
Morning Serenade

Poem by Louis Pomney
OPUS 6/1

L'oiseau dans le buisson
A salué l'aurore,
Et d'un pâle rayon
L'horizon se colore,
Voici le frais matin!
Pour voir les fleurs à la lumière,
S'ouvrir de toute part
Entr'ouvre ta paupière,
O vierge au doux regard!
O vierge au doux regard!

La voix de ton amant
A dissipé ton rêve.
Je vois ton rideau blanc
Qui tremble et se soulève,
D'amour signal charmant!

Descends sur ce tapis de mousse.
La brise est tiède encore,
Et la lumière est douce,
Accours, ô mon trésor!
Accours, ô mon trésor!

It would be hard to imagine a song of greater simplicity and purity than this charming expression of fresh, young love. The whole world seems virginal at dawn, when birds and flowers first awaken in the pale light of the new day, say the words; and the gentle chordal accompaniment offers its support for these sentiments.

The piano opens with the following chord progression: I, I^{7+}, IV^6, III. In effect this gives us a minor III chord where we might expect a V^7, a typical Fauré touch. The melody begins very simply in the tonic scale (G major for high voice) with a beautifully balanced rise and fall. In general the dynamics follow the rising and falling melodic phrases, although there are some moments of special emphasis (the strong ascending triad at "Voici le frais matin," for instance).

At the fifth measure the harmonies become more complex, with a diminished chord leading to E♭ minor and a second diminished chord leading to a beautifully altered V⁷ (the altered note is the A♭, which thus becomes part of a briefly chromatic bass line). In the next measure we return to simpler sounds, including a naive V⁷–I. The sudden unprepared shift to F major chords in the following bar provides a mildly dramatic moment. The chromatic rise in the accompaniment under the singer's "O vierge" is another focal point. A two-bar interlude, in which the piano has a simple melodic line of its own, leads us back for a full repeat of the entire song.

The bird in the thicket
Has greeted the dawn,
And with a pale ray
The horizon is colored,
Here is the cool morning!
To see the flowers in the light,
Opening up everywhere,
Open your eyes,
O virgin with the sweet expression!
O virgin with the sweet expression!

The voice of your lover
Has dispelled your dream.
I see your white curtain,
Which flutters and swells,
Charming signal of love!

Come down on this carpet of moss,
The breeze is still mild,
And the light is sweet,
Hurry, O my treasure!
Hurry, O my treasure!

Tristesse
Sadness

Poem by Théophile Gautier
OPUS 6/2

Avril est de retour,
La première des roses
De ses lèvres mi-closes,
Rit au premier beau jour,
La terre bien heureuse
S'ouvre et s'épanouit,
Tout aime, tout jouit,
Hélas! j'ai dans le coeur une tristesse affreuse!

Les buveurs en gaîté
Dans leurs chansons vermeilles

Célèbrent sous les treilles
Le vin et la beauté,
La musique joyeuses,
Avec leur rire clair,
S'éparpille dans l'air,
Hélas! j'ai dans le coeur une tristesse affreuse!

En déshabillé blanc
Les jeunes demoiselles
S'en vont sous les tonnelles
Au bras de leur galant,
La lune langoureuse
Argente leurs baisers longuement appuyés,
Hélas! j'ai dans le coeur une tristesse affreuse!

Moi je n'aime plus rien,
Ni l'homme ni la femme,
Ni mon corps ni mon âme,
Pas même mon vieux chien:
Allez dire qu'on creuse
Sous le pâle gazon
Une fosse sans nom,
Hélas! j'ai dans le coeur une tristesse affreuse!

This poignant little song certainly lives up to its name. Four times Fauré gives us the same plaintive thirteen bars of music—after the second repeat the very predictability becomes part of the woeful mood. Similar use is made of repetition by the poet, Théophile Gautier, who ends each of his four verses with the anguished refrain, "Hélas! j'ai dans le coeur une tristesse affreuse!" (Alas! I have in my heart, a dreadful sadness!)

The mode of the song is of course minor (D minor for high voice). Fauré has the piano begin with tonic chords alternating with II^{o7} chords. Although there are traditional V^7–I cadences at the final closes, Fauré often chooses interesting substitutes in the body of the song. In his mature songs he usually eschews the V^7–I cadence entirely.

The flatted D under "La première" begins a succession of lovely modulations, which rest briefly on the dominant (under "jour") and then go on to support the chromatic climb in the melody (under "jouit") and the stunning climax on "Hélas!" From this climactic moment we gradually reach the final cadence, by way of a beautiful diminished chord (after "coeur") and an even lovelier augmented chord (under "affreuse!"). The dynamic level remains high and there is considerable musical tension until the last two syllables of the refrain. Particularly effective are those moments where the piano remains on a higher note than the voice (under "coeur," "tristesse," and "affreuse").

April has returned,
The first of the roses
With half-open lips
Laughs at the first beautiful day,
The earth, very happy,
Opens and blooms,
Everyone loves, everyone revels,
Alas! I have in my heart, a dreadful sadness!

The gay drinkers
In their silvery songs
Celebrate under the arbors
Wine and beauty,
Joyous music,
With their bright laughter,
Is scattered in the air,
Alas! I have in my heart, a dreadful sadness!

In white informal robes
Young girls
Walk under the arbors
On their gallants' arms,
The languorous moon
Silvers their long-held kisses,
Alas! I have in my heart, a dreadful sadness!

I, I love nothing any more,
Neither man, nor woman,
Neither my body nor my soul,
Not even my old dog:
Go tell them to dig
Under the pale turf
A nameless grave,
Alas! I have in my heart, a dreadful sadness!

Sylvie
Sylvia

Poem by Paul Choudens
OPUS 6/3

Si tu veux savoir ma belle,
Où s'envole à tire d'aile,
L'oiseau qui chantait sur l'ormeau?
Je te le dirai, ma belle,
Il vole vers qui l'appelle,
Vers celui-là
Vers celui-là Qui l'aimera!
Vers celui-là Qui l'aimera!

Si tu veux savoir ma blonde,
Pourquoi sur terre et sur l'onde
La nuit tout s'anime et s'unit?
Je te le dirai ma blonde,
C'est qu'il est une heure au monde

Où loin du jour,
Où loin du jour veille l'amour!
Où loin du jour veille l'amour!

Si tu veux savoir Sylvie,
Pourquoi j'aime à la folie
Tes yeux brillants et langoureux?
Je te le dirai Sylvie.
C'est que sans toi dans la vie
Tout pour mon coeur,
Tout pour mon coeur, N'est que douleur.
Tout pour mon coeur, N'est que douleur.

The piano prelude, with which the song begins, gives every indication that we are to have a simple harmonic setting for this love letter to Sylvia. The tonic (Ab for high voice) and dominant chords alternate, and the only slightly unusual touch is the chromatic approach to the V⁷–I cadence two measures before the singer's entry.

When the voice enters it is with the same simple materials: scale fragments in the main key and a resting place right on home base. Suddenly, under "Il vole vers qui l'appelle," we have an extraordinary suspension over an unexpected chord formed by a diminished triad on Bb plus a major third (the Cb is the suspension which moves down to Bb in the next measure). After a climactic rise to Ab in the melodic line, which is supported by a Db major arpeggio, we have another startling measure (under the second "Vers celui-là"), which consists of a diminished chord on A♮ over the pedal point Db. This resolves to Bb major and allows the vocal line to carry us back to the tonic. These two harmonically rich moments stand out from the rest of the song, giving the entire section its emotional intensity.

The musical material is heard twice in its entirety. The beginning of the third verse is the same as in the first two, but by the singer's second measure we hear new musical ideas. The chromatic rise to E major in the third measure is especially lovely, and the dissonances under "Tes yeux brillants et langoureux" hark back to the complex measures in the earlier verses. By the climactic "pour mon coeur" Fauré has brought us back to the original melody, although the harmony doesn't fall into place until the word "coeur." From this point to the end we have a return to the original simpler harmonic setting.

A glance at the text will show why Fauré chose to change the music just when he did: the first two verses are abstractions, references to nature, circumlocutions, but in verse three the young lady is made the explicit subject of the poet's words. How much more effective this becomes when the music emphasizes the change, instead of repeating itself for each verse, as it does in so many of the earlier songs.

If you wish to know, my beauty,
Where at full speed flies
The bird who sang on the elm tree?
I shall tell you, my beauty,
He flies to whoever calls him
To him
To him who will love him!
To him who will love him!

If you wish to know, my fair one,
Why on land and sea
The night animates and unites everyone?
I shall tell you, my fair one,
It is because there is one hour in the world
When, far from day,
When far from day love awakens!
When far from day love awakens!

If you want to know, Sylvia,
Why I love to the point of madness
Your sparkling and languorous eyes?
I shall tell you, Sylvia,
It is because without you in life
Everything in my heart
Everything in my heart is but sadness!
Everything in my heart is but sadness!

In each verse the line with the most musical intensity, the highest melodic notes and the strongest dynamics, is the first of two repeated lines of verse (italicized in the above translation). The repetition of the verbal sounds is an important element in the overall dramatic effect.

Après un rêve   Poem by Romain Bussine
After a Dream   OPUS 7/1

Dans un sommeil que charmait ton image
Je rêvais le bonheur, ardent mirage.
Tes yeux étaient plus doux, ta voix pure et sonore,
Tu rayonnais comme un ciel éclairé par l'aurore;
Tu m'appelais et je quittais la terre
Pour m'enfuir avec toi vers la lumière,
Les cieux pour nous entr'ouvraient leurs nues,
Splendeurs inconnues, lueurs divines entrevues,
Hélas! Hélas, triste réveil des songes,
Je t'appelle, ô nuit, rends-moi tes mensonges,
Reviens, reviens radieuse,
Reviens, ô nuit mystérieuse!

This well known song has been transcribed for just about every imaginable instrumental combination, and it is easy to see why. The impassioned melodic line calls to the violinist or 'cellist for lush vibrato; the rich chordal accompaniment satisfies the romantic soul of the pianist. The words seem almost superfluous, and yet what wonderful, dramatic, passion-filled words they are! One is reminded of an operatic aria on the one hand, and of Fauré's own "Elegy" for 'cello and orchestra on the other.

The piano's opening minor triads establish the tonality. The singer enters on the second measure with a simple, harmonically derived melody:

> In a sleep charmed by your image
> I dreamed happiness, an ardent mirage,
> Your eyes were softer,—your voice pure and deep,
> You glowed like a dawn-lit sky;
> You called me—and I left the earth
> To flee with you towards the light,
> For us the skies opened their clouds,
> Unknown splendors, divine lights were glimpsed,

Despite small *crescendos* and *decrescendos,* the general dynamic scheme has been a gradual buildup to this point. The opening calls for a *sotto voce,* dreamlike sound and the singer must taper each long syllable (in "mir*age,*" "aur*ore,*" "*terre,*" "lum*ière*"). From the words "Les cieux" on, there is a very strong *crescendo* culminating in the singer's anguished "Hé*las*," the highest note and the most dramatic moment of the song. From this peak there is a steady falling away until the poignant—almost whispered—sound of the opening is reached again.

> Hélas, sad awakening from dreams,
> I call you, O night—
> Bring me back your lies,
> Come back, come back radiant one.

There is a secondary *crescendo* towards "radi*euse,*" but it lacks the intensity of the central climax. It is more like a remembrance of things past, a pale reflection of the passion felt in the dream and now recalled—plaintively—in vain,

> Come back, O mysterious night.

This early song shows only glimpses of the harmonic inventiveness that was to characterize Fauré's later music. Aside from the augmented chords in measures six and twenty-one, so characteristic of French music of this period, the harmonies are typical of late romantic music in general. The piano is never more than an accompaniment, a far cry from later songs such as "Clair de lune"' (Opus 46/2) in which the piano has a rich, independent song to sing.

The poem is similarly devoid of the nuances and contradictions of the Symbolist works used elsewhere by Fauré. Despite its subject—a dream of love—its syntax and use of words is normal and orderly. The poet, Romain Bussine (1821–1899), a singer and teacher who, with Camille Saint-Saëns, founded the Société Nationale de Musique, based his text on a traditional Tuscan poem.

Hymne   Poem by Charles Baudelaire
Hymn   OPUS 7/2

A la très chère, à la très belle,
Qui remplit mon coeur de clarté,
A l'ange, à l'idole immortelle,
Salut en immortalité,
Salut en immortalité!

Elle se répand dans ma vie,
Comme un air ímpregné de sel,
Et dans mon âme inassouvie
Verse le goût de l'Eternel
Comment, amour incorruptible,
T'exprimer avec verité,
Grain de musc, qui gîs invisible
Au fond de mon éternité?

A la très chère, à la très belle,
Qui remplit mon coeur de clarté,
A l'ange, à l'idole immortelle,
Salut en immortalité,
Salut en immortalité!

The meaning of the text of this song is hard to fathom unless one is aware of Baudelaire's preoccupation with a paradoxical theme: the sanctity of the sensual and the voluptuousness of the spiritual. These contradictions, barely hinted at in "Hymne," are explicitly spelled out in many of Baudelaire's other poems. Fauré's setting echoes the poem in juxtaposing the celestial and the sensual with considerable subtlety.

After the two-bar introduction, which serves merely to announce the tonality (G major for high voice), the voice and piano begin a lovely chromatic melody. There is constant harmonic motion from the fourth measure on, with especially lovely modulations under "belle" and "clarté." The chromatic feeling of the first part of the melody, which returns under "immor*telle*," continues in the accompaniment until the climactic rise to the high note on the second "immortalité." This climax concludes the terrestrial first section. The words to this point have been introductory in nature:

> To the very dear one, to the very beautiful one,
> Who fills my heart with brightness,
> To the angel, to the immortal idol,
> Greetings in immortality!
> Greetings in immortality!

We now have a piano interlude of the utmost harmonic simplicity which becomes the underlying figure for the whole next section. For ten long measures the chord remains unchanged (C major in high voice), and the melody stays within the same scale pattern. This creates the serene spirituality suitable for describing the other-worldly:

> She suffuses my life
> Like an air impregnated with piquancy,

At the word "sel," literally salt, but figuratively wit or, as here translated, piquancy, the harmony changes. This modulation was presaged by the melodic accidental in the preceding measure, but the impact is on the word "sel." This is strange imagery for an angelic creature, but Baudelaire owes us no explanation for his vision of the sublime! Despite the richer harmonic and melodic inventiveness in the next few bars, the mood remains celestial:

> And into my unsatiated soul
> Pours the taste of the Eternal.

Through much modulation Fauré arrives at a beautiful F♯ chord, which gives us a temporary resting place after "Eternel." The next section uses the very effective device of long held melodic notes over a constantly moving, highly chromatic accompaniment. This is the most dramatic part of the song, even though the dynamic level is soft until the *crescendo* under "de mon éternité?" The words are:

> How, incorruptible love,
> To explain you truthfully,
> Grain of musk which lies invisible
> At the core of my eternity?

The piano interlude gradually brings us back to the serenity of the opening. The words and music with which the song began are repeated, with the addition of one extra "Salut en immortalité," which is the most significant climax of the entire song. Note the sharp clash of the melody's high G with the piano's F♯ at this point (the lower F and C in the accompaniment should be sharped). These typical Fauré touches are always somewhat startling!

Barcarolle

Poem by Marc Monnier

OPUS 7/3

Gondolier du Rialto
Mon château c'est la lagune,
Mon jardin c'est le Lido,
Mon rideau le clair de lune.

Gondolier du grand canal,
Pour fanal j'ai la croisée
Où s'allument tous les soirs,
Tes yeux noirs mon épousée.

Ma gondole est aux heureux,
Deux à deux je les promène,
Et les vents légers et frais
Sont discret sur mon domaine.

J'ai passé dans les amours
Plus de jours et de nuits folles,
Que Vénise n'a d'îlots
Que ses flots n'ont de gondoles.

"Barcarolle" can mean any boat song, but in this case it refers clearly to a gondola on the canals of Venice. The poet, Marc Monnier, spent many years in Italy and obviously Venice was one of his favorite cities.

Like most barcarolles this one has the characteristic 6/8 rocking rhythm, but the subdivision of the eighth notes in the oft-repeated figure, first introduced by the singer, is somewhat unusual and a bit tricky because of the tied note with which the triplet sixteenth notes begin. With the exception of the two introductory and two closing bars, and three measures between the two verses, this rhythmic figure or a slight variation thereof is passed back and forth from singer to pianist throughout the song.

This leaves very few choices for the melodic line—a rise or a fall on the triplet sixteenth notes, and a continuation of the scale pattern or a little twist at the end. Note that the seventh note of the minor scale (the key is G minor for high voice) is not raised in the melodic line. This flatted seventh usually creates an antique effect.

The harmonic patterns are more varied: aside from the innumerable tonic chords, we have what amounts to a tone cluster in the fourth measure, the polytonalities of F minor over G in the following measure, and F major over G two measures later, a G^7 chord under "can*al*," which leads to an altered D^7 in the same bar (the third and fifth are flatted), which in turn introduces G major, continued progression through C minor (bar thirteen), F minor (bar fourteen), Bb⁷ (bar fifteen), E♭, E♭⁷ (bar sixteen), G, E minor seventh, D° (bar eighteen), until finally we have a solid V⁷–I cadence (D⁷–G) to end the verse. Both verses end with G major chords; in fact the lovely extended piano postlude is entirely in the major mode. This gives us a chance to hear the melody with the raised 7th (as is normal for the major scale) and the contrast is most effective.

Verse one:

Gondolier of the Rialto
My palace is the lagoon,
My garden is the Lido,
My curtain is the moonlight,
Gondolier of the Grand Canal,
For ship's lantern I have the window
Where shine every evening
Your black eyes, my bride.

The strongest dynamic marking in the first verse is at the fifth line, "Gondolier du grand canal"; these are also the highest notes in the song. Except for this phrase, the dynamic level is moderate to soft, and the overall effect is one of gentle lyricism.

Verse two:

My gondola is for the happy,
Two by two I row them
And the light and cool winds
Are discreet on my domain.
I have spent, in love affairs,
More insane days and nights
Than Venice has little islands
Than her waters have gondolas.

The dynamic scheme for the second verse is quite different from the first. The beginning is gentle, but a steady *crescendo* builds to a full *forte* on the last line. The piano continues at this dynamic level until the second bar of the postlude; from there it is a fade-out ending.

Au bord de l'eau   Poem by Sully-Prudhomme
At the Edge of the Water   opus 8/1

S'asseoir tous deux au bord du flot qui passe,
Le voir passer,
Tous deux s'il glisse un nuage en l'espace,
Le voir glisser,
A l'horizon s'il fume un toit de chaume
Le voir fumer,
Aux alentours si quelque fleur embaume
S'enbaumer,

Entendre au pied du saule où l'eau murmure
L'eau murmurer,
Ne pas sentir tant que ce rêve dure
Le temps durer,

Mais n'apportant de passion profonde
Qu'à s'adorer,
Sans nul souci des querelles du monde
Les ignorer;
Et seuls tous deux devant tout ce qui lasse
Sans se lasser,
Sentir l'amour devant tout ce qui passe
Ne point passer,
Sentir l'amour devant tout ce qui passe
Ne point passer!

To appreciate fully how strong an influence the harmonies of Fauré and other French composers of this era have had on popular music of our time, one need only play through the first six bars of accompaniment of this song, remembering that it was published in 1865. The suspensions over the B^7 and A^7 chords (analyzed in C# minor, the key for high voice) in measures four and five are now virtually clichés for the supper-club pianist—they had no such connotations a hundred years ago.

The poem is a variation on the "everything, especially love, dies" theme, but this one hints that it just might be possible for one loving pair to ignore life's woes and keep their love intact.

The opening bars are wistful enough with their stark minor chords and descending melodic line, but the suspensions discussed above enliven things a bit. This segment of music is given twice for the following words:

To sit together at the edge of the stream which goes by,
To see it go by,
Together, if a cloud glides by in the air
To see it glide by,

A rising line in the melody brings us a brighter mood, with predominantly major chords over a G# pedal point, but the falling melodic line and minor chords return after four short bars:

If on the horizon smoke rises from a thatched-roof
To see it rise,
If in the area some flower gives off a sweet scent
To wrap oneself in this scent.

There is an increasing sense of motion in the accompaniment of the next section, and the upward sweep at the ends of the melodic phrases adds to a growing sense of euphoria. Under "ne pas sentir" we find a major seventh chord, another sound frequently heard in sophisticated ballads of the 1940s. The words continue:

> To hear at the foot of the willow where the water murmurs
> The water murmur,
> Not to feel while this dream lasts
> Time goes on (The word "durer" means to last and to continue or go on)

The major chord under "durer" leads us back to the melody and harmonies of "A l'horizon," which in turn brings us back to the original descending melody of the very beginning. The remarkable structural unity of this song is the result of these imaginative interweavings of the musical material. The words in this section conclude:

> But bearing no profound passion
> Other than to adore one another,
> With no care for the quarrels of the world
> To ignore them;

The final section focuses on C♯ major as a tonal center. The beautiful augmented B♯ cord before "Ne point passer" sets off this crucial line most effectively and is a wonderful preparation for the V⁷–I cadence which follows. Again the melodic material of "A l'horizon" and "Mais n'apportant . . ." is heard, this time transposed to C♯. The major ending seems all the happier in the light of the earlier minor section. The last lines of the poem are:

> And alone together before all that wearies
> Without wearying,
> To feel love—in the face of all that vanishes—
> Not vanish at all!
> To feel love—in the face of all that vanishes—
> Not vanish at all!

La Rançon Poem by Charles Baudelaire
The Ransom OPUS 8/2

L'homme a, pour payer sa rançon,
Deux champs au tuf profond et riche,
Qu'il faut qu'il rémue et défriche
Avec le fer de la raison.

Pour obtenir la moindre rose,
Pour extorquer quelques épis,
Des pleurs salés de son front gris,
Sans cesse il faut qu'il les arrose!

L'un est l'Art et l'autre, l'Amour:
Pour rendre le juge propice,

Lorsque de la stricte justice
Paraîtra le terrible jour,
Il faudra lui montrer des granges
Pleines de moissons et de fleurs,
Dont les formes et les couleurs
Gagnent le suffrage des Anges.

As befits the philosophical nature of its text, the music for "La Rançon" is solemn and dignified. It is interesting that Fauré dedicated this song to Duparc, who was merely a seventeen-year-old student when the song was published. Neither of the two young composers could possibly have known in 1865 how high a price Duparc was to pay for his creative time on earth, for twenty years later he suffered a complete mental breakdown which ended his efforts as a musician.

An octave on the dominant (the key for high voice is E minor– E major) heralds the song's beginning. The voice enters on the same note and the melodic line remains firmly rooted in the tonic scale for the first fifteen bars. Throughout this entire section the accompaniment has consisted of rather ominous ringing octaves and a series of somber two-note phrases. At the climactic point in the vocal line ("Avec le fer") there is a strong dissonance. The words for this section are:

Man, to pay his ransom, has
Two deep and rich chalk fields,
Which he must rake and till
With the iron of his reason.

A rising scale, with two enlarged intervals, creates a sense of motion and leads to a section rich in lovely harmonic devices: the chord under "moindre," which has two intervals of a second; the diminished chord under "quelques," which is derived from the same antecedents; the progression from the diminished chord under "pleurs" to the D⁷ in the next measure, which is the result of the held octave in the bass; and the beautifully harmonized descending scale under "il faut qu'il les arrose!"

The melody in this section is equally moving, with dramatic *fortes* called for at "Des pleurs" and "Sans cesse." The words are anguished:

To obtain the smallest rose
To wrest some ears of corn,
With his grey brow's salted tears,
He must ceaselessly water them!

Fauré switches to the major mode to describe the riches with which man can ransom his life: art and love. There is a triumphant feeling in the melodic line, especially at the word "l'Art" on the tonic note, the highest note of the phrase. The actual words are:

To make the judge kind,
When with strict justice
The terrible day (judgment day) arrives,

In the final section we hear again some noteworthy harmonies: the augmented chord under "*Pleines,*" the suspensions under "*de* moissons" and "fleurs," the diminished chord which becomes a B^7 as a consequence of the tied B after "couleurs," and the suspension on the final syllable. One last suspension in the first two bars of the brief piano postlude precedes the final V–I cadence. The poem concludes:

It will be necessary to show him barns
Full of crops and flowers,
Whose forms and colors
Earn the approbation of the Angels.

This entire section has been rather mild in dynamics, but the piano has an important climax just before the last line. This should be strong enough to make the singer's voice *dolce* and *piano* on the concluding words an effective contrast.

Ici-bas!   Poem by Sully-Prudhomme
Here Below   OPUS 8/3

Ici-bas tous les lilas meurent,
Tous les chants des oiseaux sont courts,
Je rêve aux étés qui demeurent toujours!

Ici-bas, les lèvres effleurent
Sans rien laisser de leur velours,
Je rêve aux baisers qui demeurent toujours.

Ici-bas, tous les hommes pleurent
Leurs amitiés ou leurs amours.
Je rêve aux couples qui demeurent,
Aux couples qui demeurent toujours!

The sentiments expressed in this song form an ever-recurring theme found in poetry of all nations and of all eras: on this earth time changes everything . . . flowers die and love dies, and man mourns.

The simple musical setting opens with an arpeggiated dominant-seventh chord, which leads to the tonic triad (G minor for high voice) with which the melody begins. Four somber, antique-sounding chords underlie "Je rêve aux étés qui demeurent toujours!" The music of the first verse, a mere eight bars long, is repeated for the second. The words to this point are:

Here below all the lilacs die,
All the songs of the birds are short,
I dream of summers which last forever!

Here below lips brush lightly
Leaving nothing of their velvet,
I dream of kisses which last forever!

The dynamic scheme is the same for the two verses quoted above: a *crescendo* towards the highest note (under "oiseaux" and "de leur"), a *decrescendo,* and a soft dreamy sound for "Je rêve" etc.

In verse three "Ici-bas" becomes a major triad, actually part of the G⁷ chord given in the harmony. We pass through C⁷ chords as well, and when we arrive at the words "Je rêve," instead of the four somber chords, we have a big buildup to an E♭ major chord and the climactic high melodic note (at "de*meur*ent"). This is obviously the most intensely dramatic moment of the song. Fauré repeats the line of poetry to allow time to subdue this outburst and return to the original mood and key. Actually the repetition of the words becomes part of the dramatic effect. The words for the third verse are:

Here below all men weep for
Their friendships or their loves.
I dream of couples who last forever!

Nell   Poem by Leconte de Lisle
OPUS 18/1

Ta rose de pourpre à ton clair soleil,
O Juin, étincelle enivrée,
Penche aussi vers moi ta coupe dorée:
Mon coeur à ta rose est pareil.
Sous le mol abri de la feuille ombreuse
Monte un soupir de volupté:
Plus d'un ramier chante au bois écarté,
O mon coeur, sa plainte amoureuse.

Que ta perle est douce au ciel enflammé,
Etoile de la nuit pensive!
Mais combien plus douce est la clarté vive
Qui rayonne en mon coeur, en mon coeur charmé!
La chantante mer, le long du rivage,
Taira son murmure éternel,
Avant qu'en mon coeur, chère amour, O Nell,
Ne fleurisse plus ton image!

Fifteen years elapsed between the publication of Fauré's first twenty songs, Opera 1–8, and Opus 18 which appeared in 1880. These years were certainly not devoid of vocal music from his pen, however, for in 1870 he published two duets for two sopranos (Opus 10), in 1871 "Cantique de Jean Racine" for chorus, harmonium and string quartet or orchestra (Opus 11), and in 1875 "Les Djinns" for chorus and orchestra (Opus 12). While not in the scope of this study, these works are certainly of interest to singers.

From 1880 to 1892 songs for solo voice and piano once again flowed from Fauré with great regularity, one cycle almost every year. His total output in this genre, while no match for Schubert's astounding 600, reached the considerable number of ninety-six.

"Nell," the first in this second outpouring of solo songs, is full of charm and sweet sentiment. The piano part is strictly accompaniment except for two brief moments: in measure nine it separates verses one and two, and in bar twenty, it echoes the melody of the preceding measure, thus providing a countermelody to the vocal line. Hidden within the sixteenth-note figure, however, one finds subtle little melodies throughout the piano part. The key for high voice, Gb major, is the original key.

After the brief piano introduction, the melody begins with what amounts to a tonic scale. When the octave has been reached there is a drop to the lower Gb and the scale begins again, but this time the dominant is the resting place. The simplicity of the melodic line is reflected in the harmonic scheme for the first several measures, but under "mon coeur à ta rose est par*eil*," changes more typical of Fauré are heard. Particularly characteristic is the unexpected harmonization of "par*eil*"—the Ab⁷ chord under "*est par*eil" leads us to expect a resolution in Db, which is what the melody does; the accompanying figure, however, is kept ambiguous by melodic fragment in the left hand and in the absence of the Db in the Db⁷ broken chord in the right hand until the last beat of the measure.

The words for the first stanza are:

Your purple rose in your bright sunlight,
O June, sparkles drunkenly,
Tilt towards me, too, your golden cup.
My heart is like your rose.

The second verse begins like the first, but melody and harmony change under "d'un ramier." On the second beats of this and the next two measures, augmented chords color the lovely progressions, and in the following bars we have a cadence leading to a long Db resting place. The melody has a second climb to the high Gb, this one far more dramatic than the first. In fact, "O mon coeur" is the climax of the section. The words for this verse are:

Under the soft cover of the shadowy leaves
A voluptuous sigh rises;
More than one pigeon sings in the secluded wood,
Oh my heart, its love-filled lament.

The next ten bars are enormously rich harmonically and melodically. The piano echoes the vocal line in several spots, most obviously under "enflammé," more subtly under "clarté vive." Often we seem on the verge of a V⁷–I cadence, but instead of the resolution we go on to a new progression; the Db⁷–Gb between "enflammé" and "Etoile" is masked by the intervening augmented chord (on the fourth beat) and the suspension (Ab in the first beat of the next measure). This is Fauré at his subtle best! The words here are:

How sweet your pearl is in the flaming sky,
Star of the pensive night!
But how much sweeter is the keen brightness
Which shines in my heart, in my charmed heart!

A two-bar piano interlude (under the held C of "charmé") serves to bridge the harmonies from F to Gb, where the music of the beginning of the first verse is heard once again.

The singing sea, the length of the banks,
Will silence its eternal murmur,

Once again Fauré changes the music for the second half of the stanza, this third time with the most dramatic effect of all. Under "chère amour" the treble and bass accompaniment is in unison, which is in itself somewhat dramatic, but it is the rise to the Ab that is the climactic moment of the piece. The sudden *pp* at the second "ne fleurisse plus" is equally dramatic. The singer's last note, the Db, does not sound like an ending because of the Bb minor chord underlying it; two beats later, after an Eb⁷ and a Db⁷ (the dominant), we finally arrive at the tonic chord and all ends well on the following words:

Before in my heart, dear love Nell,
Your image will cease to bloom!
Your image will cease to bloom!

Le Voyageur   Poem by Armand Silvestre
The Voyager   OPUS 18/2

Voyageur, où vas-tu, marchant dans l'or vibrant de la poussière?
"Je m'en vais au soleil couchant, pour m'endormir dans la lumière.
Car j'ai vécu n'ayant qu'un Dieu,

L'astre qui luit et qui féconde,
Et c'est dans son linceul de feu
Que je veux m'en aller du monde!"

Voyageur, presse donc le pas:
L'astre vers l'horizon décline . . .
"Que m'importe, j'irai plus bas,
L'attendre au pied de la coline.
Et lui montrant mon coeur ouvert,
Saignant de son amour fidèle,
Je lui dirai: j'ai trop souffert,
Soleil! emporte moi loin d'elle!"

This song is unusual in many respects. One unique characteristic that first strikes the listener is the repetition of the dominant tone (D in the key for high voice, G minor), with which every measure in the accompaniment begins for the first twenty-three and, not counting the three final chords, the last twelve bars of the piece. Next, one might notice that, except for nine measures marked *dolce* in the middle section, the dynamics range from loud to very loud, with frequent reminders from the composer to keep loud or get louder.

The third interesting feature of the song is found in the poem, which is a dialogue between an unidentified asker of questions and a mysterious traveler. The singer must make this exchange obvious to the listener by changes in vocal color, since the dynamic level must remain fairly constant. (Shifting positions will not help on a record!)

The two-bar introduction sets the vehement mood and G minor tonality. The singer enters in a decisive manner with a melodic line that begins and ends on the dominant. The powerful chords return often to the tonic and dominant from excursions into Eb, F minor, Bb, etc.

The first line of verse is a question:

Traveler, where are you going,
Marching in the vibrant gold of the dust?

The traveler answers:

I am going to the setting sun,
To sleep in the light.
For I have lived having but one God,
The star which shines and nourishes,
And it is in its shroud of fire
That I wish to leave the world.

The *dolce* section now begins and everything changes: the mood, the accompanying figure, the dynamic level, the melodic line, the key and the mode. The piano's gentle melodic fragment in Eb brings back the questioner with a melody that shifts from F to Eb to C⁷ to F.

Traveler, hurry then:
The star sinks towards the horizon . . .

The traveler answers loudly. Is he angry, bitter or just determined?

What does it matter to me,
I shall go further down,
To wait for it at the foot of the hill.

Under this last line there is a tremendous *crescendo* and a dramatic chromatic rise, with a long pause on Db, before the climactic return to the original key and original melody. The repeated single note on the dominant and chords in the accompaniment are stronger than ever, and the dynamic is always *ff*:

And showing it my open heart,
Bleeding from its faithful love,
I shall say to it:
I have suffered too much, sun!
Carry me away far from her!

One might have known there would be a woman behind such anguish!

Automne
Autumn

Poem by Armand Silvestre
OPUS 18/3

Automne au ciel brumeux, aux horizons navrants,
Aux rapides couchants, aux aurores pâlies,
Je regarde couler, comme l'eau du torrent,
Tes jours faits de mélancolie.

Sur l'aile des regrets mes esprits emportés,
Comme s'il se pouvait que notre âge renaisse!
Parcourent en rêvant les coteaux enchantés,
Où, jadis, sourit ma jeunesse!

Je sens, au clair soleil du souvenir vainqueur,
Refleurir en bouquet les roses deliées,
Et monter à mes yeux, des larmes, qu'en mon coeur
Mes vingt ans avaient oubliées!

This melancholy song evokes nature as witness to and metaphor for man's regret at the passage of time. The poet saves for the last line the poignant revelation that this wistful yearner, who laments his lost youth, is but twenty years old!

The accompaniment opens with tonic chords (C# minor for high voice) in slowly rocking 12/8 time. The octaves in the bass are quite dramatic and form an interesting rhythmic pattern. The accent on the third eighth note must be scrupulously observed. The harmonies are unchanged for nine measures and the melodic line remains within the tonic scale for this segment, which encompasses the first two lines of the poem:

> Autumn with its foggy skies, its heart-breaking horizons,
> Its rapid sunsets, its pallid dawns,

The next two measures feature dramatic diminished chords; we then have a long progression which finally settles on the dominant, G♯ major. The words here are:

> I watch rush by, like the water of a torrent,
> Your days of melancholy.

The dynamic level has been very strong to this point, but there is a *decrescendo* to the next *dolcissimo* section. The piano establishes the new gentle mood in its sweetly melodic two-bar interlude, which is harmonized first with a diminished chord and then by E major, the relative major. The singer's melody begins gently, too, but there is a *crescendo* on the rising line from "s'il pouvait" to "notre âge." A second *crescendo*, this one marked *molto*, begins one bar later and continues to the climax on "jadis." The line ends *forte* and the *decrescendo* does not begin until the piano's solo bar. The mood is dark and dramatic, with strong supporting chords all along the way. The words are:

> On the wing of regret, my senses swept away—
> As if our early years could be reborn!—
> Wander dreaming over the enchanted hills
> Where, long ago, my youth smiled!

Having traveled far and wide, harmonically speaking, Fauré brings us back to the original key via a dominant-seventh chord. The original melody begins again over the steady tonic chords, but the dynamic level is now quiet and there are some slight variations in the melodic line. The final stanza begins:

> I feel, in the bright sunshine of triumphant memory,
> Bloom again in bouquets, the scattered roses,

Once again we have our dramatic diminished chords in the next two bars, but the end of the stanza brings a rising vocal line to the high G♯. This is the most intense line of the song and the dynamic level must remain high. The ending is very traditional in its use of dominant–tonic chords and does not yet manifest Fauré's later aversion to this overworked formula. The last lines of the poem are:

> And bring to my eyes tears that in my heart
> My twenty years had forgotten!

Poème d'un jour
Poems by Charles Grandmougin
OPUS 21/1,2,3

1. Rencontre
Meeting

J'étais triste et pensif
Quand je t'ai rencontrée:
Je sens moins, aujourd'hui, mon obstiné tourment.
O dis-moi, Serais-tu la femme inespérée
Et le rêve idéal poursuivi vainement?
O passante aux doux yeux
Serais-tu donc l'amie
Qui rendrait le bonheur au poète isolé,
Et vas-tu rayonner,
Sur mon âme affermie,
Comme le ciel natal sur un coeur d'exilé?

Ta tristesse sauvage, à la mienne pareille,
Aime à voir le soleil décliner sur la mer!
Devant l'immensité ton extase s'éveille,
Et le charme des soirs à ta belle âme est cher.
Une mystérieuse et douce sympathie
Déjà m'enchaine à toi comme un vivant lien,
Et mon âme frémit, par l'amour envahie
Et mon coeur te chérit sans te connaître bien.

The classic Aristotelian structure of this cycle with its beginning—("Rencontre"), middle—("Toujours"), and end—("Adieu") makes its performance as a unit almost mandatory. The key sequence, the meaning of the poems, and the contrasting moods and dynamic ranges are all indications of an essential cohesiveness and continuity. In fact the irony of the third song depends in large part on its following the first two.

The poems by Charles Grandmougin (1850–1930) are typical of the Symbolist school in their mysterious imagery, strange metaphors, and use of words as much for sheer sound as for sense. This is particularly striking in the final song and belies the fact that Grandmougin is usually called a Parnassien. (The Parnassiens, a slightly earlier group of poets, believed that the poet should be contemplative and wise and hide his anguish behind a mask of impersonality, antiquity, or exoticism.)

The opening song, "Rencontre" or "Meeting," is a straightforward narrative. After a one-measure introduction, which establishes the relaxed pace and B major tonality (in the original key), the words begin:

I was sad and pensive when I met you:

Underscoring the next phrase,

> I feel my persistent torment less today,

the piano has a little countermelody (indicated by double-stemmed notes) which should be brought out, but without too much emphasis. This and other countermelodies occur frequently throughout the song.

The singer continues in the same tranquil, dreamlike fashion,

> O tell me, could you be the woman I never (dared) hope for
> And the ideal dream I vainly pursued?

At the words "O passante aux doux yeux" (O soft-eyed passerby), the melodic line calls for some inner tension from the singer. Little *crescendos* build to the F♯ on "na*tal*," which is the climactic point of this section and, in fact, of the song. The words continue:

> O soft-eyed passerby
> Could you be the friend who brings happiness to the solitary poet,
> And will you shine on my closed soul,
> As the native sun on the exile's heart?

A recapitulation of the piano introduction now leads into the second verse, which begins with the marvelous sound of "Ta tristesse sauvage" (your shy sadness) with its alliterative t and s. Although the words are different, the music is the same.

> Your shy sadness, so like mine,
> Loves to see the sun sink into the sea.
> Before the vastness your ecstasy awakens
> And the charm of evening is dear to your beautiful soul.
> A mysterious and sweet sympathy
> Already binds me to you like a living bond,
> And my soul shudders, invaded by love,
> And my heart cherishes you without knowing you well.

The essentially gentle music of this song—with its shifting harmonies, its limited dynamic range, its constantly flowing broken-chord accompaniment and its long fade-out ending on the tonic—expresses the wistful, tentative nature of the poem. This is, after all, just the beginning!

2. Toujours
Always

> Vous me demandez de me taire,
> De fuir loin de vous pour jamais
> Et de m'en aller, solitaire,

Sans me rappeler qui j'amais!
Demander plutôt aux étoiles
De tomber dans l'immensité,
A la nuit de perdre ses voiles,
Au jour de perdre sa clarté!

Demandez à la mer immense
De dessecher ses vastes flots
Et quand les vents sont en démence,
D'apaiser ses sombres sanglots!
Mais n'espérez pas que mon âme
S'arrache à ses âpres douleurs,
Et se dépouille de sa flamme
Comme le printemps de ses fleurs!

The second song, "Toujours" ("Always"), brings us a sudden, tumultuous, passionate outburst. We shift from B major to E minor. The piano begins with an agitated *forte* broken-chord triplet figure and the singer enters with an accusation:

You tell me to be silent;
To flee far from you forever
And to go away alone,
Without remembering whom I loved.

There is an abrupt shift in dynamics from the furious *forte* to a *piano*, but no break in the headlong pace, which must continue throughout.

Rather tell the stars to fall into the void,
The night to lose its veils,
The day to lose its sunlight!
Tell the immense sea to dry up its vast tides
And when the winds are wildly blowing
To still their dismal sobs!

With each impossible illustration, the music increases in volume and intensity until we are once again at full *forte*. Now comes a second *subito piano*, this one marked *pp* for the pianist.
The text continues

But don't hope that my soul
Will tear itself from its bitter pain,
And throw off its flame
As the Spring does its flowers!

During this section we have another enormous *crescendo* and a tempestuous ending. Many performers prefer to ignore the *decrescendo* and *p* marked for the last chords of the accompaniment, carrying the *forte* to the end, assuring maximum contrast with the third song.

3. Adieu
Farewell

Comme tout meurt vite, la rose
Déclose,
Et les frais manteaux diaprés
Des prés:
Les longs soupirs, les bien-aimées,
Fumées!
On voit, dans ce monde léger,
Changer
Plus vite que les flots des grèves,
Nos rêves,
Plus vite que le givre en fleurs,
Nos coeurs!
A vous l'on se croyait fidèle,
Cruelle,
Mais hélas! les plus longs amours
Sont courts!
Et je dis en quittant vos charmes,
Sans larmes,
Presqu'au moment de mon aveu,
Adieu!

"Adieu" (or "Farewell") is the surprise ending to this cycle. After all the romantic storm and stress of "Toujours" comes a quiet, antique-sounding introduction. The music, a politely harmonized innocuous little tune in E major, is so bland that it gives no hint of the poet's intention. The singer enters sweetly,

Since everything quickly dies,
The rose opens
And the fresh, variegated mantles
Of the fields;
The long sighs, the loved ones,
Gone like smoke!

The above translation is at best an approximation, for the lines "Et les frais manteaux diaprés/Des prés" (here rendered "And the fresh variegated mantles of the fields"), a typical example of a Symbolist poet's use of language, seems written more for its sensual sound than for precise meaning. The aim of Symbolist poems, so often chosen by Fauré and Debussy, is to suggest rather than describe.

Throughout the first section of this ABA song, and again at the recapitulation, the composer has given very careful phrasing instructions to the pianist. There is unpedaled *legato* or semi-detached phrasing, sometimes both simultaneously. This gives a pristine, guileless sound. At the word "fumées," which means smoked, evaporated or vainly hoped for, the composer indicates the first use of pedal in the piano part. At this moment the mode changes from major to minor and the piano figuration becomes more lyric and flowing, but the words continue in the same vein:

> One sees, in this frivolous world,
> Our dreams change more quickly than waves on sand,
> Our hearts (change) more quickly than frost on flowers.

We return to the opening key and style in the piano and the voice continues, still sweetly and quietly,

> One thought oneself faithful to you,
> Cruel one,
> But alas, the longest loves
> Are short!
> And I say while leaving your charms,
> Without tears,
> Almost at the moment of my vow,
> Adieu!

The rhyme scheme of this delightful little piece of dramatic irony is unusual and effective; long lines alternate with very brief lines so the rhymed words are nearly juxtaposed; very often the irony is contained in the rhyme itself. For example,

> Mais hélas! les plus longs *amours*
> Sont *courts!*
> Et je dis en quittant vos *charmes*
> Sans *larmes,*

For the above lines to make their effect the singer must take full advantage of the rest between "charmes" and "Sans." In fact, it is probably wise to lengthen the pause a bit, even at the risk of distorting the rhythm.

The poet takes no chances with his wonderful ending punch lines,

> Presqu'au moment de mon aveu,
> Adieu!

allotting three full beats to the second syllable of "aveu," then granting an eighth note rest before allowing the singer to deliver, still sweetly and ever so softly, the final "Adieu."

Les Berceaux   Poem by Sully-Prudhomme
The Cradles   OPUS 23/I

> Le long du Quai, les grands vaisseaux,
> Que la houle incline en silence,

Ne prennent pas garde au berceaux,
Que la main des femmes balance.

Mais viendra le jour des adieux,
Car il faut que les femmes pleurent,
Et que les hommes curieux
Tentent les horizons qui leurrent!

Et ce jour-là les grands vaisseaux,
Fuyant le port qui diminue,
Sentent leur masse retenue
Par l'âme des lointains berceaux.

This is one of Fauré's most touching settings. Its eloquence and beauty are rendered all the more effective by its simplicity and economy of means. The poetry has the same virtues, and the combination is completely winning.

The piano opens with a figure suggestive of the rocking waves of the sea, which also serves to establish the tonality (C minor for high voice). This gently undulating rhythm, which never varies from beginning to end, has an almost hypnotic effect. This is abetted by the right hand octave pattern, which is also constant throughout the song.

The melody stays within the confines of the tonic scale for almost half the song, but the shifting harmonies in the accompaniment are endlessly inventive and do not seem at all constricted by the rigid tonality of the melodic line. In the singer's very first measure, for instance, the sustained note under "Quai," the seventh note of the scale, creates a dissonance with the tonic pedal point; the real harmony here is, of course, the dominant chord in the minor mode. Two measures later, under "incline," the same melody note is harmonized in E♭. In these subtle differences lies the beauty of the song. The first real harmonic change occurs under "Que la main des femmes balance": here we have an A°–G minor–D⁷–G major progression. The words to this point are:

All along the quai, the large boats,
Which the swell silently tilts,
Pay no heed to the cradles
Rocked by the women's hands.

The dynamic level for the first section is gentle and subdued, but in the following segment we have a buildup to a *forte* on the fourth line. The accompaniment contributes to this increase in intensity by the introduction of a countermelody in the bass (under "Et que les hommes"). At the climactic moment (under "leurrent") this countermelody is in octaves, and the right hand figure is reinforced by the addition of thirds. Musical tension in the melodic line is created in the usual way, that is, a rising line to a well-prepared high note. After the octave drop, the piano has two measures to calm things down again. The words for this middle verse are:

> But the day of farewells will come,
> For women must weep,
> And curious men
> Must try the horizons which lure!

The final section begins with an even softer rendition of the initial music, but after just two bars, Fauré jumps to the progression originally heard under bars 7 and 8 (A°, G minor, D⁷, G major). From "Sentent leur masse" melody and harmonies are new. A *crescendo* leads to the climax of the section ("Par l'âme . . .") and Fauré repeats the last line of the verse to give adequate time for a fade-out ending. The poem's last stanza is:

> And on that day the large ships,
> Fleeing the port which grows smaller,
> Feel their bulk held back
> By the soul of the far-off cradles,
> By the soul of the far-off cradles.

Notre amour
Our Love

Poem by Armand Silvestre
OPUS 23/2

Notre amour est chose légère,
Comme les parfums que le vent
Prend aux cimes de la fougère,
Pour qu'on les respire en rêvant.
Notre amour est chose légère!

Notre amour est chose charmante,
Comme les chansons du matin,
Où nul regret ne se lamente,
Où vibre un espoir incertain;
Notre amour est chose charmante!

Notre amour est chose sacrée,
Comme les mystères des bois,
Où tressaille une âme ignorée,
Où les silences ont des voix:
Notre amour est chose sacrée!

Notre amour est chose infinie,
Comme les chemins des couchants,
Où la mer, aux cieux réunie,
S'endort sous les soleils penchants:

Notre amour est chose éternelle,
Comme tout ce qu'un dieu vainqueur

A touché du feu de son aile,
Comme tout ce qui vient du coeur;
Notre amour, Notre amour est chose éternelle.

Here is a relative rarity—a song which celebrates happy, light-hearted, charming, sacred, eternal love! The music is suitably exuberant with its soaring melodic lines, its rapidly moving triplet figure in the accompaniment, and its almost constant major modality. The original key, which is also the key for high voice, is E major. Throughout the song we have a duple rhythm in the melody pitted against the accompanying triplets. Occasionally the piano has both rhythms simultaneously (measures 21–23, 25–27, 36, 37), but even in these cases the duple-rhythm is always melodic in nature.

The music for the first three stanzas takes its mood from the initial line of the poem: "Our love is a light thing." Even though the music is not really strophic, each of the first three stanzas begins with a rising scale fragment which descends to the dominant before rising again. The fourth and fifth verses also begin with rising scale fragments, but, as befits the more serious descriptions "infinite" and "eternal," they begin on lower pitches (the tonic) and seem weightier. In the first three verses we have small *crescendos* and *decrescendos,* but the overall dynamic level is soft and not greatly varied. In the last verse, however, a large *crescendo* leads to an impassioned *forte.*

In a way, the fourth stanza serves to bridge the emotional gap between the first three verses and the last. The duple-rhythm counter-melody in the accompaniment is introduced here, and for the first time Fauré does not repeat the opening line at the end of the stanza. The greatest difference between the earlier stanzas and the last verse is the tremendous dramatic intensity of the finale, compared to the light-hearted tranquillity of the others. This is accomplished by Fauré's holding the melodic lines in the first four stanzas to no more than a one-octave range, while in the last he allows the singer to rise from the E above middle C to the B almost two octaves above. (The singer may opt to go no higher than the A at this point.)

It is interesting that Fauré did not deem it necessary to make the music for the verse beginning "Our love is a sacred thing" any weightier than the music for "Our love is a light thing" (verses one and three are identical musically). Perhaps the poem's own definition of "sacred" is explanation for this. The words are:

Our love is a light thing,
Like the perfumes that the wind
Takes to heights of the fernery
So that one might breathe them while dreaming.
Our love is a light thing!

Our love is a charming thing,
Like the songs of the morning,
Where no regret laments,
Where a vague hope vibrates,
Our love is a charming thing!

Our love is a sacred thing,
Like the mysteries of the forests,
Where a forgotten soul trembles,
Where silences have voices:
Our love is a sacred thing!

Our love is an infinite thing,
Like the paths of the sunsets,
Where the sea and sky, reunited,
Sleep under the setting suns:

Our love is an eternal thing,
Like all that a triumphant God
Has touched with the fire of his wing,
Like all that comes from the heart;
Our love, our love is an eternal thing, is an eternal thing!

Le Secret
The Secret

Poem by Armand Silvestre
OPUS 23/3

Je veux que le matin l'ignore
Le nom que j'ai dit à la nuit,
Et qu'au vent de l'aube, sans bruit,
Comme une larme il s'évapore.

Je veux que le jour le proclame,
L'amour qu'au matin j'ai caché,
Et sur mon coeur ouvert, penché,
Comme un grain d'encens,
Il l'enflamme.

Je veux que le couchant l'oublie,
Le secret que j'ai dit au jour,
Et l'emporte avec mon amour,
Aux plis de sa robe pâlie!

The protagonist in this song is charmingly inconsistent—he cannot decide whether to keep his love his own private secret or loudly proclaim it to the world. The composer vacillates in much the same fashion between the Lydian mode (the F scale without the B♭) and the normal F major scale (in the key for high voice).

Fauré had previously used the Lydian mode within the general framework of F major in the song "Lydia" (Opus 4/2), and in fact these two settings have much in common: both begin with rather solemn chords and both aim for antique effects. In the very first bar of "Le Secret," for instance, the F–A minor progression sounds formal and old-fashioned, and it is this very progression, used in two important bridge passages as well as within the various sections, that is characteristic of the piece.

The first verse consists of three long melodic phrases, the first two beginning on, and the third ending on the dominant. The third phrase has considerable sweep—over an octave—and a dynamic swell. The words here are:

> I want the morning to be unaware of
> The name that I told the night,
> And that in the dawn's breeze,
> Noiselessly, like a tear, it might evaporate.

After the two-bar piano interlude there is a sudden *forte* and an abrupt switch to the minor mode. The music seems almost angry, but the words are bright and positive, and the C^7 chord under "proc*lame*" does temporarily lift us from the minor. At "L'amour" there is an equally sudden dynamic shift to *piano*. Here it is the F minor to A♭ progression that seems vaguely antique. A *crescendo* leads to a climactic *forte* on "comme un grain." The harmonies under this rising melodic line go from C minor (under "coeur") to C major via the diminished chord, and then to a triumphant F major right at the top of the phrase. The words for this verse are:

> I want the day to proclaim it,
> The love that I hid in the morning,
> And over my open heart, poised,
> Like a grain of incense, to inflame it.

The characteristic two-bar interlude brings us back to the music of the first verse. The dynamic level is very soft—almost a whisper, but a *crescendo* on the rising vocal line quickly brings us to a full *forte*. Since Fauré has omitted the repeat of the first melodic phrase in this verse, he has time for a new concluding line which is sung very quietly. The piano has two more opportunities to play the characteristic phrase, but now it is kept in F major with no further reference to the Lydian mode. The words to this final section are:

> I want the setting sun to forget it,
> The secret that I told the day,
> And bring it with my love,
> Into the folds of its pale robe!

Chanson d'amour
Song of Love

Poem by Armand Silvestre
OPUS 27/1

J'aime tes yeux, j'aime ton front,
O ma rebelle, ô ma farouche,
J'aime tes yeux, j'aime ta bouche
Où mes baisers s'épuiseront.

J'aime ta voix, j'aime l'étrange
Grâce de tout ce que tu dis,
O ma rebelle, ô mon cher ange,
Mon enfer et mon paradis!

J'aime tes yeux, j'aime ton front,
O ma rebelle, ô ma farouche,
J'aime tes yeux, j'aime ta bouche
Où mes baisers s'épuiseront.

J'aime tout ce qui te fait belle,
De tes pieds jusqu'a tes cheveux,
O toi vers qui montent mes voeux,
O ma farouche, ô ma rebelle,

J'aime tes yeux, j'aime ton front,
O ma rebelle, ô ma farouche,
J'aime tes yeux, j'aime ta bouche
Où mes baisers s'épuiseront.

In "Chanson d'amour" we have yet another example of Fauré's deceptively simple style, behind which one finds marvelously subtle harmonic delights. In the two-bar introduction, for instance, the bass notes give the time-honored I–IV–V progression, but the right hand figure, by retaining the median note of the tonic chord throughout the second bar (the B, when analyzing the song in G major, the key for high voice), creates a much lovelier and more characteristic sound than the strictly traditional chords would have given.

The tight structure of the song is dictated by the words, for the music underlying the first four lines of verse is repeated exactly whenever those words are heard again. This form may be stated as ABACA. The two intervening stanzas are not identical, and one of the more interesting aspects of the song is the different melodic and harmonic routes Fauré chooses as returns to the A sections.

The melodic line in the thrice-repeated section uses the gradual stretching of an interval, a device much favored by César Franck (1822–1890), the composer who exerted such a persuasive influence on all French music of Fauré's generation. This creates a feeling of intensification even without much change in dynamic level, but there is a *crescendo* to the highest note (under "O ma belle"). The word "farouche" (ferocious one) is, of course, unexpected the first time it is used, but Fauré makes it clear, from the *pp* which follows, that it is a term of endearment and not to be taken too seriously. The words for this stanza are:

> I love your eyes, I love your brow,
> O my rebel, oh my ferocious one,
> I love your eyes, I love your mouth,
> Where my kisses will exhaust themselves.

A gentle, ambling piano interlude over a tonic pedal point leads us into a contrasting section, which is more varied dynamically than the first, reaching a real *forte* at "mon enfer et mon paradis!" The harmonies are constantly shifting and highly chromatic with a rather unexpected A♭ chord under "voix." From this highest melodic note we have a descending scale, which fits so beautifully with the changing harmonies that we are scarcely aware that, until the very bottom note, it is an E♭ scale. The last two measures before the return to the A section are fascinating: Fauré first introduces the melody note D (the dominant of the original key) as part of the ascending B♭ triad under "mon enfer"; that D becomes the principal note of the dominant-seventh chord under "paradis," and is sustained over the augmented chord in the second half of the measure to become the top of the tonic triad at the return. The words for this section are:

> I love your voice, I love the strange grace of all that you say,
> Oh my rebel, Oh my angel, my inferno and my paradise!

The second contrasting section has a more readily discernible harmonic pattern than the first—the repeated shifts from E major to C♯ minor and from F♯ major to D♯ minor. This allows the melody to repeat its scale fragments in a two-part rising sequence. The final note before the return is a half step below the desired dominant tone. Fauré has the right hand figure climb chromatically with the melody note, while the bass descends a half-step to effect the return to the original key. The words for this penultimate section are:

> I love all that makes you beautiful,
> From your feet to your hair,
> Oh you towards whom my vows go,
> Oh my ferocious one, Oh my rebel,

Fauré prolongs the final stanza by repeating the last line of verse at a slower tempo, but the piano postlude returns to the moderately brisk pace of the rest of the song. Note that the dominant-seventh chord at the end of each of the solo piano passages is somewhat masked by the sustained tonic chord in the bass.

La Fée aux chansons
The Song Fairy

Poem by Armand Silvestre
OPUS 27/2

Il était une Fée
D'herbe folle coiffée,
Qui courait les buissons
Sans s'y laisser surprendre
En Avril, pour apprendre
Aux oiseaux leurs chansons.

Lorsque geais et linottes
Faisaient des fausses notes
En récitant leurs chants,
La Fée, avec constance,
Gourmandait d'importance
Ces élèves méchants.

Sa petite main nue,
D'un brin d'herbe menue
Cuilli dans les halliers,
Pour stimuler leurs zèles,
Fouettait sur leurs ailes
Ces mauvais écoliers.

Par un matin d'automne,
Elle vient et s'étonne
De voir les bois déserts:
Avec les hirondelles,
Ses amis infidèles
Avaient fui dans les airs.

Et tout l'hiver la Fée,
D'herbe morte coiffée,
Et comptant les instants
Sous les forêts immenses,
Compose des romances
Pour le prochain Printemps!

This musically sophisticated fairy tale compares most favorably with Fauré's earlier efforts in the genre (see Opus 1/1 for example). While the straightforward narrative style of the poem retains a child-like (though never childish) simplicity, the music of the *minore* section (from "Lorsque geais" to "Ces élèves méchants") is in Fauré's mature, subtle, complex style. Elsewhere the composer allows himself characteristic touches, such as the dissonance created by two moving lines in the piano interlude before "Et tout l'hiver." Therefore, if coyness is assiduously avoided by the singer, this can be as effective a recital song as any.

The piano begins the song by playing the little F major tune (the original key and key for high voice) in the bass; the singer then enters with the same melody. The harmonies are kept very simple until the beautiful D major chord under "buiss*ons*." The two bars in D major lead to two measures on a C⁷ chord. This four bar pattern is repeated once and then used as a transition to the *minore* section. The piano *crescendos* and *decrescendos* provide the only dynamic variety in this segment, for the vocal line is consistently *piano* until the *crescendo* on the last long syllable ("chan*son*"). The words for the first verse are:

> There was a fairy
> Coiffed with wild grass,
> Who ran about the thickets
> Without allowing herself to be taken by surprise
> In April, to teach
> The birds their songs.

The next section begins in the parallel minor, but the mood is more *dolce* than sad. A pattern similar to the D major–C⁷, described in the previous section, occurs in the second half of this part. Here the keys are D♭–C♭⁷. The transition leads us back to the dominant (C) by way of its dominant (G). The words here are:

> When jays and linnets
> Sang wrong notes
> While singing their songs,
> The fairy, with perseverance,
> Scolded with authority
> Her naughty students.

Despite the small dynamic swells in the previous sections, this song has thus far been on a very quiet level. The discreet *crescendos* marked in this next section do not really alter the generally subdued feeling.

We have some interesting harmonic effects in this section: the pedal point on the dominant for the first eight bars; the E♭ under what had been a G minor chord ("dans les halliers"); the C♯ after all that C natural sound (be sure to clear the pedal carefully); the diminished A chord with the major seventh under "zèles" and the similar sound under "sur." The words:

> Her little bare hand,
> With a slender blade of grass
> Plucked from the thickets,
> To stimulate their zeal,
> Spanked their wings,
> These naughty students.

The *meno mosso* section which follows is still quiet and dynamically uninflected. Its four-bar piano introduction consists of a melodic fragment, which begins with a lovely major-seventh sound the first time, and is echoed by the quarter notes in the bass for the second hearing. This four-measure pattern is repeated throughout the section, until the chromatic rise in the bass leads out of that harmonic framework and into the pedal point on D in the next section. The words:

> One autumn morning,
> She comes and is astonished
> To see the woods deserted:

The return to the original tempo brings greater dynamic variety and a new sense of excitement. At "Avaient fui" we have a full *forte* for the first time, but even the lesser *crescendo* which precedes it (under "hirondelles") is backed by tension-producing harmonies. This flurry is quickly subdued, however, for the return to the music of the opening verse. The lines before this return are:

> With the swallows
> Her unfaithful friends
> Had fled into the air.

The actual return is quite subtle because of the two notes (under "Et tout") which precede and somewhat obscure it. After only six measures, Fauré goes on to new material for the closing lines, which are the climax of the song. The unexpected E♭ melody note and A♭ chord, which underlies it at "rom*ances*," provide an especially lovely moment; but the real climax is, of course, the triumphant "prochain Printemps." The final lines of verse are:

> And all winter the Fairy,
> Coiffed with dead grass,
> And counting the minutes,
> In the immense forests,
> Composes ballads
> For the next Spring!

The piano postlude introduces harmonies not heard in the body of the song, as if to prove that Fauré's inventiveness was far from exhausted! It is a lovely passage, which gives the pianist plenty of time for an effective gradual *decrescendo* and fade-out ending.

Aurore　　　　　　　　　　　　　Poem by Armand Silvestre
Dawn　　　　　　　　　　　　　　　OPUS 39/1

Des jardins de la nuit s'envolent les étoiles.
Abeilles d'or qu'attire un invisible miel

Et l'aube, au loin, tendant la candeur de ses toiles,
Trame de fils* d'argent le manteau bleu du ciel.

Du jardin de mon coeur qu'un rêve lent enivre,
S'envolent mes desirs sur les pas du matin.
Comme un essaim léger qu'à l'horizon de cuivre,
Appelle un chant plaintif, éternel et lointain.

Ils volent à tes pieds, astres chassés des nues,
Exilés du ciel d'or où fleurit ta beauté.
Et, cherchant jusqu'à toi des routes inconnues,
Mêlent au jour naissant leur mourante clarté.

The most interesting part of this ABA song is the *minore* section in the middle. Here the piano has an independent melodic line, which sometimes coincides but often clashes with the vocal line. An added complication in this combination is the oft-repeated rhythmic oddity, whereby the accompaniment has a tied note on the first beat, keeping things slightly off balance.

The overall mood of the song is gentle and tender, but despite the *andante* indication the music moves along fast enough so that one feels a constant flow.

The first section begins with a series of churchlike chords, each of which contains the tonic note. This endows the essential I–IV–V pattern with an antique flavor. When the G (the original key and the key for high voice is G major) is finally abandoned (under *"étoiles")* it is for an unexpected III (B minor) chord, which leads to a traditional cadence. The melody is firmly rooted in the tonic scale, beginning with a triad and ending on the tonic note. At the second line of verse we move to E minor, but the altered C# leads to new modulations (the C# on the fourth beat of the sixth measure is inadvertently omitted in the E. B. Marks edition). We do return to the tonic at the end of the section, but not before much harmonic peregrination. The *crescendo* on the third line of verse leads to a climax on the highest note of the last long phrase (under "trame"). The words for the first section are:

The stars fly away from the gardens of the night,
Bees of gold attracted by an invisible honey,
And the dawn, in the distance, spreading the candor of its cloth,
Weaves the blue cloak of the sky with threads of silver.

In the center section the poet turns from the abstract to the personal and the music becomes moodier and dreamier. The mode is now minor and the piano's countermelody (all the double-stemmed notes) is extremely important. The harmonies are even more complex than in

---

* The singer should note that the final *s* is not pronounced in *fils* when it is the plural of *fil* ("thread"), unlike *fils* meaning "son."

the opening segment with none more surprising than that under the melody's E♭ on "s'en*vol*ent." The melody keeps returning to the minor triad from the lovely and varied modulations. The music for the words "sur les pas du matin" is especially interesting melodically and harmonically, with the flatted second (A) on the way up but not on the way down, and its augmented chord (under "pas") which yields to the dominant seventh two beats later. There are equally interesting suspensions under "léger" and "cuivre," and the piano's return immediately after the key change is worthy of special note. The central stanza of the poem is:

> From the garden of my heart which a slow dream intoxicates,
> My desires fly away on the steps of the morning,
> Like a light swarm which at the copper horizon,
> Calls a plaintive song, eternal and distant.

The music of the first section now returns, varied only by the increased movement in the piano figuration and the dramatic change in the dynamic scheme: where the singer's big *forte* arose in the first stanza, we now have a *ritard* and a soft, floating high note. This is undoubtedly the high point of the song, a climax of a very subtle sort. The final lines of verse are:

> They fly to your feet, stars chased from the clouds,
> Exiled from the golden sky where your beauty flourishes
> And looking for unknown routes to you,
> Mingle their fading light in the dawning day.

Fleur jetée　　　　　　　　　Poem by Armand Silvestre
Discarded Flower　　　　　　　　OPUS 39/2

Emporte ma folie
Au gré du vent,
Fleur en chantant cueillie
Et jetée en rêvant
Emporte ma folie
Au gré du vent.

Comme la fleur fauchée,
Périt l'amour
La main qui t'a touchée
Fuit ma main sans retour,
Comme la fleur fauchée,
Périt l'amour
La main qui t'a touchée
Fuit ma main sans retour.

Que le vent qui te sèche,
O pauvre fleur,

Tout à l'heure si fraiche
Et demain sans couleur,
Que le vent qui te sèche,
O pauvre fleur,
Que le vent qui te sèche,
Sèche mon coeur.

The wild, turbulent passion with which this song is infused from beginning to end makes it most unusual for its normally mild-mannered composer. The repeated octaves and chords in the accompaniment will undoubtedly remind the pianist of Schubert's "Erl King," although Fauré is much more merciful than his great predecessor in allowing the right hand moments of surcease. The *allegro energico* indication is erroneously translated into an impossible metronome marking (quarter note = 170) in the E. B. Marks edition for high voice. Perhaps an eighth note = 170 was intended, although that seems a little on the safe side. The Schirmer edition for low voice calls for a dotted quarter note = 72 which is quite fast. Obviously the performers have some leeway within the given stormy mood.

The piano begins with repeated octaves which must build in strength until the downward rush of octaves in the bass. The singer enters impetuously and angrily with a rising interval followed by a descending tonic scale fragment and triad (the original key and the key for high voice is F minor). The dynamic level drops momentarily, but only to prepare for the next *crescendo*. When the first line of verse is repeated, the voice climbs still higher for greater intensity and dramatic power, and the harmony shifts to A♭, the relative major. In the repeated line, a strange chord is created under the word "gré" by a double suspension over what becomes E♭⁷, the dominant, whereby we reach A♭ at "vent." The words for this first section are:

Carry my madness to the will of the wind,
Flower picked while (we were) singing
And thrown away while (we were) dreaming
Carry my madness to the will of the wind.

The relative balm offered by the major modality is short-lived, for an agitated scale figure in the accompaniment brings us to a diminished chord for the beginning of the next section. The anguish of the rejected lover is reflected musically by the many dissonances in this segment of the song: the ominous F, G, A♭ combination under "Périt," the melody's E♭ against the F octave in the bass, the F♭–E♭ under "touché," etc. The entire section builds from a *piano* to a tremendous *forte* on the highest note (A♭) under "Pér*it*" in the repeated line of verse, after which a *diminuendo* gradually brings the dynamic level down to a *piano*. Each of the four short lines of poetry is used twice by the composer:

> Like the cut flower
> Love perishes
> The hand which touched you
> Flees from my hand without returning

Despite all the modulations, the tonal center for the above section has remained A♭; using the A♭ octave as a pedal point, Fauré gradually brings us back to the original F minor key for the final section. We have a recapitulation of the music of the first verse for eight measures, but the poem calls for a more fiery and dramatic ending than that given to the close of the first section; Fauré then extends the poem by additional repetition, thereby allowing time for the melodic line to rise to the highest note reached in the piece, the A♮ under the last "vent." The two measures preceding this climactic moment contain its harmonic preparation: the E♭ in the bass changes enharmonically to D♯, while the right hand chord and melody note above it move to A major. We precipitously return to F minor in the following measure by way of the A♭ melody note over a C♯ minor chord, which moves to a C^{7-9}. In the last four measures, instead of alternating I–V–I chords, Fauré uses a I–VI–I pattern. This does not change the fact that the real return to the tonic was effected by a V–I cadence. The last lines of verse (including repetitions) are:

> May the wind that withers you,
> Oh poor flower
> Presently so fresh
> And tomorrow colorless
> May the wind that withers you
> Oh poor flower
> May the wind that withers you
> Wither my heart.

Le Pays des rêves   Poem by Armand Silvestre
The Land of Dreams   OPUS 39/3

> Veux-tu qu'au beau pays des rêves
> Nous allions la main dans la main?
> Plus loin que l'odeur des jasmins,
> Plus haut que la plainte des grèves.
> Veux-tu du beau pays des rêves,
> Tous les deux chercher le chemin?
> J'ai taillé dans l'azur les toiles
> Du vaisseau qui nous portera,

Et doucement nous conduira
Jusqu'au verger d'or des étoiles.

Mais combien la terre est lointaine,
Que poursuivent ses blancs sillons;
Au caprice des papillons
Demandons la route incertaine.
Ah, combien la terre est lointaine
Où fleurissent nos visions.
Vois tu: le beau pays des rêves
Est trop haut pour les pas humains.
Respirons à deux les jasmins,
Et chantons encore sur les grèves.
Vois-tu: du beau pays des rêves
L'amour seul en sait les chemins.

This long, rambling song takes on a search for the "Land of Dreams." Though we never reach our destination, the trip is so full of delights that we have no regrets.

The voyage is evidently made in a ship, for the 12/8 rocking rhythm is typical of the boat song. This particular ship is as likely to be floating on air as on sea, for the *tessitura* of the accompaniment is quite high, with both hands in treble clef more often than not. The length of the song and its relaxed tempo suggest a leisurely, even languorous trip; the gently swelling but narrow dynamic range (*p* to *mf*) indicates no storm or other disturbance to upset the even keel.

The song was originally written for high voice in the key of A♭. The piano has a two-bar introduction in which to establish the rhythm and tonality. (At no point does the piano transcend its role as accompanist.) The voice enters with a long melodic phrase, which has as its focus the dominant. After three bars of a I–III–I pattern, Fauré introduces an F⁷ chord (under "rêves Nous") which leads to a minor chord on the dominant (under "allions la main dans la"). When in the next measure the dominant is heard again in major, one has a sense of exultant upward movement. It is a beautiful sequence, which Fauré repeats immediately and then many times elsewhere throughout the song.

After the repeat of this first melodic and harmonic idea, Fauré moves farther away from the tonic, passing through C minor, G major, B⁷, and E minor before returning to A♭ by way of an augmented E♭ chord (at "le chemin"). The melodic line rises in a whole-tone scale from "Tous les deux" to "chemin," creating an ephemeral, "lost-in-the-stars" mood. The piano's lower line moves temporarily to bass clef to provide a change in color. The words for this section are:

Would you like to go hand in hand
To the beautiful land of dreams?
Further than the scent of jasmines,

Higher than the wail of the shores
Would you like us together to search for the route
To the beautiful land of dreams?

The music for the second verse is a recapitulation of the earlier material; only the transitional bars leading to the following section are different. The second verse reads:

I have fashioned sails of the sky
For the boat which will carry us,
And gently lead us
To the golden orchard of the stars.
I have fashioned sails of the sky
For the boat that will carry us.

Suddenly the piano ceases its rocking motion and we find ourselves in 4/4 time. The diminished chord under "Mais" alerts us that the voyagers are reassessing their situation but cannot stand suspended for very long, so the 12/8 barcarolle rhythm gets them underway again. For the second time, a diminished chord breaks the flow (under "Ah, combien"); when the 12/8 returns again it is on an earthbound, thrice-repeated D major chord. The text for this section is:

But how far away is the land
That its white furrows pursue;
From the whim of the butterflies
Let us ask the uncertain route.
Ah, how far away is the land
Where our vision blossoms.

In the next section Fauré continues the rocking rhythm while virtually suspending motion—the vocal line is all on one note for almost an entire measure and the accompaniment is equally static. Our voyagers are treading water, so to speak. After four bars of this strange stationary motion, the music of the first verse returns. The vocal line ends with the ascending whole-tone scale accompanied by the lovely E minor, E♭+, A♭ progression. The piano postlude allows the rolled chords to climb to the uppermost celestial register. The final lines of the poem are:

Look: the beautiful land of dreams
Is too high for human steps.
Let us both breathe the scent of jasmins,
And let us still sing on the shores,
Look: Love alone knows the paths
Of the beautiful land of dreams.

Les Roses d'Ispahan Poem by Leconte de Lisle
The Roses of Ispahan OPUS 39/4

Les roses d'Ispahan dans leur gaine de mousse,
Les jasmins de Mossoul, les fleurs de l'oranger,
Ont un parfum moins frais, ont une odeur moins douce,
O blanche Leïlah! que ton souffle léger.

Ta lèvre est de corail et ton rire léger
Sonne mieux que l'eau vive et d'une voix plus douce.
Mieux que le vent joyeux qui berce l'oranger,
Mieux que l'oiseau qui chante au bord d'un nid de mousse.

O Leïlah! depuis que de leur vol léger
Tous les baisers ont fui de ta lèvre si douce
Il n'est plus de parfum dans le pâle oranger,
Ni de céleste arome aux roses dans leur mousse.

Oh! que ton jeune amour, ce papillon léger,
Revienne vers mon coeur d'une aile prompte et douce.
Et qu'il parfume encor la fleur de l'oranger,
Les roses d'Ispahan dans leur gaine de mousse.

The structure of this lovely song is derived from its severely disciplined, symmetrical text. A glance at the words reveals the following rhyme scheme:

I	II	III	IV
mousse	léger	léger	léger
oranger	douce	douce	douce
douce	oranger	oranger	oranger
léger	mousse	mousse	mousse

Leconte de Lisle, author of this poem and spokesman for the "Parnassiens," revered the classic order of Greek art. When, as he does in "Les Roses d'Ispahan," he creates an exotic and sensual atmosphere within the formal structure, he gives us his most successful poetry.

This combination of the formalistic and the exotic is echoed in Fauré's setting. The opening melodic line provides the first example, for the first three notes are a standard tonic triad (the key for high voice is E major), but the following notes which ascend to the dominant jump from II to IV, creating a one-and-a-half step interval which sounds exotic in the context.

There is virtually no harmonic movement for the first fourteen measures, but suddenly there is an upward thrust in the accompaniment and the singer has a long phrase on a $C\sharp^7$ harmony. This occasions a dynamic rise as well, for we are heading toward the climactic

"O blanche Leïlah!" which contains the highest note and the dramatic peak of the section. The first verse of the poem is:

> The roses of Ispahan in their sheath of moss
> The jasmines of Mossoul, the flowers of the orange tree,
> Have a perfume less fresh, have an odor less sweet,
> Oh pale Leïlah! than your light breath.

The music for the second verse is identical to that of the first until the last two measures, which serve as transition to a contrasting section. Its words are:

> Your lips are of coral and your light laughter
> Rings better than running water and with a sweeter sound,
> Better than the joyous wind which rocks the orange tree,
> Better than the bird that sings near a nest of moss.

On the last word of this second verse ("mousse") Fauré abruptly changes the harmony to G♯, thus beginning the most exotic-sounding section of the piece. It is difficult to pinpoint just what in the music creates the sensual, slightly mysterious effect—the augmented chord just before the voice enters, the chromatic rise and fall on "douce," the augmented chord in the following measure, the gorgeous harmonies under the falling and rising scale fragment, the insistent F♯–C♯ combined with G major chords under "céleste" and "roses"—all these devices have a cumulative, almost hypnotic effect which is undeniable. The words for this third verse are:

> Oh Leïlah! since in their light flight
> All the kisses have flown from your lips so sweet
> There is no more perfume in the pale orange-tree
> Nor heavenly aroma in the roses in their moss.

Fauré now brings us back to the music of the opening. The dynamic indications for the last verse are also the same, but since this is the final section the *crescendo* and the fade out might be more exaggerated than they were before. Because of the *ritard,* the G♯ minor tonality under "dans leur gaîne" will also receive more emphasis than it did in the first verse (under "que ton souffle"). The last lines of verse are:

> Oh! that your young love, that light butterfly,
> Might return to my heart on a swift and gentle wing.
> And that it might perfume again the flower of the orange tree,
> The roses of Ispahan in their sheath of moss.

La nuit descend du haut des cieux,
Le givre au toit suspend ses franges,
Et dans les airs, le vol des anges éveille un bruit mystérieux.
L'étoile qui guidait les mages,

S'arrête enfin dans les nuages,
Et fait briller un nimbe d'or
Sur la chaumière où Jésus dort.

Alors, ouvrant ses yeux divins,
L'enfant couché dans l'humble crèche,
De son berceau de paille fraîche,
Sourit aux nobles pélérins.

Eux, s'inclinant, lui disent:
Sire, Reçois l'encens, l'or et la myrrhe,
Et laisse-nous, ô doux Jésus, baiser le bout de tes pieds nus.

Comme eux, ô peuple, incline-toi,
Imite leur pieux exemple,
Car cette étable c'est un temple,
Et cet enfant sera ton roi!

This is a rather strange setting for a Christmas song. The introductory bars feature a syncopated rhythm (the accents on the double-stemmed notes), which suggests a horse's gait. This "traveling" music continues for four bars after the singer's entrance and returns a few measures later. Even when the weak beat accents are discontinued, the right hand figure evokes much the same effect.

The vocal line frequently seems at odds with the accompaniment: in the very first measure where both are heard we have three consecutive intervals of a second (under "nuit descend").

In this opening section the mood seems more matter-of-fact than reverential, but the words have already begun the age-old tale:

Night descends from on high
The hoarfrost hangs its fringe on the roof,

At "Et, dans les airs," the piano figure changes, becoming more delicate, less accented, and less "busy." The simple rising melody seems less mundane, more spiritual, and the modulation to C major under "mystér*ieux*" carries us to the celestial. (The song is here analyzed in A flat, key for high voice. In the E. B. Marks edition the key signature erroneously includes a Gb for the first page.) The two lines of verse for this music are:

And in the air, the flight of angels
Evokes a mysterious sound.

A soaring C major arpeggio leads to the next section. Here the piano begins a triplet sixteenth note figure above the syncopated rhythm of the opening. Since there is less motion in the bass figure than there had been in the beginning, the celestial mood is not really disturbed. The melody for this section is of considerable scope, with wide expressive intervals (under "les mages" and "nuages"), and a fairly long chromatic fragment (from "fait briller" to "d'or"). The strongest dynamics are on "fait briller."

All this, while the accompaniment has stressed the dominant, with repeated excursions to C flat. There is a lovely augmented chord after "briller." The words for this section are:

> The star that guided the Magi,
> Finally stops in the clouds,
> And causes a golden halo to shine
> Over the thatched-roof cottage where Jesus sleeps.

The descending triplet sixteenth notes lead to a new version of our "traveling music," this one with a two-against-three polyrhythm instead of the syncopations. The melody and harmonies are a repeat of the opening section. The words are:

> Then, opening His divine eyes,
> The Child bedded in the humble crèche,
> From his cradle of fresh straw,
> Smiles at the noble pilgrims.

With very minor alterations the melody continues to repeat the original material. The harmonic scheme is also a continuation of the repeat, but the figuration is completely different, with continuous sixteenth-note broken chords in the bass and rolled chords on the weak beats in the right hand. Here the words are:

> They, bowing, say to Him:
> "Sire, receive incense, gold and myrrh,
> And allow us, O sweet Jesus,
> To kiss the tips of your bare feet."

For the last four lines of the poem we have a new vocal line, which is obviously derived from the first melody of the song. The piano figuration of the previous section is carried over for this final segment. For seven measures (from "nus" to "c'est un") there is a pedal point on the tonic, with various chords floating on top. The climactic measures of the section, and for that matter of the piece, occur when the tonic pedal point finally yields. The last line—"Et cet enfant sera ton roi!"— is of course the most important, but the *crescendo* begins two bars earlier.

Although the melody appears to have a simple V–I close, the underlying harmony at this point is III–I. The piano postlude has a combination IV–VI before the final tonic chord. The last four lines of verse are:

Like them, O people, bow down,
Imitate their pious example,
For this stable is a temple,
And this child will be your King!

Nocturne   Poem by Villiers de L'Isle-Adam
                                                    OPUS 43/2

La nuit, sur le grand mystère,
Éntr'ouvre ses écrins bleus:
Autant de fleurs sur la terre,
Que d'étoiles dans les cieux!
On voit ses ombres dormantes
S'éclairer à tous moments,
Autant par les fleurs charmantes
Que par les astres charmants.
Moi, ma nuit au sombre voile
N'a pour charme et pour clarté,
Qu'une fleur et qu'une étoile:
Mon amour et ta beauté.

This brief love song describes the night in haunting metaphors. Words and music combine to evoke the mysterious beauty of the nocturnal sky, with its stars like jewels or flowers. There is a sensuous, exotic quality to the music, similar in feeling to "Les Roses d'Ispahan" (Opus 39/4); singer and pianist share equally in creating this mood.

The two-bar piano introduction is a simple statement of the tonality (C major for high voice) and the voice enters with a predictable V–I, but in the fourth and fifth measures the harmonic changes pull the melodic line to an Ab scale fragment (under "ouvre ses écrins") before the return to the tonic at the end of the phrase. This undulation in harmony and melody is responsible for the exotic aura which continues throughout the rest of the section, aided and abetted by the weaving *minore* figure in the piano, the swaying melodic line, and above all the Ab scale over the Db chord under "dans les." This measure provides a gorgeous return to the tonic—one of Fauré's loveliest substitutions for the V⁷–I cadence. The first verse reads:

The night, on the great mystery,
Opens its blue jewelry boxes:
As many flowers on earth
As stars in the sky!

The music of the first verse is repeated while the words continue:

One sees the sleeping shadows
Being brightened at each moment,
As much by the charming flowers
As by the charming stars.

Fauré now moves to C minor, but from here to the end of the piece there is much harmonic motion. Characteristic chords, such as the F^9 at "nuit" and the combined F–C minor at "charme," exemplify Fauré's rich harmonic palette. We now have the first dynamic indication other than *p* or *dolce,* for a *crescendo* begins under "voile" which leads to the high point of the song, "Qu'une fleur." As is so often the case, this is also the highest note in the piece.

Under "étoile" we have the beginning of an eight measure pedal point on G, the dominant, but here again Fauré uses a wide variety of harmonies over this one note. Most striking is the change wrought in the measure with the Db chord and the Ab scale: the melody note is now an F, which is of course part of the Db triad; when this melody note descends to the final E, the listener expects the resolution to the tonic which had occurred in the first two verses; instead, Fauré gives us a false cadence to an E minor chord. The singer holds the E for three long measures, after which the accompaniment finally changes to a tonic chord. This harmonic shift is unprepared and is indeed a different substitute for the V–I cadence. The poem concludes:

As for me, my darkly veiled night
Has for charm and brightness,
Only one flower and only one star:
My love and your beauty.

Les Présents   Poem by Villiers de L'Isle-Adam
Gifts   OPUS 46/1

Si tu demandes quelque soir
Le secret de mon coeur malade,
Je te dirai pour t'émouvoir,
Une très ancienne ballade!

Si tu, me parles de torments,
S'espérance désabusée,
J'irai te cueillir seulement
Des roses pleines de rosée!

Si, pareille à la fleur des morts
Qui fleurit dans l'éxil des tombes,
Tu veux partager mes remords,
Je t'apporterai des colombes!

Opus 46 consists of two songs, "Les Présents" (Gifts) and "Clair de lune" (Moonlight). Related by neither the texts nor the music, these songs may be sung individually or in tandem.

The first is a gentle, melancholy song which well suits the wistful, fanciful poem by Villiers de L'Isle-Adam (1818–1894), one of the leading poets of "Le Parnasse." The poem expresses the aims of this group of poets: to eschew public avowals of personal anguish, to be impersonal, contemplative and wise. This was a reaction to the heart-on-sleeve romanticism of the preceding generation of poets.

The piano introduction is a twice-told F major to A♭ major progression, which continues as the singer enters. The vocal quality here should be as calm, cool and philosophical as the words suggest.

> If some evening you should ask the secret
> Of my sick heart,

Now, at measure nine, the harmony changes abruptly to an augmented C chord; this introduces a meandering three-measure interlude which manages to bring us back to the tonic by a remarkably original harmonic route. During these 4 bars the singer has continued,

> I shall tell you—to move you—
> A very ancient ballad!

The second segment of the poem says,

> If you speak to me of torments,
> Of hopes disabused,
> I shall go to gather only roses
> Full of dew!

The music is even more complex and haunting here, with an especially beautiful cadence (G diminished to C♭) underlying "J'irai" and a surprising variation on the old V–I (the dominant seventh chord has a raised 5th) at the end of the section.

The piano figuration develops more motion in the next section by the use of sixteenth notes instead of chords. The augmented C chord, which replaces the A♭ we have become accustomed to hearing, creates a strong harmonic effect without influencing the singer's rising line. Fauré accomplishes this by the enharmonic change from A♭ to G♯; the difference in sound is of course due to the E♮.

The singer begins the final verse with the same upward F major scale that opened each of the preceding sections. Here the words are,

> If, like the flower of the dead
> Which blooms in the exile of the grave,
> You want to share my remorse,
> I shall bring you doves!

The vocal line, from Db, Gb of "Je t'apporterai . . . ," and the supporting chords suggest a modulation to Eb and an Eb⁷–Ab cadence. Instead, we have a gorgeous false cadence, Eb⁷–F, which brings us back to the tonic. Not content with this close, Fauré give us a still stranger false cadence, D⁷–F, as the short piano postlude.

Not once in the entire song has Fauré used a normal V⁷–I close. Is this an expression of the delightful non sequiturs in the poem?

Clair de lune	Poem by Paul Verlaine
Moonlight	OPUS 46/2

Votre âme est un paysage choisi,
Que vont charmant masques et bergamasques
Jouant du luth et dansant,
Et quasi tristes sous leurs déguisements fantasques!

Tout en chantant, sur le mode mineur,
L'amour vainqueur et la vie opportune,
Ils n'ont pas l'air de croire à leur bonheur,
Et leur chanson se mêle au clair de lune!

Au calme clair de lune, triste et beau,
Qui fait rêver les oiseaux dans les arbres,
Et sangloter d'extase les jets d'eau,
Les grands jets d'eau sveltes parmi les marbres!

"Clair de lune," subtitled "Menuet," is a much more familiar song than its opus-mate. The poem, one of Paul Verlaine's most evocative, has also been set by Debussy (see pages 283 and 339).

Fauré's setting begins with a long piano prelude which is really an independent piece, with its own distinctive melodic line and harmonic structure. The unique way in which the vocal line interacts with the tune in the piano part is the most absorbing aspect of the song: often they seem to disregard one another completely; at some moments they are in close harmony (under the words "mode mineur," "la vie," "croire à"); occasionally the singer echoes the piano line; for two brief moments they are in unison ("paysage *choisi*," "d'extas*e les jets d'eau*"); and for four whole measures the piano has straight accompaniment!

The words are typical of Verlaine and later Symbolist poets, full of strange metaphors, far-fetched juxtapositions, and words chosen for their sensuous sound rather than their explicit meaning.

Your soul is an elect landscape
Where spell-binding masqueraders and dancers,

Play the lute and dance,
And are almost sad under their fantastic disguises!

As the singer continues:

While singing in the minor mode

Fauré gives us a whole measure of clearly major tonality, perhaps a private joke, perhaps an avoidance of a musical cliché.
The poem continues,

Of love, the conqueror, and opportune life,
They don't seem to believe in their happiness,
And their song blends with the moonlight.

Up to this point the piano's melodic line has actually been more singable than the singer's, but here the rôles become more traditional, with the piano playing a broken-chord accompaniment and the singer reveling in a lovely *espressivo e dolce* phrase.

In the calm moonlight, sad and beautiful,
Which makes the birds dream in the trees,

The crucial word in this last line, "rêver" (dream), is hard to hear because its first syllable falls on a weak beat. The singer must take pains to separate "fait" from "rêver" to make the meaning clear.
Meanwhile the piano has already returned to its own song. The words continue:

And (makes) the fountains sob with ecstasy,
The tall, slim streams amid the statues!

The piano ends the song with a postlude similar to the prelude. The minor modality is firmly established in the last two measures after an unusual VI–I cadence (major–minor) has been heard twice. Once again, as is his wont, Fauré has avoided the V⁷–I cadence while steadfastly insisting on a clear tonic ending. His resourcefulness in inventing new final cadences borders on the miraculous!

Larmes   Poem by Jean Richepin
Tears   OPUS 51/1

Pleurons nos chagrins, chacun le nôtre;
Une larme tombe, puis une autre:
Toi, qui pleures-tu? ton doux pays, test parents lointains, ta fiancée.
Moi, mon existence dépensée en voeux trahis!

Pleurons nos chagrins, chacun le nôtre;
Une larme tombe, puis une autre.

Semons dans la mer ces pâles fleurs!
A notre sanglot qui se lamente
Elle répondra par la tourmente de flots hurleurs.

Pleurons nos chagrins, chacun le nôtre;
Une larme tombe, puis une autre.
Peut-être toi-même, ô triste mer,
Mer au gout de larme acre et salée,
Es-tu de la terre inconsolée le pleur amer!

"Tears," which is part of a larger work called *The Sea* by Jean Richepin, is an intensely dramatic song from beginning to end. Its two measures of piano introduction consist of a stormy, choppy figure in which C minor (the tonic in the key for high voice), Eb (the relative major) and Eb augmented chords alternate. This is the characteristic piano figure which reappears throughout the song.

The first two lines of verse, "Pleurons nos chagrins, chacun le nôtre;/Une larme tombe, puis une autre" (Let us cry for our sorrows, each for his own;/One tear falls, then another) are like a refrain, although they begin, rather than end each stanza. Each time these words are repeated, the original melodic line and chordal pattern are heard, but the pitch moves up one half step at each repeat. This steplike rise in pitch adds to the turbulence and excitement. In the final repeat the melody rises an additional half step for the second of the two lines, pushing us towards the tremendous *crescendo* and climactic final notes. The melody for these two lines is in itself dramatic, with a V–I opening interval and a half-step rise to the dominant at the end of each line.

After the opening lines discussed above, the first stanza continues with a question and some possible answers. The music becomes gentle under the words "ton doux pays . . . fiancée." These more tranquil measures are less personal—they muse over another's tears—but from the word "Moi," as the poet's thoughts return to his own woes, the intensity of his own sorrow brings back his pain, which is reflected in the greater intensity of the music. The first stanza reads:

Let us cry for our sorrows, each for his own;
One tear falls, then another:
You, why do you cry? for your sweet land,
Your distant relatives, your fiancée.
Me, I cry for my existence wasted on vows betrayed.

The key change which allows the opening lines of the second stanza to be heard on the higher pitch actually occurs under the last line of the first stanza. This will not be true for the transition between stanzas two and three, where the key change occurs right on the refrain. The gentler section in the second stanza is even shorter than its counterpart in the first stanza. In this section it coincides with the lines of text in which tears are called "pale flowers" which are sown into the sea. This second stanza has a strong climax on "Elle répondra . . . hurleurs." The accompaniment here abandons its characteristic figure in favor of strong octaves, for the most part in unison with the vocal line. The piano is given but one brief measure, at the end of the stanza, in which to pull back the dynamic level so that the final stanza can make its point. The words for this center section are:

> Let us cry for our sorrows, each for his own;
> One tear falls, then another.
> Let us scatter on the sea our pale flowers!
> To our sigh which bemoans itself
> She (the sea) will respond by the torment of her howling waves.

The third and final stanza begins softly, albeit with the characteristic melodic line and chordal pattern. Under the second line of text a new piano figure is heard, an ominous dotted-eighth-plus-sixteenth-note octave figure in the bass. An enormous *crescendo* begins at "Es-tu de la terre" and continues right to the climactic high note at the end of the vocal part. The melody ends on the dominant in this remarkably tonal song, and the chords of the postlude are mostly tonic-dominant combinations, although the dominant is augmented, thereby avoiding any banality in the V–I sequence. The main function of the postlude is the *diminuendo* from the singer's climax to the *pp* C minor final cord. The last lines of verse are:

> Let us cry for our sorrows, each for his own;
> One tear falls, then another.
> Perhaps you yourself, O sad sea,
> Sea which tastes like tears, acrid and salty,
> Are you of the unconsolable land the bitter tears!

Au cimetière   Poem by Jean Richepin
At the Cemetery   OPUS 51/2

Heureux qui meurt ici,
Ainsi que les oiseaux des champs!
Son corps, près des amis,
Est mis dans l'herbe et dans les chants.

Il dort d'un bon sommeil vermeil,
Sous le ciel radieux.
Tous ceux qu'il a connus, venus,
Lui font de longs adieux.

A sa croix les parents, pleurants,
Restent agenouillés;

Et ses os, sous les fleurs, de pleurs
Sont doucement mouillés.

Chacun, sur le bois noir,
Peut voir s'il était jeune ou non,
Et peut, avec de vrais regrets,
L'appeler par son nom.

Combien plus malchanceux
Sont ceux qui meurent à la mé,
Et sous le flot profond
S'en vont loin du pays aimé!

Ah! pauvres! qui pour seuls linceuls
Ont les goémons verts,
Où l'on roule inconnu, tout nu,
Et les yeux grands ouverts!

Heureux qui meurt ici,
Ainsi que les oiseaux des champs!
Son corps, près des amis,
Est mis dans l'herbe et dans les chants.

Il dort d'un bon sommeil vermeil,
Sous le ciel radieux.
Tous ceux qu'il a connus, venus,
Lui font de longs adieux.

"Au cimetière," the second song of this two-part opus, presents another aspect of the sea as seen by poet Jean Richepin. In the preceding song the sea is thought of as the bitter tears shed by the inconsolable Earth; here the sea is described as the most horrible and inhospitable of all graves, in contrast to which the cemetery is tranquil and consoling.

Aside from its vivid imagery the most interesting feature of the poem is its brilliant rhyme scheme, according to which contiguous words, be they the last word of one line and the first word of the next, or the last two words of the same line, rhyme. Other inner rhymes abound, and of course we have the normal end-sound rhyme scheme (*abab*/*cded*/etc.). The example quoted below illustrates the complexity of the rhyme patterns:

Heureux qui meurt ici,	*a*
Ainsi que les oiseaux des champs!	*b*
Son corps, près des amis,	*a*
Est mis dans l'herbe et dans les chants.	*b*
Il dort d'un bon sommeil vermeil,	*c*
Sous le ciel radieux.	*d*
Tous ceux qu'il a connus, venus,	*e*
Lui font de longs adieux.	*d*

Since the subject matter is the relative merits of a traditional earth burial versus a watery grave, it is no surprise to find the music sombre and slow. The sections devoted to descriptions of the cemetery itself are serene in their sorrow, but the central verses, which deal with the horrors of being buried at sea, are stormy and anguished.

The piano begins with a minimal introduction—simple minor triads on the tonic (D minor for high voice). Like so many of Fauré's melodic lines, the first vocal phrase begins and ends on the dominant; in fact, the first six lines hover around the dominant note, A, and it is not until the end of the second verse that the vocal line descends to the tonic. Under the word "chants" the accompanying chords shift to the major mode, lightening the mood until the doleful cadence under "longs adieux." The words to this point are:

> Happy is he who dies here,
> Like the birds in the fields!
> His body, near friends,
> Is one with the grass and the songs.
>
> He sleeps a good rosy sleep,
> Under the radiant sky.
> All those whom he has known come,
> To say their long goodbye.

The next two stanzas continue to reflect the sombre but reconciled mood of the beginning. Although we return to the original D minor triads at the beginning of the section, interesting modulations—many of them quite antique-sounding—bring us to A major at "mouillés." The melodic line rises optimistically from "A sa croix" to "agenouillés," only to fall again to the low D of the tonic scale. The minor ending of this section seems a bit heavier in mood than its counterpart in the first part. The words are:

> At his cross relatives, crying,
> Remain kneeling;
> And his bones, under the flowers, with tears
> Are sweetly dampened.
>
> Each person, under the dark wood,
> Can see if he was young or not.
> And can, with true regrets,
> Call him by name.

A brief piano interlude on all D minor chords now provides the opportunity for a tremendous *crescendo*, for now the stormy section is about to begin. Fauré's instructions to the singer say *declamato*, "in a declamatory style." The dynamic level begins at a *forte* and builds relentlessly to a double *forte*. The pitch rises chromatically, twice at four-bar intervals and again after eight bars, in melody and accompaniment; the tessitura is consistently high in comparison to the rest of the song as the vocal line proceeds in half or whole steps, each four measure phrase using but three contiguous notes. An interesting note on the text—the word "mer" has been altered to "mé," a dialect usage, for the sake of its rhyme with the following word "Et." The words are:

> How much more unfortunate
> Are those who die at sea,
> And under the deep waves
> Go far from their beloved homelands.
>
> Ah! poor souls! who for their only shroud
> Have green seaweed,
> Where one is tossed about, unknown, all nude,
> And with eyes opened wide!

Crashing bass notes and chords accompany this gruesome imagery, but a rapid *diminuendo* brings us back to the serenity of the earlier sections. For the last time D minor chords introduce the original melody, words, and harmonies as the entire first section is repeated. A few closing chords are added, increasing the solemnity of the final measures.

Spleen   Poem by Paul Verlaine
OPUS 51/3

> Il pleure dans mon coeur comme il pleut sur la ville.
> Quelle est cette langueur qui pénètre mon coeur?
> O bruit doux de la pluie
> Par terre et sur les toits!
> Pour un coeur qui s'ennuie
> O le chant de la pluie!
> Il pleure sans raison
> Dans mon coeur qui s'écoeure.
>
> Quoi! nulle trahison?
> Mon deuil est sans raison?
> C'est bien la pire peine de ne savoir pourquoi . . .
> Sans amour et sans haine
> Mon coeur a tant de peine!

Several poems by Verlaine have been set to music by both Debussy and Fauré, notably "Clair de Lune," "En Sourdine," "Green," "C'est L'Extase," and "Mandoline." Each of these composers has also written a song called "Spleen" to a poem by Verlaine, but in this case two different texts are used: the famous "Il pleure dans mon coeur" by Fauré and a poem whose first line is "Les roses étaient toutes rouges" by Debussy. To add to the confusion, Debussy has also set the poem "Il pleure dans mon coeur," but like Verlaine he gives the first line of the poem as its title.

The Debussy and Fauré settings of "Il pleure dans mon coeur" are almost exactly contemporaneous, Fauré's having been written circa 1889 and Debussy's in 1888. There are of course similarities—both composers start with a raindrop figure in the piano introduction and both continue the figure throughout the song—but the extensive use of whole-tone patterns, broken by significant downward half-step intervals in the Debussy version, surrounds the words with an aura of vague discontent, which this listener finds more beautiful and more appropriate than that of Fauré. This is of course a matter of opinion totally subject to dispute! For a complete discussion of the Debussy version see page 310.

The impact of the opening line of the poem hinges on the similarity of the words "pleuvoir" and "pleurer," to rain and to cry, in the third person singular (il pleure, il pleut). No translation, literal or free, can do justice to the phrase as it sounds in French. An old adage says that a translation is like a woman—if it's beautiful it's not faithful and if it's faithful it's not beautiful. In places like this where the sound is half the significance, it is hard for the translation to be either!

Fauré's music seems a little less sad than the words which inspired it. The *andante quasi allegretto* tempo indication and the repeated "raindrop" staccato notes assure a sense of movement, and warn the performers not to bog down. In the second and third measures of the introduction, the bass line has a V–I melodic interval (the key for high voice is E minor) which is echoed by the singer's opening notes. As is so common with Fauré, the vocal part focuses on the dominant for the first phrase.

Just before the words "O bruit doux," the raindrop figure yields to a gentle triplet on the tonic in the accompaniment. At "sur les toits," the triplets become sixteenth notes and the mode changes to a soothing major, which lasts but one measure. The next line, "Pour un coeur qui s'ennuie," is sung all on one note while the harmonies shift in the accompanying triplets. The raindrop figure now alternates with the triplets until a climax is reached under "Il pleure sans raison." This is a real cry of anguish, which leads to a descending scale, a rapid *diminuendo,* and a break in the vocal part. The words thus far are:

> It weeps in my heart
> As it rains in the city.
> What is this languor
> That pervades my heart?

The soft sound of the rain
On the ground and on the roofs!
For a heart that grows weary
Oh the sound of the rain!

It cries without reason
In this disheartened heart.

The music in the piano part is gentle under the beginning of "s'écoeure," but the strong discord in the measure of the last syllable of that word underscores once again the pain expressed in these two important lines of text.

After these words the piano has one measure of raindrop music before the vocal part continues. The exclamation "Quoi" is given an entire measure, which sets off the climactic rise at "nulle trahison?" The music for "nulle trahison," and the descending line which follows, is reiterated from the second line of the first section, making the word "Quoi" a truncated stand-in for the opening line, an effective structural device. There is another *crescendo* under "de ne savoir pourquoi" and another climax at "Sans amour et sans haine." The last five words are sung to a sorrowful descending scale which ends on the tonic. This five-note minor scale fragment is repeated in the postlude, first in octaves, then in single notes. The E minor tonality is stressed here and throughout the song to a degree unusual in the works of this composer. The second part of the poem reads:

What! No teachery?
This mourning is without cause?
It is by far the worst pain
Not to know why,
Without love and without hate,
My heart has so much pain.

La Rose (Ode Anacréontique)   Poem by Leconte de Lisle
The Rose   OPUS 51/4

Je dirai la Rose aux plis gracieux.
La Rose est le souffle embaumé des Dieux,
Le plus cher souci des Muses divines.
Je dirai ta gloire, ô charme des yeux,
O fleur de kypris, reine des collines!

Tu t'épanouis entre les beaux doigts
De l'Aube écartant les ombres moroses;
L'Air bleu devient rose et rose les bois;
La bouche et le sein des vierges sont roses!

Heureuse la vierge aux bras arrondis
Qui dans les halliers humides te cueille!

Heureux le front jeune où tu resplendis!
Heureuse la coupe où nage ta feuille!

Ruisselante encor du flot paternel,
Quand de la mer bleue
Aphrodite éclose
Etincela nue aux clartés du ciel,
La terre jalouse enfanta la rose;

Et l'Olympe entier, d'amour transporté,
Salua la fleur avec la Beauté!

It is hard to imagine a more typically "Parnassien" poem than "La Rose" (Ode Anacréontique) by Leconte de Lisle, on which Fauré based this song. All the aims of the Parnassien poets, of whom de Lisle was chief spokesman, are here fulfilled: the poem is impersonal and "cool," it has references to Classical Greece, it is concerned with beauty for beauty's sake, and its language is elegant and crystal clear. *Anacréontique* is a Gallicized Greek word meaning bacchic and convivial, but our accustomed view of Bacchus as a wine-imbibing, slightly ribald figure is obviously far from the image de Lisle wished to evoke—nothing could be more delicate and innocent than this Ode to a Rose.

The poet's imagery is delightful: he sees the rose as the embodied breath of the Gods, as the jealous earth's rival to Aphrodite, beautiful daughter of the sea. Fauré's delicately flowing music well matches the lyric grace of the text. The sixteenth notes in the accompaniment support the melodic line without disruption; the dynamics undulate with gradual *crescendos* and *diminuendos* uninterrupted by harsh accents; the vocal part is virtually continuous, with only one short break before "Ruisselante encore."

The accompaniment opens with a characteristic melodic fragment based on the tonic scale and triad (the key for high voice is F major). The melody enters with a V–I interval followed by a gently arched phrase which ends on the dominant. The piano unites with the voice on this dominant note (C) and continues its own melodic phrase. This melodic overlapping between singer and piano is a constant feature of the music, one which helps create the sense of uninterrupted flow that characterizes the song.

For the most part the harmonies for this song are quite traditional. In the first section the only mildly jarring note is the Ab under "char*me*," but the resolution on "yeux" in the next beat immediately soothes the ear. There is, however, much harmonic motion, but the modulations are so seamless that they, too, are part of the flow.

The rhyme scheme for the poem is equally traditional—*abab/ cdcd*/etc. The first and last verses differ from the others in that the first has an introductory line (its pattern becomes *aabab*) and the last is a rhymed couplet. The words for the first two verses are:

> I shall speak of the Rose with its graceful folds.
> The Rose is the embodied breath of the Gods,
> The most cherished care of the divine Muses.
> I shall speak of your glory, Oh delight for the eyes,
> Oh flower of kypris, queen of the hills!

> You unfold between the beautiful fingers
> Of the Dawn casting aside the morose shadows;
> The blue air becomes pink and pink the woods;
> The mouth and breasts of virgins are pink!

At the beginning of the third verse the music seems to begin a repeat, but in the last beat of the next measure (under "Qui") the piano leads to new harmonic paths. This verse reads:

> Happy is the virgin with round arms
> Who gathers you in the damp thickets!
> Happy the young forehead you adorn!
> Happy the cup in which your leaf floats!

The mood now becomes even more tranquil as the piano part becomes less of a partner and more of an accompanist. From this very quiet music a large *crescendo* grows, leading to a *forte* on "Aphrodite." The vocal part remains loud until the end, and the *tessitura* is rather high in this climactic section. The steady sixteenth notes in the piano part keep the music flowing despite these dynamic changes, and the postlude allows the dynamics to return to their gentle level. The last two verses are:

> Still dripping from the paternal waters,
> When from the blue sea Aphrodite emerged
> Sparkled nude in the brilliance of the sky,
> The jealous earth gave birth to the rose;

> And all Olympus, transported by love,
> Saluted the flower with the Beauty!

Mandoline   Poem by Paul Verlaine
Mandolin   OPUS 58/1

Les donneurs de sérénades
Et les belles écouteuses
Echangent des propos fades
Sous les ramures chanteuses.

C'est Tircis et c'est Aminte
Et c'est l'éternel Clitandre

Et c'est Damis qui, pour mainte cruelle,
Fit maint vers tendre.

Leurs courtes vestes de soie,
Leurs longues robes à queues,
Leur élégance, leur joie
Et leurs molles ombres bleues

Tourbillonnent dans l'extase
D'une lune rose et grise,
Et la mandoline jase
Parmi les frissons de brise.

Les donneurs de sérénades
Et les belles écouteuses
Echangent des propos fades,
Sous les ramures chanteuses.

"Mandoline" is one of the several poems from Verlaine's collection, *Les Fêtes galantes,* set to music by both Debussy and Fauré. (For a discussion of the Debussy song see page 279.) The entire collection, which includes such familiar poems as "Clair de lune" and "En Sourdine," was inspired by the sensuous paintings of the French artist, Watteau. This poem evokes Watteau's pastoral scenes, with their elegantly attired aristocratic young lords and ladies flirting and playing on manicured lawns to the music of strummed mandolins.

The music is jaunty and carefree. The piano part is largely composed of staccato chords reminiscent of plucked strings, although it is frequently called upon to sing a duet with the vocalist. The initial melodic phrase is a simple rising tonic scale, varied only by the triplets on "*séré*nades" (the key for high voice is Ab). This gay, optimistic, upward line is heard often during the song, although its ending may be changed, as it is in the second melodic phrase, where it soars higher in the scale. The last word of the first section, "chanteuses," is stretched to accommodate a charming cadenzalike ornamental phrase, which is taken over by the piano and then used as a harmonic bridge to the next section. In the Debussy setting a similar feeling is created by the "la, la, la" refrain. The words are:

The serenaders
And beautiful listeners
Exchange idle chatter
Under the singing branches.

The next verse begins with the same music we had in the first, but in the second measure the piano echoes the melodic line, giving it the ending of the second phrase in section one. There is a *crescendo* under the measure leading to a modest climax at "cru*elle*," which is harmonized by an effective augmented chord. This verse, like the first, ends with a long ornamented syllable, this time on the word "tendre." Again the piano echoes the beginning of the cadenza, but completes the figure with an exciting ascending scale. The words for verse two are:

It is Tircis and Aminte
And the eternal Clitandre
And Damis, who makes tender verses
For many a cruel woman.

A word about the characters named: Tircis and Damis are shepherds and Aminte and Clitandre are from the Italian comic opera. For a while it had been the vogue for French royalty to play at being shepherds and shepherdesses—Marie Antoinette had an entire play-farm built near Versailles. Of course, as we can tell by the description of the costumes in the next verse, the real work of farming was never even contemplated!

The ascending scale in the accompaniment announces a vigorous section full of verve and bounce. At "leurs molles ombres bleues" a *diminuendo* leads to a much gentler mood as the scene changes from sunlight to moonlight. This hushed aura lasts through the verse:

Their short silk vests,
Their long gowns with trains,
Their elegance, their joy
And their soft blue shadows,

Whirling in the ecstasy
Of a red and grey moon
And the mandolin chatters
In the chill of the breeze.

Once again the piano figure leads us to a new mood, this time to the original one of jaunty insouciance. The music is essentially a repeat of the opening bars, but now the piano is a full-fledged partner from the beginning. The words of the first verse are repeated and the song ends gaily but softly.

En sourdine   Poem by Paul Verlaine
Muted   OPUS 58/2

Calmes dans le demi-jour
Que les branches hautes font,
Pénétrons bien notre amour.
De ce silence profond,
Mêlons nos âmes,

Nos coeurs et nos sens extasiés,
Parmi les vagues langueurs
Des pins et des arbousiers.

Ferme tes yeux à demi,
Croise tes bras sur ton sein
Et de ton coeur endormi
Chasse à jamais tout dessein.
Laissons-nous persuader
Au souffle berceur et doux
Qui vient, à tes pieds, rider
Les ondes des gazons roux.

Et quand, solennel, le soir
Des chênes noirs tombera,
Voix de notre désespoir,
Le rossignol chantera.

"En sourdine" is another of the poems from Verlaine's collection, *Les Fêtes galantes,* set to music by both Debussy and Fauré. For the analysis of the Debussy song see page 337. The title may be translated as "Muted," and that adjective well describes the music and the mood. We are in the chiaroscuro of half-light; there is profound silence; the gentle breath of air barely ruffles the grass—everything is hushed and still. Into this quiet landscape the poet interjects a personal note, "our love," "our souls," "our hearts and our ecstasy-filled senses," and towards the end of the poem "our despair." His advice to his beloved— "Close your eyes half way,/ Cross your arms on your breast/ And from your sleeping heart/ Chase all design forever"—tells her to abandon herself to the solemnity of the evening, to the vague languors of the dark trees.

Fauré's setting is appropriately gentle and languid. The sixteenth-note broken-chord pattern of the accompaniment provides a constantly flowing background for the equally gentle vocal part. Frequently the piano has a countermelody riding above its sixteenth notes, and from "des*sein*" to "gazons roux" the piano's melody is a full partner to the singer's line.

The piano's single introductory measure establishes the tonality, F♯ major for high voice. The singer enters with a long held note on the first syllable, which immediately underscores the serene mood of the song. Before the third line of verse ("Pénétrons . . .") the piano's first countermelody, marked *espressivo,* is heard. There is a *crescendo* under this line resulting in the *forte* for "Nos coeurs . . . ." The *diminuendo* does not begin until the last syllable of "extasiés," but once begun it brings us quickly to the *p* and *pp* lines which follow. The eight lines of verse for the above described music are:

Calm in the half-light
Created by the high branches
Let us steep our love deeply
In this profound silence.

Let us plant our souls, our hearts
And our ecstasy-filled senses,
Amid the vague weariness
Of the pine and arbutus trees.

The next section is marked *dolcissimo*. One small *crescendo* to
a *mezzoforte* is permitted under "Et de ton coeur endormi," but the
first two lines ("Ferme tes yeux . . ." and "Croise tes bras . . .") are
almost hypnotic with their quiet dynamics and limited intervalic
range. It is in this section that the piano's countermelody is so
beautiful.

Close your eyes half way,
Cross your arms on your breast,
And from your sleeping heart
Chase all design forever.

Let us be persuaded
By the gentle and rocking breeze
Which comes, to your feet, to ruffle
The waves of the reddish lawn.

A *crescendo* in the piano part at the end of the last line quoted
above bring us to a *forte,* which lasts no more than two brief measures
before the *diminuendo* under "chênes noirs tombera." Once again the
piano makes a *crescendo* to allow the voice its *forte* entrance on "Voix."
This whole line, "Voix de notre désespoir" (Voice of our despair) is
loud—an anguished outcry breaking through the calm detachment of
so much of the song. The last line is soft again, however, passion yielding to serenity. The concluding words are:

And when solemnly, the evening
Falls from the black oak trees,
Voice of our despair,
The nightingale will sing.

Green   Poem by Paul Verlaine
                                             OPUS 58/3

Voici des fruits, des fleurs, des feuilles et des branches
Et puis voici mon coeur qui ne bat que pour vous.
Ne le déchirez pas avec vos deux mains blanches
Et qu'à vos yeux si beaux l'humble présent soit doux.

J'arrive tout couvert encore de rosée
Que le vent du matin vient glacer à mon front,
Souffrez que ma fatigue un instant reposée
Rêve des chers instants qui la délasseront.

Sur votre jeune sein laissez rouler ma tête
Toute sonore encor de vos derniers baisers,
Laissez la s'apaiser de la bonne tempête
Et que je dorme un peu puisque vous reposez.

Compared to the Debussy setting of this poem (see page 318) the Fauré song is rather bland and impersonal. In the Debussy a whole little scenario unfolds—the arrival of the breathless lover who has rushed at dawn to his beloved's side, the dew frozen on his brow, bearing fruits, flowers, leaves and branches as gifts. As he rests his head on her breast, the music reflects his tenderness towards her and his wish to rest for a moment beside her.

Fauré does convey the lover's breathless arrival with the short, choppy phrases of "Voici des fruits, des fleurs, des feuilles et des branches," but the ensuing sense of relaxation and then erotic fatigue is not reflected as clearly in the music.

The piano opens with simple tonic chords (the key for high voice is Ab major) which allows the melody's sixteenth notes to enter between beats, providing the desired effect of haste. The piano has a big *crescendo* under "branches" setting off the exuberant "Et puis voici mon coeur" (And then here is my heart), which is sung *forte*. The sudden drop to *p* changes the singer's exhilaration to pleading for "Ne le déchirez pas" (Don't tear it to bits), but this *crescendo* to the climactic high note (Ab in this key) at "yeux" brings us back to a *forte*. The repeated Eb at the end of the phrase is the occasion for another rapid *diminuendo,* and the word "doux" is sung softly and sweetly. The words thus far are:

Here are fruits, flowers, leaves and branches,
And then here is my heart, which beats only for you.
Don't tear it to bits with your two white hands,
And in your eyes so beautiful may the humble present be sweet.

Despite minor ups and downs, the second verse builds in one large *crescendo* from the *dolce* beginning of "J'arrive" to the *sempre forte* of "Rêve . . . délasseront." There are many intricate harmonic changes, but Ab as a frame of reference, heard under "J'arrive" and "rosée" and implied by the Eb chords under "glacer" and "délasseront," is always understood. The excitement one inevitably senses in the music for "Rêve des chers instants qui la délasseront" (Dreams of the cherished moments which will take its weariness away) would seem to indicate that Fauré interprets Verlaine's words quite differently from Debussy—Fauré's "Rêve" is an active wish rather than a languid dream. The verse reads:

I arrive still all covered with dew
Which the morning wind has just frozen on my brow.
Allow my fatigue, placed at your feet,
To dream of the dear moments which will refresh it.

Very subtly the piano leads us back to a recapitulation of the music of the opening bars, as the final stanza begins. The melody must be much more *legato* than it was at the beginning (there are no choppy breathing marks here), for now the words describe a much less hectic activity. The dynamic levels shift as rapidly as they did in the first stanza, with two impassioned *fortes*—at "Toute sonore" and at "Laissez la s'apaiser"—and intervening *diminuendos*. The last two lines are *sempre dolce* and we finally do have a feeling of fatigue and repose. The concluding words are:

On your young breast, let my head rest
All ringing still from your last kisses.
Let it be appeased after the good storm,
And let me sleep a little while you rest.

A Clymène
To Clymène

Poem by Paul Verlaine
OPUS 58/4

Mystiques barcarolles
Romances sans paroles
Chère
Puisque tes yeux
Couleur des cieux
Puisque ta voix étrange
Vision qui dérange
Et trouble l'horizon
De ma raison
Puisque l'arôme insigne
De ta pâleur de cygne
Et puisque la candeur
De ton odeur
Ah! pour que tout ton être
Musique qui pénètre
Nimbes d'anges défunts
Tons et parfums
A sur d'almes cadences
En ses correspondances
Induit mon coeur subtil
Ainsi soit-il!

This is a strange little song, as fragile and wispy as a spiderweb. Its poem is not in the least concerned with narrative cohesiveness—it is a series of brief and fanciful descriptive phrases. The vocal part created by Fauré reflects the disconnected, ephemeral nature of the words, especially at the beginning and the end, where short melodic phrases are separated by long piano interludes. Only in the accompaniment do we find any sense of continuity, although even here the oft-repeated pattern of six eighth notes and one-and-a-half beats of rest in the left hand adds to the stop-and-start character of the piece.

The title of the poem is "To Clymène," but the young lady in question is never mentioned in the song. Clymène was a figure in Greek mythology, but just what part she played is somewhat obscure. She is variously mentioned as the possible mother of Prometheus, daughter of Helius (the sun-god), granddaughter of Minos of labyrinth fame, wife of Nauplius the navigator, consort of Zeus, etc. She may or may not have been turned into a poplar tree at the water's edge by an irate Zeus for participating in an ill-fated ride in Helius' sun chariot. In any case she is most certainly adored in this poem.

The first line of the poem, "Mystiques barcarolles" (mysterious barcarolles), obviously inspired Fauré's setting, with its gently-rocking 9/8 rhythm so typical of the barcarolle. The piano immediately introduces the rhythm, the tonality (E minor for high voice), and a strong melodic line. The singer enters with a short, two-word phrase, lengthened by stretching the last two syllables of "barcarolles" over two long measures. The D–G–D intervals seem awkward here—one must be careful not to swoop down and up. The piano repeats its opening melodic line, and then the singer repeats his four measures to another brief phrase, "Romances sans paroles" (Songs or ballads without words). After the three-bar piano interlude, the singer has a long sustained high note which drops an octave for the second syllable of the word "Chère." Then at last the vocal line begins to move; the tempo becomes a little faster and the accompaniment's triplets move along without the break at the end of each measure. The rhythm changes to 4/4, so that the barcarolle effect is temporarily suspended, and there is a big *crescendo* to the climactic "l'horizon." This spurt of energy is short lived, for after the *forte* the original tempo, rhythm, and character return. The words for the first section are:

Mysterious barcarolles
Songs without words
Dear one
Since your eyes
Color of the skies
Since your voice—strange

Vision which deranges
And troubles the horizon
Of my reason

At "l'horiz*on*" the piano's original melody is heard again, but this time the vocal line joins the piano for the second half of the line. Although the dynamics are subdued again, the vocal line remains active. There is a small *crescendo* to the high note on "candeur" and a larger *crescendo* to the greater climax at "ton être." Despite these dynamic fluctuations the big moment has yet to come, that is, the *forte* on the long F♯ of "par*fums*." The accompaniment becomes quite ecstatic here. The words to this point are:

Since the characteristic scent
Of your swanlike pallor
And since the freshness
Of your aura
Ah! for all your being
Music which penetrates
The halos of angels long gone
Sounds and perfumes

A rapid *diminuendo* brings back the *dolce* mood of the beginning, and the melody gradually becomes wispier and more fragmented, as it was in the opening verse. The loveliest moment of the song is at the very end of the vocal part, where the singer holds an E, while the underlying harmonies shift until they reach the final E major chords with which the song closes. The last lines of the poem, which seem to be a cryptic and personalized distillation of Baudelaire's "Correspondances" (see page 297), are:

With certain cadences
In their correspondences
Lead my subtle heart on—
Thus may it be!

C'est l'extase   Poem by Paul Verlaine
This Is Ecstasy   OPUS 58/5

C'est l'extase langoureuse,
C'est la fatigue amoureuse,
C'est tous les frissons des bois
Parmi l'étreinte des brises,
C'est vers les ramures grises
Le choeur des petites voix.

O le frêle et frais murmure
Cela gazouille et susure

Cela ressemble au bruit doux
Que l'herbe agitée expire,
Tu dirais, sous l'eau qui vire,
Le roulis sourd des cailloux.

Cette âme qui se lamente
Et cette plainte dormante
C'est la nôtre, n'est-ce pas?
La mienne, dis, et la tienne
Dont s'exhale l'humble antienne
Par ce tiède soir tout bas.

Of the five songs in Opus 58, all but one, "A Clymène," have been
set to music by Debussy as well as Fauré. (For a discussion of the
Debussy song see p. 307.) It is easy to see why this particular poem
appealed to both composers: the subject, the languid fatigue that follows erotic passion, is perfectly suited for the sensuous harmonies and
limpid melodic lines characteristic of their styles; the sound of its language is so musical ("la frêle at frais murmure/ Cela gazouille et
susure," "Le roulis sourd des cailloux," "Cette âme qui se lamente")
that even when spoken it seems to have been sung.

The Debussy setting is more hushed and atmospheric than the
Fauré. Where the poet uses the strange metaphor of muted pebbles
rolling under swirling water, Debussy gives us onomatopoeic chromatic figures. This direct transposition of words into musical effects
does not occur in the Fauré.

Like the other songs in this opus, "C'est l'extase" is quite traditional in its harmonic structure, beginning and ending on simple tonic
chords (the key for high voice is Eb). The piano opens with a downward I–V interval which is repeated, then echoed by the singer. The
syncopated rhythm of the accompanying chords must be subdued and
gentle to avoid any hint of bouncy exuberance. The first two lines of
text are sung to the same languid melody, but at "C'est tous les frissons"
there is an upward surge in the vocal part. From this point the melodic
line has considerable sweep and range both in pitch and dynamics, but
the section ends quietly at "des petites voix." The words to this point
are:

This is languid ecstasy,
This is erotic fatigue.
This is all the trembling of the woods
In the embrace of the breezes
This is, through the gray branches,
The chorus of little voices.

The piano, which has already had considerable melodic interplay
with the voice, now has a beautiful tune of its own. This melodic frag-

ment is used many times in the remainder of the song and should always be heard, even when the vocal part is above it.

The rising melody under "Cela gazouille" culminates in the wide octave interval at "susure." The voice immediately leaps up an octave for the next phrase, after which the melody continues in its broad scope until the restful pause after "Le roulis sourd des cailloux." These lines of verse are:

> Oh the frail and fresh murmur
> It twitters and whispers
> It resembles the soft cry
> That the ruffled grass emits
> One would call it, under the swirling water,
> The muted rolling of pebbles!

The first and second lines of the final section are sung to the same melody, a sinuous, undulating phrase which is echoed in the piano part. For a full ten measures we have a lovely duet between equals, rather than a song for soloist and accompanist. This is the climactic portion of the song, where one finds the strongest dynamics and the greatest dynamic contrasts. The question, "C'est la nôtre, n'est-ce pas?" is begun dramatically but fades to a *piano* as the melody falls. The next phrase, "La mienne, dis, et la tienne," also begins vigorously and falls off to a *piano*, but the *crescendo*, which starts on "Dont s'exhale," leads to a climactic *forte* which lasts two full bars before the final fade out of the ending. The drop in dynamics at "ce tiède" is underscored by the octave descent in the melodic line, the second such use of this wide interval in the song. The melody ends gently on the tonic note, while the accompanying chords play a traditional V^7–I cadence. The last lines of verse are:

> This soul which laments
> In this quiet plaint
> It is ours, isn't it?
> Mine, tell me, and yours,
> Which exhales the humble hymn,
> Of this mild evening so quietly.

En prière   Poem by Stéphan Bordèse
In Prayer

> Si la voix d'un enfant peut monter jusqu'à vous,
> O mon Père,
> Ecoutez de Jésus, devant Vous à genoux,
> La prière!

Si Vous m'avez choisi pour enseigner vos lois
Sur la terre,
Je saurai Vous servir, auguste Roi des rois,
O Lumière!
Sur mes lèvres, Seigneur, mettez la verité
Salutaire,
Pour que celui qui doute, avec humilité
Vous révère!

Ne m'abandonnez pas, donnez-moi la douceur
Nécessaire,
Pour apaiser les maux, soulager la douleur,
La misère!
Révélez Vous à moi, Seigneur en qui je crois
Et j'espère:
Pour Vous je veux souffrir et mourir sur la croix,
Au calvaire!

Since this song was published in 1890, it belongs chronologically somewhere between Opus 51 and Opus 61. Fauré has given it no opus number of its own.

The text is of a childlike simplicity, but the idea of overhearing Jesus at prayer is a somewhat theatrical one. The music mirrors the poet's considerable sensitivity, but here, too, theatrical effects crop up. Particularly obvious is the augmented chord at "prière," which is repeated under "nécessaire." Elsewhere Fauré's harmonic vocabulary seems well-suited to the text, and characteristic devices such as the change from D major to F major under "lois" (analyzed in F major, the key for high voice) do not disturb the mood.

The accompaniment begins with broken tonic chords in a characteristic triplet figure that continues throughout most of the song. The melody hovers around the dominant for the first eight bars. While this constant returning to one note is characteristic of Fauré, it is also typical of liturgical chants in general.

After the augmented chord under "prière" there is much harmonic motion. The melody rises in a *crescendo* to climax on the high tonic note at "Roi des rois," but the harmonies continue to change, providing no resting place. We finally find a dominant-seventh chord under "Lumière," but its resolution is to the minor of the tonic. It is not until the very end of the verse that a final-sounding tonic chord is reached. The words for the first verse are:

If the voice of a child can ascend to You,
Oh my Father,
Listen to, before You on his knees,
Jesus' prayer!
If You have chosen me to teach Your laws
On earth,

I shall know how to serve You, august King of kings,
  Oh Light!
On my lips, Seigneur, place the salutary
  Truth,
That those who doubt, with humility
  Might revere You!

The second verse begins with music from the first section (Fauré repeats measures six through ten), but the composer changes everything by quickly providing the V^7–I close (under "*misère*") that was so long delayed in the earlier part of the song. The remaining bars are actually a long coda, in which chords frequently replace the triplet figure in the accompaniment, and the melodic line becomes less flowing because of the steady quarter notes and long dotted half and whole notes.

The gentle ending, with its tender harmonies, *sempre dolce* dynamics, and overall tranquillity, seems somewhat at odds with the anguish evoked by mention of the agony of the Crucifixion. Nevertheless, it is quite convincing musically. The words for this second half are:

Do not abandon me, give me the necessary
  Gentleness,
To lessen pain, to comfort sorrow,
  Misery!
Reveal Yourself to me.
Seigneur in Whom I believe
And I hope:
For You I am willing to suffer and to die on the Cross,
At Calvary!

La Bonne Chanson
Poems by Paul Verlaine
OPUS 61

1. Une Sainte en son auréole
A Saint in Her Halo

Une Sainte en son auréole,
Une Chatelaine en sa tour,
Tout ce que contient la parole humaine
De grâce et d'amour;
La note d'or que fait entendre
Le cor dans le lointain des bois,
Marié à la fierté tendre
Des nobles dames d'autrefois;
Avec cela le charme insigne

D'un frais sourire triomphant
Eclos dans des candeurs de cygne
Et des rougeurs de femme enfant,
Des aspects nacrés blancs et roses,
Un doux accord patricien,
Je vois, j'entends toutes ces choses
Dans son nom Carlovingien.

Fauré's Opus 61, "La Bonne Chanson," consists of settings of nine of the twenty-one poems by Paul Verlaine which were written in the first flush of happiness occasioned by the poet's betrothal to Mathilde Mauté de Fleurville. The poems are filled with ecstasy. They call on nature to witness and share in the boundless joy of requited love. There is a purity and innocence to the verses that bathes them in sunlight, giving them a surprisingly nonerotic character. Only one, the third in the cycle, describes evening, "l'heure exquise," the exquisite hour. Although the fifth song expresses the fear of losing such great happiness, and the fourth contrasts the poet's former gloomy existence with his new-found bliss, the overall effect of the cycle is one of tranquil joy.

In "Une Sainte en son auréole," the first song in the cycle, Verlaine piles image upon image—a haloed saint, the golden note of a horn, the pride of noblewomen of ancient times, the purity of a swan, the pearl-like hues of a blush—and then tells us that he sees and hears all this in his beloved's name. This is indeed the "universal analogy," the *correspondance* of all things, that made Verlaine the hero of the symbolist poets.

Fauré's setting begins with a well-developed melody in the piano part. In fact, the character of this oft-repeated melodic line is stronger and more easily identifiable than the vocalist's melody. The two melodic lines overlap, the pianist's theme beginning while the singer's phrase ends. Each of these fresh beginnings should be brought out to make the most of the lovely duet, which continues through the first four lines:

A Saint in her halo,
A Chatelaine in her tower,
Everything contained in human speech
Of grace and love;

After this impassioned line, the piano melody ceases and a rich chord (a suspension over E♭, the dominant, spiced by F♭) is heard in the accompaniment. This sound, alternating with the C⁹ chord that follows, supports the singer's next two lines:

The golden note which makes one hear
The horn in the far-off woods,

The next two lines have a charming antique quality, especially the cadence under "d'autre-fois." This is, of course, a deliberate underscoring of the text:

> Wedded to the tender pride
> Of the noblewomen of long ago;

At this cadence the piano resumes its melody. There is a *crescendo* to an exultant *forte* at "triomphant," where the singer's high note is part of a strong suspension over an E^7 chord.

> With this the great charm
> Of a fresh triumphant smile

The mood suddenly changes to one of utmost gentleness and calm. For the next ten bars the piano has quiet accompanying harmonies, while the singer continues the sweetly flowing melody:

> Blossoms with the purity of a swan
> And the blushes of a woman-child,

The duet between piano and singer begins again, but the aura of tranquillity is unchanged.

> The pearllike looks, white and red,
> A sweet patrician harmony,

The pause in the vocal part and the B^9 chord in the piano part serve to set off the two final crucial lines of the poem:

> I see, I hear all these things
> In your Carlovingien name.

The key syllables "nom" (name) and "Carlovingi*en*" are sung on the tonic note (Ab), but the intervention of the piano's melody postpones the feeling of return to the principal tonality until the last Ab chords at the end of the postlude. The penultimate chord, a II^7 rather than the usual V^7, provides a strange and rather disconcerting approach to the final tonic chord.

2. Puisque l'aube grandit
Since Dawn Grew Bright

Puisque l'aube grandit, puisque voici l'aurore,
Puisqu'après m'avoir fui longtemps l'espoir veut bien
Revoler devers moi qui l'appelle et l'implore,
Puisque toute ce bonheur veut bien être le mien,
Je veux guidé par vous, beaux yeux aux flammes douces,
Par toi conduit, ô main où tremblera ma main,

Marcher droit que ce soit par des sentiers de mousse
Ou que rocs et cailloux encombrent le chemin;
Et comme pour bercer les lenteurs de la route,
Je chanterai des airs ingénus,
Je me dis qu'elle m'écoutera sans déplaisir sans doute,
Et vraiment je ne veux pas d'autre Paradis.

This second song in the cycle *La Bonne Chanson* has a free-flowing quality, which sweeps the listener along through constantly shifting harmonies. The piano part is nothing more than a series of arpeggiated chords, which support the undulating melody without establishing a distinctive character of its own. The melody surges from phrase to phrase, rarely pausing, exhilarated, ecstatic.

A simple introduction in the key of G (the original key) prepares the singer's entry. We are immediately caught up in the melody which first descends from the dominant, only to rise exultantly on the word "aurore." The dynamics follow the line of the melody, soaring to a *forte* on "aur*ore*." There is a drop to *p* on the wistful words "Puis-qu'après m'avoir fue longtemps," and a joyful surge for "L'espoir veut . . . l'implore." These rapidly changing dynamics continue throughout the song.

Towards the end of the piece (at "Et comme pour bercer les len-teurs") we have a built-in *ritard* in the accompaniment, for the six sixteenth-note figure is changed first to four sixteenth notes, and then to triplet eighths. This rhythmic alteration will make the music seem slower without a real change in tempo.

Careful attention to the words will clarify the dynamic and rhyth-mic instructions:

Since dawn grew bright and sunrise is here,
Since, having long fled from me, hope wishes
To turn towards me who calls and begs her,
Since all this happiness wants to be mine,
I would be guided by you, beautiful eyes with tender flames,
By you led, oh hand in which my hand will tremble,
To walk ahead whether through paths of moss
Or where rocks and pebbles obstruct the way;
And as though lulling the languors of the route,
I shall sing ingenuous tunes,
I tell myself that she will doubtless listen to me without displeasure,
And in truth I need no other Paradise.

3. La Lune blanche luit dans les bois
The White Moon Shines in the Woods

La lune blanche luit dans les bois,
De chaque branche part une voix

Sous la ramée,
O bien-aimée!
L'étang reflète, profond miroir,
La silhouette du saule noir
Où le vent pleure.
Rêvons, c'est l'heure!
Un vaste et tendre apaisement
Semble descendre du firmament
Que l'astre irise;
C'est l'heure exquise.

In "La Lune blanche luit dans les bois," Verlaine describes a hauntingly beautiful night landscape. The white moon shines in the trees; the pond—as still as a mirror—reflects the black willow tree. Although the wind weeps in the willow, all is calm. It is the time for dreams, the exquisite hour.

Fauré's setting of this misty poem is surprisingly operatic. It has two passionate climaxes, one for voice and piano under "O bien aimée!" and one for piano alone after "Rêvons c'est l'heure." In both these places one feels an unabashed romanticism not too often encountered in Fauré's works.

The piano opens with a series of tender F♯ major chords (the original key). The modulation under "blanche" to an F♯ minor⁷ chord creates a mysterious aura well-suited to the verbal image of the moon shining in the trees. At the end of the singer's first phrase, the piano has a lovely little countermelody, which continues when the voice reenters. This section is hushed and dreamy, with the gently rocking triple meter (9/8 time) suggesting a lullaby or a barcarolle. The words for this portion are:

The white moon shines in the woods;
From each branch comes a voice
Under the foliage*

Under the second and third syllables of "ramée" Fauré gives the piano the opening phrase of his earlier song, "Lydia." We shall encounter this melodic reference elsewhere in the cycle.

The pause in the vocal part before the next line, "O bien aimée,"

Oh beloved

makes the ensuing *crescendo* all the more dramatic. The melody rises to the high F♯ and then falls to the octave below, while the accompaniment revels in its own passionate outpouring. At the high note, the tonic harmony prevails, and the piano holds this tonality, at full *forte*,

* The French word should be "ramée," not "ramee," as it is in the International Music Co. edition.

for two complete measures. The change to F♯ minor on the second beat of the next bar signals a dramatic drop in dynamics, in preparation for the singer's calm delivery of the words

> The pool reflects, deep mirror

The next phrase,

> The silhouette of the black willow

has a dramatic quality, despite its quiet dynamic level, because of the rise to the upper E♭ and the ensuing drop to the E♭ an octave below in the melodic line, but the section that follows is clearly marked *dolce:*

> Where the wind weeps.
> Let us dream, this is the hour!

When the singer's phrase ends, the piano, which has been quietly singing its countermelody, bursts forth in a glorious surge to an E major chord. The *diminuendo* under the bass line's arpeggiated version of this chord must be exaggerated, for the singer enters quietly in the same measure. There is a lovely duet between voice and piano, the vocal line rising while the piano descends, under "Un vaste et tendre apaisement." The dynamics remain hushed for the rest of the song, as, with all passion spent, the lovers sense

> A vast and tender calm
> Seems to descend from the firmament
> That the star makes radiant.
> It is the exquisite hour.

To create this aura of blessed calm, Fauré gradually lightens the piano part, substituting rests and held chords for the formerly ubiquitous triplets. The vocal line drops in *tessitura,* pausing after "l'astre irise" to allow the murmured scales of the piano's concluding figure to be heard. An interesting suspension under "des*cen*dre" leads to a series of modulations, which seem to pull the music far from the main tonality; but a dominant-seventh chord in the piano interlude brings us back to the tonic two measures before the words "C'est l'heure exquise." The repetition of this progression adds to the blissful tranquillity of the ending.

4. J'allais par des chemins perfides
I Wandered on Treacherous Paths

J'allais par des chemins perfides,
Douloureusement incertain,

Vos chères mains furent mes guides;
Si pâle à l'horizon lointain
Luisait un faible espoir d'aurore—
Votre regard fut le matin!
Nul bruit, sinon son pas sonore,
N'encourageait le voyageur,
Votre voix me dit: Marche encore!
Mon coeur craintif, mon sombre coeur
Pleurait, seul, sur la triste voie;
L'amour, délicieux vainqueur,
Nous a réuni dans la joie!

This fourth song in the cycle *La Bonne Chanson* steps back in time to paint the portrait of the doleful poet before love transformed his life. We see him wandering along treacherous paths, painfully uncertain, until the guiding hands of his beloved give him courage to go on. Finally love unites the poet and the maiden in joy.

The poem is really an intimate confession, for Verlaine had led the life of a decadent vagabond before his betrothal to Mathilde. After a very brief period of marital happiness, his homosexual relationship with fellow poet Rimbaud lured him from home, back to those very treacherous paths he describes. Of course, in 1870, when the poems were published, neither he nor Mathilde had any idea how short-lived this oasis of calm in his troubled life would be.

To express the poet's unsettled past, Fauré begins the song with a four-bar introduction in which the piano shifts uneasily from harmony to harmony. The tonic chord, F♯ minor, occurs only once, on the third beat of the first measure, leaving the tonality quite ambiguous. The piano's short melodic phrases in the first three bars descend in melancholy sighs. In the fourth bar the melody rises, to allow for a repeat of the piano's four-bar sequence while the singer enters. The tonal ambiguity heard in the introduction is reinforced by the opening phrase in the vocal part, which begins with a I–V melodic interval in F♯ minor and ends with a I–V melodic interval in the minor of the relative major. The second line of text is sung to similar music, but the chord progression changes, leading out of the circular harmonic pattern. The first two lines read:

I wandered on treacherous paths,
Painfully uncertain

The first of a series of rising scales in the accompaniment heralds a more hopeful mood. The *crescendo* and ascent in the melodic line (under "furent mes guides") sweeps us to a moving climax on the E♭ in the vocal line and even further, to the piano's D^{7+} chord in the next measure. Here the words are

Your dear hands were my guides;

There is a sudden drop in dynamics as the poet describes in awe-struck tones the first glimmer of his salvation, but passion once again bursts forth as he is moved by thoughts of his love:

So pale in the distant horizon
There shone a weak hope of dawn—
Your glance was the morning light!

At this climactic statement the piano soars in rising octaves, tapering off at the repetition of the opening figure. Once again the poem recalls the lonely past, when

No sound, save his sonorous steps,
Encouraged the traveler.

But the beloved's voice comes to the poet, inspiring him (and the music) to a new peak of excitement. A rich D major chord supports the climactic "Votre *voix*" before the return of the familiar shifting harmonies. The words are

Your voice said to me: "Walk on!"

Still unable to dismiss the memory of his miseries, the poet gives us two more sorrowful lines:

My fearful heart, my somber heart,
Wept alone, on the sad way;

Finally, however, the key changes to F♯ major and the mood becomes one of peace and contentment. The accompaniment has lovely, feathery scales in the left hand, while the right hand's melodic line, although clearly derived from the initial introductory music, is transformed into warm, tranquil phrases. The voice reenters with a rising octave interval on the tonic note. Scales in both hands accompany the vocal line, with all parts joining in a beautiful augmented chord at "déli*cieux*." The harmonies are still ephemeral, although we are clearly being led to the tonic. Even when the singer arrives at the triumphant F♯ at "la joie," a G♯ in the accompanying F♯ chord complicates the sound. It is not until the last two chords of the postlude that we hear a completely unadulterated tonic chord.

The last two lines of the poem are:

Love, delicious conqueror,
Has reunited us in joy!

To emphasize this onrush of bliss, at the last word, "joie," the accompanying scales quicken from eighth notes to triplets, just as one's pulse might quicken at such emotion.

5. J'ai presque peur, en vérité
I Am Almost Afraid, In Truth

J'ai presque peur, en vérité,
Tant je sens ma vie enlacée
A la radieuse pensée
Qui m'a pris l'âme l'autre été;
Tant votre image à jamais chère
Habite en ce coeur tout à vous,
Ce coeur uniquement jaloux
De vous aimer et de vous plaire.
Et je tremble, pardonnez-moi,
D'aussi franchement vous le dire,
A penser qu'un mot, qu'un sourire
De vous est désormais ma loi,
Et qu'il vous suffirait d'un geste,
D'une parole ou d'un clin d'oeil
Pour mettre tout mon être en deuil
De son illusion céleste!

Mais, plutôt, je ne veux vous voir,
L'avenir dut-il m'être sombre
Et fécond en peines sans nombre,
Qu'à travers un immense espoir;
Plongé dans ce bonheur suprême,
De me dire encore et toujours,
En dépit des mornes retours
Que je vous aime, que je t'aime!

The agitated minor chords in the opening bars of "J'ai presque peur, en vérité" express the anxiety felt by the poet when contemplating his enraptured state. His very life is so intertwined with his feelings, his heart is so filled with his beloved's image, he is so vulnerable to her words and moods, that he trembles with fear lest she destroy his celestial dream. His one great happiness is to repeat again and again, "I love you, I love you."

In French there are two forms of the pronoun "you," *vous* and *tu*. While *vous* is always used in the plural, in the singular form *vous* indicates formality and *tu* is reserved for intimate friends and family. It is significant that in the last line of the poem Verlaine allows himself to progress from the somewhat distant "Je vous aime" to the intimate "Je t'aime."

The poems in this cycle, presented to his fiancée by Verlaine as a pre-nuptial gift, are a personal chronicle of their meeting, falling in love, courtship, and betrothal. The words "qui m'a pris l'âme l'autre été" are a tender reference to the summer during which their romance began. As we know from the history of their life together, his fears of her moods were groundless; it was his own restlessness that ended their marriage after less than two years.

The song divides itself into two distinct parts, the opening minor section with its restless nervous energy, and the calmer portion in the major mode which follows. The change occurs in the two-bar piano interlude before "Mais plutôt." Fauré indicates three times in this *dolce* section that there is to be no ritard; the change in mood is accomplished by the switch from minor to major and—even more important —by the cessation of the accompaniment's agitato chords and the substitution of lyric phrases in the piano part. At the last line, "Que je vous aime, que je t'aime," the sweet calm yields to passionate excitement, but this is an excitement full of joy and hope rather than nervous anxiety.

As is his wont, Fauré emphasizes the earlier uneasy mood by the use of rapidly changing harmonies. Although the E minor tonality is clearly established in the beginning and reinforced at the first piano interlude (after "l'autre été") the music eddies swiftly from key to key. There is much less harmonic motion in the second section, and the last five bars remain at rest on the tonic chord. For the second time in the cycle we hear the opening phrase of "Lydia" in the accompaniment, this time under the words "de vous aimer et de vous plaire." These subtle quotations act as a unifying factor in the long cycle. The poem reads:

> I am almost afraid, in truth,
> So much do I sense my life enlaced
> With the radiant thought
> Which seized my heart that summer,
> So much your image, always cherished,
> Lives in this heart which is all yours,
> This heart solely desirous
> Of loving you and pleasing you.
> And I tremble, forgive me
> For so frankly telling you,
> To think that a word, a smile
> From you is henceforth my law,
> And that a gesture from you would suffice,
> A word or a wink of the eye,
> To put my entire being in mourning
> For its heavenly illusion!
>
> But if I should not wish to see you,
> The future would be dark
> And filled with numberless woes,
> Across an immense hope;
> Plunged into this supreme happiness
> To tell myself again and forever
> In spite of sad memories
> That I love you, that I love you!

6. Avant que tu ne t'en ailles
Before You Go

Avant que tu ne t'en ailles, pâle étoile de matin,
Mille cailles chantent, chantent dans le thym!
Tourne devers le poète dont les yeux sont pleins d'amour,
L'alouette monte au ciel avec le jour!
Tourne ton regard que noie l'aurore dans son azur,
Quelle joie parmi les champs de blé mur
Et fais luire ma pensée là-bas, bien loin!
Oh bien loin! La rosée, gaiment brille sur le foin!
Dans le doux rêve où s'agite m'amie endormie encore.
Vite, vite, car voici le soleil d'or!

The first half of this shimmering song is marked by vivid contrasts, as music of pallid, but stately, solemnity alternates with sections filled with rippling motion. Despite the differences between sections, an overall celestial quality unifies the song, allowing the contrasting segments to flow into one another. Further to insure against a disjointed feeling, Fauré often uses the last melody note of one section enharmonically in the opening chord of the following section. For example, the first chord in the measure before "Tourne devers le poète" has a Db octave, which is held over from the C♯ octave in the preceding bar.

The alternation between stillness and motion is a wonderfully apt interpretation of the words. In the first line of text we are made to sense that mysterious moment of *chiaroscuro* when the pale blue sky is just grey enough for us to see the last star, and night is gradually yielding to day. This is expressed by the slowly moving chords. In the next line we are to picture a thousand quail singing in the thyme, so of course we must have motion. In the poem, as in the music, this pattern continues, but the differences become less marked as day completely vanquishes night and the poet's thoughts become more animated. By "Quelle joie," the halfway mark in the text, the *adagio* indication vanishes from the score and a more earthy aura prevails. Further changes in degree of animation are accomplished by use of sixteenth notes instead of triplets for the line "La rosée, gaîment, brille sur le foin."

Since most music divides itself into four-bar units and multiples thereof, it is interesting to note how Fauré deliberately avoids this rhythmic superstructure. The first section (in Db major) has seven bars plus an upbeat, while the second unit (in A major) consists of exactly seven measures; after the return to the original key signature we have a segment six bars long, followed by a B major section lasting seven measures, etc. In the entire song only the music under "La rosée . . . le foin" is the traditional eight bars in length. That this unusual arrangement is not necessitated by the words is clear, for the piano interludes between words are themselves irregularly spaced. Since the ear does not hear stopping points in the expected places, the ability of the music to flow smoothly from section to section is enhanced.

The song is a very beautiful one. The high *tessitura* of the piano part contributes to the ethereal, other-worldly quality of the music. (This is a foretaste of the even more celestial music in the opening song of Fauré's Opus 95, *La Chanson d'Eve,* discussed on pages 132–135.) The I–flatted III progressions—under "Mille cailles chantent, chantent dans le thym!" and "L'alouette monte au ciel avec le jour"—lift the music heavenward as do the rising melodic lines and exhilarating *crescendi* with which these words are sung. Again, the music is remarkably apt for the words. At the end of each of these lines the I chord (A for the first, B for the second) becomes a V^7 which leads to the new tonality of the next section. The words thus far are:

> Before you go, pale morning star,
> A thousand quail sing in the thyme!
> Turn towards the poet whose eyes are full of love
> The lark soars to the sky with the day!

There is one more set of slow-fast lines, which once again ends with a glorious rising melodic line and an impassioned *crescendo:*

> Turn your glance which drowns the dawn in blue,
> What joy amid the fields of ripe wheat!

This time the music for the second line is somewhat extended— nine measures instead of the usual seven—and the harmonic pattern is more complex: $G\sharp^7$–$C\sharp^7$–$F\sharp^7$–C augmented–D^7–B^7. This last B^7 chord leads to the key change and the second half of the song.

Although there is no obvious break between the two halves, there is a considerable difference in moods. The lower, deeper accompanying chords make the music warmer, earthier, more human. Only under the words "Dans le doux rêve où s'agite m'amie endormie encor" (In the sweet dream in which my love, still sleeping, is stirred) does the celestial aura return. The cadence under "endormie encore," D to G♭ with the F♯ changing enharmonically to G♭, is especially evocative of the former mood.

There are no further key changes in the second half, but the harmonies shift endlessly nevertheless. The central tonality, D♭, is established under "Car voi*ci,*" but the strange D♮ in the last beat of the measure—a repeat of the equally strange sound two measures earlier— disturbs the ear, so that the listener is not really satisfied with the tonic harmony until "d'or!" The last eleven bars are one long passionate *crescendo* as the sun bursts forth in all its golden glory. It is a marvelous ending! The words for the second half are:

And make my thoughts shine there, far away!
Oh, very far! Dew gaily glitters on the hay!
In the sweet dream in which my love, still sleeping, is stirred,
Quickly, quickly, for here is the golden sun!

7. Donc, ce sera par un clair jour d'été
Thus It Will Be On a Clear Summer Day

Donc, ce sera par un clair jour d'été
Le grand soleil, complice de ma joie,
Fera, parmi le satin et la soie
Plus belle encore votre chère beauté;
Le ciel tout bleu, comme une haute tente,
Frissonera somptueux, à long plis,
Sur nos deux fronts qu'auront pâlis
L'émotion du bonheur et l'attente;

Et quand le soir viendra, l'air sera doux,
Qui se jouera, caressant, dans vos voiles,
Et les regards paisibles des étoiles
Bienveillamment souriront aux époux!

In "Donc, ce sera par un clair jour d'été," the seventh of the nine-song cycle *La Bonne Chanson,* the poet paints the picture of his forth-coming wedding day. It will take place on a clear summer day, and the glowing sun will increase the beauty of the bride in her silks and satins. When evening comes its gentle air will play caressingly in her bridal veils and the stars will shine benevolently on the couple.

These idyllic musings are swathed in an appropriately lyric setting by Fauré. The accompaniment for the first two-thirds of the song consists primarily of rapidly flowing arpeggiated chords, whose constantly shifting harmonies are often based on augmented triads. Since the overall tonality is major and the augmented sound is so frequently heard, there is a spirit-lifting buoyancy to the music. The piano part alternates between sections of sheer accompaniment, when nothing but arpeggiated chords are heard, and measures filled with rich countermelodies, which sometimes soar above the vocal line. The melody expresses joy and exhilaration. Almost every phrase rises to F or F♯, usually preceded by the note C♯. The anxieties expressed in some of the previous songs in the cycle have obviously been assuaged as the wedding plans have become definite.

There is a clearcut division between the first part of the song, described above, and the closing portion. This is based on the text, which deals with the sun-filled day for the first eight lines and then describes the long-awaited evening in the remaining four. The music echoes this

dichotomy, for the active arpeggiated chord figure ceases in the interlude introducing the words "Et quand le soir viendra," And when
evening comes. The tempo becomes much slower (*molto piu lento*)
and the sense of exhilaration is replaced by tender serenity.

Although there is no change of key signature, the second section
clearly begins with a sustained D major chord. The modulation to C
major in the third bar of the new section is very lovely and should be
emphasized. Even more effective is the shift to A♭ under "vien*dra*" after
the D to C progression has been repeated. The D tonality, this time in
the minor mode, is used tellingly once again in the final bars, where
it precedes the dominant seventh (F⁷) before the tonic, giving us a
III–V⁷–I under "souriront aux époux!" The poem reads:

> Thus it will be on a clear summer day
> The great sun, accomplice to my joy
> Will make, mid the satin and the silk,
> Still more beautiful your dear beauty:
> The sky all blue, like a tall tent,
> Will flutter sumptuously, in long pleats,
> On our two brows which the emotions
> Of happiness and expectation will have made pale;
>
> And when evening comes, the air will be gentle,
> And will play, caressingly, among your veils,
> And the peaceful regard of the stars
> Will smile benevolently on the newlyweds!

8. N'est-ce pas?
Isn't It True?

> N'est-ce pas? Nous irons, gais et lents, dans la voie,
> Modeste que nous montre en souriant l'Espoir,
> Peu soucieux qu'on nous ignore ou qu'on nous voie.
> Isolés dans l'amour ainsi qu'en un bois noir,
> Nos deux coeurs exhalant leur tendresse paisible,
> Seront deux rossignols qui chantent dans le soir.
> Sans nous préoccuper de ce que nous destine le sort,
> Nous marcherons pourtant du même pas
> Et la main dans la main avec l'âme enfantine
> De ceux qui s'aiment sans mélange. N'est-ce pas?

One would be hard put to find a more charming paean to young
love than this penultimate song of *La Bonne Chanson*. The opening
and closing words, "N'est-ce pas?" are the French idiom with which
one asks for confirmation of one's views when one is fairly certain of
receiving it. The closest English equivalent is the questioning "Right?"

which would sound too coarse in a setting such as this. "Don't you agree?" is much too cold, so we'll reluctantly submit "Isn't it true?" as the best translation. In any case a romantic young fiancée would be unlikely to disagree with this idealized picture of what married life would be like—the joyous couple strolling hand in hand along the road, oblivious to the regard of others, isolated in love, their hearts singing like nightingales. Verlaine says that so pure a love presupposes the rare innocence of "l'âme enfantine," the childlike soul. His final "N'est-ce pas?" gives no hint of doubt or cynicism.

The language of the poem is straightforward, with none of the convoluted syntax or mysterious ellipses and analogies common to symbolist poetry. The "wa" sound of the "oi" vowel combination is frequently heard, giving a softness to the words. The phrase "qu'en un bois noir" is hard to pronounce, because of the subtle difference between "en" and "un" and because of the repetition of the "wa" in "bois" and "noir." Careful attention to this phrase is suggested. A meticulous elision of the "n" (enun) will help.

For such an optimistic, idyllic picture of the future, Fauré quite naturally elects to provide a gentle setting in the major mode. Nothing disturbs the flowing accompaniment and the harmonies are relatively free from discord. This by no means indicates lack of complexity, as the progression from A to Bb under "gais et lents" proves in the very first line. The augmented chord under "souri*ant*" leads to a G chord with a raised seventh which eventually yields to B major (under "voie"). The melody develops a repetitious "sing-song" quality while these modulations beguile the ear. The B major in turn becomes augmented, as the endless harmonic changes go on.

The salient characteristic of the song is the way in which the vocal and piano parts are inextricably intertwined. Some obvious examples are the use of the melody note in the augmented chord at "dans l'am*our*," the F♯ at "*ain*si" heard as the top of the piano's counter-melody and the beginning of the singer's phrase, the arrival on B of the piano's melodic line one-and-a-half beats before the singer's use of the same note at "qu'en," and the piano's downward scale fragment echoed by the voice on the long held word "chantent." Often the two parts are in unison, but the duet is all the lovelier when these divergencies and reunions occur. Is it too romantic to explain this as a musical interpretation of the loving couple traveling through life together?

The poem reads:

Isn't it true? We shall go, gayly and slowly, along the path,
The modest way which Hope shows us while smiling,
Caring little that we are ignored or seen.

Isolated in love as in a dark forest,
Our two hearts, exhaling their peaceful tenderness,
Will be two nightingales who sing at night.
We shall walk in the same steps
And hand in hand with the childlike souls
Of those who love without mixed feelings. Isn't it true?

9. L'Hiver a cessé
Winter is Over

L'Hiver a cessé, la lumière est tiède
Et danse, du sol au firmament clair,
Il faut que le coeur le plus triste cède
A l'immense joie éparse dans l'air.

J'ai depuis un an le printemps dans l'âme,
Et le vert retour du doux floréal,
Ainsi qu'une flamme entoure une flamme,
Met de l'idéal sur mon idéal.

Le ciel bleu prolonge, exhausse et couronne
L'immuable azur où rit mon amour.
La saison est belle et ma part est bonne
Et tous mes espoirs ont enfin leur tour.

Que vienne l'Eté! Que viennent encore
L'Automne et l'Hiver! Et chaque saison
Me sera charmante, ô toi, que décore
Cette fantaisie et cette raison!

With this song, the cycle *La Bonne Chanson* comes to an end. Ended, too, is the long winter, the time of waiting. Spring is here and summer, the season of the wedding day, will soon follow. To express the exuberant joy of the poet, Fauré provides a piano prelude bursting with high spirits and expectancy. After a subtle, halting introductory measure, the dotted sixteenth notes and resulting thirty-second notes gain in speed and energy. There is a rapid *crescendo* to a full *forte* followed by a *diminuendo* and a second *crescendo,* this one heralding the singer's entrance. The vocal line is swept up in this second *crescendo* but another *diminuendo* brings the music back down to a *pp*. These roller-coaster dynamics continue throughout the song, adding to the aura of youthful exhilaration.

The text of this song is irresistible in its boundless happiness. The beautiful line "J'ai depuis un an le printemps dans l'âme" refers to the year-long betrothal, which is now to culminate in Verlaine's marriage to his Mathilde. The poet is so happy he thinks everyone must share his rapture at winter's end—"Il faut que le coeur le plus triste cède/ A l'immense joie éparse dans l'air," "The saddest heart must yield/ To the enormous joy scattered in the air." He is unable even to imagine the melancholia of those whose moods do not match the bright season.

Since joy is usually far less complicated than sorrow, Fauré begins his setting with a straightforward harmonic scheme focusing on B♭ major, the main key. The first unusual modulation occurs at the singer's second note, the E♭ on "hiver," where one expects an E♭ chord but hears instead a diminished chord with G♭ as the root. By the end of the phrase ("cessé"), Fauré has returned to the tonic where he stays through the singer's second phrase. He then moves on to C♯ minor for the wonderfully affirmative melodic upswing of "du sol au firmament," which culminates in the F♮ at "clair" where we find an F^7 chord. There is a characteristic augmented chord under "joie" and a satisfying V^7–I (F^7–B♭) at "dans l'air." The words for this tumultuous first section are:

> Winter is over, the light is soft
> And dances from the earth to the clear firmament,
> The saddest heart must yield
> To the immense joy scattered in the air.

Despite small *crescendi* and *diminuendi* the next section is more docile, less hectic. There is one *crescendo* to a *forte* at "mon idéal," but it seems less emphatic than those in the earlier section. The *dolce* mood continues through the E major measure (before "La saison"), but there is a strong *crescendo* leading back to the tonic key at "enfin leur tour," where the opening figure is again repeated. This takes us through the verses

> For a year I have had Springtime in my soul,
> And the green return of the sweet flowering time,
> Like a flame encircling a flame,
> Puts the ideal on my ideal.
>
> The blue sky extends, heightens and crowns
> The immutable blue where my love laughs.
> The season is beautiful and my share is good,
> And all my hopes finally have their turn.

The feeling of passionate intensity, brought back by the *crescendo* at the end of the last verse, carries through the next line, but the words "Et chaque saison" introduce a more gentle sound. The music pauses after the word "charmante"—the first break in the headlong rush of notes in the accompaniment—and the next four measures are slow and contemplative. Suddenly, for the last two words, the original rapid tempo and the sweep of sixteenth notes in the accompaniment return. The melody ends on the dominant, and it is the task of the four-bar postlude to establish the tonic and to fade out gently. The last lines of verse are:

Let Summer come! Let come also
Autumn and Winter! And each season
Will be charming for me, Oh thou who are adorned by
This fantasy and this thought!

Sérénade   Poem by Molière
Serenade   (1893)

Je languis nuit et jour et ma peine est extrême,
Depuis qu'à vos rigueurs vos beaux yeux m'ont soumis!
Si vous traitez ainsi, belle Iris, qui vous aime,
Hélas! Hélas! que pourriez-vous faire à vos ennemis!

In the first act of Molière's *Le Bourgeois Gentilhomme,* the dancing master and the music teacher attempt to awaken their patron, a nouveau riche bourgeois who would like to become a "Gentleman," to the delights of their arts. As part of the lesson the music teacher has his student sing a Serenade of his own composition for M. Jourdain, the totally uncultivated bourgeois in question. M. Jourdain dismisses this air as too lugubrious, and suggests instead a ridiculous popular ditty, which he then bleats out in a raucous bray.

Since it was Molière's intention to mock the pretentious "masters" of dance and music as well as the insensitive bourgeois, in most productions of the play the "Serenade" is sung abominably to dreadful music. The fact that M. Jourdain's choice is even worse does not make the "serious" piece one whit better.

Fauré's setting of the silly quatrain, which is in absolutely correct Alexandrines (the twelve-syllable rhymed couplet was the favored form of versification in the 17th century when this play was written), is quite lovely and to this ear devoid of satiric intent. The harmonies are typical of Fauré, and the only concession to seventeenth-century style is the singer's cadenza just before the end of the vocal part. In fact, the lovely accompaniment and flowing melody lend an undeserved dignity to the words and the song is quite touching.

The piano begins with a typical broken-chord figure on the tonic (F minor is the original key). The gently rocking 9/8 rhythm is equally suitable for a barcarolle, a lullaby, or a serenade. The melodic line has considerable scope, moving freely within the octave from F above middle C to the F above that.

To extend the brief poem and give the song more impact, Fauré repeats the word "Hélas" several times and then uses the whole last line twice. The anguished little exclamations are well-spaced to add to their dramatic power. The octave drop in the melodic line before each "que pourriez-vous" is another dramatic device. There is a powerful dissonance at "aime," the singer's C clashing harshly with the piano's D♮, again for dramatic effect.

Fauré was not the only composer drawn to this play. Molière's original musical collaborator was the French composer Lully; Richard Strauss wrote incidental music for the play and originally intended to include "Ariadne auf Naxos" in the play as the entertainment M. Jourdain plans for his ladylove. The Strauss score is also heard as a suite for concert performance. The Fauré song is not listed in *Groves Dictionary of Music and Musicians, Fifth Edition* and has no opus number. The words of the quatrain are:

> I languish night and day, and my pain is extreme,
> Since your beauty has made me submit to your will:
> If you treat thus, beautiful Iris, him whom you love,
> Alas, what would you do to your enemies?

Le Parfum impérissable　　　　　Poem by Leconte de Lisle
The Imperishable Perfume　　　　　　OPUS 76/1

> Quand la fleur du soleil, la rose de Lahor,
> De son âme odorante a rempli goutte à goutte
> La fiole d'argile ou de cristal ou d'or,
> Sur le sable qui brûle on peut l'épandre toute,
>
> Les fleuves et la mer inonderaient en vain
> Ce sanctuaire étroit qui la tint enfermée,
> Il garde en se brisant son arôme divin
> Et sa poussière heureuse en reste parfumée!
>
> Puisque par la blessure ouverte de mon coeur
> Tu t'écoules de même ô céleste liqueur,
>
> Inexprimable amour qui m'enflammais pour elle!
> Qu'il lui soit pardonné, que mon mal soit béni!
> Par delà l'heure humaine et le temps infini
> Mon coeur est embaumé d'une odeur immortelle!

"Le Parfum impérissable" ("The Imperishable Perfume"), while dealing with intensely emotional subject matter, maintains such an aura of cool reserve that its final prayerlike verse seems entirely in keeping with the rest of the song. Fauré well understood Leconte de Lisle's poetic aims of symmetry, beauty and avoidance of excessive romantic effusiveness. This is not a denial of passion—it would be hard to find a more compelling image than that of the "open wound of my heart" ("la blessure ouverte de mon coeur") from which the "heavenly liqueur" ("céleste liqueur"), the "inexplicable love" ("inexprimable amour") flows away—it is passion expressed within the structures of elegance of style and form.

The poem has an unusual rhyme scheme and stanza arrangement, which can be shown by the end sounds:

I	II	III	IV
Lahor	envain	coeur	pour elle
goutte	enfermée	liqueur	béni
d'or	divin		infini
toute	parfumée		immortelle

This particular division lends emphasis to the two focal lines from which the above quotes are taken. As we shall see, these lines are also given suitable dynamic strength in the music.

The piano opens with three solemn tonic chords (Gb major is the key for high voice) and the vocal line begins with a tonic triad. The piano's upper notes are more or less in unison with the voice, and both make a discreet *crescendo* under "âme odorante" and an immediate *diminuendo* at the end of the phrase. Under "Sur le sable qui brûle," the piano part rises above the highly chromatic vocal part (the piano is providing a harmony in thirds) and the *crescendo* is much more pronounced. (There is a misprint in the Marks Edition for high voice on the word "sable," where the first syllable should be an eighth note, not a sixteenth note.) The first verse reads:

> When the flower of sunshine, the rose of Lahor,
> With its fragrant soul has filled drop by drop
> The phial of china, crystal or gold,
> One can scatter it all on the burning sand,

The first verse flows without a break into the second, and the dynamics continue their modest ups and downs. The melodic phrase under "sa poussière heureuse en reste parfumée" is almost identical to the comparable line of verse in the first stanza; this structural device sets the stanzas in relief without the usual piano interlude. The words continue:

> The ocean's waves will inundate in vain
> This narrow sanctuary which holds it enclosed,
> It retains even though broken its divine aroma
> And the happy dust remains scented with it!

A rising Gb arpeggio (actually a Gb⁷ because of the Fb in the bass) leads precipitously to the climactic rhymed couplet. At this point, the *forte* dynamics and the impassioned chords make these two lines and the first line of the next verse dramatic and relatively unrestrained. For the sake of narrative clarity and musical structure these three lines belong together, although this is not the case in the rhyme scheme:

> For from the open wound of my heart
> You too flow away, O heavenly liqueur,
> Inexplicable love which enflamed me for her!

Suddenly there is a hushed sense of reverence as the singer intones his prayer, first on one note and then with a beautifully arched phrase. As the prayer progresses, a *crescendo* builds until we reach one last *forte* at "Mon coeur," after which we have a *diminuendo* and a descending melodic line. The piano finishes as it began on solemn tonic chords. The last three lines of verse are:

> May it be pardoned, may my woe be sanctified!
> Beyond the hour of man and infinite time
> My heart is embalmed with an immortal fragrance!

Arpège   Poem by Albert Samain
Arpeggio   OPUS 76/2

L'âme d'une flûte soupire
Au fond du parc mélodieux
Limpide est l'ombre où l'on respire
Ton poème silencieux,

Nuit de langueur, nuit de mensonge,
Qui pose, d'un geste ondoyant,
Dans ta chevelure de songe
La lune bijou d'Orient.

Sylva, Sylvie et Sylvanire
Belles au regard bleu changeant
L'étoile aux fontaines se mire,
Allez par les sentiers d'argent,

Allez vite l'heure est si brève
Cueillir au jardin des aveux
Les coeurs qui se meurent du rêve
De mourir parmi vos cheveux!

The brooding, melancholy, murky text of this song is typical of the style of its author, Albert Samain. In the poem, "the soul of a flute sighs melodiously/ Deep in the park." One inhales a silent poem in a limpid shadow; and night wears tresses of dreams of which hearts die. Clearly narrative clarity is not the desired effect—words are used for their musical sound or for the aura they evoke.

The title of the piece, "Arpège," has a strong commercial connotation today due to its well-advertised association with a perfume. The
real meaning of the word however is musical—it is the French equivalent of the Italian *arpeggio*. Since the majority of Fauré's accompaniments are arpeggiated figures anyway, it is no surprise that he chose to
interpret the title literally, and most of the accompaniment consists of
arpeggiated chords. With "Arpeggio" as its name and the "soul of the
flute" as its first image, this poem is a natural choice for a musical
setting.

There are four four-line stanzas in the poem, but Fauré presents
stanzas one and two as a unit, making the first real break in the vocal
part after "bijou d'Orient." The music for this section is limpid and
flowing. The piano has a beautiful introductory melody, ending in a
trill which brings the vocal line in. The 9/8 rhythm has a slightly unusual effect because of the rest on the last beat of every group of three.
Dovetailing this halting triplet in the accompaniment with the ongoing melody creates a subtle and beautiful rhythmic tension.

The melody enters on the dominant (the key for high voice is F♯
minor) and is dominant oriented for the first four bars. The lowered F
and G under "parc melodieux" allows Fauré to use a whole-tone
scale back up to the C♯. The harmonic changes are extremely subtle,
especially those under the enharmonically altered notes at "l'on
respire."

Under "Nuit de langueur" the piano's original solo melody is
heard again. This is the only indication that the second stanza has begun. In fact, the repeated notes in the vocal part, bridging "silen*cieux*"
and "Nuit," emphasize continuity rather than separation. Throughout
the section the dynamic scale has been low, but a *crescendo* begins to
build at "Dans ta chevelure" and we have a modest climax at "La
lune." The first two stanzas read:

> The soul of a flute sighs melodiously
> Deep in the park.
> Limpid is the shadow where one inhales
> Your silent poem,
>
> Night of languor, night of lies,
> Which puts, with an undulating gesture,
> In your dreamlike hair
> The moon, jewel of the Orient.

After the brief piano interlude, the third stanza begins with three
names, all variants on Sylvan (growing in the woods). Sylvie is also the
name of a bird, the warbler. There is much less movement in the
accompaniment here, as sixteenth notes yield to eighth notes. The key

has shifted to the relative major with considerable use of augmented chords. The words for this short section are:

Sylva, Sylvie, Sylvanire
Beauties with fickle blue eyes
The star is reflected in the fountains
Go by way of the silver paths,

The piano's opening melody returns again, this time as a solo, and the trill is used again to usher in the vocal part. By way of the chromatic melodic line under "l'heure est si brève," Fauré brings us to F♯ major for the concluding segment. Here we have a combination of the original accompanying figure, with its sixteenth notes and rests in the bass and the more legato eighth notes in the treble. The singer begins the only really climactic *crescendo* in the song under "Cueillir au jardin"; from "jardin" to "*se meur*ent," the top of the phrase and the climax of the *crescendo,* the vocalist has a chromatic melody which is reinforced by the piano's upper line. The piano part is rich here in countermelodies (double-stemmed notes under "brève," "aveux," "meurent," and "rêve de mourir"), broken chords, long held notes, and supporting melodic notes. From the *forte* at "se meurent" there is a steady *decrescendo* to the end. The vocal part ends with a long final syllable on the dominant, under which the piano begins its solo melody. As the voice fades away, the piano plays its tune one final time before it, too, fades away on major tonic chords. The ending is truly beautiful. The last stanza reads:

Go quickly the time is so brief
To gather vows in the garden
Hearts which die from the dream
Of dying amid your hair.

Prison
Poem by Paul Verlaine
OPUS 83/1

Le ciel est, par dessus le toit,
Si bleu, si calme,
Un arbre, par dessus le toit,
Berce sa palme;

La cloche, dans le ciel qu'on voit,
Doucement tinte,
Un oiseau, sur l'arbre qu'on voit,
Chante sa plainte.

Mon Dieu, mon Dieu, la vie est là,
Simple et tranquille!
Cette paisible rumeur-là
Vient de la ville.

Qu'as-tu fait, ô toi que voilà,
Pleurant sans cesse
Dis, qu'as-tu fait, toi que voilà,
De ta jeunesse?

This anguished poem was written by Verlaine in 1873, while he was serving a two-year prison sentence for having wounded his friend and fellow poet, Rimbaud, during a quarrel. The story of the friendship between Verlaine and Rimbaud is strange and difficult to understand. In 1870 Verlaine had been married—happily as far as anyone knew—to Mathilde, the woman who had inspired his beautiful collection *La Bonne Chanson* (for a discussion of the nine poems from this collection set to music by Fauré, see pages 91 to 108). The following year they had a child, but Rimbaud, already a friend of the family, convinced Verlaine to leave home and with him wander through Belgium, leading a wild Bohemian life. There was a tug of war between Mathilde and Rimbaud, and Verlaine was torn between the two life styles. Eventually Mathilde left Verlaine, but shortly thereafter there was a rupture between Verlaine and Rimbaud as well. The rest of Verlaine's life was a struggle for normalcy, periods of emotional disturbance alternating with years of stability.

This poem, called "Le Ciel est par-dessus le toit . . ." by its author, is one of his most famous. It is a masterpiece of concentration, in three very brief stanzas conveying the sweetness and peacefulness of everyday life, and in the fourth riveting one's attention on the poor wretch, crying ceaselessly, who is prohibited from enjoying it. Verlaine was twenty-nine years old at the time; robbed of his wife, his child, his friend, and his freedom by his own ridiculous action, his misery must have been boundless.

The *abab* rhyme scheme is rendered somewhat unusual by the use of repetition: in each stanza the first and third lines end with the same word, not just the same sound. In fact, in all but the third stanza a considerable part of lines one and three are identical. Somehow this repetition is soothing where simple, peaceful life is described, and heartrending in the last stanza.

Fauré's setting of the poem emphasizes the drama inherent in its words. He makes no attempt to extend the length of the poem by piano preludes, interludes, or postludes, nor does he linger over any end syllables. The rhythm of the poem is therefore faithfully reproduced in the music.

The piano opens with simple tonic chords (the key for high voice is E minor) and the singer enters with an equally simple tonic melody. A dominant-seventh chord brings us to a natural resting place on "calme," after which this material is repeated, concluding the first stanza:

> The sky is above the roof
>> So blue, so calm!
> A tree above the roof
>> Waves its branch.

The chord under "doucement" vaguely suggests the bell mentioned at the beginning of the line, which once again ends with a pause on the dominant. The second half of the stanza offers the first variant ending as the melody descends from the F♯, which is still part of the dominant-seventh chord, to an E, which is harmonized in C major. This is a brilliant lead to the dramatic outburst which follows. The second stanza reads:

> The bell in the sky which one sees
>> Sweetly rings,
> A bird on the tree which one sees,
>> Sings its lament.

Suddenly the voice leaps an octave for the next dramatic phrase, which begins *forte* and then tapers as the line descends. The accompanying chords are intensely dramatic, the ostinato F♮ on top harmonized by rich, constantly changing combinations. The entire scheme is repeated one half-step up for the second half of the stanza, the rise in pitch increasing the dramatic intensity. The third stanza is:

> My God, my God, life is there,
>> Simple and tranquil.
> That peaceful clamor there
>> Comes from the city.

The last stanza begins angrily on a still higher pitch, but, instead of an immediate descent and *diminuendo,* we have a rise to the dominant at the end of the first half of the stanza, the final *decrescendo* held in reserve for the second half. Just as Verlaine exempted the third stanza from his scheme of verbal repetition, Fauré abandons the comparable musical device in the final stanza. The C minor chord under "Dis," the diminished chord under "qu'as-tu," and the E$^9_7$ under "fait" make this line particularly beautiful and moving.

There is an ostinato E in the bass from the word "fait" to the end of the song. It is absolutely necessary to catch the E-G grace notes in the third measure from the end in the pedal, so the C chords may be revealed as suspensions over the E minor chord. This same suspension occurs in the vocal line, and the resolution on the last syllable brings the song to a mournful end on the tonic. The last stanza reads:

What have you done, oh you over there
   Crying ceaselessly,
Say, what have you done, you over there
   With your youth?

Soir   Poem by Albert Samain
Evening   OPUS 83/2

Voici que les jardins de la nuit vont fleurir.
Les lignes, les couleurs, les sons deviennent vagues;
Vois! le dernier rayon agonise à tes bagues.
Ma soeur, entends-tu pas quelque chose mourir?

Mets sur mon front tes mains fraîches comme une eau pure,
Mets sur mes yeux tes mains douces comme des fleurs,
Et que mon âme où vit le goût secret des pleurs
Soit comme un lys fidèle et pâle à ta ceinture!

C'est la pitié qui pose ainsi son doigt sur nous,
Et tout ce que la terre a de soupirs qui montent,
Il semble qu'à mon coeur enivré le racontent
Tes yeux levés au ciel si tristes et si doux.

"Soir" is in almost every way the exact opposite of "Prison," its
opus mate. Rambling rather than concentrated, lyric rather than dramatic, vague rather than concise, "Soir" provides excellent contrast to
Prison," although there is no indication whatsoever that Fauré wanted
them performed in tandem.

Despite the impressionistic nature of its text, the poem itself is in
strict Alexandrines (lines of twelve syllables) and has a traditional
rhyme scheme:

	I	II	III
a	fleurir	pure	nous
b	vagues	fleurs	montent
b	bagues	pleurs	racontent
a	mourir	ceinture	doux

The piano introduction consists of three arpeggiated tonic chords
(the key for high voice is Eb). These quiet single notes, which continue as the singer enters, create an aura of calm and vague mystery.
The melodic line rises in a simple scale from tonic to dominant in the
next measure, but the music becomes more complex and less bland in
the latter part of the stanza. A very small *crescendo* on the long syllable
"pas" is immediately squelched and the dynamics for this segment are
subdued. The words are:

Now the gardens of the night will blossom.
The lines, the colors, the sounds become vague;
See! the last ray dies in your rings.
My sister, don't you hear something die?

As the last syllable fades, the piano introduces a lovely melody of its own. The increased activity in the piano part makes the music sound livelier, although there is no tempo change. The voice joins the piano in this melodic effusion for most of the stanza, except where the singer holds a low F for over a measure ("pleurs Soit comme un") and then sings its own melody in counterpoint with the piano. There is a *crescendo* from "pâle" to "ceinture" where the two melodic lines meet on a *forte*. The piano ends the stanza with a continuation of its melody. The words are:

Put on my forehead your hands cool as pure water
Put on my eyes your hands soft as flowers,
And may my soul, where the secret taste for tears lives,
Be like a lily, faithful and pale at your waist!

The single-note broken chords of the opening bars now return, but there is a little countermelody on the first of each group of sixteenth notes (the double-stemmed notes) and the harmonies move gradually from G minor until they reach the tonic at "nous." The vocal part does begin with a recapitulation of the opening line, but it soon soars to new heights, first at "Il semble," then at "racontent," and finally at "ciel." The singer's melody has unusual sweep in these last three lines, rising and falling in a more dramatic way than the earlier sections of the song would suggest. It is here that we have our dynamic climaxes as well, with a *crescendo* to a *forte* at "racontent" and continued strength through "ciel." The inevitable *decrescendo* begins at "tristes" and continues through the pretty postlude. The final stanza is:

It is pity which places its finger thus upon us,
And all the sighs of the earth which rise,
It seems that to my drunken heart they recount
Your eyes raised to heaven, so sad and so sweet.

Dans la forêt de Septembre　　　　Poem by Catulle Mendès
In the Forest of September　　　　　　OPUS 85/1

Ramure aux rumeurs amollies,
Troncs sonores que l'âge creuse,
L'antique forêt douloureuse
S'accorde à nos mélancolies.

O sapins agriffés au gouffre,
Nids déserts aux branches brisées,
Halliers brûlés, fleurs sans rosées,
Vous savez bien comme l'on souffre!

Et lorsque l'homme, passant blême,
Pleure dans le bois solitaire,
Des plaintes d'ombre et de mystère
L'accueillent en pleurant de même.

Bonne forêt! promesse ouverte
De l'exil que la vie implore,
Je viens d'un pas alerte encore
Dans ta profondeur encor verte.

Mais d'un fin bouleau de la sente,
Une feuille, un peu rousse, frôle
Ma tête et tremble à mon épaule;
C'est que la forêt vieillissante,
Sachant l'hiver, où tout avorte,
Déjà proche en moi comme en elle,
Me fait l'aumône fraternelle
De sa première feuille morte!

"Dans la forêt de Septembre" is one of Fauré's loveliest, most evocative songs. Its harmonies create an atmosphere at the same time antique, mysterious, passionate and peaceful. The alternation of flowing
sixteenth notes and somber chords in the accompaniment provides variety, while the quasi-strophic structure of the music assures unity and
cohesiveness.

The poem is typical of the genre which uses nature as a metaphor
for the human condition. In this case the sadness of the old forest
corresponds to man's melancholia. Everything in the forest speaks of
desolation and abandonment—deserted nests in broken branches,
burned-out thickets, flowers without dew. Since the forest suffers this
desolation, it can understand man's pain when the winter of life or love
is near, and in fraternal charity offers to the poet who wanders deep
within, its first dead leaf.

Catulle Mendès, author of this poem and of the second text of
Fauré's Opus 85, which follows, was one of the founders of a literary
magazine called *La Revue fantaisiste,* in which many poems of the
Parnassiens were published. Elegance of style, richness of rhyme, regularity and symmetry of rhythm, an avoidance of excessive romantic
Angst—the "art-for-art's sake" aims of the Parnassiens are manifest in
this poem.

The poem is a long one, six stanzas of four lines with the *abba/
cddc/effe/*, etc., rhyme scheme. The language itself is very musical and

full of alliterations such as "Rameurs aux rumeurs," "agriffés au gouffre," and "branches brisées."

Fauré's musical style, with its constantly shifting harmonies and gently flowing figures, is perfectly suited to this sort of poetry. Due to the length of the poem, Fauré opted for a compromise between the strophic structure (where each subsequent stanza has a recapitulation of the music of the first), which he had abandoned after his earliest songs, and the straight-through type of composing where the material is always new for each section of verse. In this song we have a recapitulation of the piano part and part of the vocal line after the second stanza. A similar repeat, involving the accompaniment and melody, occurs after the third line of the fifth stanza. Neither of these reiterations lasts for the whole stanza, but enough material is repeated to lend cohesiveness to the rather long song.

The piano opens with a two-bar introduction in which solemn chords set a mood of sobriety and melancholia. Each of the first three measures begins with a tonic chord (Ab in the key for high voice), with the singer entering on the piano's top melodic note. At the end of the first vocal phrase there is an antique-sounding cadence (at "amoll*ies*"). This effect is repeated at the end of the next line (under "creuse"), where the cadence is almost churchlike. This is excellent psychological preparation for the words "L'antique forêt." An unexpected and exquisite false cadence, from Bb⁷ to Cb, is heard under "douloureuse," and an equally telling suspension under "*à* nos" leads back to the tonic at "mélanco*lies*," making this brief stanza enormously rich harmonically. The crest of the vocal line is at "doulou*reu*se," but the general dynamic level remains *piano* throughout. The words for this stanza are:

> Branches with softened sounds,
> Sonorous trunks which age makes hollow,
> Ancient mournful forest
> Corresponds to our melancholia

The next section has less harmonic intensity, as single-note figures replace the chords in the accompaniment. Nevertheless, an aura of mystery is created by the half-step intervals in the piano figure at "gou*ff*re," "brisées," "brûl*és*," and "rosées." This time the return to the tonic at the end of the stanza is accomplished by way of the relative minor, F minor. The singer has a fairly strong *crescendo* to "Halliers brûlés" but then returns to a *piano*. The second stanza reads:

> Oh pine trees clutched by the whirlpool,
> Deserted nests in broken branches,
> Burned-out thickets, flowers without dew,
> You know well how one suffers!

The accompaniment now returns to its original chords, and the vocal line joins the recapitulation in time for the cadence at "blême." Although there is a variance in the melodic line (it is flattened out in this repeat) the harmonies remain the same for these four bars. The return to the tonic comes only after three additional bars in this musically abbreviated segment:

> And while man, passing wan,
> Cries in the lonely woods,
> Laments of shadow and mystery
> Assail him, crying as he does.

The mood now changes to one of benign tenderness as the poet extolls the forest. The broken chords are predominantly major and there is a free-flowing quality to the vocal line. No further references in words or music are made to antiquity.

> Good forest! candid promise
> Of the exile which life implores,
> I come with a still lively step
> To your still green depths.

The last two lines, quoted above, imply that the poet's life is not yet spent, just as the forest is not yet totally denuded. The music continues with no discernible break between stanzas in mood or figuration.

> But from a slender birch tree on the path
> A leaf, slightly reddish, grazes
> My head and trembles on my shoulder.

The piano's interlude, which comes before the last line of the stanza, is a harmonic bridge back to the tonic and to a recapitulation of the music of the opening bars. The chords bring back the more somber mood, and the words hold back the melodic line even when the sixteenth note figure reappears. The climax of the song, the only genuine *forte*, occurs at "Me fait l'aumône." From that peak we have the usual fade-out ending on the tonic. The last five lines of verse are:

> It is that the aging forest,
> Knowing winter, where all is aborted,
> Already near in me, as in her,
> Gives me the brotherly charitable gift
> Of its first dead leaf.

La Fleur qui va sur l'eau Poem by Catulle Mendès
The Flower on the Water OPUS 85/2

Sur la mer voilée
D'un brouillard amer

La Belle est allée,
La nuit, sur la mer!

Elle avait aux lèvres
D'un air irrité,
La Rose des Fièvres,
La Rose Beauté!

D'un souffle farouche
L'ouragan hurleur
Lui baisa la bouche
Et lui prit la fleur!

Dans l'océan sombre,
Moins sombre déjà,
Où le troismats sombre,
La fleur surnagea.

L'eau s'en est jouée,
Dans ses noirs sillons;
C'est une bouée
Pour les papillons.

Et l'embrun, la Houle
Depuis cette nuit,
Les brisants où croule
Un sauvage bruit,

L'alcyon, la voile,
L'hirondelle autour,
Et l'ombre et l'étoile
Se meurent d'amour,

Et l'aurore éclose
Sur le gouffre clair
Pour la seule rose
De toute la mer!

There seems to be an unlimited number of ways in which the piano can be used to evoke the sound of the sea. In this song Fauré has hit upon a particularly effective figure to convey the sea's surging energy and turbulence.

The poem which inspired this setting is, like the first of this opus, by Catulle Mendès. In both these poems Mendès anthropomorphizes nature, first the forest, then the sea. "La Fleur qui va sur l'Eau" has an unusually large number of stanzas—eight in all—but each line is only five syllables long, so the overall length is not inordinate. Because of the brevity of each line there is almost constant rhyme, and the musical phrases tend to be short. Fauré does allow brief pauses in the vocal line between stanzas, but the constantly moving accompaniment prevents a stop-and-start effect.

The meaning of the opening stanzas is somewhat mysterious: a beautiful woman goes to the sea at night, in a bitter fog, with a rose in her lips and an air of irritation. Why does she go? Does she drown herself in the water? The poet doesn't tell us. In the third stanza the focus shifts to the rose itself, which is snatched from her lips by the winds and tossed about in the somber ocean, where it floats as a buoy for the butterflies. The shadows and stars die of love for the rose, as dawn blossoms for her, the only rose of the sea. Has the woman become the flower? Were they always one and the same? We do not know.

The piano begins with the agitated figure that represents the sea. This figure, equally effective whether loud or soft, is heard under the first four stanzas. Its most interesting versions are under "Elle avait aux lèvres . . . Fièvres," where we find suspensions in the first half of each measure and augmented chords in the second half. The half notes in the piano's bass make a little countermelody at "baisa la bouche Et lui prit," and there are lovely harmonic changes under the repeated notes in the vocal line from "prit la" to "l'océan sombre" including an augmented chord under "océan." The dynamics add to the turbulence, with important *crescendos* to "Beauté" and "la fleur" and several lesser ups and downs. The first four stanzas read:

> On the sea, veiled
> By a bitter fog
> The Beauty went,
> The night, on the sea!
>
> She had in her lips
> With an irritated air,
> The Rose of Fevers,
> The Beauty Rose!
>
> With a ferocious wind
> The howling hurricane
> Kissed her mouth
> And took the flower from her!
>
> In the dark ocean
> Already less dark,
> Or threemaster dark,
> The flower floated.

At this point the restless accompaniment begins to calm down, as a much more tranquil figure is introduced in the piano part. We now have a melody for left hand, largely in quarter notes, with broken triads for harmony in the right hand. Here Fauré marks the vocal part *dolce* and *piano*. This pattern, which lasts for eight bars, is based on simple major, minor, or dominant-seventh chords. The last measure of this figure introduces the first line of the following stanza, so the musical and poetic divisions are not simultaneous. The fifth stanza, given below, is *dolce* from beginning to end:

> The water frolicked with it,
> In its dark furrows;
> It is a buoy
> For the butterflies.

The next line of verse, "Et l'embrun, la Houle," leads us to a third accompanying figure, this one in bold eighth notes, with half-note bass notes for the first three bars. The dynamics are once again tempestuous, with a big *crescendo* to "Un sauvage bruit," a *subito piano,* and another climactic rise to "la seule rose," the highest note and most passionate outcry of the song. There is an interesting harmony under "la voile" and a strong suspension at "l'ètoile." The vocal part ends *forte* but the accompaniment tapers to a *piano* at the close. The last three stanzas are:

> And the spray, the Billows
> Since that night,
> Breaking them where crashes
> A savage noise
>
> The kingfisher, the sail,
> The swallow nearby,
> And the shadow and the star
> Die of love
>
> And the dawn blooms
> On the clear whirlpool
> For the only rose
> In all the sea!

Accompagnement   Poem by Albert Samain
Accompaniment   OPUS 85/3

> Tremble argenté tilleul, bouleau ...
> La lune s'effeuille sur l'eau ...
> Comme de longs cheveux peignés au vent du soir,
> L'odeur des nuits d'été parfume le lac noir,
> Le grand lac parfumé brille comme un miroir.
> Ma rame tombe et se relève,
> Ma barque glisse dans le rêve
> Ma barque glisse dans le ciel
> Sur le lac immatériel!
> En cadence les yeux fermés,
> Rame, ô mon coeur, ton indolence
> A larges coups lents at pâmés.

Là-bas la lune écoute, accoudée au côteau,
Le silence qu'exhale en glissant le bateau.
Trois grands lys frais coupés meurent sur mon manteau ...
Vers tes lèvres, ô nuit voluptueuse et pâle.
Est-ce leur âme, est-ce mon âme qui s'exhale?
Cheveux des nuits d'argent peignés aux longs roseaux ...
Comme la lune sur les eaux,
Comme la rame sur les flots
Mon âme s'effeuille en sanglots!

This is one of the least regular and most fascinating poems chosen as a text by Fauré. Its twenty-one lines are unevenly divided according to the following rhyme scheme:

boul*eau*	relève	fermés	pâle
l'eau	rêve	indolence	exhale
soir	ciel	pâmés	ros*eaux*
noir	immatériel	côt*eau*	*eaux*
miroir		bat*eau*	*flots*
		mant*eau*	sang*lots*

(*aa bbb ccdd efe aaa gg aaaa:* the italicized end sounds are the same.) Some of the lines are eight syllables long, others are twelve. The imagery is full of mystery and fantasy, with an overall air of vague melancholia typical of Albert Samain, its author. The syntax defies the grammarian—sentences are begun and left to float unfinished in the mist, with total disdain for exactness of meaning.

Fauré's setting is replete with augmented chords, the vaguest of harmonies. The vocal line often proceeds by chromatic or enharmonic changes, allowing for constantly shifting tonalities. It takes a while for Fauré to cut loose from his tonal moorings, and in the first two bars held tonic and dominant bass notes provide anchorage (the key for high voice is Ab major). After two bars, which contain an augmented chord and a chromatic rise (under "La lune s'effeuille"), Fauré brings us back to the tonic (under "l'eau"). The next several measures have much flux and several consecutive augmented chords, but at "miroir" we return again to the tonic. Despite the irregularity of the stanza divisions, a natural resting place seems intended at this point. The words thus far are:

Silvery aspen, linden, birch ...
The moon sheds its leaves on the water
Like long hair combed by the evening breeze
The scent of summer nights perfumes the black lake,
The great perfumed lake shines like a mirror.

A *crescendo* has led us to a *forte* at "miroir," and the subsequent music has considerable strength. The image of the poet rowing on the lake is an active one, and this is reflected in the music. With the words "dans le rêve," the poet makes it clear that this is all a dream, and the music becomes soft and dreamy again, even though the piano figuration remains the same. The vocalist's high notes come in the first part of this section, where the words and music are less ephemeral.

> My oar falls and rises
> My boat glides in the dream
> My boat glides in the sky
> On the imaginary lake!
> In rhythm with closed eyes
> Row, Oh my heart, your indolence
> With large strokes slow and swooning.

A new figure in the accompaniment announces a new, even more tranquil section. There is less motion in the vocal line, with many syllables repeated on the Ab and with no note higher than a D♮. The piano has a languid countermelody over its running-note figures, which is repeated three times in one key and then throughout the section in various keys. The vocal line pauses after "manteau," a likely stanza division, but the accompaniment's pattern continues. When the voice reenters, the *tessitura* is higher and some excitement builds towards the modest climax at "mon âme." There is an overlap, as the last stanza of verse begins before the comparable change in the music:

> Over there the moon listens, leaning to the side,
> To the silence which the gliding boat exudes.
> Three large lilies, freshly cut, die on my sleeve . . .
> Towards your lips, Oh night voluptuous and pale,
> Is it their soul, is it my soul which breathes?
> Hair of silvery nights combed in the long dew . . .

On the word "roseaux," the first rhyme word of the last stanza, we have an interesting dissonance, E♮ in the vocal part, Eb in the accompaniment. Despite the *pp* indication, this marvelous sound should be heard. The Eb in the bass brings back the accompanying figure of the introductory bars with the strong tonic-dominant focus. With the exception of the two measures at the beginning of the 4/2 rhythm, this tonic-dominant underpinning continues until the end of the song. Augmented chords play a part in the harmonic scheme in the closing bars (the chords with Fb instead of Eb), and, of course, in the music under "Mon âme s'effeuille," which is a repeat of the comparable phrase in the first section. In the final segment Fauré has the melody rise with each short phrase: "Comme la lune . . . ," "Comme la râme . . . ," and finally "Mon âme. . . ." The climax is, of course, at "Mon âme," after which we have a fade-out ending. The final lines of verse are:

Like the moon on the waters
Like the oar on the waves
My soul sheds its leaves and sighs!

Le plus doux chemin (Madrigal)   Poem by Armand Silvestre
The Sweetest Path   OPUS 87/1

A mes pas le plus doux chemin
Mène à la porte de ma belle,
Et, bien qu'elle me soit rebelle,
J'y veux encor passer demain.

Il est tout fleuri de jasmin
Au temps de la saison nouvelle,
Et, bien qu'elle me soit cruelle
J'y passe, des fleurs à la main.

Pour toucher son coeur inhumain
Je chante ma peine cruelle,
Et bien qu'elle me soit rebelle,
C'est pour moi le plus doux chemin.

Webster's *Dictionary* defines "Madrigal" as "a little amorous poem, sometimes called a pastoral poem, containing some tender and delicate, though simple thought, suitably expressed." As secondary meanings are listed "a setting for such a poem" and "a glee, a part song." (A glee is a vocal composition in three or more parts.) Although musicians are likely to think of the wonderful part songs of Monteverdi, Gesualdo, and Jannequin, in this song the subtitle "Madrigal" obviously refers to the charming little poem, since the setting is for solo voice with the simplest of accompaniments.

The poem itself is a perfect example of the dangers of judging an author from a small sample of his output, for Armand Silvestre was well known for his humorous short stories, which were often in dubious taste, and for his dramatic opera libretti, while this poem is the personification of innocence and delicacy.

There are but two end sounds in the twelve lines of verse, for which the rhyme scheme is *abba/abba/abba*. The first and last lines of the poem are the same and the overall structure is tightly knit.

Fauré's music matches Silvestre's text in ingenuous naïveté, but behind the single notes and sparse chords lies a sophisticated harmonic scheme. In the key for high voice G minor is the tonal center for most of the song, but the last six bars are in G major. Within the piece the 6th and 7th steps of the scale are frequently raised, creating major-minor ambiguity. This is true of the two introductory bars and the first

bar of the vocal part. At the half notes under "chem*in*," "*be*lle" and
"re*be*lle," we have matching dominant-seventh chords, but the expected resolutions do not follow.

There is no break in the vocal line between the first and second
stanzas, but at the end of the second stanza a rise in the melody to the
dominant note, a strong V⁷–I cadence, and a charming little piano
interlude create a clear separation. The first two stanzas read:

> To my steps the sweetest path
> Leads to the door of my beauty,
> And, even though she is unyielding to me,
> I wish to go there again tomorrow.
>
> It is all abloom with jasmine
> At the time of the new season,
> And even though she is cruel to me
> I go there, flowers in my hand.

The focal point of the first section occurs at "bien qu'elle me
soit," where we find the highest notes of the song. The more intense
climax of the second section is found on the repeated E♭ of "peine
cruelle," the most heartfelt words of the poem. Even though there is a
two bar *crescendo* to this point, the dynamics are not to exceed *mezzo
forte*—this is a gentle pastoral without much *Sturm und Drang*. The
vocal part ends with the same melodic fragment that brought section
one to a close, leaving us on the dominant. The tender postlude is in
the major mode. The final stanza is:

> To touch her inhuman heart
> I sing of my cruel pain,
> And even though she is unyielding to me
> It is for me the sweetest path.

Le Ramier   Poem by Armand Silvestre
The Ring Dove   OPUS 87/2

Avec son chant doux et plaintif,
Ce ramier blanc te fait envie:
S'il te plait l'avoir pour captif,
J'irai te le chercher, Sylvie.

Mais là près de toi dans mon sein,
Comme ce ramier mon coeur chante,
S'il t'en plait faire le larcin,
Il sera mieux à toi, méchante.

Pour qu'il soit tel qu'un ramier blanc,
Le prisonnier que tu recèles,

Sur mon coeur, oiselet tremblant,
Pose tes mains comme deux ailes.

This touching little song is as succinct as its opus-mate, "Le plus doux chemin," but its mood is much darker and more sophisticated. The poem's message, although couched in complex syntax, is simple: the loved one is tempted by the beautiful song of the ringdove; the poet is willing to find one for her, but offers his heart, which sings like a ringdove when near her, as a better gift. The last stanza complicates the metaphor by comparing the beloved's hands to a bird's wings, a slightly confusing bit of poetic license.

The poem is in three stort stanzas with the standard *abab/cdcd/efef* rhyme scheme. The music follows the poem's rhythmic structure, with suitable pauses in the vocal line at the end of each stanza.

The piano opens with a curiously halting rhythmic figure. Each of the first three measures begins with a tonic chord (F♯ minor for high voice), but on the second beat the bass note leads to IV minor-seventh and diminished-plus-major-third chords. The overall effect of these shifting harmonies and the long note in the bass is dark and somber. The vocal part enters in this rather melancholy mood, but at the beloved's name, Sylvie, the mood brightens a bit. Actually the name is a pun, for Sylvie or Sylvia is the ornithological word for another type of bird, the warbler. The words thus far are:

With its sweet and plaintive song
This white ring dove tempts you:
If it should please you to have it for a captive,
I shall go to look for it, Sylvia.

There are some interesting harmonic ideas in the next section, in particular the F♯ major chord suspended over the bass note D in the measure which includes the words "S'il t'en plait," and the resolution to the relative major (A major) at the end of the stanza (under "méchante"). There is a small *crescendo* at the beginning of the section but no real climax. The second stanza reads:

But there near you in my breast
Like this dove my heart sings,
If it pleases you to steal it,
It would be better yours, wicked one.

The word "méchante," wicked one, is sung so gently and sweetly above the major chord that it is clearly a term of endearment!

In the final section we have a *crescendo* leading to a modest climax at "Pose." The melody for the last line of verse has considerable scope, with an octave jump up and back from the first syllable of "ailes." The song ends quietly, with a recapitulation of the halting figure of the opening bars plus a tranquil tonic chord. The last four lines read:

> For it to be like a white dove,
> The prisoner that you receive,
> On my heart, trembling little bird,
> Place your hands like two wings.

Le Don silencieux   Poem by Jean Dominique
The Silent Gift   OPUS 92

> Je mettrai mes deux mains sur ma bouche, pour taire
> Ce que je voudras tant vous dire, âme bien chère!
> Je mettrai mes deux mains sur mes yeux, pour cacher
> Ce que je voudrais tant que pourtant vous cherchiez.
> Je mettrai mes deux mains sur mon coeur, chère vie,
> Pour que vous ignoriez de quel coeur je vous prie!
> Et puis je les mettrai doucement dans vos mains,
> Ces deux mains-ci qui meurent d'un fatigant chagrin . . .
> Elles iront à vous, pleines de leur faiblesse,
> Toutes silencieuses, et même sans caresse,
> Lasse d'avoir porté tout le poids d'un secret
> Dont ma bouche et mes yeux et mon front parleraient.
> Elles iront à vous, légères d'être vides,
> Et lourdes d'être tristes, tristes d'être timides;
> Malheureuses et douces, et si découragées
> Que peut-être, mon Dieu, vous les recueillerez.

This little-known song by Fauré is suffused with a gentle melancholia that is really quite appealing. In it the timid lover says he will cover his mouth, his eyes, and his heart lest the words, glances and thoughts of his passion—which he desperately wants to reach his beloved—should reach her. And yet, despite his discretion, he hopes that somehow she will receive his sad, discouraged but sweet manifestations of love.

Fauré's setting is tender and flowing. Frequently we find expressive suspensions in the accompaniment (under "dire, âme bien chère!" "coeur, chère vie," "faiblesse," "légères," and "lourdes"), a characteristic harmonic device in Fauré's "mélodies." Other outstanding harmonic effects are the progression under "pour cacher"—a combined E♭ minor–C♭ major chord to an F⁷—and the augmented chord which follows immediately, the major 7th under "prie," and the whole-tone-based chord under "et mon par*leraient*." The overall harmonic structure is rather simple, as the song begins and ends on E major and there is even a traditional V⁷–I cadence at the end. (The V⁷ chord is slightly altered by the inclusion of the E♮.)

The vocal line is subdued in range and dynamics, with many stretches of *recitativo*like repeated notes. Each time a rising line seems about to soar, Fauré suppresses the excitement by turning the melody downward again. At "ces deux mains," the rising interval and suggested *crescendo* create a small climax, but once again the melodic line and dynamics fall away. The most intense feeling occurs at the couplet

> Lasse d'avoir porté tout le poids d'un secret
> Dont ma bouche et mes yeux et mon front parleraient.

But once again there is a *decrescendo* and lessening of tension. The last few lines are wistful and poignant, a mixture of hope and discouragement. The words are:

> I shall put my two hands over my mouth, to silence
> What I would so much like to say to you, dearest soul!
> I shall put my two hands over my eyes, to hide
> What I would however so like you to seek.
> I shall put my two hands over my heart, cherished life,
> That you may not know with how much heart I pray!
> And then I shall put them sweetly in your two hands,
> These two hands here which die of a wearying sorrow . . .
> They will come to you, full of their weakness,
> All silent, and even without caress,
> Weary of having carried the weight of a secret
> Of which my eyes and face would speak.
> They will come to you, light from being empty,
> And heavy from being sad, sad from being timid;
> Unhappy and gentle, and so discouraged
> That perhaps, my God, you will receive them.

Chanson   Poem by Henri de Régnier
Song   OPUS 94

> Que me fait toute la terre
> Inutile où tu n'as pas
> En marchant marqué ton pas
> Dans le sable ou la poussière!
>
> Il n'est de fleuve attendu
> Par ma soif qui s'y étanche
> Que l'eau qui sourd et s'épenche,
> De la source où tu as bu.
>
> La seule fleur qui m'attire
> Est celle où je trouverai

Le souvenir empourpré
De ta bouche et de ton rire;

Et, sous la courbe des cieux
La mer pour moi n'est immense
Que parce qu'elle commence
A la couleur de tes yeux.

Although obviously one of Fauré's slighter efforts, "Chanson" has a gentle charm all its own. Its text is a simple set of variations on one romantic theme: nothing on earth has any meaning unless it is somehow touched by the beloved.

Like so many of Fauré's later songs, its minimal accompaniment—root notes and alternating vertical and broken chords—maintains the same rhythmic pattern from beginning to end. Its basic tonality moves from E minor to E major for the last of the four four-line stanzas, but the overall wistfulness of the song is scarcely affected by the change of mode.

Despite the delicate transparency of the music, Fauré's masterful harmonic sense is everywhere in evidence. Particularly lovely are the unexpected G major chord at "La mer," in the final stanza (a B major chord would ordinarily be found in this context), and the G♯ in the next measure (a note extraneous to the otherwise B^7 chord) under "immense."

The melody flows easily from one measure to the next with no unusual leaps and no climactic high notes. Its range is in fact quite limited—from the B below Middle C to the D a little more than an octave above. The pivotal melodic note—again a Fauré characteristic—is the dominant (B), to which and from which the other notes lead. The composer's indications call for a modest dynamic scale, with *mezzo forte* topping the *crescendi;* it would be self-defeating to over-interpret the wispy little piece.

What good is all the land to me
Useless where you have not,
Walking, marked your step
In the sand or the dust!

No stream is awaited
By my thirst which is quenched there
But the water which rumbles and flows
From the stream where you have drunk.

The only flower which attracts me
Is that on which I shall find
The lavender memory
Of your lips and your laugh;

And, under the arc of the skies,
The sea is immense to me
Only because it begins
With the color of your eyes.

La Chanson d'Eve
Poems by Charles van Lerberghe
OPUS 95

1. Paradis
Paradise

C'est le premier matin du monde,
Comme une fleur confuse exhalé dans la nuit,
Au souffle noveau qui se lève des ondes,
Un jardin bleu s'épanouit.

Tout s'y confond encore et tout s'y mêle,
Frissons de feuilles, chants d'oiseaux
Glissements d'ailes
Sources qui sourdent, voix des airs, voix des eaux,

Murmure immense
Et qui pourtant est du silence.
Ouvrant à la clarté ses doux et vagues yeux,
La jeune et divine Eve s'est éveillée de Dieu,

Et le monde à ses pieds s'étend comme un beau rêve.
Or, Dieu lui dit: Va, fille humaine,
Et donne à tous les êtres
Que j'ai créés, une parole de tes lèvres,
Un son pour les connaître.

Et Eve s'en alla, docile à son seigneur,
En son bosquet de roses,
Donnant à toutes choses
Une parole, un son de ses lèvres de fleur:

Chose qui fuit, chose qui souffle, chose qui vole ...
Cependant le jour passe, et vague, comme à l'aube,
Au crépuscule, peu à peu,
L'Eden s'endort et se dérobe
Dans le silence d'un songe bleu.

La voix s'est tue, mais tous l'écoute encore,
Tout demeure en l'attente,
Lorsqu'avec le lever de l'étoile du soir,
Eve chante.

Opus 95, *La Chanson d'Eve,* is the most ambitious of Fauré's song cycles. Its ten songs, all to texts by the Belgian symbolist poet Charles van Lerberghe, were composed over a period of three years from 1907 to 1910. Only *La Bonne Chanson,* Opus 61, with its nine settings of poems by Verlaine, and *Le Jardin Clos,* Opus 106, another group of eight songs by Van Lerberghe, approach *La Chanson d'Eve* in length and seriousness of purpose.

"Paradis," the first song in the cycle, has one of the most beautiful openings in the entire repertoire. With utmost simplicity Fauré expresses the awesome wonder of creation. The piano hesitantly intrudes on the silent void with a single note, the tonic (E minor is the original key). The singer then echoes this note while the piano moves to the dominant for harmony. After the singer rises to the dominant, the piano plays a dissonant C against the vocal B, but both resolve to an A minor chord before the singer's return to the tonic note. The piano then surrounds this tonic E with a pristine C major chord. The stunning words here are "C'est le premier matin du monde," "It is the first morning of the world," and one can well believe it! The entire first stanza continues in this celestial style. The words are:

> It is the first morning of the world,
> Like an obscure flower exhaled in the night,
> In the new breath which rises from the shadows,
> A blue garden blooms.

At the last syllable of the first stanza there is a change from minor to major, and the accompaniment suddenly develops a totally new style. Rhythmic subdivisions become important—in some measures the basic half note is subdivided into two quarters, in others into triplet quarter notes—and the harmonies are complex and in constant flux. The melodic line moves slowly, allowing the accompaniment to swirl about its many repeated notes. There is an exciting rise in the melody under "voix des airs, voix des eaux, Murmure immense," the first big climactic moment of the song. The music for this section is a splendid expression of the meaning of the text, which explains that everything is mingled and mixed together. The overall feeling is still gentle despite strong dissonances on "Frissons" and elsewhere in the accompaniment.

> Everything mingles there and everything mixes,
> Trembling of leaves, songs of birds
> Gliding of wings,
> Murmuring springs, sound of air, sound of water,
> Immense murmur
> And which, nevertheless, is silence.

A piano interlude brings us back to the awestruck music of the beginning, but after a few measures the accompaniment halts to permit the singer to declaim dramatically that Eve "was awakened by God." This moment of great triumph is reflected in the strong major chords and equally strong dynamic level, beginning on the word "Dieu" (God). The accompaniment is similar to that of the second section, with even greater emphasis on triplet subdivisions of the half note beats.

> Opening her gentle and vague eyes to the light,
> The young and divine Eve
> Is awakened by God
> And the world lies at her feet like a beautiful dream.

The next section begins with a new key and a new mood. An F major chord provides the backdrop for the *recitativo*-like "Or, Dieu lui dit" (Then, God said to her). The harmonies here are beautiful and ethereal, the melody replete with repeated notes which climb chromatically or change enharmonically over the shifting chords.

> Then, God said to her: Go human girl
> And give to all the beings
> That I have created a word from your lips,
> A sound by which we may know them.
> And Eve went, obedient to her Lord

The music changes again after the first line of the following stanza, giving considerable significance to "seigneur." We now move back to E major but the accompaniment is much more free-flowing and easy-going, less complex, less thorny. All the harmonic devices of the first E major accompaniment—the dissonances, suspensions, shifts—are heard again, but the simplicity of the rhythmic pattern softens their effect in this recapitulation. The vocal part is still notable for its repeated notes, chromatic rises and enharmonic changes. There is a *crescendo* towards the climactic C♮ at "vole," which is further dramatized by the octave drop on the second syllable.

> In her thicket of roses
> Giving to all things
> A word, a sound, from her flowerlike lips:

After a brief interlude the music becomes as still and spare as it was at the beginning. An F major chord, similar in effect to the chord before "Or, Dieu lui dit," provides the harmonic underpinnings for a long *recitativo* in which the poet describes the end of the first day, when twilight brings silence and Eden sleeps. The F minor chord after "s'endort," the D♭ major chord under "dérobe," and the modulation to C minor under "bleu" are exquisite moments comparable to the opening measures of the song.

Thing that glides, thing that breathes, thing that flies . . .
However the day passes and, vague, as at dawn
In the twilight, little by little, Eden sleeps and disrobes
In the silence of a blue dream.

For the last few lines the accompaniment shifts to a tenderly flowing eighth note figure. Once again we have moments of exquisite beauty—under "enco*re*" (an unexpected C minor), under "attente," and at the conclusion of the vocal line. The postlude brings back the more complex patterns of the earlier E major section, another example of the remarkable skill with which Fauré provides structural unity for this long, rambling song with its irregular text. This is a song that deserves more frequent performances than it receives; it is surprisingly little known. The final stanza reads:

The voice is stilled, but everything still listens for it,
Everything waits,
When with the rising of the evening star
Eve sings.

2. Prima verba
First Words

Comme elle chante dans ma voix
L'âme longtemps murmurante des fontaines et des bois.
Air limpide du paradis,
Avec tes grappes de rubis,
Avec tes gerbes de lumière,
Avec tes roses et tes fruits.
Quelle merveille en nous à cette heure!

Des paroles depuis des âges endormies,
En des sons, en des fleurs sur mes lèvres enfin prennent vie.
Depuis que mon souffle a dit leur chanson,
Depuis que ma voix les a créées,
Quel silence heureux et profond
Naît de leurs âmes allégées!

"Prima verba," the second song of *La Chanson d'Eve,* Fauré's Opus 95, is a much slighter effort than "Paradis," the first song of the cycle. Again we are dealing with an aspect of creation, this time Eve's joy at her "First Words," but here the text is short and homogeneous rather than long and diffuse, as it was in "Paradis."

The poem is highly irregular rhythmically, with lines ranging from eight to sixteen syllables in length. The rhyme scheme is equally quixotic, with a rhymed couplet before each of the two *abab* four-line stanzas:

voix	rubis	endormies	chanson
bois	lumière	vie	créées
	fruits		profond
	heure		allégées

The internal rhyme of "paradis" and "rubis" makes one wonder whether to break the line midway, giving us two eight syllable lines instead of the inordinately long sixteen syllable line, but adding a seventh line to the first half of the poem, thereby destroying its symmetry.

Fauré copes with this structural complexity by providing a steady quarter-note accompaniment, which marches with serene gravity from beginning to end. Pauses in the vocal part are dictated by meanings of the words, rather than by rhymed end-sounds or stanza subdivisions.

The piano begins with a tonic (Gb) chord. The median note of the triad (Bb) is repeated ostinato-fashion throughout the first three measures, while the melody notes are heard on the off-beats between the chiming octaves. The shifting harmonies under the D flats (dominant notes) of "limpide du paradis" are very lovely. After this measure the melody begins to climb chromatically and a *crescendo* leads to a climax at "tes fruits." There are two misprints in the original *Heugel et Cie* edition: under "de rubis" the accompaniment should have a C♮ to match the melody note, and in the measure after the next, "Avec" is misspelled "Aves." The last line of the stanza is a long *diminuendo* and melodic descent. The words thus far are:

> How it sings in my voice
> The long-murmuring soul of the fountains and the woods.
> Clear air of paradise, with its cluster of rubies
> With its sheaves of light,
> With its roses and its fruits.
> What marvel is in us at this hour!

The second part of the song, which is much shorter than the first, begins softly again, but the *crescendo* and melodic rise come quite soon. Both are encapsulated versions of the larger buildup in the first section. There is a wonderful false cadence under "prennent vie," and then some subtle harmonic shifts under the held note at "vie." At "Depuis que ma voix," the music of the opening bars returns—only the last few notes are changed to make a suitable tonic ending. The words for this second segment are:

> Words asleep for ages,
> In sounds, in flowers on my lips come to life.
> Since my breath has said their song,
> Since my voice has created them,
> What a happy and profound silence
> Is born from their lightened souls!

3. Roses ardentes
Fiery Roses

Roses ardentes
Dans l'immobile nuit,
C'est en vous que je chante
Et que je suis.

En vous, étincelles
A la cime des bois,
Que je suis éternelle
Et que je vois.

O mer profonde,
C'est en toi que mon sang
Renâit, vague blonde,
Et flot dansant

Et c'est en toi, force suprême,
Soleil radieux,
Que mon âme elle-même
Atteint son dieu!

The third song sung by Eve, "Roses ardentes," is an ecstatic affirmation of her oneness with the universe, with the flowers, the sea, and above all the radiant sun, through which her soul reaches God.

This time the text supplied by poet Charles van Lerberghe is regular in form and rhyme scheme. Each of its four stanzas consists of four lines with alternating rhymed end sounds (*abab/cdcd/*etc.).

Fauré's setting is full of ardor. The melodic line seems to rise continually, because each drop in pitch is followed by a new ascent. There are many gorgeous harmonic effects, such as the augmented chord under "vous que je chante," but the overall harmonic scheme is traditional, with a clearly tonic (E major) opening and close.

The piano begins with simple tonic chords. The melody starts on the dominant and immediately rises to the VI. In the second melodic phrase, the melody returns to the dominant, this time to ascend a step higher, to the flatted VII. The harmony is lovely here, B minor over the ostinato G♯. After an augmented chord harmonizing the raised B in the melody, we return to the tonic for the end of the stanza.

Fiery roses
In the still night
It is in you that I sing
And that I exist.

The second stanza begins like the first, but the augmented chord is now based on F over a G♮ in the bass. Despite this change, Fauré manages to bring us back to the tonic for the close of this stanza. Lovely harmonic shifts constantly change the effect of the long A♮, which is the melody note for nine long syllables.

> It is in you, flames
> It is in the summit of the woods
> That I am eternal
> And that I see.

The third stanza ends with a lovely B⁷ which changes to an augmented B chord. Since there is no return to the tonic here, the third and fourth stanzas melt into one another. In fact, the augmented B moves to an augmented C in an unbroken line which rises to the climactic word "suprême." The song continues to grow dramatically and dynamically until the very end, with a beautiful augmented sound under "âme" and a wonderful V–I melodic interval for the last two syllables. Eve's radiant joy is indeed well conveyed in this lovely song. The last two stanzas are:

> Oh deep sea
> It is in you that my blood
> Is reborn, vague, pale,
> And dancing waves.

> And it is in you, supreme force
> Radiant sun,
> That my soul itself
> Reaches its God!

4. Comme Dieu rayonne
How Radiant Is God

> Comme Dieu rayonne aujourd'hui,
> Comme il exulte, comme il fleurit parmi ces roses et ces fruits!
> Comme il murmure en cette fontaine!
> Ah! comme il chante en ces oiseaux . . .
> Qu'elle est suave son haleine
> Dans l'odorant printemps nouveau!
> Comme il se baigne dans la lumière
> Avec amour, mon jeune dieu!
> Toutes les choses de la terre
> Sont ses vêtements radieux.

In this fourth song of the cycle *La Chanson d'Eve* we hear for the first time traces of "church" music. The piano part in the second and fourth measures has a cadence strongly associated with early religious music, the minor IV–I, (C minor to G minor, a temporary IV–I, as the actual key of the song is C minor) and the first two lines have an overall antique quality. Fauré's own harmonic style is beautifully blended with this evocative early sound—a combination we have already come across in other songs such as "Lydia" (see page 12).

The poem is a glowing tribute to the physical beauty of God. Seldom does one find God described in quite this way, radiant and in full flower of youth. We must remind ourselves that Eve is singing this song about "my young God," not about a lover.

Charles van Lerberghe, the poet, uses a structure previously encountered in his texts: one rhymed couplet followed by two four-line stanzas with alternating rhymed end sounds (*abab/cdcd*). The rhythm is unusually regular for this poet—each line has eight syllables.

The piano begins with single notes, which overlap to provide C minor and F minor harmonies, one melting into the other. The mood is tender and reverent. The special religious quality of the first two lines has already been discussed.

> How radiant God is today,
> How He exults, how He blooms amid His flowers and fruits!

In the next four lines of verse the harmonies become more typical of Fauré, with fewer references to antiquity:

> How He murmurs in the fountain!
> Ah! how He sings in His birds . . .
> How sweet is His breath
> In the fragrant new springtime!

At the end of the stanza there is a change of style in the accompaniment: a flowing sixteenth note figure, with its own melodic line, now replaces the slower-moving pattern of the beginning. The religious reverence yields to an ardent expression of love—if we did not know the true subject matter we might even say passion. The melody has wide expressive intervals under "lumière," "amour," and "jeune Dieu." For the last five bars Fauré moves to the major mode, and the last melodic interval, the sixth from G to high E on "radieux," allows the song to float away gently, tenderly, and, indeed, radiantly. The last four lines read:

> How He is bathed in light
> With love, my young God!
> All things of the Earth
> Are His radiant raimants!

5. L'Aube blanche
The White Dawn

L'aube blanche dit à mon rêve:
Eveille-toi, le soleil luit.
Mon âme écoute et je soulève
Un peu mes paupières vers lui.

Un rayon de lumière touche
La pâle fleur de mes yeux bleus.
Une flamme éveille ma bouche,
Un souffle éveille mes cheveux.

Et mon âme, comme une rose
Troublante, lente tout le jour,
S'éveille à la beauté des choses
Comme mon âme à leur amour.

"L'Aube blanche" ("The White Dawn"), is the fifth of ten songs in the cycle *La Chanson d'Eve* (*The Song of Eve*). It is an extremely simple expression of Eve's pleasure in the beauty and love inherent in all things of the Earth.

The poem, in straightforward narrative language, has a traditionally symmetrical structure: three four-line stanzas with an *abab/cdcd* rhyme scheme, each line eight syllables in length. Fauré's setting is equally traditional and uncomplicated, beginning and ending on tonic (Db) chords. There is only one rhythmic figure in the accompaniment which is heard throughout the song.

The piano opens with broken Db chords, which set the stage for the first quiet vocal phrase. At the second line of verse, "Eveille-toi, le soleil luit" (Awaken, the sun is shining), there is a sudden ascent in the melody to the Db an octave above middle C. This is accompanied by a quick *crescendo* and a wonderful false cadence from Bb^7 under "soleil" to A^9 (spelled as Bbb) under "luit." This is the most dramatic moment in the song. The rest of the stanza is harmonically rich, with an augmented chord under "soulève" and a strong suspension—A♮ in the melody over Ab in the bass—at "paupières." The stanza closes with a return to the tonic.

The white dawn said to my dream:
Awaken, the sun is shining.
My soul listens and I raise
My eyelids a little towards Him.

The music for the second stanza revolves around the tension-creating device of suspension: sometimes the accompaniment's bass note moves to the next chord before the melody note, as in "Un rayon," and sometimes the melody note precedes the chord change, as on the following beat. The strongest effects are created when the melody note is unchanged and a new bass note is heard. This happens on the first beats of the measures under "rayon," "touche," "fleur," "bouche," and "souffle." The climactic moment of the section is at "Une flamme," where the wide melodic interval to the highest note of the song and the accompanying *crescendo* suggest dramatic intensity.

> A ray of light touches
> The pale flower of my blue eyes.
> A flame awakens my mouth,
> A breeze awakens my hair.

The final stanza begins quietly, but we soon have another buildup to a *forte,* which lasts until the penultimate measure of the vocal part. The chords are particularly strong under "tout le jour," with a B♮ used as a bass note for the C♯ in the melody and the C♯ and A♯ in the upper piano line. Eventually Fauré brings us back to the gentle tonic chords for the *dolce* close. The last stanza reads:

> And my soul, like a perplexed
> Rose, slowly all day,
> Awakens to the beauty of things
> As my soul to their love.

6. Eau vivante
Running Water

> Que tu es simple et claire,
> Eau vivante,
> Qui, du sein de la terre,
> Jaillis en ces bassins et chantes!
>
> O fontaine divine et pure,
> Les plantes aspirent
> Ta liquide clarté.
> La biche et la colombe en toi se désaltèrent.
>
> Et tu descends par des pentes douces des fleurs et des mousses,
> Vers l'océan original,
> Toi qui passes et vas sans cesse et jamais lasse
> De la terre à la mer et de la mer au ciel . . .

"Eau Vivante" is one of the few songs by Fauré in which we have an onomatopoeic accompaniment. Obviously the sixteenth note scale fragments and broken chords heard throughout the piece represent the clear running water which Eve is praising in this, her sixth song.

At first, the water murmurs quietly as it gently bubbles along in C major (the original key). The first melodic phrase consists of two notes from the tonic triad, and the words are simple and direct. In the second half of the first stanza, more complex harmonies are introduced as the scale fragments veer towards whole-tone intervals, without completely abandoning the half step. The words for the first stanza are:

> How simple and clear you are
> Running water,
> Which from the bosom of the Earth,
> Splashes in these basins and sings!

Strong augmented chords and mainly whole-tone scales characterize the second stanza, which reaches a climax at "clarté." The last line of the section, which is gentle and murmuring again, ends with an octave drop in the melody.

> Oh divine and pure fountains,
> The plants ingest
> Your liquid clarity.
> The hind and the dove quench their thirst in you.

The last stanza is the most interesting harmonically. Fauré uses dissonance in the one measure interlude between stanzas and then again in the next two bars, making the E major chord—the sound for the word "mousses"—as soft and welcoming as the grassy moss it describes. Discords even more strident return under "Toi qui passes," and continue through the *crescendo* to the climactic "De la terre à la mer," where an augmented chord and *diminuendo* combine to calm things down and prepare for the return to the original C major tonality. The poem ends:

> And you descend by the sweet slopes of flowers and mosses,
> Towards the original ocean,
> You who come and go ceaselessly and without tiring
> From the land to the sea and from the sea to the sky.

7. Veilles-tu, ma senteur de soleil
Are You Awake, My Aroma of Sunlight

Veilles-tu, ma senteur de soleil,
Mon arôme d'abeilles blondes,
Flottes-tu sure le monde,
Mon doux parfum de miel?

La nuit, lorsque mes pas
Dans le silence rodent.

M'annonce-tu, senteur de mes lilas
Et de mes roses chaudes?

Suis-je comme un grappe de fruits
Cachés dans les feuilles,
Et que rien ne décèle,
Mais qu'on odore dans la nuit?

Sait-il, à cette heure,
Que j'entrouvre ma chevelure,
Et qu'elle respire?
Le sent-il sur la terre?

Sent-il que j'étends les bras
Et que des lys de mes vallées,
Ma voix qu'il n'entend pas
Est embaumée?

The text for this seventh song in the cycle *La Chanson d'Eve* is free and complex, with an irregular rhyme scheme and lines of widely varied lengths. Internal rhymes are sometimes more striking than end rhymes, and in some places we approach blank verse. Only in the second and last groups of four lines do we have bona fide stanzas, with regular *abab* rhyme schemes. The first two lines give an example of important internal rhyme:

Veilles-tu, ma senteur de so*leil*,
Mon arôme d'ab*eilles* blondes,

"Soleil" rhymes with "abeilles," but the line ends with "blondes" which rhymes with "monde," the last sound of the next line. Since the pattern here is *abba* we expect the last line to end with another rhyme word for "soleil"; van Lerberghe gives us "miel," which is more of a visual than aural match and not even a very good visual one.

The fourth stanza consists of a more-or-less rhymed couplet ("heure" and "chevelure") plus two unrhymed lines ("respire" and "terre"). The four lines are united by their common "re" endings, but this would be an inadmissible rhyme in a classical poem.

As he has done before, Fauré counterbalances the irregularities of the poem with a monochromatic accompaniment, for a single pattern is repeated in the piano part throughout the song. This gives rise to a certain monotony, which is alleviated by the beautiful harmonies encompassed by the piano figure and by the melody, which ascends to climactic peaks in several places only to drop dramatically before rising again.

The piano begins with the broken tonic chord (D major in the original key) and the melody enters calmly and gently. There is an immediate rise in the vocal part to "abeilles," where the tonic melodic note is colored by an augmented chord. The melody drops at the end of the line and climbs back to the dominant at "monde," where once again Fauré chooses an augmented chord for harmony. The last line of the stanza remains fairly level:

> Are you awake, my aroma of sunlight,
> My perfume of blond bees,
> Do you waft over the earth,
> My sweet scent of honey?

In the second stanza the focal point is "de mes roses." A *crescendo* has accompanied the rising line and the high E is sung *forte*.

> Night, while my steps
> Roam in the silence
> Are you announcing to me, scent of lilacs
> And of warm roses?

The third stanza begins quietly, with little motion in the melodic line until "Mais qu'on odore," which merits a *crescendo* and subsequent *diminuendo*. The piano interlude which follows should be quite expressive.

> Am I like a cluster of fruits
> Hidden among the leaves,
> And that nothing reveals
> But what one smells in the night?

The highest note in the vocal part occurs in this stanza under "respire." The composer indicates that he wants the *crescendo* to continue through this note to the next note, which is an octave below. In other words the loudest part of the *forte* is reached by singer and piano on the last syllable of the word "respire." The last line of the stanza rises again. Since the dynamics climb right back up to *forte,* this whole section has an aura of joyous excitement.

> Does he know, at this time,
> That I loosen my hair,
> And that it breathes?
> Does he sense it on Earth?

After all this excitement we have a quiet beginning for the final section. Nevertheless, there is one last buildup, which culminates in the dramatic interval "Ma voix." From this high point we have a steady *diminuendo* to the fade-out ending.

> Does he sense that I extend my arms
> And that the lilies of my valleys,
> My voice that he does not hear
> Is perfumed?

This is a rather pantheistic and sensual statement from our Eve, more evocative perhaps of a Greek nymph than an Old Testament character!

8. Dans un parfum de roses blanches
In a Perfume of White Roses

Dans un parfum de roses blanches,
Elle est assise et songe;
Et l'ombre est belle comme s'il s'y mirait un ange...
L'ombre descend,
Le bosquet dort;
Entre les feuilles et les branches,
Sur le paradis bleu s'ouvre un paradis d'or;
Une voix qui chantait tout à l'heure murmure...
Un murmure s'exhale en haleine et s'éteint.
Dans le silence il tombe des pétales...

This song is to be sung about Eve rather than by her. The poem describes her day-dreaming about the white roses in the beautiful shadows. Once again we have a sensual text that appeals to one's sight, smell, and hearing. The poet has moved far from the first poems in the cycle, in which Old Testament tales of Creation are evoked, to a pantheistic celebration of nature.

The poem itself is very free and, indeed, approaches the genre known as prose-poem, which had been initiated by Charles Baudelaire. There are some end rhymes—"blanches" and "branches," "dort" and "d'or"—but no consistent rhyme scheme, and no rhymes at all for the last three lines. The poem seems to divide itself logically into three sections, each consisting of three lines. There is a preponderance of soft sounds—"songe," "ombre," "murmure," "ange," etc.—and the language is very lovely.

Fauré's setting is less repetitious, more varied, in this song than it had been in the two or three preceding songs in the cycle. A glance at the printed page will show that there are two basic ideas in the accompaniment: moving quarter notes in the bass with short sixteenth note phrases for harmonic filler, and a combined eighth note and sixteenth note pattern for the right hand. These two elements allow for interesting combinations within the basically simple framework.

The melody flows gently without reaching any climactic peaks. The *tessitura* is quite low, with no note higher than a D one octave above middle C in the original key of G major. Aside from a strong suspension at "mirait," the harmonies are bland and pleasant—there is nothing to disturb the aura of tranquillity.

The song begins with two measures of introduction, in which the quarter notes in the bass part have their own melodic line. This melodic bass is almost always present, as a solo voice in the piano interludes and in duet with the singer elsewhere. The right hand figure for the piano has melodic content too, in the double-stemmed notes. The richer this accompaniment can be made, the more interest the song will have. A free-flowing tempo is also essential—*andantino* can be thought of as synonymous with *allegretto*.

This is the last of Eve's songs in which the poet evokes nature as witness to and metaphor for her happiness, for in the ninth and tenth songs we meet sadness and death. The words are:

> In a perfume of white roses
> She sits and dreams;
> And the shadow is as beautiful as if an angel were reflected there . . .
> The shadow descends, the thicket sleeps
> Among the leaves and the branches,
> On the blue paradise a golden paradise opens;
> A voice which sang now murmurs . . .
> A murmur wafts on the air and is silenced.
> In the silence some petals fall . . .

9. Crépuscule
Twilight

> Ce soir, à travers le bonheur,
> Qui donc soupire, qu'est-ce qui pleure?
> Qu'est-ce qui vient palpiter sur mon coeur,
> Comme un oiseau blessé?
> Est-ce une voix future, une voix du passé?
> J'écoute, jusqu'a la souffrance,
> Ce son dans le silence.
>
> Ile d'oubli, ô Paradis!
> Quel cri déchire, dans la nuit,
> Ta voix qui me berce?
> Quel cri traverse
> Ta ceinture de fleurs,
> Et ton beau voile d'allégresse?

With "Crépuscule" ("Twilight") the cycle *La Chanson d'Eve* begins to draw to a close. The opening bars have the same dreamlike reverent quality found in "Paradis," the first of the ten songs, which began with the words "C'est le premier matin du monde" (It is the first morning of the world). Now we have the first evening and Eve's first experience with melancholy. This prepares for the final song, in which Eve embraces death.

For the first six measures, accompaniment and vocal line vacillate between D minor, the main key for most of the piece, although there is a change to D major at the end, and Bb major. The chords must be as ethereal as possible. At "qu'est-ce qui pleure?" the melody climbs to F, then drops an octave and the chords modulate to A minor. This is a particularly lovely moment and Fauré repeats the harmonic scheme under the next phrase. The words for this part are:

> This evening, through the happiness,
> Who then sighs, who cries?
> What comes to palpitate in my heart
> Like a wounded bird?

Gradually, the accompaniment becomes thicker and less celestial. The quarter note chords have an earthbound heaviness, which is perhaps meant to remind us that Eve has fallen from Paradise. There are many harsh dissonances, such as those in the measure before "J'écoute," where Fauré gives us a G# in the bass against a G♮ and F♮ in the treble of the piano part. These harmonies are repeated under "souffrance," suffering.

At "Ce son dans le silence," the voice rises again to an F one-and-a-half octaves above middle C and then drops to the F an octave below. The dynamics are interesting here—the voice has a *forte* while the piano is still soft; then a *crescendo* builds in the piano part to the same dissonances described above. Both taper off together.

> Is it a voice from the future, a voice from the past?
> I listen, until the point of suffering, to
> This sound in this silence.

The following section begins softly, with Eve evoking her lost Paradise. The long piano interlude is loud and dissonant, expressing an anguish hitherto undreamed of in this cycle. As Eve remembers the caressing voice that once cradled her ("Ta voix qui me berce"), the music becomes gentle again. The dynamics continue to fluctuate, giving us two full *crescendos*, but the harmonies remain largely consonant. A soothing D major tonality during the last seven bars gradually becomes ascendant, and the song ends quietly and peacefully despite the inconsolable words:

> Isle of forgetfulness, Oh Paradise!
> What cry lacerates, in the night,
> Your voice which cradles me?
> What cry cuts through
> Your girdle of flowers,
> And your beautiful veil of joy?

10. O mort, poussière d'étoiles
O Death, Dust of Stars

O mort, poussière d'étoiles
Lève-toi sous mes pas!
Viens, ô douce vague qui brille
Dans les ténèbres.
Emporte-moi dans ton néant!
Viens, souffle sombre où je vacille,
Comme une flamme ivre de vent!
C'est en toi que je veux m'étendre,
M'éteindre et me dissoudre,
Mort où mon âme aspire!
Viens, brise-moi comme une fleur d'écume,
Une fleur de soleil à la cime des eaux!
Et comme d'une amphore d'or
Un vin de flamme et d'arome divin,
Epanche mon âme en ton abîme,
Pour qu'elle embaume
La terre sombre et le souffle des morts.

This last song in the cycle *La Chanson d'Eve* is more than an acceptance of mortality; it is an ecstatic reaching towards death. Eve beckons Death and begs it to carry her off into its void. When she sings "Mort où mon âme aspire" (Death to which my soul aspires), the rising melody and vibrant chords fill us with joy, not dread.

Throughout the poem the language is ardent and passionate. This is not an old person weary of life, this is a young woman whose soul is "Comme une flamme ivre de vent," Like a flame drunk with wind. In death she senses the ultimate union with the universe—her soul will pour into the abyss and perfume the dark earth.

For this poem Charles van Lerberghe abandons rhymed endings completely. There are two sets of rhymed end-sounds, "brille"— "vacille" and "néant"—"vent," but their irregular placement indicates that they are more or less accidental. Certainly they are incidental to the beauty of the poem.

As befits the subject, Fauré's setting is solemn but not anguished. The basic modality is major (Db major in the original key) and the brief introduction and postlude are tranquil. The melody enters on the dominant and stays on that note for the entire first phrase. On the first two beats of the third bar, Fauré gives us a very strange sound combination, dark and discordant, but the resolution to the tonic which follows immediately (under "Lève-*toi*") soothes the ear. Similar harmonies are heard under "Comme une flamme" (here the resolution is to an augmented chord) and "Viens, brise-moi."

Despite small fluctuations in the dynamics there is but one real climax, the high E♭ of "Viens, brise-moi," which follows the ecstatic chords in the measures of "Mort où mon âme aspire."

This song is unusually dramatic for Fauré and the chord combinations are far from typical of his style. It is a beautiful and fitting conclusion to this major cycle which is so full of exquisite music. The sense of affirmation in the poetry—its celebration of life, of the word, of physical beauty, of nature and finally of death—reverberates in the music. It is a cycle that should be far better known than it seems to be at the present time. The words are:

> Oh death, dust of stars,
> Arise under my steps!
> Come, oh sweet vagueness which shines
> In the shadows.
> Transport me to your void!
> Come somber breeze in which I waver,
> Like a flame drunk with wind!
> It is in you that I wish to extend myself
> Extinguish myself and dissolve myself,
> Death to which my soul aspires!
> Come, break me like a flower of spray,
> A flower of sun in the depths of the waters!
> And like a golden amphora
> A wine of flame and divine aroma,
> Pour out my soul into your abyss,
> That it may perfume
> The somber earth and the breath of the dead.

Le Jardin Clos
Poems by Charles van Lerberghe
OPUS 106

1. L'Exaucement
Benediction

Alors qu'en tes mains de lumière
Tu poses ton front défaillant,
Que mon amour en ta prière,
Vienne comme un exaucement.

Alors que la parole expire
Sur ta lèvre qui tremble encor,
Et s'adoucit en un sourire de roses,
En des rayons d'or;

Que ton âme calme et muette,
Fée endormie au jardin clos,

En sa douce volonté faite,
Trouve la joie et le repos.

Fauré's Opus 106, *Le Jardin Clos,* consists of eight short songs to texts by Charles van Lerberghe. The songs which immediately precede *Le Jardin Clos* in a chronological listing of Fauré's works, the ten songs of Opus 95, *La Chanson d'Eve,* are also settings of poems by van Lerberghe. In the five-year hiatus between these two cycles, Fauré produced five barcarolles, three nocturnes, nine preludes and an impromptu for piano solo, and a serenade for 'cello and piano, all this despite the facts of his increasing deafness and advancing age.

In *Le Jardin Clos* Fauré's characteristic restraint and subtlety are carried to an extreme. Only after repeated hearings do the songs yield their charm and beauty. The songs lack strong individual profiles, perhaps because the poems are rather bland, perhaps because Fauré wishes to reinforce the idea of the secret garden behind high walls whose delights can only be sensed from afar. The previous cycle, *La Chanson d'Eve,* is a much more ambitious work in number and length of songs, in variety of moods, and in power of musical and poetic imagery.

The cycle opens with a sweet, tender song in which the idea of the walled or closed garden is introduced. We have a charming picture of a young girl with her head bowed in prayer. The poet says that her soul is like a sleeping fairy in a closed garden. The image of the sleeping beauty, waiting for a kiss from the lover to awaken her from her enchantment, is a popular one in folk literature all over the world.

The title of the song, "L'Exaucement," has no exact English equivalent. It means the granting of what is prayed for. We have translated it here as "Benediction." The structure of the poem is traditional: three four-line stanzas with *abab* rhyme scheme.

Fauré's setting is simple and masterful. The liquid, melodic lines allow the words to flow naturally, so that end-rhymes and textual meanings are easily heard and understood. The minimal accompaniment has a bittersweet flavor attributable to the many suspensions and discords, which prevent any cloying quality. The original key is C major and the vocal range is limited to less than an octave—from the E above middle C to C'. The words are:

When in your luminous hands
You lay your bowed head
In your prayer, may my love
Come like a benediction.

When words die
On your still trembling lips

And melt into a smile
Of roses in rays of gold

May your calm and silent soul,
Sleeping fairy in a walled garden,
In its sweet will
Find joy and repose.

2. Quand tu plonge tes yeux
When You Plunge Your Eyes in Mine

Quand tu plonge tes yeux dans mes yeux,
Je suis toute dans mes yeux.
Quand ta bouche dénoue ma bouche,
Mon amour n'est que ma bouche.
Si tu frôles mes cheveux,
Je n'existe plus qu'en eux.
Si ta main effleure mes seins,
J'y monte comme un feu soudain.
Est-ce moi que tu as choisie?
Là est mon âme, Là est ma vie.

For the second song in the cycle Fauré uses a poem in rhymed couplets, a somewhat unusual form for a musical setting. In fact the texts of this opus are quite varied in form, ranging from this tightest of structures to blank verse. To achieve his matched end sounds, van Lerberghe uses the same word at the end of lines one and two ("yeux") and also at three and four ("bouche"). Since this device soon grows tiresome, it is a relief to hear more genuine rhymes (cheveux-eux, seins-soudain, choisie-vie) for the other couplets.

With "Quand tu plonge . . ." we move from the quasi-religious purity of the young girl in prayer, portrayed so lovingly in the opening song, to an overtly sensuous statement. The woman speaks (we know for "toute" and "choise" have the requisite feminine endings) fervently of how her entire being in concentrated in whatever part of her body her lover touches. This is a far cry from the chaste progression from maiden to wife, to mother, to widow in Schumann's cycle *Frauen liebe und leben,* of which one is vaguely reminded.

Fauré's setting begins quietly with the tonic note in the bass (the original key is F major). Although the melody climbs right up the tonic scale, the underlying chords wander vaguely through various tonalities. There is a strange dissonance just before "Je suis," and one feels no resting place until the tonic chord under the final "yeux." The music continues in a similar style with the next solid chord, an A^7, at the end of the next couplet (the second "bouche"). No such solace is offered at the close of the third couplet ("qu'en eux") where the harmonies continue to ramble on. The high F, at "Je n'*existe* plus," is the focal point of the section, but there is no dynamic emphasis on it.

The next couplet brings us the most impassioned music of the song. The ascending melodic line well suits the words "J'y monte comme un feu soudain." A satisfying B♭ chord underscores the *forte* at "Est-ce moi," as does the C major harmony under "tu *as* choisi," but the vague, wandering, somewhat dissonant chords continue until the tonic ending at "vie." The words are:

> When you plunge your eyes in mine,
> I am completely in my eyes.
> When your lips open my lips,
> My love is only in my lips.
> If you touch my hair,
> I exist no longer except in it.
> If your hand grazes my bosom
> I mount there like a sudden flame.
> Is it I whom you have chosen?
> There is my soul, there is my life.

3. La Messagère
The Messenger

> Avril, et c'est le point du jour.
> Tes blondes soeurs qui te ressemblent,
> En ce moment, toutes ensemble,
> S'avancent vers toi, cher Amour.
>
> Tu te tiens dans un clos ombreux
> De myrte et d'aubépines blanches;
> La porte s'ouvre sous les branches;
> Le chemin est mystérieux.
>
> Elles, lentes, en longues robes,
> Une à une, main dans la main,
> Franchissent le seuil indistinct
> Où de la nuit devient de l'aube.
>
> Celle qui s'avance d'abord
> Regarde l'ombre, te découvre,
> Crie, et la fleur de ses yeux s'ouvre
> Splendide, dans un rire d'or.
>
> Et jusqu'à la dernière soeur,
> Toutes tremblent, tes lèvres touchent leurs lèvres,
> L'éclair de ta bouche
> Eclate jusque dans leur coeur.

The twenty-line poem, on which this third song of Opus 106 is based, is the longest in the set. It describes a strange scene, perhaps all youthful innocence of sisters at play, perhaps with Sapphic overtones. The poet's beloved is still in her walled garden where she waits in a shadowy close of myrtle and white hawthorne. Her sisters, dressed in long gowns, enter the garden, find her in the shadows and, all atremble, kiss her lips. The last lines read "The lightning flash from your lips/Explodes in their very hearts," strong language if a nonerotic effect is intended!

To accommodate the length of the text without upsetting the symmetry of the cycle, Fauré moves the words along at a fairly rapid narrative clip. The accompaniment consists of a typical all-purpose Fauré arpeggiated figure, in itself bland and not too interesting, but the harmonies are often pungent and apt. The original key is G major and, as is true of the cycle as a whole, its vocal range is limited, with no note above E′ in this song.

After a very brief introduction, the singer enters with a cheerful I–V rising interval, which is then echoed in the piano part. The dynamics are strong, and remain so until a sense of mystery begins to creep in as the words describe the girl hidden in the shadows ("Tu te tiens . . ."). There is a steady *diminuendo* and then an atmospheric augmented chord under "mystérieux." This takes us through the first two stanzas which read:

> April, and it is daybreak.
> Your blond sisters who resemble you,
> At the moment, all together,
> Advance towards you, dear Love.
>
> You keep yourself in a shadowy close
> Of myrtle and white hawthorne;
> The door opens under the branches;
> The path is mysterious.

At this point the accompaniment changes from the sixteenth note figure to a more tranquil series of eighth notes. The many suspensions create musical tension, but the real buildup begins after the return of the original accompanying figure. From "Regarde l'ombre" to "d'or" there is an overall *crescendo,* with peaks at the melodic leap to "Crie" and the high note at "Splendide." This encompasses stanzas three and four:

> They slowly, in long gowns,
> One by one, hand in hand,
> Cross the indistinct threshold
> Where night becomes dawn.
>
> The one who comes first
> Looks at the shadow, discovers you,

Cries, and the flower of her eyes opens,
Splendid, in a golden laugh.

The last stanza starts softly and builds to a strong ending. The *crescendo* begins at "Tes lèvres," and once the *forte* has been reached at "L'éclair" the high dynamic level is maintained. No other plan would suit these passionate last words:

And to the last sister
Each trembles, your lips touch
Their lips, the lightning flash from your lips
Explodes in their very hearts.

4. Je me poserai sur ton coeur
I Shall Place Myself on Your Heart

Je me poserai sur ton coeur,
 Comme le printemps sur la mer,
Sur les plaines de la mer stérile,
Où nulle fleur ne peut croître
A ses souffles agiles
Que des fleurs de la lumière.

Je me poserai sur ton coeur
Comme l'oiseau sur la mer,
Dans le repos de ses ailes lasses,
Et que berce le rhythme éternel
Des flots et de l'espace.

Je me poserai sur ton coeur
Comme l'oiseau sur la mer.

With this fourth song of *Le Jardin Clos* we move from the enclosed garden to the wide open sea. An even more interesting change occurs in the poet's attitude towards his beloved: in the earlier songs she was young and sheltered; here she represents the motherly sea, upon whose vast bosom he wishes to rest his head.

Technically, too, this poem represents a departure from the others. There is very little rhyme in it, and the first two lines are twice repeated, refrainlike, at uneven intervals (after the next four lines and then again after only three lines). Within the nonrefrain lines there are two sets of end rhymes, "stérile-agiles" and "lasses-espâce." Below is an outline of the end-sounds:

coeur	stérile	coeur	lasses	coeur
mer	croître	mer	éternel	mer
	agiles		espace	
	lumière			

Fauré's setting is very bland and rather bleak. There are two moments of great beauty, at "lumière" and at the final "Je me poserai," but on the whole the song lacks great appeal. The key is Eb and the vocal range modest—from Eb above middle C to the Eb one octave above. The words are:

> I shall place myself on your heart,
> Like the springtime on the sea,
> On the plains of the sterile sea,
> Where no flower can grow
> In its supple breezes,
> Save flowers of light.
>
> I shall place myself on your heart
> Like the bird on the sea,
> In the repose of its weary wings
> And rocked by the eternal rhythm
> Of the waves and of space.
>
> I shall place myself on your heart
> Like the bird on the sea.

5. Dans la nymphée
In the Nymph Garden

> Quoique tes yeux ne la voient pas,
> Pense en ton âme qu'elle est là,
> Comme autrefois divine et blanche.
> Sur ce bord reposent ses mains.
> Sa tête est entre ces jasmins,
> Là ses pieds effleurent les branches.
>
> Elle sommeille en ces rameaux,
> Ses lèvres et ses yeux sont clos,
> Et sa bouche à peine respire.
> Parfois, la nuit, dans un éclair,
> Elle apparait, les yeux ouverte,
> Et l'éclair dans ses yeux se mire.
>
> Un bref éblouissement bleu
> La découvre en ses longs cheveux,
> Elle s'éveille, elle se lève,
> Et tout un jardin ébloui s'illumine
> Au fond de la nuit,
> Dans le rapide éclair d'un rêve.

In the fifth song of the cycle the poet fantasizes that a beautiful nymph once played in the enclosed garden. He asks the listener to see with his soul what he cannot see with his eyes, the white goddess, her head among the flowers, her feet grazing the branches, blue lightning mirrored in her eyes. So dazzling is she that she illuminates the whole garden.

The poem is lovely. Each of its three stanzas is composed of six lines, with the rhyme scheme *aabccb,* a pattern seldom encountered in these songs. Fauré's setting is equally felicitous, one of the prettiest in the cycle. Indeed, of these eight songs it is the one closest in style to Fauré's earlier works in this genre, with its atmospheric half-step drops at "La voient pas" and "qu'elle est là," its chromatic ascents under "pieds effleurent les branches" and "bref éblouissement bleu," and its dreamy harmonies all contributing to the unmistakable Fauré sound. Nevertheless the strange dissonances that characterize this cycle more than any other body of Fauré songs are also present—see in particular the chord before "Et sa bouche," which pits a G♮ against an A♭ (in the original key of D♭ major), and the chords after "blanche" and under "*bran*ches."

The overall dynamic level is quiet, with a dreamlike quality. The one important *crescendo* leads only to a *mezzo forte* at "Elle s'éveille" (She awakens). The ending is harmonious and tranquil. The words are:

> Even though your eyes don't see her,
> Think in your soul that she is there,
> As in former times, divine and white.
> On this bank her hands rest.
> Her head is among the jasmines,
> There her feet graze the branches.
>
> She sleeps in these boughs,
> Her lips and her eyes are closed,
> And her mouth scarcely breathes.
> Sometimes at night, in a flash of light,
> She appears, her eyes open,
> And the lightning is mirrored in her eyes.
>
> A brief blue dazzlement
> Discovers her with her long hair.
> She awakens, she rises,
> And the whole dazzled garden
> Is illuminated in the middle of the night,
> In the rapid flash of a dream.

6. Dans la pénombre
In the Shadows

> A quoi, dans ce matin d'Avril,
> Si douce, et d'ombre enveloppée,
> La chère enfant au coeur subtil
> Est-elle ainsi toute occupée?

Pensivement, d'un geste lent,
En longue robe, en robe à queue,
Sur le soleil au rouet blanc
A filer de la laine bleue,

A sourire à son rêve encor
Avec ses yeux de fiancée,
A travers les feuillages d'or,
Parmi les lys de sa pensée.

"Dans la pénombre" brings us back to the original picture of the
young woman, sweet, shy, rapt in rêverie, that was presented to us in
the first song of the cycle. Though dressed in a long gown with a train,
she is busily spinning blue wool at the white spinning wheel. Unlike
poor Gretchen, she smiles, for her thoughts are those of a happy
fiancée.

The poem is sweet and tender, its three stanzas in traditional *abab*
rhyme. The setting is yet another curious mixture of tender romantic
harmonies and strange dissonances and suspensions. The music flows
most naturally under "Pensivement . . . de la laine," and then again
from "A travers" to the end. Elsewhere the accompaniment seems halting and sparse. Interestingly enough, the harsh sounds at "geste" and
"rouet" do not disturb the ear, perhaps because they occur within the
most fluid bars. The loveliest sounds are heard from "sa pensée" to the
end. The original key is E major and the vocal line has the limited
range of D♯ above middle C to the D♮ less than an octave above. There
is no real climax, no strong *crescendo*, no reason to raise the dynamic
level above *mezzo forte*. The words are:

With what, in this April morning,
So sweet, and enveloped with shadow,
Is the dear child with the understanding heart
Thus completely occupied?

Thoughtfully, with slow gestures,
In a long gown, in a gown with a train,
In the sun at the white spinning-wheel
Spinning blue wool,

Still smiling at her dream
With her eyes of a fiancée
Across the golden foliage,
Among the lilies of her thought.

7. Il m'est cher, Amour
It Is Dear To Me, Love

Il m'est cher, Amour, le bandeau
Qui me tient les paupières closes,

Il pèse comme un doux fardeau
De soleil sur de faibles roses.

Si j'avance, l'étrange chose!
Je parais marcher sur les eaux;
Mes pieds plus lourds où je les pose,
S'enfoncent comme en des anneaux.

Qui donc a delié dans l'ombre
Le faix d'or de mes longs cheveux?
Toute ceinte d'étreinte sombre,
Je plonge en des vagues de feu.

Mes lèvres où mon âme chante,
Toute d'extase et de baisers,
S'ouvrent comme une fleur ardente
Au dessus d'un fleuve embrasé!

The seventh song of Opus 106, "Il m'est cher, Amour," has more individuality and more substance than the earlier songs of the cycle. The text is a strange one, in which the beloved says that the blindfold that keeps her eyelids closed is dear to her. The aura is clearly erotic—someone has loosed her golden hair, she plunges into waves of fire, her lips open like an ardent flower, her soul sings of ecstasy and kisses—but there are obscure images which leave much to the reader's imagination: why the blindfold? is it figurative or real? Perhaps some symbolist poems are better left unexplained!

Fauré's setting responds to the ardor of the poem. It is marked *allegro,* and the sixteenth note figure in the accompaniment moves along with a steady hum of excitement. The two important climaxes of the song are sung on the relatively high note E♭, in both instances at full *forte.* There are many beautiful moments in the harmonic scheme, notably the false cadence from E^{7o} to D major under "paupières closes," the G minor chord under "eaux," and the augmented chords for "Toute ceinte." In several places Fauré gives us interesting harmonic shifts under repeated melody notes. Examples are the repeated A at "pèse comme," where the harmonies move from the tonic (F major) to a dissonance and a suspension, and the E flats at "feu. Mes lèvres," where we have a strong dissonance first, then an A♭, a C♭^{7}, and finally an F^7.

As is characteristic of the cycle, dissonances and suspensions abound. None is less expected than that under the last note of "baisers," a word usually accompanied by tender, *dolce* sounds. Here we have, instead, the bittersweet feeling that pervades the composition. The words are:

It is dear to me, Love, the blindfold
Which holds my eyelids closed;

It weighs like a sweet burden
Of sun on the weak roses.

If I move forward, strange thing!
I seem to walk on water;
My feet heavier where I put them,
Sink like rings.

Who then has untied in the shadow
The golden weight of my long hair?
All girdled in a somber embrace,
I plunge into the waves of fire.

My lips where my soul sings,
All of ecstasy and of kisses,
Open like an ardent flower
Above an enflamed river!

8. Inscription sur le sable
Inscription in the Sand

Toute, avec sa robe et ses fleurs,
Elle, ici, redevint poussière,
Et son âme emportée ailleurs
Renaquit en chant de lumière.

Mais un léger lien fragile,
Dans la mort brise doucement,
Encerclait ses tempes débilés
D'impérissables diamants.

En signe d'elle, à cette place,
Seule, parmi le sable blond,
Les pierres éternelles tracent encor
L'image de son front.

With "Inscription sur le sable" we come to the end of *Le Jardin Clos*. As in the preceding cycle, *La Chanson d'Eve*, the last song deals with death as a solemn, but not terrible phenomenon. The words have a somewhat mystic quality, for the poet says that the soul of the dead woman, carried elsewhere, is reborn as a song of light.

The music is warm and tender despite the gravity of its somberly paced chords. At the word "diamants" we have a limpid C major chord to underscore the triumphant melodic rise to E♮, the highest note reached in the cycle. The A⁷ chord at "chant" is equally affirmative, but the song ends with a rather mournful downward melodic interval and melancholy E minor (tonic) chords. The words are:

All, with her gown and her flowers,
She becomes dust again here,

And her soul carried elsewhere
Is reborn in a song of light.

But a light fragile tie,
In death softly broken,
Circled her feeble temples
With imperishable diamonds.

As a sign of her, in this place,
Alone, among the blond sand,
The eternal rocks still trace
The image of her face.

Les Mirages
Poems by La Baronne de Brimont
OPUS 113

1. Cygne sur l'eau
Swan on the Water

Ma pensée est un cygne harmonieux et sage
Qui glisse lentement aux rivages d'ennui
Sur les ondes sans fond du rêve, du mirage,
De l'écho, du brouillard, de l'ombre, de la nuit.

Il glisse, roi hautain fendant un libre espace,
Poursuit un reflet vain, précieux et changeant,
Et les roseaux nombreux s'inclinent quand il passe,
Sombre et muet, au seuil d'une lune d'argent;

Et des blancs nenuphars chaque corolle ronde
Tour-à-tour a fleuri de désir et d'espoir . . .
Mais plus avant toujours, sur la brume et sur l'onde,
Vers l'inconnu fuyant, glisse le cygne noir.

Or j'ai dit, "Renoncez, beau cygne chimérique,
A ce voyage lent vers de troubles destins;
Nul miracle chinois, nul étrange Amérique
Ne vous acceuilleront en des havres certains;

Les golfes embaumés, les îles immortelles
Ont pour vous, Cygne noir, des récifs périlleux,
Demeurez sur les lacs où se mirent, fidèles,
Ces nuages, ces fleurs, ces astres, et ces yeux."

In 1919 Fauré published four songs based on poems of La Baronne
de Brimont. The first of these, "Cygne sur l'eau" (Swan on the Water),
is a beautifully harmonious mating of words and music. The song
seems to flow as effortlessly as its subject glides on the water.

It is interesting to see how the poet creates this sense of continuous flow: each line has twelve syllables (the typical Alexandrine) and there is the usual pattern of alternating rhymed end sounds (*abab*); within the stanza however there are inner rhymes which lead one across the twelve-syllable units, creating a seamless entity.

> Ma pensée est un cygne harmonieux et *sage*
> Qui glisse lentement aux *rivages* d'ennui
> Sur les *ondes* sans *fond* du rêve, du *mirage,*
> De l'écho, du brouillard, de l'ombre, de la nuit.

In the first stanza, quoted above, the rhyme of "sage" and "mirage" is echoed by "rivages," and "ondes sans fond" is an inner rhyme. Of course the end sounds "ennui" and "nuit" also rhyme. The word "ennui" comes as a surprise, for the adjectives "harmonious" and "wise" have predisposed us to anticipate some felicitous end to the thought. Instead we find boredom, weariness, lassitude. The last word of the third stanza, "noir," is another surprise, for nothing has led us to picture a black swan. Fauré emphasizes this with a strong dissonance on the word "noir," as we shall see when we reach that section.

Fauré based the structure of his setting on the meaning of the text. Thus the first and last stanzas are accompanied by quiet, discreet chords, with nothing to disturb or threaten. A feeling of intensity begins to build towards the end of the second stanza, and the dramatic peak is in the middle of the third. Calm gradually returns during the fourth stanza, leading us back to the original mood. The music is the same for beginning and end, so we have a loose ABA form, with the B section divisible into three segments.

The melody for the entire first stanza consists of the five notes from the tonic (F in the original key) to the dominant. There is only one accidental in the accompaniment for the whole section, which is very unusual for Fauré, but the harmonies are far from simplistic. The beautiful minor chord under "ennui" underscores the sadness attached to the thought, and the many suspensions sustain interest. The words are:

> My thought is a swan, harmonious and wise,
> Which glides slowly on the rivers of boredom
> On the unsupported waves of dream, of mirage,
> Of echo, of mist, of shadow, of night.

For the second stanza Fauré gives us a broken-chord figure in the piano which provides more movement. Augmented chords color the accompaniment and there is more frequent modulation. The melodic line now ranges over a full octave, and there is a definite *crescendo* to the end of the stanza. The words are:

> He glides, haughty king, ploughing a free space,
> A vain reflection follows, precious and changing,

And the numerous reeds bow when he passes,
Somber and silent at the threshold of the silver moon.

Augmented chords become more frequent, as a vaguely ominous feeling touches the interlude before the third stanza. There is a marvelous buildup under "tour-à-tour a fleuri de désir," and an even greater one under "mais plus avant . . . vers l'inconnu." These rising melodic lines, aided by accompaniment and dynamics, sweep the music to potent climaxes. The dissonance under the unexpected word "noir" and the minor resolution bring the stanza to a dramatic close.

And each round corolla of the white water-lilies
One at a time has flowered with desire and with hope . . .
But always onward, on the spray and on the waves,
Fleeing towards the unknown, glides the black swan.

A new piano figure of detached chords marks the beginning of the fourth stanza. For these four lines the melodic line is restricted to a span of four whole steps, from the tonic F to B♮. The accompaniment is rich in interesting harmonies for this static melody, often transforming what seem to be repeated notes into audible enharmonic changes. The words offer philosophical advice:

Then I said, "Beautiful mystical swan, renounce
This slow journey towards troubled destinies;
No Chinese miracle, no strange America
Will welcome you in safe harbors;

For the last stanza we return to the music of the first. The only changes are the tonic conclusion of the vocal part, and the use of broken chords instead of single notes in the accompaniment after measure five. The poem ends:

The perfumed gulfs, the immortal isles
Have for you, black Swan, perilous reefs;
Stay on the lakes where are mirrored, faithfully,
These clouds, these flowers, these stars, these eyes.

2. Reflets dans l'eau
Reflection in the Water

Etendue au seuil du bassin,
Dans l'eau plus froide que le sein
        Des vierges sages,
J'ai refleté mon vague ennui,
Mes yeux profonds, couleur de nuit
        Et mon visage.

Et dans ce miroir incertain
J'ai vu de merveilleux matins . . .
      J'ai vu des choses
Pâles comme des souvenirs
Sur l'eau que ne saurait ternir
      Nul vent morose.

Alors au fond du Passé bleu,
Mon corps mince n'était qu'un peu
      D'ombre mouvante,
Sous les lauriers et les cyprès
J'aimais la brise au souffle frais
      Qui nous évente . . .

J'aimais vos caresses de soeur,
Vos nuances, votre douceur,
      Aube opportune;
Et votre pas souple et rythmé,
Nymphes au rire parfumé,
      Au teint de lune;

Et le galop des aegypans;
Et la fontaine qui s'épand
      En larmes fades . . .
Par les bois secrets et divins
J'écoutais frissoner sans fin
      L'hamadryade.

O cher Passé mystérieux
Qui vous refletez dans mes yeux
      Comme un nuage,
Il me serait plaisant et doux,
Passé, d'essayer avec vous
      Le long voyage! . . .

Si je glisse, les eaux feront
Un rond fluide . . . un astre rond,
      Un autre à peine . . .
Et puis le miroir enchanté
Reprendra sa limpidité
      Froide et sereine.

This long (seven-stanza) poem by the Baroness of Brimont has been set with considerable economy by Fauré. Even at the slow tempo indicated, the syllables move along in quasi-recitativo style, and one stanza flows imperceptibly into the next. Only in the last few lines do we find pauses in the vocal part, and these are used specifically to convey the returning stillness of the water after the ripples caused by the disturbance have gradually ceased.

The format of the poem is somewhat unusual: there are two lines of eight syllables each and one line of four syllables in the pattern, and two such groups make a stanza. The rhyme scheme is *aabccb*.

Fauré begins his setting with an almost motionless melodic line, which well represents the stillness of the water in the basin. At "couleur de nuit" the melody begins to rise. The concomitant rise in dynamics gives us a small climax at "visage." The accompaniment to this point has been gentle and quiet, but it is distinguished by the constant use of intervals of a major or minor second, giving an acrid aura to what might otherwise have become sentimental. The first stanza reads:

> Leaning over the rim of the basin,
> In the water colder than the breast
> > Of wise virgins,
> I saw reflected my vague ennui,
> My deep eyes, color of the night,
> > And my face.

The music continues in much the same mood for the next two stanzas, but there is a bit more motion in the melodic line. Three wonderful chords (actually the same intervals on three pitch levels) are heard—under "Passé," under "ce n'était" in the following measure, and under "lauriers" in the bar after that. These chords each contain an augmented triad based on the note a whole step below the root note in the bass. A rising melodic line and *crescendo,* similar to the music at the end of the first stanza, brings the third stanza to a close. The top note is the same—the C above middle C, but here we have a dramatic drop of an octave. The words are:

> And in this uncertain mirror
> I have seen wondrous mornings . . .
> > I have seen things
> As pale as memories . . .
> On the water which no morose wind
> > Knows how to tarnish.

> Then in the depths of the blue Past,
> My thin body was no more than a small
> > Moving shadow,
> Under the laurels and the cypress
> I loved the breeze in the fresh breath
> > That fans us . . .

The music changes for the next stanza: the *tessitura* of the melody is higher for the first three lines, the rhythm changes from 4/4 to 3/2, and the moving figure is in the accompaniment's bass, with strong right hand chords supporting the melody. More excitement is generated by this new music at the beginning of the segment, but gradually, through a series of lovely modulations and a descending melodic line, calm is restored. This stanza reads:

I loved your sisterly caresses,
Your nuances, your tenderness,
Opportune dawn;
And your supple and rhythmic step,
Nymphs with scented laughter,
In the moon's light;

The melodic line becomes more and more restricted as we gradually return to the calm of the opening bars. For the fourth time, Fauré uses the augmented chord over a nonrelated bass note. This combination can also be analyzed as an A♭ minor chord with a major third added—the wonderful sound remains either way! It is an appropriate accompaniment to the esoteric word "l'hamadryade" (water nymph), which ends the stanza.

And the galop of the aegypans;
And the fountain which spends itself
In stale tears
In the secret and divine woods
I heard the wood nymph
Tremble endlessly.

The sixth verse is rather uneventful musically. The augmented chord after "nuage" lacks the spice of the others previously mentioned. The melody becomes almost motionless for the last stanza, with twenty long syllables (from "glisse" to "à peine") on the repeated note E, for instance. Triplet eighth-note chords, which yield to regular eighth notes, are introduced in the accompaniment to represent ripples in the water which widen their circles before disappearing, leaving the surface as glassily smooth as before. The last two stanzas are:

Oh dear blue, mysterious Past
Which you mirror in my eyes
Like a cloud
It would be pleasant and sweet to me
Past, to try the long voyage
With you! . . .

If I glide the waters will make
A fluid circle, another circle,
Scarcely one other,
And then the enchanted mirror
Will reassume its limpid clarity
Cold and serene.

3. Jardin nocturne
Nocturnal Garden

Nocturne jardin tout rempli de silence,
Voici que la lune ouverte se balance
En des voiles d'or fluides et légers;
Elle semble proche et cependant lointaine . . .
Son visage rit au coeur de la fontaine
Et l'ombre pâlit sous les noirs orangers.

Nul bruit, si ce n'est le faible bruit de l'onde
Fuyant goutte à goutte au bord des vasques rondes,
Ou le bleu frisson d'une brise d'été,
Furtive parmi des palmes invisibles . . .
Je sais, ô jardin, vos caresses sensibles,
Et votre languide et chaude volupté!

Je sais votre paix délectable et morose,
Vos parfums d'iris, de jasmins et de roses,
Vos charmes troublés de désirs et d'ennui . . .
O jardin muet! L'eau des vasques d'égoutte
Avec un bruit faible et magique . . . J'écoute
Ce baiser qui chante aux lèvres de la Nuit.

"Jardin nocturne" is the third of the four songs which constitute Fauré's Opus 113, *Les Mirages*. Although these songs are published as a unit, the first three are so similar in mood and expression that performers would be hard-pressed to provide enough variety to sustain interest if they were sung consecutively. The individual songs are certainly long enough to be programmed as entities within a French or all-Fauré group.

The structure of this poem is almost identical to that of the preceding text: two lines of twelve syllables each, one slightly shorter line (eleven syllables in this case) and a repeat of the pattern to make up each stanza, with a rhyme scheme of *aabccb*. Whereas "Reflets dans l'eau" had seven stanzas, "Jardin nocturne" has only three, so of course the song is much shorter. Since each line of text has many syllables, Fauré moves the vocal line rather quickly, rarely lingering on a syllable unless the end of a phrase, sentence, or stanza has been reached. This makes for considerable motion in the vocal part, which is somewhat counteracted by a quiet, unrushed accompaniment.

The melodic line rises and falls constantly—a style not really typical of Fauré. In the first three lines, for instance, we rise from G to C (there are small detours along the way) and then descend to G again at "légers." The harmonies shift often under this melody, leading us from G minor and E♭, the chords in the introductory bars, through F major, A minor, G major, B minor, a lovely augmented E♭ under "ouver*te*," C minor, A♭, and finally the striking cadence from a D minor[7] to the unexpected C major chord at "légers." Although this music could be used to create excitement, the dynamic level is kept low, and the words suggest a hushed, diaphanous delivery.

After the pause on "légers," the melody becomes more static. A new accompanying figure which is replete with interesting alterations, suspensions, and dissonances quietly surrounds the melodic line. At "fontaine" the melody begins to rise again and there is a *crescendo* to "orangers," the last word of the stanza. The words thus far are:

> Nocturnal garden, all filled with silence,
> Here the full moon is poised
> In light and fluid veils of gold;
> She seems near and yet far . . .
> Her face laughs in the heart of the fountain
> And the shadow pales under the dark orange trees.

The second stanza begins quietly, with a pleasant countermelody atop the eighth note piano figure. Once again the accompanying figure changes midstanza, this time reverting to the original pattern. There is no break in the music between the second and third stanzas, as the melodic rise begun at "Je sais" continues until the D of "charmes troublés," and the musical phrase does not end until "et d'ennui." This ascent, emphasized by a sizable *crescendo,* is longer and more dramatic than its counterpart at the beginning of the song, leading to the climactic "charmes troublés." The words "morose" and "ennui" are unexpected in the context (see translation below) and the harmonic changes accompanying them are equally unsettling. The innocuous word "roses" has a similarly unusual chord, obviously for musical rather than textual reasons.

For the last three lines we return to the eighth note piano figure, with double-stemmed notes supplying a countermelody which we first encountered in the second half of the second stanza. The sounds of the harmonies may not be as appealing as some of Fauré's—they have an overcast grey aura at times—but the final resolution to the E♭ major tonality is soothing and comforting. Stanzas two and three read:

> No noise, but perhaps the faint sound of the wave
> Fleeing, drop by drop from the edge of the round basins,
> Or the blue shudder of a summer breeze,
> Furtive among the invisible palms . . .
> I know, oh garden, your sensitive caresses,
> And your languid and warm voluptuousness!
>
> I know your delightful and morose peace
> Your scents of iris, of jasmine and of roses,
> Your charm troubled by desire and ennui

Oh silent garden! The water of the basins drips
With a weak and magic sound . . . I listen to
This kiss which sings on the lips of the Night.

4. Danseuse
Dancer

Soeur des Soeurs tisseuses de violettes,
Une ardente veille blémit tes joues . . .
Danse! et que les rythmes aigus dénouent
    Tes bandelettes.
Vase svelte, fresque mouvante et souple,
Danse, danse, paumes vers nous tendues,
Pieds étroits fuyant tels des ailes nues
    Qu'Eros découple . . .
Sois la fleur multiple un peu balancée,
Sois l'écharpe offerte au désir qui change,
Sois la lampe chaste, la flamme étrange,
    Sois la pensée!
Danse, danse au chant de ma flûte creuse,
Soeur des Soeurs divines. La moiteur glisse,
Baiser vain, le long de ta hanche lisse . . .
    Vaine danseuse!

"Danseuse," the final song of Opus 113, might be subtitled "An Apotheosis to the Dancer." The words suggest a wild frenzy—the feverish energy and pale cheeks, the constant motion and total self-absorption, of the dedicated dancer. This is diametrically opposed to the calm stillness that pervades the three other songs of *Mirages*, and finally provides much-needed contrast.

The poem has an interesting structure—(the Baroness of Brimont was quite skilled in the manipulation of complex forms): the first three lines of the four-line stanzas have ten syllables each, while the concluding line has only five. There are four complete stanzas whose rhyme scheme is *abba/cddc*, etc.

Fauré's setting is a wonderfully simple distillation of rhythm and harmony. The accompaniment immediately establishes an undulating, semi-hypnotic figure which is repeated unchanged for the first ten measures. The vocal line is heavily dominant-oriented in the first half of the song (the original key is D minor), with four of the first six lines beginning and/or ending on the dominant note. This sinuous melody and repetitious accompaniment create an exotic effect—this is neither a classical ballerina nor a Can-Can girl. Is she the danacer on a Greek vase, caught forever in her frenetic pose, or is she as real as the sweat on her hip would imply? She dances to the sound of a hollow flute—is it a Greek aulos or a snake charmer's pipe? The words do not really tell us:

> Sister of sisters, weaver of violets
> A scorching sleeplessness makes your cheeks pale
> Dance! and let the sharp rhythms untie
>   Your fillets.

The accompaniment for the entire first stanza (quoted above) is in the simple single-note figure. For the second stanza, Fauré softens the contours by adding some harmonizing notes. The melody remains quite constrained until the little scale rises to the sinuous ornament on "nues" (nude or bare). The dance is obviously erotic as well as exotic!

> Svelte vase, moving and supple fresco,
> Dance, dance, palms extended towards us
> Slender feet flying like bare wings
>   That Eros unbinds

In the third stanza, the exotic element is much reduced by the change in the accompaniment. Now the music has an almost popular flavor. Only the rhythmic figure in the bass of the accompaniment retains the original spirit.

> Be the multiple flowers swaying a bit,
> Be the scarf offered to changing desire,
> Be the chaste lamp, strangely burning,
>   Be the thought!

The music for the final segment is the most frenzied in the song. At a faster speed, the chromatic figure in the accompaniment can suggest a whirling dervish, but nowhere is an *accelerando* indicated. Although the words mention the flute here, this music is too low and dense to be flutelike. The *crescendo* under "La moiteur glisse" leads only to a *mezzo-forte,* and then the music begins to become calmer. The *tessitura* for the last two lines is quite low, which contributes to the feeling of winding down. The piano has four long measures in which to fade away on a tonic chord. The last stanza reads:

> Dance, dance to the song of my hollow flute,
> Sister of divine sisters. Moisture slides,
> Vain kiss, along your lithe hip ...
>   Vain dancer!

C'est la Paix!   Poem by Mlle. Georgette Debladis
Peace Is Here!   OPUS 114

> Pendant qu'ils étaient partis pour la guerre,
> On ne dansait plus, on ne parlait guère,

On ne chantait pas.
Mes soeurs, c'est la paix!
La guerre est finie.
Dans la paix bénie
Courons au devant de nos chers soldats.
Et joyeusement, toutes en cadence,
Nous irons vers eux en dansant la danse
Qu'on danse chez nous.
Nous les aimerons! la guerre est finie.
Ils seront aimés, dans la paix bénie
Sîtot leur retour.
Pour avoir chassé la horde Germaine
Ils auront nos coeurs, au lieu de la haine.
Ils auront l'amour.

It is all too evident when listening to "C'est la Paix!" (Peace is here!) that the upbeat, patriotic sentiments (expressed in its less-than-inspired text) were not the material to bring out the best in Fauré. Were it not for the four songs of Op. 118 which follow "C'est la Paix" chronologically, one would suspect that the seventy-five-year-old composer had begun to run dry by the time this song was written (1919–20). Fortunately this was not the case.

The poem celebrates the end of World War I, particularly the victory of the French over the Germans. It promises the returning soldiers song, dance, and above all, love. The first three lines of verse describe the wartime mood:

While they were gone to the war
We danced no more, we scarcely spoke,
We did not sing—

Fauré sets this much of the text in the minor mode (A minor), but his use of a martial dotted rhythm in the accompaniment right from the first bar prevents too lugubrious a mood. At the words "Mes soeurs, c'est la paix!" (My sisters, peace is here!), we have a triumphant A major chord (the parallel major) and a strongly declamative vocal line on the median note (C♯). The melody rises exultantly for "La guerre est finie" (The war is over) and maintains a fairly high *tessitura* for the next several bars. The rising interval under "Mes soeurs . . . " is repeated for "Nous les aimerons!" (We shall love them!), where strong tonic (A major) chords continue to support the melodic line.

In typical Fauré fashion, much of the melody is dominant-oriented, but that pivotal E is harmonized with a bona fide V chord exactly once (under the upbeat E's at "Nous les aimerons!") in the entire song. Elsewhere we meet C chords (under "*chers* soldats"), A minor chords with chromatically rising unrelated bass notes (under "Ils au*ront nos coeurs*"), F♯ minor[7] chords, and so forth. Paradoxically, despite all this harmonic activity, the song does not seem harmonically interesting, nor, for that matter, is the melody catchy or in any way memorable. The text continues:

> My sisters, peace is here!
> The war is over.
> In blessed peace
> We shall run before our dear soldiers,
> And joyously, all in cadence,
> We shall go towards them dancing the dance
> We dance at home.
> We shall love them! the war is over.
> They will be loved in the blessed peace
> Immediately upon their return.
> For having chased the German horde
> They shall have our hearts, instead of hate.
> They shall have love.

L'Horizon Chimérique
Poems by Jean de la Ville de Mirmont
OPUS 118

1. La Mer est infinie
The Sea Is Infinite

La mer est infinie et mes rêves sont fous.
La mer chante au soleil en battant les falaises
Et mes rêves légers ne se sentent plus d'aise
De danser sur la mer comme des oiseaux soûls.

Le vaste mouvement des vagues les emporte,
La brise les agite et les roule en ses plis;
Jouant dans le sillage, ils feront une escorte
Aux vaisseaux que mon coeur dans leur fuite a suivis.

Ivres d'air et de sel et brûlés par l'écume
De la mer qui console et qui lave des pleurs,
Ils connaîtront le large et sa bonne amertume;
Les goëlands perdus les prendront pour des leurs.

The four songs of Opus 118 were the last to come from Fauré's pen. Composed two years before his death in 1924, they are followed by only three later works: Nocturne for piano, Opus 119; Trio for violin, 'cello, and piano, Opus 120; and String Quartet, Opus 121. Since Fauré's Opus 1, published in 1865, consists of two songs (see pages 1 to 4), this analysis of his compositions for solo voice and piano spans his career from his twentieth to his seventy-seventh year. These last songs are not among his most powerful expressions in the genre—certainly no one would value them as highly as "Après un rêve," "Au Bord de l'Eau," the three songs of *Poëme d'un Jour,* "Nell," "Aurore," "Clair de lune," "Les Roses d'Ispahan" or "Prison," to name a few favorites. Nevertheless, their many beautiful moments indicate that Fauré's gift for this form remained strong throughout his life.

The overall title for the cycle, *L'Horizon Chimérique* (*The Mythical Horizon*), the interrelated subject matter of the four poems, and the cyclical scheme of the key signatures—the first and last poems are in the same key (D major), and the second and third songs are in keys related by proximity (the second is one half step down from the first; the third is a whole step up from the second, which means that one must once again go one half step down for the fourth)—are indications that poet and composer both envisioned these as a group. Actually each song is rather short and too lacking in internal contrast to be effective if sung singly. A look at the individual titles reinforces this impression, for the poet has not really named each song, he has simply given the first few words of text as title.

The first poem, "La Mer est infinie," is written in twelve-syllable Alexandrines. Its rhyme scheme is a bit irregular, with stanza one having *abba* and stanzas two and three *cdcd/efef*. The first line is stunning: "La mer est infinie et mes rêves sont fous." The French word "fou" has all the connotations the English word "mad" carries, from seriously insane to wildly devil-may-care or merely foolish. The poet says his dreams are as wild as the sea is vast; his dreams dance on the sea like drunken birds. Aside from the word "fou" we have two words for intoxicated, "soûls" and "ivres." Obviously the poem, at least until the last three lines, has an impetuous, heady flavor.

Interestingly enough, this exuberance is only mildly reflected in the music. The sixteenth note piano figure is a sort of all-purpose Fauré accompaniment, which suggests the sea only in a few dissonant places (the best example is under "roule en ses plis"). The vocal part begins with a simple rising tonic scale which pauses on the dominant before continuing. There is a detour in the scale, and we arrive at the top (at "fa*laises*") after a modulation to B♭ major. This is the occasion for a strong *forte,* the culmination of the *crescendo* that was begun two bars earlier. The *subito piano* (at the return to the high D at "Et mes rêves") is very effective, as it allows singer and pianist to reflect the lightness implied in the words. Another *crescendo* grows to a *forte* on "comme des oiseaux soûls," and the dynamics remain fairly high until the last six bars of the song.

The music most accurately echoes the words in the lovely resolution at "pleurs." The poet has just described the sea as a consoling element which washes away one's tears, and the beautiful E major chord at "pleurs" expresses this feeling of solace. The mood of the last stanza becomes much more pensive and melancholy; the fading dynamics of the end underscore this change. The text is:

> The sea is infinite and my dreams are mad.
> The sea sings in the sunshine while beating the cliffs
> And my light dreams are beside themselves
> With the joy of dancing on the sea like drunken birds.
>
> The vast motion of the waves carries them,
> The breeze agitates and rolls them in its folds;
> Playing in the furrows, they will be an escort
> To the ships that my heart followed in their flight.
>
> Drunk with the air and the salt and burned by the spray
> Of the sea which consoles and which washes away tears,
> They will know the open sea and its good bitterness;
> The lost seagulls will take them for their own.

2. Je me suis embarqué...
I Set Sail

> Je me suis embarqué sur un vaisseau qui danse
> Et roule bord sur bord et tangue et se balance.
> Mes pieds ont oublié la terre et ses chemins;
> Les vagues souples m'ont appris d'autres cadences
> Plus belles que le rythme las des chants humains.
>
> A vivre parmi vous, hélas! avais-je une âme?
> Mes frères, j'ai souffert sur tous vos continents.
> Je ne veux que la mer, je ne veux que le vent
> Pour me bercer, comme un enfant au creux des lames.
>
> Hors du port, qui n'est plus qu'une image effacée,
> Les larmes du départ ne brûlent plus mes yeux.
> Je ne me souviens pas de mes derniers adieux...
> O ma peine, ma peine, où vous ai-je laissée?

Despite the gaiety of the opening lines of its text, this second song of Opus 118 is much more somber than its predecessor. The piano figure with which the song begins is an unlikely musical approximation of the sea—perhaps it is meant to portray the clumsy terrestrial gait of the sailor. (In American music comparable figures often symbolize the cowboy on or off his horse!) As was the case in "La mer est infinie . . . ," the roar of the sea is best evoked by the dissonances in such places as "d'autres cadences."

Fauré abandons the characteristic accompanying figure in three places in the song, each time in favor of an accompaniment better suited to the words. "A vivre parmi vous, avais-je une âme? Mes frères, j'ai souffert sur tous vos continents." (Had I the soul to live among you? My brothers, I have suffered on all your continents.) This poignant question and plaint elicits tender, melancholy harmonies, although the dotted figure reappears once under "une âme." For the words "Pour me bercer, comme un enfant, aux creux des lames" (To rock me, like a child, in the hollow of the surging waves), the piano supplies a gently rocking accompaniment. The climax of the song, "o ma peine, ma peine" (Oh my grief, my grief), is accompanied by strong chords, first augmented, then major, minor, major, and minor in turn. The melody is sung all on one note in these three powerful measures, the harmonic changes seething below.

The poem begins gaily and ends in sorrow and bewilderment. Its three stanzas are not quite symmetrical, the first having five lines (*aabab*) and the others four lines each (*cddc, effe*). The meaning of the text is subject to various interpretations: in the first stanza the protagonist seems to have chosen the sea because it tantalized him, but in the second stanza we learn that he turned to the sea because he had suffered on land. The third stanza is the most puzzling—he once cried upon leaving port but he no longer remembers his last farewells; does he cry out in suffering or because he has lost his anguish? The actual words are:

> I set sail on a ship which dances
> And rolls from side to side and pitches and rocks.
> My feet have forgotten the land and its ways.
> The supple waves have taught me other cadences
> More beautiful than the weary rhythm of human songs.
>
> To live among you, alas! had I a soul?
> My brothers, I have suffered on all your continents.
> I want only the sea, I want only the wind
> To rock me, like a child, in the hollow of the waves.
>
> Far from the port, which is no longer more than a faded image,
> The tears of parting no longer burn my eyes.
> I don't remember my last farewells.
> Oh my grief, my grief, where have I left you?

3. Diane, Séléné...
Diana, Goddess...

Diane, Séléné lune de beau métal,
Qui reflète vers nous, par ta face déserte,

Dans l'immortel ennui de calme sidéral
Le regret d'un soleil dont nous pleurons la perte.

O lune, je t'en veux de ta limpidité
Injurieuse au trouble vain des pauvres âmes,
Et mon coeur, toujours las et toujours agité,
Aspire vers la paix de ta nocturne flamme.

This third song of *L'Horizon Chimérique* never mentions the sea, but it is not hard to imagine that the starlit night with its brilliant moon is seen from a ship's deck.

The most remarkable things about this brief song are the strange dissonances Fauré has written into the accompaniment. The first such sound occurs at "métal," and from that point on they are frequent indeed. The entire accompaniment is in four part harmony and the dissonances occur as natural results of the convergence of the four moving lines. With the exception of two measures in which short countermelodies are heard, the piano part consists of evenly spaced, semi-detached chords. The E♭ tonality is stressed in the piano intro-duction, in the first two measures of the vocal part, in the one measure interlude before "O lune," as well as at those climactic words, and in the last three bars of the piece. Since the song is only twenty-two bars long, we feel the constant pull of the home key.

Like so many of Fauré's melodies, this one is dominant-oriented. The downward interval from dominant to tonic and its upward return are heard in the original key at "Diane, Séléné" and then a half step up at "Dans l'immortel ennui." The first and last phrases end on the dominant.

The poem, like others of the cycle, is in twelve-syllable Alexan-drines. It has only two stanzas, whose rhyme scheme is *abab/cdcd*. Despite the *Lento* tempo indication, the words must be sung fairly rapidly if one is to fit all the syllables in the given number of beats. Once again the poem's message is obscure, calling upon Diane, God-dess of the moon, at the same time praising her, berating her, and hop-ing to imitate her. The words are:

Goddess, Séléné, moon of beautiful metal,
Which reflects towards us, by her deserted façade,
In the immortal boredom of the starry calm
The yearning for a sun whose loss we mourn,

Oh moon, I begrudge you your limpidity
Harmful to the vain sorrow of the poor souls,
And my heart, always weary and agitated,
Longs for the peace of your nocturnal glow.

4. Vaisseaux, nous vous aurons aimés...
Ships, We Shall Have Loved You...

Vaisseaux, nous vous aurons aimés en pure perte;
Le dernier de vous tous est parti sur la mer.
Le couchant emporta tant de voiles ouvertes
Que ce port et mon coeur sont à jamais déserts.

La mer vous a rendus à votre destinée,
Au delà du rivage où s'arrêtent nos pas.
Nous ne pouvions garder vos âmes enchaînées;
Il vous faut des lointains que je ne connais pas.

Je suis de ceux dont les désirs sont sur la terre.
Le souffle qui vous grise emplit mon coeur d'effroi,
Mais votre appel, au fond des soirs, me désespère,
Car j'ai de grands départs inassouvis en moi.

The final poem in this cycle, the last Fauré was ever to set to music, is a fitting finale. Its last line, "Car j'ai de grands départs inassouvis en moi" (For I have great unsatisfied departures in me), expresses regret at opportunities missed, adventures passed by; it explains the poet's ambivalence toward the sea, which simultaneously lures and frightens him.

The structure of the poem is strictly classical—three four-line stanzas with alternating rhymed end sounds (*abab/cdcd/efef*) and symmetrical, twelve-syllable lines. The "vaisseaux" (ships, vessels) are obviously stand-ins for the adventurous souls who seek the unknown, the uncharted.

Fauré's setting is calm and reflective. Once again he eschews any piano figuration whose sound imitates the sea,* giving us instead a simple broken chord pattern for accompaniment. Like the other songs in the cycle, "Vaisseaux, nous vous aurons aimés . . ." adheres closely to its tonal center (D major). Fauré uses many classic modulatory devices, such as the descending bass line from "parti sur la mer" to "tant de voiles," but he also infuses the song with his favorite harmony, the augmented chord. A particularly lovely sound is created by the confluence of these two elements at "empor*ta*," where the low note E is part of the descending line and the chord above is an augmented D.

Despite small dynamic fluctuations earlier in the music, the song has only one forceful *crescendo*. Beginning on "Le souffle," it builds steadily to the climax of the piece, "inassouvis en moi." The octave drop to D above middle C for the last two syllables is not accompanied by a drop in dynamic level—the *diminuendo* begins after the note is

* For some examples wherein Fauré chooses to portray the sea musically, see Opus 85/2, pages 120 to 123, and Opus 23/1, pages 45 to 47.

begun. This final fadeout should be very controlled, so that the sound dies away so imperceptibly that one is scarcely aware of the exact point at which it is no longer heard. The words are:

Ships, we shall have loved you in vain;
The last of you are all gone on the sea.
Sunset brings so many open sails
That this port and my heart are forever deserted.

The sea has returned you to your destiny
Beyond the shores where our steps halt.
We could not keep your sails enchained;
You must have far-away places that I do not know.

I am among those whose desires are on land.
The wind which intoxicates you fills my heart with fear,
But your call, in the depth of the nights, makes me despair,
For I have great departures unsatisfied in me.

Ernest Chausson

Nanny   Poem by Leconte de Lisle

OPUS 2/1

Bois chère aux ramiers, pleurez doux feuillages,
Et toi, source vive, et vous, frais sentiers;
Pleurez, ô bruyères sauvages,
Buissons de houx et d'églantiers.
Printemps, roi fleuri de la verte année,
O jeune Dieu, pleure!
Eté murissant, coupe ta tresse couronnée,
Et pleure, automne rougissant.
L'angoisse d'aimer brise un coeur fidèle.
Terre et ciel, pleurez!
Oh! Que je l'aimais!
Cher pays, ne parle plus d'elle;
Nanny reviendra jamais!

This early piece, Chausson's first published song, was written in
1882, when the composer was already twenty-seven years old. Chausson decided on music as a career relatively late in life and his mature
style is in evidence from his earliest works.

The poem, by Leconte de Lisle, strongly visual and detailed, like
so many of his works, calls upon nature to share man's pain.

One of Chausson's favorite devices—and "Nanny" is a perfect example of this—is the use of an unvarying pattern in the piano accompaniment, in this case sixteenth notes in the right hand against triplets
in the left. The chromatic melody is first given by the piano and then
immediately echoed by the singer. This descending melodic line is a
steady lament, well-suited to the melancholia of the poem. The pianist
should take care not to let the half note C♯ in measure two become two
quarter notes. Judicious pedaling will allow the first C♯ to carry over
to the second.

Woods dear to the doves, cry, sweet foliage,
And you, lively spring, and you, cool paths;

The *crescendo* to F♮ is most effective if the D♯ preceding it is a strict sixteenth note.

Weep, oh wild heather

Here the mournful descending chromatic line returns, but the gentle F major measure (under "sauvages") suggests a short-lived moment of balm.

Bushes of holly and sweetbriar.

Actually solace, even joy, comes in the next line, which is in B major:

Spring, flower-laden king of the green year.

But the G♯ minor of the next line brings the return of sadness.

Oh young God, weep!

This alternation of major-minor, happiness-sadness continues:

Ripening summer, cut your crowned tresses
And cry reddening Autumn

The section describing the seasons has been more animated and alive dynamically as well as in tempo. The *ritard* on "rougiss*ant*" brings us back to the slower pace and the sorrowful chromatic melody of the beginning.

The anguish of loving breaks a faithful heart.
Earth and sky weep!

Nevertheless, the real climax of the song is here on

Oh! how I loved her!

The G♮ is the highest note in the song and is well-prepared by the rising line under "Terre et ciel pleurez!" After this passionate outburst there is a sense of weariness and ultimate despair. Once again we have our chromatic descent and these sorrowful final words:

Beloved countryside, speak of her no more;
Nanny will never return.

Le Charme   Poem by Armand Silvestre
The Charm   OPUS 2/2

Quand ton sourire me surprit,
Je sentis frémir tout mon être,

Mais ce qui domptait mon esprit,
Je ne pus d'abord le connaître.

Quand ton regard tombas sur moi,
Je sentis mon âme se fondre,
Mais ce que serait cet emoi,
Je ne pus d'abord en répondre.

Ce qui me vainquit à jamais,
Ce fut un plus douloureux charme;
Et je n'ai su que je t'aimais
Qu'en voyant ta première larme.

Like so many of Chausson's songs, this one is a little gem, simple, naive, and touching. There is no grand climax and no virtuosic display to distort the wistful, almost childlike clarity of expression. Without introduction, piano and voice begin together:

When your smile took me by surprise,
I felt my entire being tremble
But what conquered my spirit,
I didn't recognize at first.

The D minor chord under "Je" (in measure seven), analyzed in G, key for high voice, gives a sudden sense of awe. A little *tenuto* might be effective here.

When your glance fell on me,
I felt my soul melt,
But what that emotion might be
I could not at first respond to

The ABA form of the song now dictates the return of the original musical material:

What vanquished me forever,
Was a sadder charm;
And I did not know that I loved you,
Until I saw your first tear.

The final plagal cadence (C minor to G) reinforces the somewhat melancholy feeling of the song, but the major resolution takes away any real sting of sorrow.

Les Papillons   Poem by Théophile Gautier
Butterflies   OPUS 2/3

Les papillons couleur de neige
Volent par essaims sur la mer;

Beaux papillons blancs, quand pourrai-je
Prendre le beau chemin de l'air?

Savez-vous, ô belle des belles,
Ma bayadère aux yeux de jais,
S'ils me voulaient prêter leurs ailes,
Dîtes, savez-vous, où j'irais?

Sans prendre un seul baiser aux roses,
A travers vallons et forêts,
J'irais à vos lèvres mi-closes
Fleur de mon âme, et j'y mourrais.

"Butterflies" is an unusually lively and upbeat song for this characteristically moody composer. The piano accompaniment is a light figure meant to suggest the flight of butterflies; it is particularly effective in measures eleven through fourteen and in the six soaring measures at the end of the song. The major modality contributes to the light-hearted mood.

The poem, by Théophile Gautier, is an example of "l'art pour l'art," art for its own sake. Gautier felt that all things, especially poetry, are beautiful in inverse proportion to their usefulness. Poetry must serve no didactic or moralistic ends; "roses are as necessary as potatoes!"

The color white had special significance for Gautier. In his poem "Symphonie en Blanc Majeur" (Symphony in White Major), he stresses the purity and coolness of white. We have hints of this preoccupation in this poem.

Butterflies the color of snow
Fly in swarms over the sea;
Beautiful white butterflies, when shall I be able
To take the blue road of the air?

Do you know, oh beauty of beauties,
My dancing-girl with eyes of jade,
If they would lend me their wings,
Tell me, do you know where I would go?

Under "O belle des *belles*" the insistent G major chords change to G minor; we also have slightly more adventurous harmonization under "ailes" (wings). The obligatory augmented chord comes in the next line, under "prendre un seul baiser aux . . .".

Without taking a single kiss to the roses,
Across valleys and forests

The high point of the vocal line occurs on the F♮ under "forêts." From this point we have three consecutive *decrescendos* and a fade-out ending. The final lines read

I would go to your half-closed lips,
Flower of my soul, and die there.

When the piano figure finally comes to a halt (under the last line),
the contrast between it and the held chords which replace it is stunning.
On the singer's last syllable the butterflies resume their flight and soar
out of view. Since it is clear that the poet will die only of pleasure on
the lips of his beloved, no note of sadness invades the end of the song.

La Dernière feuille   Poem by Théophile Gautier
The Last Leaf   OPUS 2/4

Dans la forêt chauve et rouillée
Il ne reste plus au rameau
Qu'une pauvre feuille oubliée,
Rien qu'une feuille et qu'un oiseau.

Il ne reste plus en mon âme
Qu'un seul amour pour y chanter;
Mais le vent d'automne, qui brame,
Ne permet pas de l'écouter.

L'oiseau s'en va, la feuille tombe,
L'amour s'éteint, car c'est l'hiver.
Petit oiseau, viens sur ma tombe
Chanter quand l'arbre sera vert.

After the lightness and gaiety of Opus 2/3, this song brings a
return to the brooding melancholia so characteristic of most of Chausson's songs. The poet is once again Théophile Gautier, but in contrast
to the description of a butterfly-filled, benign natural setting, as in the
first song, we now have a cold, mournful winter scene.

The piano begins with an attention-getting A♯. This must be
played boldly and allowed plenty of time to fade. The piece really begins on the next measure with somberly paced chords (B minor–G♯
diminished in the original key). The feeling of sadness already conveyed by the chords is reinforced by the use of G♯ in the rise of the
melody and G♮ when the melody falls.

In the bare and blighted forest

The chords are now in a higher register, but their morose harmonic effect (minor to diminished) is unchanged.

There is nothing left on the branch
But one poor forgotten leaf,
Nothing but one leaf and one bird.

The rising melody and cadence to G♯ on "ois*eau*" lend an air of expectancy and hope. The E major chord under "Il ne" (the next measure) seems to fulfill this happy expectation as does the slightly faster tempo ("un peu plus vite" indication), but the minor chord and G♮ in the melody squelch the inchoate joy. The dissonance under "am*our*" is particularly disturbing and should probably be stressed. The same dissonance occurs seven measures later, but the greater interval blunts its force.

> Nothing remains in my soul
> Except a single love to sing there
> But the wind of autumn, which bellows,
> Doesn't allow one to listen to it.

Although the section quoted above ends with grim words, the last two measures of music provide a soothing C♯–F♯ major cadence. In the final section, however, words and music are equally haunting:

> The bird goes away, the leaf falls
> Love dies away, for it is winter.
> Little bird, come to my tomb
> To sing when the tree is green again.

The words for "fall" ("la feuille tombe"—the leaf falls) and "tomb" ("sur ma tombe"—to my tomb) are the same in French, which greatly increases the power of the imagery.

The aura of this piece, especially in the weighty chords towards the end, is strongly reminiscent of a song by Henri Duparc, called "Lamento." Interestingly enough, the poet for that Duparc song was also Théophile Gautier.

| **Sérénade italienne** | Poem by Paul Bourget |
| *Italian Serenade* | OPUS 2/5 |

Partons en barque sur la mer
Pour passer la nuit aux étoiles,
Vois, il souffle juste assez d'air
Pour enfler la toile des voiles.

Le vieux pêcheur italien
Et ses deux fils, qui nous conduisent
Ecoutent mais n'entendent rien
Aux mots que nos bouches se disent.

Sur la mer calme et sombre, vois,
Nous pouvons échanger nos âmes,
Et nul ne comprendra nos voix
Que la nuit, le ciel et les lames.

In direct contrast to the previous song in this opus, "Italian Serenade" is a blissful expression of ardor. In it the young lover invites his beloved to sail through the star-filled night with him. Unlike Duparc's "L'Invitation au voyage," discussed on page 249, this is a practical invitation with details worked out in advance!

The two introductory bars establish the principal piano figuration, which of course suggests the motion of the sea—a very gentle and calm sea. The little left hand melody in measure two introduces a two-against-three rhythmic pattern, which is most often carried out in the vocal line with eighth notes while the triplets continue in the piano.

> Let us go in a small boat on the sea
> To spend the night under the stars.
> See, there's just enough breeze
> To fill the cloth of the sails.

The piano figures under "d'air" and "voiles" suggest a jaunty light breeze.

> The Italian fisherman
> And his two sons who guide us,
> Listen but understand nothing
> Of the words our lips say.

As the boat picks up speed, the piano figuration changes to a more rapidly-moving one.

> On the sea calm and somber,
> See,

Voice and piano must make a *crescendo* and then a *decrescendo* on this long D♯ under "Vois." It is undoubtedly the climax of the song.

> We exchange our souls,
> And no one will understand our voices
> But the night, the sky and the waves.

The postlude, replete with B major and G♯ minor chords (the original key is B major), is saved from banality by the odd arpeggio in the penultimate measure. Nevertheless, this seems to be one of Chausson's least original songs.

Hébé   Poem by Louis Ackermann
Hebe   OPUS 2/6

> Les yeux baissés, rougissante et candide,
> Vers leur banquet quand Hébé s'avançait,

Les Dieux charmés tendaient leur coupe vide,
Et de nectar l'enfant la remplissait.

Nous tous aussi, quand passe la jeunesse,
Nous lui tendons notre coupe à l'envi.
Quel est le vin qu'y verse la Déesse?
Nous l'ignorons; il enivre et ravit.

Ayant souri dans sa grâce immortelle,
Hébé s'éloigne; on la rappelle en vain.
Longtemps encor sur la route éternelle,
Notre oeil en pleurs suit l'échanson divin.

Hébé, the Greek goddess of youth, is ostensibly the subject of this charming little song; but man's desire for eternal youth, his tears when his cup of youth is empty, his vain attempt to recall youth once it has flown—these melancholy thoughts are the underlying message of the poem.

Chausson's setting is a model of touching simplicity, in which ingenious use is made of the Phrygian mode (D to D' on the piano with no black notes). For the first four lines of verse, while the poet is describing the Greek gods at their banquet (Hébé can fill their cups as often as they like for they have the gift of eternal youth), this antique mode is featured. Under the words "Vers le banquet . . ." we have a series of parallel fourths to reinforce the antique sound, and the III–IV progression after "s'avançait" provides yet another modal effect. The words thus far are:

Eyes lowered, blushing and candid,
When Hebe drew near their feast,
The enchanted Gods held out their empty cups,
And the child refilled them with nectar.

At "remplissait," however, the G^7–C cadence subtly shifts the harmonic aura from the modal to the familiar tonic-dominant major-minor scheme of post-sixteenth-century music. This is accomplished without the use of accidentals, so there is no outward sign of key change. Obviously, Chausson chose to make this transition to mark the difference between the text's description of the Greek gods and us poor mortals, for the words continue:

All of us, too, when youth has passed,
We extend our cups to her in emulation.
What is the wine that the goddess pours there?
We do not know; it intoxicates and enraptures.

For the last four lines of the poem Chausson reverts to the antique-sounding music of the opening section. This is heralded by the IV–I

cadence (major-minor because the sixth is not flatted) at "Ayant souri."
Once again we have the parallel fourths (under "s'éloigne") and the
III–IV progression (before "Longtemps"). The melody's return to the
tonic note, a IV–I melodic interval, is harmonized by a II (E minor)
chord, avoiding any hint of the V–I cadence associated so strongly with
major-minor music. In the piano postlude we do finally hear the V–I
ending, but since the V (A minor) is kept in the minor mode, the antique feeling is not lost. The concluding lines are:

> Having smiled with immortal grace,
> Hebe goes away; one recalls her in vain.
> For a long time, still on the eternal route,
> Our tearful eyes follow the divine cupbearer.

Le Colibri   Poem by Leconte de Lisle
The Hummingbird   OPUS 2/7

> Le vert colibri, le roi des collines,
> Voyant la rosée et le soleil clair,
> Luire dans son nid tissé d'herbes fines,
> Comme un frais rayon s'échappe dans l'air.
> Il se hâte et vole aux sources voisines,
> Où les bambous font le bruit de la mer,
> Où l'açoka rouge aux odeurs divines
> S'ouvre et porte au coeur un humide éclair.
> Vers la fleur dorée, il descend, se pose,
> Et boit tant d'amour dans la coupe rose,
> Qu'il meurt, ne sachant s'il l'a put arir!
> Sur ta lèvre pure, ô ma bien aimée,
> Telle aussi mon âme eut voulu mourir,
> Du premier baiser, qui l'a parfumée.

"Le Colibri" ("The Hummingbird") completes Chausson's Opus
2. Like most of its opus mates, this song summons nature as witness to,
and allegory for erotic love. Texts by poet Leconte de Lisle open and
close this cycle, but while the style is obviously the same, there is a
vast difference in mood: in the first song ("Nanny") we have the despair
of lost love; in this last all is ecstasy.

This seventh song seems more sophisticated musically than its
predecessors. The 5/4 rhythm is a departure from more common
meters and the harmonies are richer and more varied. The four bar
piano introduction is based on an ostinato Ab, the dominant key
(original key). The third measure is a particularly lovely A♮ triad over
the Ab pedal point. The 5/4 time has no special effect in the introduction, but in the body of the piece it tends to push the music precipi-

tously from one measure to the next. In other words, one feels that a sixth beat is missing. This is especially true in the measures with descending eighth note figures.

> The green hummingbird, king of the hills,
> Seeing the dew and the clear sunlight
> Shine in his nest woven of sweet-smelling grasses,
> Like a bright beam escapes into the air.

> He hurries and flies to nearby springs

Under this last line the 5/4 rhythm aids the sense of flight, and now the tempo actually moves forward a bit ("en pressant peu à peu" means get faster little by little).

The next few lines of poetry are typical of Leconte de Lisle in his quest for the exotic. Like most poets of the Parnassian School, de Lisle loved the strange-sounding names of tropical flora and fauna.

> Where the bamboo reeds make the sound of the sea,
> Where the divinely scented red hibiscus
> Blooms and carries a moist flash to the heart.

Under these lines the music has been working its way towards the song's climax. There are several long *crescendos* to the *forte* on "Vers." The intensity and sound level are maintained for four bars, then the gradual pulling-back in tempo and dynamics begins. The four climactic measures repeat the harmonies found in the piano introduction, but now the chords are arpeggiated and the melody rides on top.

> Toward the gilded flower he descends, poses,

> At "bois" (drinks) the climax begins to fade:

> And drinks so much love from the red cup
> That he dies, not knowing whether he would have been able to drain it!

Now the melody with which the voice first entered is repeated:

> On your pure lips, oh my beloved,
> Thus my soul also wished to die,

On the word "mourir" (to die) we have a secondary climax, by no means as intense as the first. The piano has a falling, dying line under the held note. The final phrase is gentle and wistful:

> Of the first kiss, which sweetened it.

Nocturne　　　　　　　　Poem by Maurice Bouchor

La nuit était pensive et ténébreuse;
A peine quelques épingles d'or scintillaient dans l'ébène
De ses grands cheveux déroulés,
Qui, sur nous, sur la mer lointaine et sur la terre
Ensevelie en un sommeil plein de mystère,
Secouaient des parfums ailés.
Et notre jeune amour, naissant de nos pensées,
S'éveillait sur le lit de cent roses glacées
Qui n'avaient respiré qu'un jour;
Et moi, je lui disais, pâle et tremblant de fièvre,
Que nous mourrions tous deux, le sourire à la lèvre,
En même temps que notre amour.

This charming little song makes its appeal through its simplicity and sweetness. The melody floats above a seamlessly flowing piano figuration in which chords occur every third eighth note. Since the meter is 4/4, the first beat of the measure is unaccented two out of every three measures, hence the fluidity.

With the exception of the characteristic augmented chords (under "à peine, quelques épingles," for instance), the harmonies are straightforward and uncomplicated. Similarly the melody is basically diatonic with few surprises. The poem, on the other hand, is more elusive:

The night was pensive and overcast;
Scarcely a few pins of gold shone in the ebony
Of its flowing hair
Which, on us, on the far sea, and on the earth
Shrouded in a sleep full of mystery,
Threw off winged fragrances.

This entire first section is marked *piano,* with no change in dynamics. The piano interlude has a *crescendo* and *decrescendo* all on the tonic (E major) chord. When the voice enters again there is a sudden shift to the minor modality. The piano remains high in register and the voice is more than two octaves below the highest piano notes. This is always a celestial effect.

And our young love, born of our thoughts,
Awakens on a bed of a hundred icy roses
Which breathed no more than a day

Augmented chords introduce the final section, which contains the most interesting melodic fragment (under "pâle et tremblant de fièvre") and the dynamic peak (the *crescendo* under "Que nous mourrions tous deux").

And I, I told her, pale and trembling with fever,
That we shall both die, a smile on our lips,
When our love dies.

Amour d'antan
Love of Yesteryear

Poem by Maurice Bouchor

OPUS 8/2

Mon amour d'antan, vous souvenez-vous?
Nos coeurs ont fleuri tout comme deux roses
Au vent printanier des baisers si doux.
Vous souvenez-vous de ces vielles choses?
Voyez-vous toujours en vos songes d'or
Les horizons bleus, la mer soleilleuse
Qui baisant vos pieds lentement s'endort?
En vos songes d'or peut-être oublieuse?
Au rayon pâli des avrils passés
Sentez-vous s'ouvrir la fleur de vos rêves,
Bouquet d'odorants et de frais pensers?
Beaux avrils passés là-bas, sur les grèves!

Another song of charm and simplicity, "Amour d'antan," continues in the mood of the first song of this opus. The E major of the earlier song leads right into the E minor of this second.

An ostinato B (the dominant) in the piano introduces the song and continues under the vocal entry. The pianist must take pains to let the B♮ ring through the B♭ in the opening measure, so that both the ostinato B♮ and the downward chromatic line under it are heard.

My love of yesteryear, do you remember?
Our hearts flowered just like two roses
In the springlike breeze from such sweet kisses.

The B♮ is again prominent in the piano interlude and the melody, so its change to B♭ (under "choses") becomes a "big moment."

Do you remember these old things?

The piano now has a nice little melody, played by the left hand crossing over the right.

Do you always see in your golden dreams
The blue horizons, the sun-filled sea
Which slowly falls asleep kissing your feet?

The scale passage in the piano interlude is a lovely and unusual grouping of half step, whole step, and step-and-a-half intervals. It leads to the climax in the vocal line, which occurs at the end of the next line, on "oublie*use*" (the F♯).

In your golden dreams perhaps forgetful?

Calm once again, the singer continues:

In the pale rays of past Aprils
Do you feel the flower of your dreams open,
Bouquet of fragrant and fresh thoughts?
Beautiful bygone Aprils there, on the sands.

Printemps triste
Sad Spring

Poem by Maurice Bouchor

OPUS 8/3

Nos sentiers aimés s'en vont refleurir
Et mon coeur brisé ne peut pas renaître.
Aussi chaque soir me voit accourir
Et longuement pleurer sous ta fenêtre,
Ta fenêtre vide où ne brille plus
Ta tête charmante et ton doux sourire;
Et comme je pense à nos jours perdus
Je me lamente, et je ne sais que dire.
Et toujours les fleurs et toujours le ciel
Et l'âme des bois dans leur ombre épaisse
Murmurant en choeur un chant éternel
Qui se répand dans l'air chargé d'ivresse!
Et la mer qui roule au soleil levant,
Emportant bien loin toutes mes pensées...
Qu'elles aillent donc sur l'aile du vent
Jusques à toi, ces colombes blessées!

"Printemps triste" is Chausson's most extended effort in the song form to this point, and one of his most successful. Its mood is unmitigatedly grief-stricken, even in the usually consoling middle section. Composers, from Schubert on, have used the section of the poem where the lost love is remembered to lighten the mood, often switching to the major mode ("Gretchen at the Spinning Wheel" comes to mind), but in this song Chausson chooses to leave the intense melancholia unalleviated. Instead of solace, for musical variety Chausson offers us a frenzied section towards the end, where the poet seems wild with grief.

The piano begins with a C minor–C diminished (original key) progression, which includes many chromatic passing notes. Its chromatic melody (in thirds) seems more descriptive of howling Winter winds than of Spring. As is his wont, Chausson uses this piano figure throughout the first section. After four bars the voice enters with a highly chromatic melodic line:

Our beloved lanes will soon bloom again
And my broken heart can not be reborn.

The high F (under "Et mon") is especially effective—a real cry of anguish. The contrast between joyous, ever-fresh spring and unrelenting human grief, expressed in the first two lines of the poem, sums up the entire song.

> Thus every evening sees me hasten
> To cry for a long time under your window.

There is a beautiful harmonic change under the long Db of "ac*courir*." In fact, the last four bars of this section are extraordinarily rich harmonically. The voice descends as the piano's melodic line rises in the last two of these bars—another most effective device.

The 9/8 section begins with a Bb minor harmonic center, but after four measures the whole section becomes one constant modulation. The scale figure, in the inner voice of the piano, gradually assumes importance through repetition and leads back to the original melody and harmonies.

The words for the above section continue to express the poet's despair:

> Your empty window where no longer shines
> Your charming head and your gentle smile;
> And when I think of our days gone by

At the words "Et comme" the singer must leap an octave.

> I lament, and know not what to say.

The next section is polyrhythmic: 12/8 time in the right hand and 4/4 in the left. This merely serves to clarify the three-against-two figure, which suggests more movement and agitation than we had at the beginning of the song. Short, choppy phrases begin to build tension:

> And always the flowers,
> And always the sky,

As the outpouring of grief becomes more intense, phrases grow longer and more fluid:

> And the soul of the woods in their deep shadows
> Murmuring in chorus an eternal song
> Which floats in the air drunk with rapture!

The enormous climax, now being prepared, will culminate in the singer's high note, G on the word "pens*ées*." These next two lines contain the final outburst:

> And the sea which rolls under the rising sun,
> Carrying all my thoughts very far away . . .

The all-important G is supported by a strong C♯ octave and a cascading E minor arpeggio. This combination, a diminished chord with an added major third, carries over into the next two measures as the music gradually becomes less turbulent. It takes the piano four long measures to subdue the storm, but when the singer reenters, there is a deadly calm. Crucial to this change has been the abrupt substitution of the much slower-sounding regular sixteenth notes for the triplet sixteenth-note pattern. This occurs just before the singer's final words:

Would that they could go on the wings of the wind
To you, these wounded doves!

The octave interval reappears in the last line of the song. This time it gives emphasis to the word "toi" (you) at the high note. The last five measures ride on a tonic pedal point, but only in the first and last of these measures do we have a pure C minor chord. The accompaniment's richly varied harmonies in between yield to C minor by way of two chromatic lines in contrary motion: the suspension A♭–G in the upper line and F, F♯, G in the lower. Meanwhile the melody has already arrived at the E♭ by way of a rather large interval, increasing the poignancy of the final word, "blessées" (wounded).

Nos souvenirs   Poem by Maurice Bouchor
Our Memories   OPUS 8/4

Nos souvenirs, toutes ces choses
Qu'à tous les vents nous effeuillons
Comme des pétales de roses
Ou des ailes de papillons,
Ont d'une joie évanouie
Gardé tout le parfum secret,
Et c'est une chose inouïe
Comme le passé reparaît.
A de certains moments il semble
Que le rêve dure toujours
Et que l'on soit encore ensemble
Comme au temps des défunts amours;
Pendant qu'à demi l'on sommeille
Bercé par la vague chanson
D'une voix qui charme l'oreille,
Sur les lèvres voltige un nom;
Et cette heure où l'on se rappelle
Son coeur follement dépensé
Est comme un frissonnement d'aile
Qui s'en vient du joyeux passé.

"Nos souvenirs" completes Chausson's Opus 8. If one plays first the brief piano introduction to #1 of this opus, then the postlude to #4, it seems evident that Chausson intended the four songs to be sung as a cycle (this despite the fact that some editions do not even present the songs in order!), for the two passages are very closely related. The key relationships, the fact that one poet is responsible for all four texts, and the logical progression of the poems also point to this conclusion.

The first poem tells of young love; the second reminisces with the beloved on love's first blossoming; the third cries out in pain over the loss of love, and the fourth looks back on love with the serenity that only the passage of time can bring.

After one brief measure in the piano to establish the tonality (C# minor in the original key) the voice enters:

Our memories, all these things
Which we scatter to the winds
Like rose petals
Or butterflies' wings,
Have kept of a vanished joy
All the secret aura
And it is an extraordinary thing
How the past reappears.

Although the words seem merely philosophical and nostalgic, the music is quite sad. The rising melodic line under "Comme des pétales de roses ou des" creates a good deal of tension, as do the harsh chords under "Gardé," "secret," and "Et c'est une chose."

At the beginning of the second verse, Chausson creates a sense of increased motion by use of the device he employed in the third song of this opus—the triplets against eighth notes where formerly both hands had eighth notes. The singer is consistently with the bass line's eighth notes.

At certain moments it seems that the dream still lasts
And that we are still together
As (we were) in the time of lost loves;

The triplet figure continues in the accompaniment but without the cross-rhythm. The mood becomes dreamier and less sad:

While half asleep, rocked by the vague song
Of a voice which charms the ear,
On one's lips a name flutters

At the *tempo I°* there begins a pedal point on the dominant (G#), which lasts five measures, disappears for six bars, and then returns for another five bars, ending only at the postlude. The melody, too, begins and ends on the dominant. In fact, the vocal line ends with a feeling of incompleteness: there is no resolution until the piano postlude.

> And that hour when one recalls
> One's heart madly flung away

There are very few dynamic indications in this song: the pianist has a *p* at the beginning, a *decrescendo* and *pp* in the interlude between "les défunts amours" and "Pendant qu'à demi l'on sommeille," a return to *p* at the *tempo I°*, and a few hints in the postlude; the singer has exactly one clue—the *p* at the start. Obviously, there must be nuances within the song—a small *crescendo* seems called for under the rising line at "Comme des pétales de roses," for instance—but to the writer the real climactic moment is at the words quoted above: "Son coeur *follement* dépensé."

> Is like a quivering of wings
> That return from the joyous past.

With the exception of four measures, the entire postlude is supported by a pedal point on C♯. Since frequent pedal changes are required within the measures, holding the low C♯ and the B in the fourth bar with the sustaining pedal is a great help. Although all the double-stemmed notes are important, none is more crucial than the A, G♯, G♯, G♯ in the last four bars. These echo the singer's last plaintive phrase.

Apaisement   Poem by Paul Verlaine
Appeasement   OPUS 13/1

> La lune blanche luit dans les bois,
> De chaque branche part une voix
> Sous la ramée,
> O bien-aimée!
> L'étang reflète, profond miroir,
> La silhouette du saule noir
> Où le vent pleure.
> Rêvons, c'est l'heure!
> Un vaste et tendre apaisement
> Semble descendre du firmament
> Que l'astre irise:
> C'est l'heure exquise.

With remarkable economy of means, Chausson has created an enchanted setting for the beautiful poem "Apaisement" by Paul Verlaine. In 1891–92, six years after the publication of the Chausson song, Fauré included this same poem in his cycle *La Bonne Chanson* (Opus 61/3, see pp. 94–96), and it is interesting to compare the two songs. Chausson's is far more atmospheric, with hardly any motion in the accompaniment, just exquisite chords on which the melody floats. Fauré's setting, which goes under the title of the first line of text, "La lune blanche luit dans les bois," is quite operatic in feeling, with two passionately romantic climactic moments.

Be it coincidence or subtle allusion, the opening chords in the Chausson song are identical to those which begin Mendelssohn's famous "Wedding Music" from "Midsummer Night's Dream." This is totally appropriate, since the poem, like the twenty others in Verlaine's collection *La Bonne Chanson,* was written in celebration of the poet's betrothal to Mathilde Mauté de Fleurville.

Immediately following the two-bar introduction, the piano strikes an open tonic chord in the bass. The sound rings through the next eighteen bars and is then used as an arpeggiated full tonic chord for the following four. Above this tonic pedal point the singer has a melody totally derived from the tonic scale, with stopping points on the dominant and tonic. What prevents boredom or a feeling of banality are the subtly changing right hand chords. Not until the singer's last note (on "ramée") does the right hand chord meet the left hand in a tonic triad, and the chord combinations chosen by Chausson before this point are distinctive and beautiful.

The piano halts after the E minor arpeggio while the singer intones four *a capella* measures, first on the tonic and then one half step down on E♭. On this syllable ("aimée") the accompanying chords recommence, first with A♭ as a tonal center, then modulating through several keys until an A major arpeggio is sounded. The melodic motion is somewhat restricted in this section. The words thus far are:

The white moon shines in the forest,
From each branch comes a voice
Under the foliage,
Oh beloved!
The pool reflects, deep mirror,
The silhouette of the black willow

A C♯ chord heralds the central word of the song: "Rêvons," "let us dream." The opening "wedding" chords are heard again, and an open E chord in the bass leads us to expect a recapitulation of the first section. Instead, we have a descending melodic line from the high E of "apaise*ment*" to the F♯ of "iridise" harmonized by a bass with its own line of motion. There is a pause on the dominant chord at the end of "iridise," another reprise of the opening chords followed by a twice-told variation on them, and then the four penultimate magical notes of the melody, a remarkable ascent to high G. The singer holds this

hushed, floating tone while the harmonies change from A minor to
E minor (IV–I) and the top note of the chords echo the singer's climb
to G. The melody then drops to a low E for the last two syllables. It
is not only "l'heure exquise," it is an exquisite ending. The second half
of the poem reads:

> Where the wind weeps.
> Let us dream, this is the hour!
> A vast and tender calm
> Seems to descend from the firmament
> Which the star makes radiant.
> It is the exquisite hour.

Sérénade
Serenade

Poem by Jean Lahor
OPUS 13/2

> Tes grands yeux doux semblent des îles
> Qui nagent dans un lac d'azur;
> Aux fraîcheurs de tes yeux tranquilles
> Fais-moi tranquille et fais-moi pur.
> Ton corps a l'adorable enfance
> Des clairs paradis de jadis;
> Enveloppe-moi de silence,
> Du silence argenté des lys.
> Alangui par les yeux tranquilles
> Des étoiles caressant l'air
> J'ai tant rêvé la paix des îles,
> Sous un soir frissonant et clair!

The fragile beauty of this song makes one almost reluctant to submit it to analysis. There are so many beautiful moments, magical
modulations—how deflating it is to reduce them to minor II chords
and plagal cadences! The poem is lovely, too, full of evocative metaphors and youthful rapture.

The piano opens with a five bar introduction, based primarily on
the tonic chord (E major in the original key) with references to D minor
and B^7 in the fifth bar. The singer begins simply enough with a fragment
of the E scale, but the F♮ on "deux" lifts the song out of the diatonic
framework. The harmony in this measure is based on a D minor
chord. This E major–D minor combination occurs again at the end of
the song. There is constant modulation from here to the gorgeous return to the tonic on "d'azur." In the two measures preceding this resolution we have a lovely duet between singer and piano, the singer's line
falling in what might be analyzed as an A minor scale, while in the
piano a countermelody soars. The text to this point has been

> Your large soft eyes seem to be islands
> Which float in an azure lake;

To constantly shifting harmonies, the voice continues

> With the freshness of your tranquil eyes
> Make me tranquil
> And make me pure.

A *crescendo* begins to develop in this section, leading one to expect a climax on the word "pur." Instead, we have a dramatic buildup on "Et fais-moi" and a *subito piano* on "pur." The modulation here from Eb to F♯ minor is particularly effective, partially because of the chromatic drop in the bass note. The next downward chromatic step in the bass gives us an augmented chord under the singer's long note, another telling effect.

After the piano harmonies shift once again, a new tonal center seems to develop around the key of F (under "ton corps"). This lasts for four bars and then, after more harmonic motion, we sense a new resting place on D (in the measure after "jadis"). This pattern of several measures of constantly shifting harmonies, alternating with a few measures of harmonic stability, proves a most effective device.

The text for the above section is:

> Your body has the adorable youth
> Of the clear paradise of yore;

Once again an important harmonic change occurs under the singer's long note (on "jadis").

> Envelop me in silence
> In the silvered silence of lilies.

The dynamic level for most of this section has been very hushed. Nevertheless, the voice must be even softer at the *pp* ("Du silence"). The song has been at rest harmonically (D major) for nine measures, but after "lys" harmonic motion begins again. The C♮ octave under "argenté" actually announces the coming change, but the vocal line is clearly allowed its resolution in D.

> Made languid by the tranquil eyes
> Of the stars caressing the air
> I so dreamed the peace of the islands
> In an evening trembling and clear.

The one real climax allowed the singer comes on the highest note of the song, the A of "J'ai." The piano must prepare for this by making the most of the *crescendo* marked in the previous measure. The return to the tonic is accomplished under "rêvé," and the original harmonic pattern (E major–D minor) is reiterated. The singer has an extraordinary leap from F♮ to G♯ an octave above on the last two syllables. This final G♯ floats over the piano's descending arpeggio. The postlude fades away as quietly as possible.

L'Aveu   Poem by Villiers de l'Isle-Adam
The Vow   OPUS 13/3

> J'ai perdu la forêt, la plaine,
> Et les frais Avrils d'autrefois.
> Donne tes lèvres, leur haleine,
> Ce sera le souffle des bois.
> J'ai perdu l'océan morose;
> Son deuil, ses vagues, ses échos;
> Dis-moi n'importe quelle chose,
> Ce sera la rumeur des flots.
> Lourd d'une tristesse royale,
> Mon front songe aux soleils enfuis;
> Oh! cache-moi dans ton sein pâle!
> Ce sera le calme des nuits!

Despite long sections and important endings in the major mode, this song has a rather gloomy overall effect. The poem is far from jolly, even though it expresses the hope of solace in the bosom of the loved one. A look at the text shows us many a discouraging word: "perdu" (lost), "deuil" (mourning), "tristesse" (sadness). The ocean, which the poet regrets having lost, was nonetheless "morose"; the yearned-for bosom is "pale." No wonder the song is no *scherzo!*

The dirgelike piano introduction begins on a D minor chord (the tonic in the original key) and passes immediately to a C minor chord. This haunting I–VII progression seems to be a favorite of Chausson's. Equally striking is the D minor–B♭ minor in measures three and four.

The piano's extended melodic line is highly chromatic and leads right into the vocal line, which echoes it. At the singer's entrance the D minor–C minor, D minor–B♭ minor progressions are repeated. The poem begins:

> I have lost the forest, the plains,
> And the fresh Aprils of other times.

A D minor broken chord leads to the new section, which is livelier, in 6/8 time, and in the major mode (B♭). Once again the piano states the new melody before the singer. The modulations here are based on alternating Bb–Eb roots, with one interesting chord based on fourths (Eb, Ab, Db, Gb).

> Give me your lips, their breath,
> Will be the breath of the woods

There is a *crescendo* under "Ce sera le souffle." The D major grace-note arpeggio to the high F# under "*souffle*" helps the singer's climactic ascent. The section ends on a soothing D major chord.

The second verse begins with an abbreviated version of the original piano introduction, but the vocal line enters with new melodic material which is even heavier with gloom:

> I have lost the morose ocean
> Its mourning, its waves, its echoes;

The piano has an impassioned countermelody under the singer's falling line. The short phrases of "Son deuil, ses vagues, ses échos" are anguished; the piano's *legato* accompaniment sets them in relief. The rich piano interlude which follows (primarily in Eb minor) continues the lament.

Under the singer's D# ("Dis-moi") the harmony changes to B major. The tempo picks up briefly, too, but the mood remains sad and wistful:

> Tell me anything, no matter what,
> That will be the roaring of the waves.
> Heavy with a noble sadness
> My brow thinks of vanished sunlight;

The piano passage before "Mon front" is chromatic and meandering. It leads to the singer's dramatic Ab, Db, C ("Mon front songe"), which is sung to a solid Db accompanying arpeggio.

The singer's most beautiful passage, prepared by the piano interlude, now begins with the high F under "Oh!" This is the pivotal note for the last section, gaining in intensity with each repetition and yielding at the most exciting moment to F# ("Ce sera"). Each time the F is sung there is a different harmony supporting it (Bb, F^+, E^9, F°); the last F (under "le") has for its harmony another chord based on fourths (G, C, F, Bb). The words are passionate and almost desperate:

> Oh! hide me in your pale bosom!
> That will be the calm of night.

With the words "calme des nuits," the *ritard* and *decrescendo* have begun to extinguish the burning intensity. The song fades away on a D major chord.

La Cigale   Poem by Leconte de Lisle
The Grasshopper   OPUS 13/4

O Cigale, née avec les beaux jours,
Sur les verts rameaux, dès l'aube posée,
Contente de boire un peu de rosée,
Et telle qu'un roi, tu chantes toujours.

Innocente à tous, paisible et sans ruses,
Le gai laboureur, du chêne abrité,
T'écoute de loin annoncer l'Eté.
Apollon t'honore autant que les Muses,

Et Zeus t'a donné l'Immortalité!

Salut, sage enfant de la terre antique,
Dont le chant invite à clore les yeux,
Et qui, sous l'ardeur du soleil attique,
N'ayant chair ni sang, vis semblable aux Dieux.

"La Cigale" (The Grasshopper), the last of the four songs of Chausson's Opus 13, comes as a complete surprise, for it is totally different in mood and style from the three that precede it. The choice of text—a light-hearted poem in praise of the grasshopper, "wise child of the ancient land" whose innocent voice announces summer—obviously determined the general tenor of the setting, which is lively and gay. It is also extremely simple in its rhythmic pattern, a jaunty 6/8 which changes to a steady 2/4 for the last stanza. Nowhere in the song does one find the haunting chords, misty harmonies, and floating melodic notes with which Opus 13, Nos. 1, 2, and 3 abound, for nowhere are they called for.

Nevertheless, there is one aspect of this song which is complex and sophisticated, and shows the mastery of Chausson: its harmonic structure. The most obvious manifestation of this harmonic sophistication is the unexpected choice of the minor mode—not usually associated with the childlike innocence implied by the words and rhythm—for the overall sound. Each section, of course, has its excursions into major chords, but the general effect is minor until the second stanza ("Innocente à tous . . ."), which describes the grasshopper as innocent and without guile, and is the only section in which extended use is made of the major mode.

The piano opens with the principal melody in the top notes of its eighth-note figure (the dotted notes). The singer echoes this tune after the six-bar introduction. Chausson avoids V–I cadences in the introduction (and subsequently in the body of the song) by substituting diminished chords in the second and fourth bars. In the latter instance a major third has been added to the diminished chord. The melody's two quarter notes against three eighth notes (under "les beaux" and "Sur les verts rameaux") lend some rhythmic interest to the otherwise repetitive pattern. Under *"contente"* we find another diminished chord, this one with a major seventh and a minor ninth added and voiced to emphasize its dissonance. The last line of the stanza, "Et telle qu'un roi, tu chantes toujours" is quite similar to the opening measures. The words are:

> Oh Grasshopper, born with the fair weather,
> Perched on the green branches since dawn,
> Content to drink a little dew,
> And like a king always singing.

The first three lines of the second stanza, in which Chausson moves briefly to the innocent sounds of C and G major under "sans ruses," read:

> Innocent of everything, peaceful and without guile,
> The happy workman, sheltered by the oak tree,
> Listens to you announce from afar the Summer.

There is an enormous climax at "l'Eté," with the singer's climb to a high A accompanied by a grand *crescendo*. The triumphant high note is supported by a D minor arpeggio, which is followed by the first real break in the rhythm, four bars of four eighth notes to a half measure instead of three. The dynamics change to *p* before the next line, and a new thought, which relates to Greek mythology, is introduced. In other words, the four-line stanza structure of the poem is at odds with the gist of the words and the music.

> Apollo honors you as do the Muses,

The next line,

> And Zeus has given you immortality!

seems not to belong to either the stanza that precedes it or the one that follows, as far as the rhyme scheme is concerned. Because it is included, the poem has thirteen lines rather than the customary twelve.

After this odd line the rhythm changes to 2/4, and the piano begins a steady sixteenth note figure which continues to the end of the song. The change from triplets to sixteenth notes gives the illusion of greater speed though there is no real change in tempo. Melodically and harmonically this concluding section is very similar to the music of the first two stanzas, but with an even more rousing climactic ascent to the high B on the final syllable. The poem ends:

> Hail, wise child of the ancient earth,
> Whose song invites one's eyes to close,

And who, under the warmth of the Attic (early Greek) sun,
Having neither flesh nor blood, lives like the Gods!

La Caravane Poem by Théophile Gautier
The Caravan OPUS 14

La caravane humaine, au Sahara du monde
Par ce chemin des ans qui n'a plus de retour,
S'en va, trainant le pied, brûlée aux feux du jour,
Et buvant sur ses bras la sueur qui l'inonde.
Le grand lion rugit et la tempête gronde;
A l'horizon fuyard, ni minaret, ni tour.
La seule ombre qu'on ait c'est l'ombre du vautour
Qui traverse le ciel cherchant sa proie immonde.
L'on avance toujours et voici que l'on voit
Quelque chose de vert que l'on se montre au doigt!
C'est un bois de cyprès semé de blanches pierres.
Dieu, pour vous reposer, dans le désert du temps,
Comme des oasis a mis les cimetières.
Couchez-vous et dormez, voyageurs haletants!

It would be hard to imagine a musical setting more descriptive of
its poem than "La Caravane." The relentless quarter-note chords of the
accompaniment graphically depict mankind's endless, painful march
across "the Sahara of the world"; the organlike chords towards the end
evoke the religious solemnity of the cemetery.

The piano introduction begins the slow, inexorable march in the
key of E minor (in the original key). Even quarter notes in the left hand
beat time, while the right hand establishes a characteristic rhythmic
pattern. The repetition of E minor in measures two and three and the
return to this tonality in bar six seem to suggest a treadmill—man
marches but goes nowhere. This feeling is enhanced by the pedal point
on the tonic, which lasts eight bars. The singer enters softly:

The human caravan, in the Sahara of the world
On this road of the years, which has no more returning,
Goes on, dragging its feet, burned by the fires of the day,
And drinking from its arms the sweat that pours from it.

The melody centers on the dominant (B) until the word "brûlée."
At this point tension begins to mount in the vocal line as the singer rises
to F on "jour" and "buvant." The *crescendo* accompanying these
phrases results in a strong *forte,* which lasts until the melodic line begins its descent. The harmonies at the climax are dissonant and powerful. From "re*tour*" to "bras" we once again have a pedal point on the
tonic. The singer's downward line is continued by the piano until a new

tonal center, A minor, is reached. The new key serves to introduce a new section, marked "faster." The melody begins chromatically, but falls an octave under the word "gronde." Here resignation seems to have yielded to anger, as piano and voice grow louder and more dramatic. The stormy music and bitter words continue:

> The great lion roars and the storm growls,
> On the fleeing horizon, neither minaret nor tower.
> The only shade one has is the shadow of the vulture that crosses the sky,
> Looking for its unclean prey.

The tension built in this section is almost unbearable: the singer climbs higher and higher at full voice before descending in chromatic steps under "vautour qui traverse le ciel"; the accompanying chords are almost maniacal in their endlessly rising and falling pitches. Although the vocal line remains *forte* throughout, the piano has enormous *crescendos* and *decrescendos,* creating further turbulence. The singer's falling intervals under "sa proie immonde" are chilling.

The gentler chords of the following piano interlude seem to bring back the more resigned mood of the beginning. The chords stop for one brief measure, while the singer intones

> It moves on and on.

The march begins again more forcefully and the singer enters on a high note (E)

> And it is here that they see something green that they point out to one
> another!

At the word "voit," the singer's F♮, there is a *subito p* and a completely unexpected F major chord. Although the vocal line culminates in the high A on "doigt," the change of mood that affects the entire remainder of the song really occurs at this splendid modulation. Suddenly there is a feeling of triumph and exaltation. The *ff* chords in the accompaniment are still marching, but no longer do they constitute a funeral march. Now they are a processional, dignified and joyous.

When the piano's last chord fades from *ff* to *pp* the voice enters quietly:

> It is a cypress grove strewn with white stones.

The piano begins the next section with an unusual progression: I–III major (E major–G♯ major). This seems to express religious solemnity and tranquility. The melody is simple, diatonic, and equally serene:

> God, to give you rest, in the desert of time
> Like an oasis, has put cemeteries,

The piano halts on an E major chord while the singer—on the tonic—continues:

Lie down and sleep, breathless travelers.

On the word "dor*mez*" there is a beautiful C major chord. The final chord under these words is a dominant seventh, leading back to E major for the celestial postlude.

Les Morts
The Dead

Poem by Jean Richepin
OPUS 17/1

Ne crois pas que les morts soient morts!
Tant qu'il y aura des vivants
Les morts vivront.

Lorsque le soleil s'est couché,
Tu n'as qu'à fermer tes deux yeux
Pour qu'il s'y lève, rallumé.

L'oiseau s'envole, l'oiseau s'en va;
Mais pendant qu'il plane là-haut,
Son ombre reste sur la terre.

Le souffle que tu m'as fait boire
Sur tes lèvres, en t'en allant,
Il est en moi.

Un autre te l'avait donné en s'en allant,
En m'en allant, je le donnerai à un autre.
De bouche en bouche il a passé;
De bouche en bouche il passera.
Ainsi jamais ne se perdra.

Chausson's Opus 17 consists of two songs, "Les Morts" and "La Pluie," grouped under the title, *Chansons de Miarka*. Apparently extracted from a longer dramatic work by Richepin, only the first of the two songs remains in print; even the archives of La Bibliothèque Nationale in Paris could not locate a copy of "La Pluie."

The text of "Les Morts" (The Dead) is philosophical and comforting, expressing in blank verse the tenet that the dead are not truly dead, for they live on in the memory of the living; the breath of life is eternally passed from one soul to another.

Despite the affirmative nature of the words, the overall impact of the music is melancholy. The piano opens with a suspension over a minor IV chord (F♯ minor) which leads to the tonic (C♯ minor in the original key). This pattern is reiterated as the singer enters with quiet, carefully paced quarter notes. The first modulation (to E, the relative major) is initiated by way of the raised note (A♯) at the word "que," and ends with a lovely major IV–I cadence in the temporary key. Chausson brings us back to the original C♯ minor for the words "les morts vivront" (the dead shall live), a rather gloomy cadence for such encouraging words.

When the poet says that one has only to close one's eyes for the dead to rise, "rallumé" (revived, rekindled), the key moves from C♯ minor to C major and the melodic line rises triumphantly stepwise from B to E, each melody note having its own harmony. These measures, the brightest in the song, are bolstered by a *crescendo* to a *forte*. At the climax the piano plays a bell-like scale passage, still in a major key (E), further emphasizing the exalted mood. A *diminuendo* then brings us to a more reflective passage; but a melodic ascent to a high G♮ and a concomitant harmonic move back to C major lighten the spirits for the second time, as the words describe the bird hovering above the earth ("Mais pendant qu'il plane là-haut").

Shifting harmonies characterize the next section, but we return to the tonic for the crucial words "Il est en moi, Il est en moi" (It is in me, it is in me). The climactic melodic line for these words features an octave drop—always a dramatic device. The triumphant melodic rise and harmonic shift from C♯ minor to C major, followed by the E major chimelike scale originally found under the words "Pour qu'il s'y lève, rallumé," is now repeated for the words "En m'en allant, je le donnerai à un autre" (In leaving I shall give it to another), the only significant repeat in this through-composed song. This time, however, the mood of exaltation continues for another eight bars, and there is a secondary climax on a diminished chord at the word "bouche" (mouth). Chausson then returns to the original minor mode, ending this quietly lovely song in a wistful, reflective mood.

> Don't believe that the dead are dead!
> As long as there are the living
> The dead will live.
>
> When the sun has set,
> You have only to close your two eyes
> For him to rise, revived.
>
> The bird flies away, the bird goes;
> But while he hovers above,
> His shadow remains on the earth.
>
> The breath that you made me drink
> From your lips, in departing,
> It is in me.
>
> Another had given it to you in departing,
> In departing, I shall give it to another.

From mouth to mouth it has passed;
From mouth to mouth it will pass.
Thus it will never be lost.

Le Temps des lilas   Poem by Maurice Bouchor
The Time of Lilacs   OPUS 19

Le temps des lilas et le temps des roses
Ne reviendra plus à ce printemps-ci;
Le temps des lilas et le temps des roses
Est passé, le temps des oeillets aussi.
Le vent a changé, les cieux sont moroses,
Et nous n'irons plus courir, et cueillir
Les lilas en fleur et les belles roses;
Le printemps est triste et ne peut fleurir.
Oh joyeux et doux printemps de l'année,
Qui vins, l'an passé, nous ensoleiller,
Notre fleur d'amour est si bien fanée,
Las! Que ton baiser ne peut l'éveiller!
Et toi, que fais-tu? pas de fleurs écloses,
Point de gai soleil ni d'ombrages frais;
Le temps des lilas et le temps des roses
Avec notre amour est mort à jamais.

"Le Temps des lilas" is actually an extract from a larger work for voice and orchestra called "Poème de l'Amour et de la Mer." Since that piece is the composer's Opus 19, we shall refer to the song as Opus 19-with-an-explanation!

Like so many of the poems used by Chausson, "The Time of Lilacs" evokes nature as a metaphor for the human condition, specifically the end of the flowering of spring and the death of love.

The piano begins with a simple statement of the sad little tune which is the mainstay of the melodic line. The tonic chord (D minor in the original key) is the sole harmony for the entire introduction, and the melody, in typical Chausson fashion, hovers around the dominant. The singer enters in unison with the piano's ongoing melody, but there is harmonic movement after only one measure, changing the effect of the third airing of the tune (under "Ne reviendra plus"). The constantly modulating accompaniment finally brings us back to the tonic. For the fourth repeat ("Le temps des lilas") the melody itself is altered (B♮ instead of B♭), and the lovely accompaniment leads us to a D major resolution (the tonic parallel major). This completes the first section.

The words to this point have been sad and wistful, but not tormented. The gently flowing melodic line and mildly undulating dynamics reflect this mood:

The time of the lilacs and the time of the roses
Will return no more this spring;
The time of the lilacs and the time of the roses
Is gone, the time of the carnations too.

In the next section tension begins to develop as the vocal line rises
in pitch and volume. The E♭ under "cieux" pulls against the accompaniment until the chord is filled in by the right hand, and the E♭ in
the next measure creates even more tension. The thrice-repeated climb
to F is, of course, the climax of the section. Immediately after the last
and most important F, we hear once again the original melody ("les
lilas en fleur"). The long *diminuendo* which follows brings us back to
the calmer mood and the original key. The words are now more personal and more pained:

The wind has changed; the skies are morose,
And no longer shall we run to gather
The flowering lilacs and the beautiful roses;
The spring is sad and cannot blossom.

The piano now has a five-bar interlude, very similar in feeling to
the music in another Chausson song, "Les Heures" (Opus 27/1). In
both cases the right-hand octaves seem to be a bell tolling the hours,
mourning the passage of time. There is a *crescendo* and an *accelerando*
in the last two bars of the interlude and then a sweeping arpeggio introduces a wild and stormy section.

At first the words seem ecstatic, but the fact that in this case the
memory of lost love brings anguish, not pleasure, is made clear in the
music, which is agitated (see the angular cross rhythm under "joy*eux
et doux prin*temps," the octave leap on "ensol*eiller*," the dissonance
under "fan*é*") and intense.

Oh! joyous and sweet springtime of the year,
Which came, last year, to engulf us in sunlight,
Our flower of love is so completely faded,
Alas, your kiss cannot reawaken it!

The climax is obviously at the G♯ on "Las," but the voice remains
strong until the end of the line. The accompaniment, however, has a
big *decrescendo* on its countermelody, so that the harmonic resolution
on the tonic is quiet.

The singer now asks a plaintive question:

And you, what are you doing? no budding flowers,
No gay sunshine or cool shade;

This is to be sung simply; the harmonies, while in constant motion,
are nevertheless simple major or minor triads. A dominant seventh
leads us back to a recapitulation of the opening bars:

The time of lilacs and the time of roses

There are important alterations in the melodic line for this last, most moving statement, namely the octave interval under "roses" and the rise which precedes it. The last line is completely new:

With our love is dead for ever.

It is a long sigh, beginning on the tonic, pausing on the dominant, and coming to rest on the mediant, where it intones the mournful "à jamais." The piano's brief coda whispers the refrain one last time before fading away.

Serres chaudes
Poems by Maurice Maeterlinck
OPUS 24

1. Serre chaude
Hothouse

O serre au milieu des forêts!
Et vos portes à jamais closes!
Et tout ce qu'il y a sous votre coupole!
Et dans mon âme en vos analogies!
Les pensées d'une princesse qui a faim,
L'ennui d'un matelot dans le desert,
Une musique de cuivre aux fenêtres des incurables.
Allez aux angles les plus tièdes!
On dirait une femme évanouie un jour de moisson,
Il y a des postillons dans la cour de l'hospice.
Au loin passe un chasseur d'élan devenu infirmier.
Examinez au clair de lune.
Oh! rien n'y est à sa place.
On dirait une folle devant les juges,
Un navire de guerre à pleines voiles
Sur un canal
Des oiseaux de nuit sur des lis
Un glas vers midi
(Là-bas sous ces cloches!)
Une étape de malades dans la prairie
Une odeur d'éther un jour de soleil
Mon Dieu! Mon Dieu!
Quand aurons-nous la pluie
Et la neige
Et le vent dans la serre!

The five songs of the cycle *Serres chaudes*, Chausson's Opus 24, are settings of poems from an early (1889) collection bearing the same title by Belgian-born Maurice Maeterlinck (1862–1949). Three years later this same writer published his *Pelléas et Mélisande,* on which Debussy's only completed opera is based.

Serres chaudes and *Pelléas* are examples of Materlinck's early style, in which his preoccupation with mystic symbolism borders on the surrealistic. The poems are full of strange, morbid images and there is a fairy-tale atmosphere of bizarre metaphors couched in the simplest of terms. We are often deep in a forest, far from familiar territory, fearful of being lost. In true symbolist fashion hothouses become hospitals, hunters turn into nurses, the thoughts of a hungry princess are compared to the boredom of a sailor in a desert, nocturnal birds lie on lilies, while a death knell tolls at high noon. As Maeterlinck says, "rien n'y est à sa place"—nothing is in its proper place.

Chausson's settings echo the vaguely threatening gloom of the poems. Nowhere in the cycle is there real solace or peace, much less pleasure or joy. Here the image of the hothouse, which can evoke happy associations of flowers and greens, brings to mind stifling heat and forced, unnatural growth.

The music of the first song is wild and passionate. The accompaniment is full of turbulent motion and the overall modality is minor. The piano begins with a broken-chord figure that continues through the first section, after which it is replaced by other sixteenth-note patterns. Only for the last ten bars of this extended song does the headlong motion in the piano part cease. The opening measures create a sense of foreboding and mystery as the singer begins in declamatory style:

> O hothouse in the middle of the forests!
> And your doors forever closed!

The piano rises above the vocal line at "à jamais closes!" and the strong sound of a B^9 chord is heard under the last word of the phrase. Excitement continues to build as the singer rises to Eb, the climactic note of the first section, after which there is a *diminuendo* and a brief pause to set off the words "en vos analogies!"

> And everything under your cupola!
> And in my soul in your analogies!

A short piano interlude in a higher register of the instrument creates a gossamer, fairy-tale effect. The words are intoned in long phrases of repeated notes, with only the last note breaking the monotone. The music is replete with hemiolas—2/4 time in the accompaniment superimposed on the 3/4 meter. The words exemplify the sealed hothouse's analogies—they are mysterious and bizarre:

The thoughts of a hungry princess,
The boredom of a sailor in the desert,

For the next phrase the melody develops some motion; a *cre-scendo* at its conclusion brings us a strong augmented chord on the high E.

A music of copper at the windows of the hospital for incurables

There is less turbulence for the next section despite the increased motion in the melodic line, which climbs to a high F at "infirmier."

Go to the warmest corners!
One would say there is a woman who has fainted on a harvest day,
There are coaches in the hospital's courtyard.
In the distance a deer-hunter turned nurse passes.

Another hemiola brings back the fairy-tale gossamer accompaniment, as the words offer an explanation of the strange imagery of the preceding verses:

Look closely in the moonlight.
Oh! Nothing is in its place there.

Pale, shimmering music accompanies the recitativo vocal lines:

One would say a madwoman before the judges,
A warship at full sail
On a canal

Rich chords under the continuing sixteenth notes display the full range of the impressionist composers' harmonic palette—diminished chords with major thirds on top, augmented chords, and a beautifully placed C major chord (under "Là-bas") which bursts forth like a ray of sunshine. Chausson shifts these resplendent sounds back and forth until the tremendous climax at "jour de soleil":

Nocturnal birds on lilies
A death toll towards noon
· (There, under these bells!)
A resting place for the sick in the prairie
An odor of ether, a day of sunshine!

A cascading arpeggio leads to a tremolo in the piano part, over which the singer cries:

My God! My God!

Finally the tremolo fades, yielding to solemn quarter notes, which inexorably march in the new 4/4 time until the end of the song. B minor, the key of the piece, is stressed in this coda, but the final chord is, surprisingly enough, on B major. The vocal line stays on the high F♯ for four long syllables and then returns to that note—the dominant—two bars later. The singer's last note is on the F♯ one octave below, but the supporting chord contains such a strong supension that we do not feel the arrival on the tonic until the very last chord, by which time the voice has faded away. A very strange ending to a very strange, very beautiful song. The last lines read:

> When will we have rain
> And snow
> And wind in the hothouse!

2. Serre d'ennui
Hothouse of Boredom

> O cet ennui bleu dans le coeur!
> Avec la vision meilleure,
> Dans le clair de lune qui pleure,
> De mes rêves bleus de langueur!
>
> Cet ennui bleu comme la serre,
> Où l'on voit closes à travers
> Les vitrages profonds et verts,
> Couvertes de lune et de verre
>
> Les grandes végétations
> Dont l'oubli nocturne s'allonge,
> Immobilement comme un songe
> Sur les roses des passions.
>
> Où de l'eau très lente s'élève
> En mélant la lune et le ciel
> En un sanglot glauque éternel
> Monotonement comme un rêve.

"Serre d'ennui," the second of the five *Serres chaudes,* is a little masterpiece. Its mood is languorous and melancholy, with solace finally offered by an ending in the major mode.

To grasp the meaning of the poem one must realize that "ennui" implies much more than boredom, its usual English translation: the French word connotes a mood compounded of weariness, dejection, and lack of energy or will, as well as boredom. After the defeat of Napoléon I and the crumbling of France's dreams of imperial glory, this condition was known as "le mal du siècle," the illness of the century, and most fashionable young men claimed to be afflicted with it. In this later symbolist generation, as Verlaine said, it was a worse pain, for its cause was unknown:

C'est bien la pire peine
De ne savoir pourquoi . . .
Sans amour et sans haine
Mon coeur a tant de peine!
Il pleure dans mon coeur

In true symbolist fashion, Maeterlinck equates this mood with a color, blue. Even in our anti-poetic era we claim to feel "blue" when depressed. Later in the poem he describes a sigh as "glauque," a pale sea green color, an image for which we have no counterpart. Everything in the poem is bathed in moonlight, moonlight that weeps on the dreamlike scene, moonlight that mingles with glass to cover the hothouse, the central image of the cycle.

Chausson's setting beautifully expresses the enervated languor of the text. For the first six measures the accompaniment's bass has a recurring tonic chord (E minor), alternating with varying harmonies. This repeated pull back to the tonic gives a melancholy, weary aura to the music. The melody begins on the high tonic note, which is held for three-and-a-half beats, and then descends pessimistically. The pianist must pedal the fifth measure discreetly, so that one hears the E minor chord created when the E and G whole notes held from the previous measure join the final eighth note of that bar. The melody rises again to the high E under "lune," only to fall once more at "pleure." The harmonization of "pleure" is the lovely diminished chord-plus-major third, so characteristic of this era. The chord under "rêve" is equally atmospheric, as is the ninth at "serre." The constantly shifting harmonies create an overall chromaticism well-suited to the vague scene described by the words:

Oh this blue ennui in my heart!
With the better vision
In the weeping moonlight,
Of my dreams, blue with languor!

This ennui, blue as the hothouse,
Where one sees it through
Closed windows deep and green,
Covered with moon and glass

A rather prosaic dominant seventh chord having brought the first half of the song to a close, one expects a tonic chord in the next bar, ("Les grandes . . .") but Chausson chooses to support the melodic V–I interval with a VI chord (C major). He then continues with an augmented D chord, followed by constantly shifting harmonies until we reach an E major^9, which halts the accompaniment's motion while the vocalist slowly sings "Immobilement." On the last syllable of this weighty word, we have a lovely double suspension resolving on an A^7 chord. This pattern, similar to the one used by Fauré in "Au bord de l'eau" (see p. 30), is graceful and charming, and Chausson repeats it under "songe" and "Monoton*ement*."

At "Où de l'eau" we have a recapitulation of the music of the first six bars of the song (the first measure in the recapitulation encapsulates bars one and two of the opening). The remaining measures refer to ideas previously encountered in the piece, until we reach the beautiful major ending. Without detracting from Chausson's genius, we should like to point out the close affinity of this work to songs of Duparc and Fauré. It is not a question of imitation, but of a shared aesthetic. The poem concludes:

> The great vegetations
> Which nocturnal oblivion lengthens,
> Immovably like a dream
> On the roses of passions.
>
> Where the water very slowly rises
> Mingling the moon and the sky
> In an eternal sea green sigh
> Monotonously like a dream.

3. Lassitude
Weariness

> Ils ne savent plus où se poser ces baisers,
> Ces lèvres sur des yeux aveugles et glacés;
> Désormais endormis en leur songe superbe,
> Ils regardent rêveurs comme des chiens dans l'herbe,
> La foule des brebis grises à l'horizon
> Brouter le clair de lune épars sur le gazon.
> Aux caresses du ciel, vague comme leur vie,
> Indifférent et sans une flamme d'envie
> Pour ces roses de joie écloses sous leur pas
> Et ce long calme vert qu'ils ne comprennent pas.

Four of the five songs of *Serres chaudes*, all but the first, are variations on the theme of world-weariness, apathy, boredom, absence of joy. While the first and fourth songs are quite tempestuous and therefore provide contrast, the moods of numbers two, three and five resemble one another, suggesting subdued, pessimistic melancholia. Most alike in musical setting are numbers three and five, in which solemnly paced quarter notes march inexorably from beginning to end. In both of these songs, but even more obviously in "Lassitude," the third, Chausson uses excessive repetition to underscore the agonizing weariness and sorrow that afflict the poet. During the course of this third song the opening bar is heard five times, and two additional measures begin the same way, changing only on the third beat. Since there are only twenty-eight measures in the piece (exclusive of the long held final chord), and since the repeated measure is three half notes long while many of the other measures are only two half notes in length, this repetition becomes oppressive, well conveying the dreariness of the mood.

The melody also makes much use of repetition, as one may see from the singer's very first phrase, which is sung all on one note. When the pitch finally changes it is only by a half step, and the new note is then repeated. There is a melodic interval of a third under "poser," but Chausson soon brings us back to the original note, the tonic. A chromatic rise to an A follows and then that, too, is repeated. This is characteristic of the vocal line for the major portion of the song.

The chords in the first two measures—heavy F♯ minor chords in the first and a G⁷⁺ in the second—set the harmonic style for the entire song. In the third measure the piano begins a countermelody, which must be brought out by very legato playing of the stemmed-up notes. The mood continues to be ponderous. The sudden change to a D minor chord (under "gardent") seems to lighten the mood momentarily, but the C♯ minor chord before "comme des chiens" is once again heavy and dramatic. This music, very much dominated by the F♯ minor tonality, takes us through the first six lines of verse:

> They no longer know where to put themselves, these kisses,
> These lips, upon eyes blind and cold;
> Even now, asleep in their superb dream,
> They, dreamers, like dogs in the grass, watch
>   the mass of grey ewes on the horizon
> Nibbling the sparse moonlight on the lawn.

At this point the central tonality shifts to D♯ minor. Even though the mode is still minor, the rise in *tessitura* for both voice and piano gives the music a lift. The E major chord under "vie" is a welcome excursion into the major mode, and the rising melodic line brings with it excitement and passion. The dynamics reflect this surge of life, thus we have a large *crescendo* to and beyond the high E's at "flamme" and "envie."

At "Pour ces roses" the melody begins its descent, accompanied by a *diminuendo*. On the way down, there is a lovely augmented chord under "roses" and another under "pas." At "Et ce long," the accompaniment returns to the much-repeated music of the opening, but the melody floats high above the chords, only gradually descending again and then never actually coming down as far as the low F♯. It is left to the piano to resolve the singer's last G♮ with a final tonic chord. The last four lines of this poem, which is written in rhymed couplets of Alexandrines (the classic twelve-syllable line), are:

> In the embrace of the sky, vague like their lives,
> Indifferent and without a flame of envy
> Towards these roses of joy open under their feet
> And this long calm green that they do not understand.

4. Fauves las
Weary Beasts

> O les passions en allées,
> Et les rires et les sanglots!
> Malades et les yeux mi-clos
> Parmi les feuilles effeuillées,
>
> Les chiens jaunes de mes péchés,
> Les hyènes louches de mes haines
> Et sur l'ennui pâle des haines
> Les lions de l'amour couchés!
>
> En l'impuissance de leur rêve
> Et languides sous la langueur
> De leur ciel morne et sans couleur
> Elles regarderont sans trève
>
> Les brebis des tentations
> S'éloigner lentes une à une
> En l'immobile clair de lune
> Mes immobiles passions!

In this poem it is the beasts who are weary, but they are the beasts that lie within man, the beasts of his passions—the yellow dogs of his sins, the hyenas of his hatreds, the lions of his loves. These once savage passions are immobilized by lassitude; they have become languid, impotent.

Chausson's setting is one of his most adventurous in terms of harmonic structure. The key signature of the piece is four flats, but one is left with no feeling of tonal center on either A♭ or F minor, the two possibilities. The last chord is an unresolved C^9 which might serve as a dominant to F minor, but nowhere do we have a satisfactory F minor chord. The only tonal guidelines are the several pedal points: the opening one on C, which lasts for five measures and moves to F, the second brief one on C beginning before "En l'impuissance," the eleven-bar passage on F which begins at "couleur," and the six-measure pedal point on C, which ends the piece. The constant harmonic motion above the stabilizing pedal points creates a curious effect—on the one hand we are rushing headlong from one sound combination to another, yet simultaneously we are bound to a single note for long stretches of time. One might risk interpreting this as Chausson's way of dealing with the innate contradiction of dispassionate passions. In any case if we had to define it, we might settle for "atonal with a strong pull towards F."

The music opens with a spurt of energy, all the more welcome after the oppressive heaviness of the previous song. Although the vocal line begins with groups of repeated notes, its rhythmic intensity and insistent chromatic rise assure exciting musical tension. When not using repeated notes for dramatic emphasis, the melody has unusual sweep and scope, rising and falling with great freedom. Interestingly enough, its becomes low-keyed and motionless at the phrase "Les lions de l'amour," surrounding the very words one might expect to arouse the strongest response with a hushed calm. This lull creates the first break in the flow of the words:

> Oh the long-gone passions!
> Both the smiles and the sighs!
> Sick and eyes half-closed
> Among the fallen leaves,
> The yellow dogs of my sins,
> The squinty-eyed hyenas of my hatreds
> And on the pale boredom of the hatreds
> The lions of love bedded!

After this brief moment of relaxation, we have what seems to be the beginning of a recapitulation. Although the music soon veers off in new directions, this repeat of the C pedal point we heard in the beginning serves as a structural signpost. We have already described the long pedal point on F, which affects most of the second half of the song. With the words "des tentations," calm begins to pervade the music; there is less motion in melody and harmony, as though in preparation for Maeterlinck's repeated use of the word "immobile." For four measures, under "une/En l'immobile," we hear nothing but F's in the accompaniment and mostly F's in the melody, but in its last five notes the vocal line rises to D♭, where it hangs suspended over a C^7 chord. At the singer's last syllable the piano begins its final pedal point on C. The expectation of an ultimate resolution to F is certainly raised, so the unresolved C^9 chord leaves one feeling vaguely unsatisfied. It is nevertheless a beautiful ending, one well-suited to the mood of the text. The poem concludes:

> In the impotence of their dream
> And languid under the languor
> Of their mournful and colorless sky
> They will watch without truce

The flock of temptations
Slowly depart, one by one
In the motionless moonlight
My motionless passions!

5. Oraison
Prayer

Vous voyez, Seigneur, ma misère!
Voyez ce que je vous apporte
Des fleurs mauvaises de la terre
Et du soleil sur une morte.

Voyez aussi ma lassitude,
La lune éteinte et l'aube noire;
Et fécondez ma solitude
En l'arrosant de votre gloire.

Ouvrez-moi, Seigneur, votre voie,
Eclairez mon âme lasse
Car la tristesse de ma joie
Semble de l'herbe sous la glace.

"Oraison," the last of the *Serres chaudes,* is a poignant prayer in which the poet describes his misery and begs God to show him His way. The last two lines of the text are the key to the central image of the cycle, the hothouse, although in this poem the term is never used:

Car la tristesse de ma joie
Semble de l'herbe sous la glace.

For the sadness of my joy
Seems like grass under glass.

Unfortunately the inescapable rhyme of "grass" and "glass" trivializes the thought in English. In French the word "glace" means ice as well as plate glass and mirror, rendering the image far more chilling in the original than in translation. Earlier in the poem the phrase "Des fleurs mauvaises de la terre" (Evil flowers of the earth) summons up Baudelaire's *Les fleurs du mal,* the seminal work for the entire symbolist movement.

Chausson's setting for this sorrowful litany is appropriately gloomy. The tempo indication "Pas trop lent" warns the interpreters against turning the solemn marchlike quarter notes into a funeral dirge, but it would be even more inappropriate to pace the piece too quickly. Despite rhythmic intricacies, the accompaniment's quarter notes move inexorably from measure to measure. One is reminded of a similar rhythmic inevitability created by Chausson in "La Caravane" (p. 202).

A single tonic chord (Eb minor) sets the stage for the singer's entry on Bb, the dominant. After five syllables on this note, the melodic line descends until we reach the end of the first phrase, after which a repeat of the first measure begins on the second line. The singer's next phrase is similar to the first, but the voice rises to a high Eb for "De fleurs mauvaises," and in the climactic line "Et du soleil sur une morte" we have a Gb and then a G♮. The musical tension produced by this high *tessitura* is emphasized by the forceful *crescendo* to and beyond the word "morte." The *diminuendo* in the next line, "Voyez aussi ma lassitude," follows the abruptly falling melody, which beautifully expresses the idea of lassitude. Although the harmonies selected by Chausson are all enormously evocative, none is so appropriately chilling as the D^{7+} on the last syllable of "solitude."

Unlike most music, which consists of four-bar units and multiples thereof, in this song the phrases are three measures long. This seems to push the music from line to line, with little pause between verses except after "de votre gloire," the end of the second stanza. The words to this point are:

> You see, Lord, my misery!
> See what I bring you
> Evil flowers of the earth
> And sun on a corpse.
>
> See also my weariness,
> The moon extinguished and the dawn black;
> And make my solitude fertile
> By sprinkling it with your glory.

The music for the last stanza is an encapsulated version of the setting of the first two. At "Ouvrez-moi" we have a recapitulation of the opening chords, and the melody is similar to the first two vocal phrases. The voice rises for "Eclairez," but this time goes no higher than F♮. Under the words "Car la tristesse de ma joie," the bass notes of the accompaniment descend chromatically to the Eb and then jump a fourth down, making the declamatory repeated notes and pathetic falling scale fragment of the melody even weightier and more lugubrious. The chord before "sous la glace," a wonderful combination of Bb and Ab minor, is a powerful suspension which makes the dominant seventh, to which it resolves, an arresting "beginning of the end." The final syllables are accompanied by yet another repeat of the opening measures, which finally melt into the tonic chord. The last stanza reads:

> Open your path to me, Seigneur,
> Brighten my weary soul

For the sadness of my joy
Seems like grass under glass.

Les Heures   Poem by Camille Mauclair
The Hours   OPUS 27/1

Les pâles heures, sous la lune
En chantant jusqu'à mourir
Avec un triste sourire,
Vont une à une

Sur un lac baigné de lune
Où, avec un sombre sourire
Elles tendent, une à une,
Les mains qui mènent à mourir;

Et certains, blêmes sous la lune,
Aux yeux d'iris sans sourire
Sachant que l'heure est de mourir,
Donnent leurs mains une à une

Et tout s'en vont dans l'ombre et dans la lune,
Pour s'alanguir et puis mourir
Avec les heures une à une,
Les heures au pâle sourire.

This brief song is a gem of structural unity. The tolling bell, the piano's right hand rhythmic figure on the dominant (the original key is E minor) never ceases from the first measure to the last, and the melody slowly pirouettes around the same note, but the beautiful harmonies prevent any sense of boredom or repetitiveness. The poem, with its refrainlike phrase, "une à une" (one by one), and its oft-repeated rhymes (each of the four verses has the same four final words: "lune," "mourir," "sourire," and "une"), is equally unified. Because of the repeated end sounds, the simplest word changes within the line become significant, and one feels no lack of interest in the text.

The bell tolls for one measure and then the singer begins:

The pale hours under the moonlight
Singing until death
With a sad smile,
Go, one by one

From the beginning the left hand of the piano joins the singer in a lovely duet. At "jusqu'à mou*rir*," the melody and its harmonization in the piano clash mournfully with the ostinato B. A highly chromatic measure leads to the next verse:

On a lake bathed in moonlight
Where, with a somber smile
They hold out one by one
Their hands which lead to death;

Once again, this time under "Elles tendent une à une," we have the melody note C clashing with the ostinato B. The clanging of bells often gives dissonant overtones, but these are so very doleful!

The third verse is heralded by two important notes in the piano:

And certain (hours), wan in the moonlight,
With rainbow-colored, unsmiling eyes
Knowing that this is the hour of death
Offer their hands one by one

The chords under "blêmes sous la lune," so characteristic of Chausson and Duparc, are particularly lovely; the E♯ G in the right hand under "l'heure" is ominous, as befits the words that follow.

At the beginning of each verse, including this last, the harmony returns to the tonic. This fourth verse closely resembles the first in lines one through three; in it the clash of the C against the B is more emphatic than ever (under "dans *l'ombre et dans la lune*").

And all go off into the shadow and the moonlight
To languish and then to die
With the hours one by one,

The final line is a long descent from E′ to E by way of the triad and the last three notes of the scale. The words are enigmatic:

The hours of the pale smile.

The dynamic scope of this song is severely limited. There are a few small *crescendos* within the *p* framework, but the strongest dynamic indication is the *mf* for piano before verse three. The last long *decrescendo*, starting as it does from a *p*, must fade away in a whisper.

Ballade   Poem by Camille Mauclair
                                                          OPUS 27/2

Quand les anges se sont perdus
Qui s'en venaient sur la mer
Les oiseaux les ont attendus
En criant éperdus
Dans le vent amer.

Quand les vaisseaux se sont perdus
Qui s'en venaient sur la mer,

Les oiseaux les ont attendus,
Puis, s'en sont állés dans le vent amer.

S'en sont allés jusqu'aux chaumières
Qui dorment au bord de la mer;
Et ils ont dit qu'étaient perdus
Les anges attendus.

S'en sont allés aux clochers des églises
Qui chantent selon la brise,
Et ils ont dit qu'étaient perdus
Les vaiseaux attendus.

Et la nuit les enfants étranges
Ont vu les ailes des anges
Comme des vaisseaux flotter au ciel,
Ont vu des voiles comme des ailes
Planer vers les étoiles.

Et mêlant les ailes, les voiles,
Et les navires et les anges,
Ils ont prié les enfants frêles,
Dans une ignorance blanche.

Of the three "mélodies" which comprise Opus 27 (published in 1896 under the bilingual heading "Trois lieder") only the first, "Les Heures," is well-known at the present time. That seems a shame, for "Ballade" is a pretty song, less powerful than its more famous opus mate, but full of lovely harmonies and certainly worthy of being heard.

All three texts were written by Camille Mauclair (1872–1945), a rather obscure poet who was better known as an art historian and fervent admirer of the Impressionist painters. In this poem he skillfully evokes the rocking rhythm of the sea. The hypnotic monotony of the sea's waves is reflected in his repetitious use of key words and phrases; the predominantly soft sounds ("anges," "oiseaux," "vent," etc.) are as fluid as the water.

The setting is typical of Chausson in its combined simplicity and sophistication. The opening tonic (A major) chord immediately yields to a characteristic augmented whole tone-based harmony, and the rhythmic pattern is the sparest possible rocking or barcarolle figure. The melody reflects the harmonic augmentation (with its altered note, F♮, on "se sont perdus") and the barcarolle rhythm. In the third bar we are gently led away from the tonic, as Chausson, in his characteristic style, begins to glide from harmony to harmony. The first verse reads:

When the angels became lost
Who were to come to the sea
The birds awaited them

Crying distractedly
In the bitter wind.

On the word "amer" Chausson reaches E minor, the minor of
the dominant. From that point he begins to create considerable musical
tension. The progression under "les ont attendus" six bars later is
quite compelling. It seems to settle on E major, but Chausson immediately moves to G♯ minor so that the harmonic motion persists. The
rhythm becomes more insistent as the piano figure changes under "le
vent amer." At this point we have reached A minor. The most interesting harmonic progression in the section is under "au bord de la mer"
(C minor to B♭⁺).

> When the ships became lost
> Which were to come to the sea,
> The birds awaited them,
> Then went off in the bitter wind.
>
> They went as far as the thatched cottages
> That sleep at the edge of the sea;
> And they said that were lost
> The awaited angels.

The rocking rhythm, halted in melody and accompaniment at
"Et ils ont dit," returns after "anges attendus." This pattern is repeated in the next verse, in which we also find a chord progression
similar to the one described above (under "selon la brise").

> They went to the bell towers of the churches
> Which sing according to the breeze,
> And they said that were lost
> The awaited ships.

(Grammatically we should naturally prefer "And they said that the
awaited angels [or ships] were lost," but that translation does not convey the cadence of the words.)

The music of the opening section now returns for the beginning of
the following stanza:

> And during the night foreign children
> Saw the wings of the angels
> Like ships sailing in the sky.

Chausson gives us a new melody for the fourth line:

> They saw the sails like wings,

At the end of this line an inner voice in the piano part (which must
be heard) leads directly to the closing section. The change in music

occurs before the logical division of the stanzas, one line later. Here we have a new figure in the accompaniment as well as fresh melodic material. The high point in this fairly limited vocal part (a half step more than an octave, from the E♭ above middle C to the E♮ above) occurs at the very end, but the *tessitura* is somewhat raised from "les enfants frêles" on. The melodic climb from "Ils ont prié" creates some tension in this rather bland song, and would seem to call for a *crescendo,* although none is indicated. However, the final ascent on the tonic triad (under "Dans une ignorance blanche") would probably be more effective as a fade out. The final lines read:

> Soar towards the stars.

> And mingling the wings, the sails,
> The ships and the angels,
> They prayed, the delicate children,
> In a pure innocence.

Les Couronnes   Poem by Camille Mauclair
The Crowns   OPUS 27/3

> C'est la fillette aux yeux cernés,
> Avec son air étonné
> Et ses trois frêles couronnes:

> L'une de fraîche pimprenelle,
> L'autre de vigne en dentelle,
> Dans la troisième une rose d'automne.

> Le pimprenelle est pour son âme,
> La vigne est pour l'amuser,
> La rose à qui voudra l'aimer.

> Beau chevalier! Beau chevalier!
> Mais il ne passe plus personne,
> Et la fillette aux yeux cernés
> A laissé tomber les couronnes.

The final song of Opus 27 is plaintive and tender. It describes a young girl with dark circles under her eyes who has bedecked herself in three leafy crowns, one of wildflowers, one of lacy vines, and one boasting a single autumn rose. Each tiara has a *raison d'être:* the first is for her soul, the second to amuse her, and the third for the handsome chevalier who will love her. But alas, no handsome chevalier appears, and the maiden allows her crowns to fall to the ground.

    Chausson's setting is elegant and innocent. The harmonies slip delicately from minor to major and back again throughout the song, beginning on A minor, settling on C major for the entrance of the vocal line, and drifting off on a unexpected C minor chord at the end. The melody proceeds diatonically step-by-step, with only one relatively wide leap at "La rose," the high point of the section. This brief phrase and the two "Beau chevalier!" phrases provide what little drama the song contains. The Db minor chord under "Mais il ne *passe* plus personne" has an appropriately chilling effect. The last three notes in the melody seem to call for a final resolution to an Eb chord. Instead Chausson gives us C minor, which ends the song with a curiously unresolved feeling. The words are:

> It is the maiden with darkly circled eyes,
> With her astonished air
> And her three fragile crowns:
>
> One of fresh burnet,
> Another of lacy vine,
> In the third an autumn rose.
>
> The burnet is for her soul,
> The vine is to amuse her,
> The rose for whoever wishes to love her.
>
> Handsome chevalier! Handsome chevalier!
> But no one else passes by,
> And the maiden with the darkly-circled eyes
> Has let the crowns fall.

Chanson de Clown Poem by Maurice Bouchor
Song of the Clown OPUS 28/1

Through alternating periods of Anglophobia and Anglomania, the French have always had special affection for one English writer, William Shakespeare. The Romantics of the 1830s, led by young Victor Hugo, regarded him as *the* important model for French writers, for his plays, unlike the works of the French seventeenth-century classicists (Racine, Corneille, and Molière), present a true-to-life mixture of tragedy and comedy, nobility and coarseness, strength and weakness.

Using the rather free French renditions of poet Maurice Bouchor, Chausson set to music four excerpts from Shakespearean dramas: "Chanson de Clown," "Chanson d'amour," "Chant funèbre," and "Chanson d'Ophélie." Of these only the third, "Chant funèbre," is not explored in this study, for it is written for chorus rather than for solo voice.

"Chanson de Clown" is based on a song sung by Clown, Olivia's servant, in the play *Twelfth Night* (translated by Bouchor as "Le Soir des Rois," which is the French equivalent of the Feast of Epiphany, the twelfth day after Christmas). The Duke, hopelessly in love with Olivia, asks to hear this "silly" song that "dallies with the innocence of love" (Act II, Scene IV). When heard out of context, the song seems to be a serious lament, and it is treated as such by Chausson. Perhaps Shakespeare was indulging in dramatic irony when he put these bitter words in the mouth of a clown.

We quote three versions of the text: Shakespeare's, Bouchor's rendition, and our own translation of Bouchor's lines.

Shakespeare:

> Come away, come away, death;
> And in sad cypress let me be laid;
>   Fly away, fly away, breath,
> I am slain by a fair cruel maid.
> My shroud of white, stuck all with yew,
>   O, prepare it!
> My part of death no one so true
>   Did share it.
>
>   Not a flower, not a flower sweet,
> On my black coffin let there be strown;
>   Not a friend, not a friend greet
> My poor corpse where my bones shall be thrown;
> A thousand thousand sighs to save,
>   Lay me, O where
> Sad true lover never find my grave,
>   To weep there!

Bouchor:

> Fuis mon âme, fuis!
> Je meurs sous les traits de la plus cruelle des vièrges.
> Viens, ô mort!
> Qu'on m'étende à la lueur des cierges
>
> Dans un cerceuil de noir cyprès. Qu'on m'en sevelisse loin d'elle
> Dans le blême linceul couvert de branches d'if,
> Qui, partageant mon sort, ami sûr mais tardif,
> De moins me restera fidèle.
>
> Que pas une fleur, une pauvre fleur
> Sur ma tombe ne soit semée,
> Pour moi que nul ami que nul voix aimée
> N'ait des paroles de douleur.
>
> Que je sois seul avec mes peines,
> Et laissez au désert blancher mes ossements,
> De peur que sur ma tombe, hélas! les vrais amants
> Ne versent trop de larmes vaines.

Translation from the French:

Flee my soul, flee!
I die under the strictures of the cruellest of virgins.
Come, oh death!
Let them lay me out in the glimmer of candles

In a casket of black cypress. Let them bury me far from her
In the pale shroud covered with branches of yew,
Which, sharing my fate, friend sure but late,
At least will remain faithful to me.

Let not a flower, a poor flower
Be scattered on my tomb,
For me let no friend, let no beloved voice
Have words of grief.

Let me be alone with my sorrows,
And let my bones whiten in the desert,
Lest on my tomb, alas! true lovers
Might shed too many vain tears.

Chausson's setting is heavy and sad. The voice, necessarily a low male voice, often moves downward in pitch while the upper line of the accompaniment rises. This device, used in the opening three bars, emphasizes the despair of the poor protagonist. A similar and even more lugubrious effect is created by the three measures at the end of the second stanza ("fidèle"), which are repeated at the end of the song.

The music is in the key of E minor, and, although the harmonies are in constant flux, the minor mode is fairly unrelieved. Chausson opens the song with an interesting harmonic progression—E minor to A diminished with a major third added, and back to E minor, a form of I–IV–I—and uses it with increasing effectiveness at various points in the song. We hear the I–IV–I under "vièrges/Viens," but the progression is to E♭ minor at "mort." Under "Qui, partageant mon sort, ami sûr" the progression is completed and extended (I–IV–I–IV). From the last syllable of "semée" to the word "aimée" we have I–IV–I–IV–I–IV–I and at its final appearance, from "De peur" through "hélas!" we hear I–IV–I–IV (the altered form of the IV, a diminished chord with a major third added, is understood). Obviously this very dramatic and passionate combination colors most of the song. One other progression should be noted—the antique sounding D minor–A minor–E minor after "douleur."

Chanson d'amour   Poem by Maurice Bouchor
Song of Love   OPUS 28/2

This second Chanson de Shakespeare is much lighter in feeling than the first. Sung by a higher male voice, accompanied in part in very high registers of the piano, it offers the hope that the cruel loved one might be touched by her swain's sadness and return his kisses after all. *Measure for Measure,* the play from which the song is taken, is, of course, a comedy where all ends well.

The song seems extraneous to the plot of the play, but actually describes the plight of one of the heroines, Mariana. It is sung, at the beginning of Act IV by an unidentified "boy," to the sadly troubled woman. When the Duke appears, Mariana apologizes for listening to the music. He replies ". . . music oft hath such a charm/To make bad good and good provoke to harm."

Mariana explains that this music suits her mood, for "My mirth it much displeased but pleas'd my woe." Chausson expresses this sentiment with the sad little chords which comprise the brief piano introduction. After the vagueness of the first two bars, he settles on a D minor (tonic) chord over which the singer enters. Melody and harmony are alike free and inventive, with much use made of diminished chords and suspensions. The melody rises passionately at "ces lèvres que j'adore," but its most effective moment is the half step down on "mensonge" (lie), a wonderful evocation of the dark evil of the word. Under the next word, "fut," we have a V^7 chord which cries for a I resolution. Chausson does not actually deny us the I chord, but he softens it with a beautiful suspension, thereby expressing in music the word "doux."

Under "le matin jaloux" we have a descending chromatic line in the vocal part countered by an ascending chromatic line in the accompaniment, a very charming device. At this point the first two lines of text are repeated. The music for this recapitulation is similar to the original in harmonic outline, but broken chords give much more motion than at first. At the word "doux," Chausson manages an equally soft effect with a different variant of the I chord and a change of rhythmic pattern.

Suddenly there is an impassioned outburst in the accompaniment, high in register. The singer joins in this new excited mood and the words now express hope ("Mai si malgré tout . . ."). As the singer remembers the kisses so vainly proffered in the past, the sense of exultation fades and the somber mood returns to end the song. Since Bouchor's poem is a free adaptation rather than a literal translation, we quote the original Shakespeare, the French text, and a translation of that text.

Shakespeare:

Take, O take those lips away,
    That so sweetly were forsworn;

And those eyes, the break of day,
    Lights that do mislead the morn;
But my kisses bring again, bring again;
Seals of love, but seal'd in vain, sealed in vain.

Bouchor:

Loin de moi, loin de moi ces lèvres que j'adore
Et dont le mensonge, hélas! fut si doux.
Ces beaux yeux que le ciel de mai prend pour l'aurore
Ces yeux qui rendraient le matin jaloux

Loin de moi, loin de moi ces lèvres que j'adore
Et dont le mensonge hélas! fut si doux.

Mais si malgré tout ma douleur te touche
Ah! rends-moi, rends-moi mes baisers ,
Sceaux d'amour qui furent posés
En vain sur tes yeux, tes yeux et ta bouche.

Translation of above text:

Far from me, far from me these lips that I adore
And whose lies, alas, were so sweet.
Those beautiful eyes that the May sky takes for the dawn
Those eyes which made the morning jealous

Far from me, far from me these lips that I adore
And whose lies, alas, were so sweet.

But if, in spite of all, my sadness touches you
Ah! bring back, bring back my kisses,
Seals of love which were placed
In vain on your eyes, your eyes and your mouth.

Chanson d'Ophélie   Poem by Maurice Bouchor
Ophelia's Song   OPUS 28/4

The text of this song is a translation by Maurice Bouchor of a
song Ophelia sings to the Queen in Act IV, Scene 5 of Shakespeare's
Hamlet. This is Ophelia's famous mad scene. The original English
words are:

He is dead and gone, lady,
    He is dead and gone;
At his head a grass-green turf,
    At his head a stone.
White his shroud as the mountain snow,
    Larded all with sweet flowers;
Which bewept to the grave did not go
    With true-love showers.

The song is brief, simple, and touching. In the play Ophelia accompanies herself by strumming on a lute. Chausson keeps his accompaniment to a minimum, most often using simple chords. The first really striking harmony comes in measure seven, before the words "une pierre." This is a foreboding sound. Equally ominous is the chord two measures later, just before "Un tertre," which resolves to the dominant minor (B minor in the original key of E minor). Bouchor's translation:

Il est mort ayant bien souffert, Madame;
Il est parti; c'est une chose faite.
Une pierre à ses pieds et pour poser sa tête
Un tertre vert.
Sur le linceul de neige à pleines mains semées
Mille fleurs parfumées,
Avant d'aller sous terre avec lui sans retour
Dans leur jeunesse épanouie
Ont bu, comme une fraîche pluie,
Les larmes du sincère amour.

Since the French words are quite different from Shakespeare's, it is necessary to translate them anew:

He is dead having suffered much, Madame;
He is gone; it is done.
A stone at his feet and—to rest his head—
A green turf.

The French words "tête" and "tertre" are quite similar in sound, so the singer must make sure that the r's sound clearly in the latter.

The melodic line for this first verse has been of limited range and color. The second verse has a little more motion in the accompaniment and the singer rises to an E on "Ont bu," giving the vocal line a bit more scope. Nevertheless, the overall effect is one of withdrawal, as Ophelia's dazed mind shrinks from painful realities.

On the snowy shroud freely are strewn
Thousands of perfumed flowers,
Before going under the earth with him forever
In their merry youth
They have drunk, like a fresh rainfall,
The tears of sincere love.

The most touching note in the whole song seems to be the flatted II on "sincere." This is, of course, supported by the F major chord, which resolves to E minor in the lovely final cadence.

La Chanson bien douce
The Very Gentle Song

Poem by Paul Verlaine
OPUS 34/1

Ecoutez la chanson bien douce
Qui ne pleure que pour vous plaire.
Elle est discrète, elle est légère:
Un frisson d'eau sur de la mousse.
La voix vous fut connue et chère,
Mais à present elle est voilée
Comme une veuve désolée;
Pourtant comme elle encore fière,
Et dans les longs plis de son voile
Qui palpite aux brises d'automne
Cache et montre au coeur qui s'étonne
La vérité comme une étoile.
Elle dit, la voix reconnue,
Que la bonté c'est notre vie
Que de la haine et de l'envie
Rien ne reste, la morte venue.
Accueillez la voix qui persiste
Dans son naïf épithalame.
Allez, rien n'est meilleur à l'âme
Que de faire une âme moins triste.
Elle est en peine et de passage,
L'âme qui souffre sans colère
Et comme sa morale est claire . . .
Ecoutez la chanson bien sage.

Much of the meaning of this song depends on the similarity of the two French words "pleurer" (to cry) and "pleuvoir" (to rain). In some forms they sound very much alike, hence the famous lines of another poem by Verlaine, "Il pleure dans mon coeur/Comme il pleut dans la ville" (set to music by Debussy). Awkwardly, but literally translated, this means "It cries in my heart as it rains in the city." This "Very Gentle Song" cries (pleure), but the accompaniment seems to suggest a gentle rain, and the fourth line, "Un frisson d'eau sur de la mousse," is a watery metaphor ("a trembling of water on the moss").

In characteristic fashion, Chausson establishes a piano figure and keeps it going through large sections of the piece. The mode is major (Eb major in the original key) and the overall effect is gentle. The singer begins immediately:

Listen to the very gentle song
Which cries only to please you.
It is discreet, it is light
A trembling of water on the moss.

At this point the ripply piano figure yields to a warmer accompaniment, in which the right hand has a beautiful *legato* melody and the left hand has rich arpeggios, some of them minor, some augmented, some highly chromatic. Under "voilée," raindrops are suggested by the left hand figure, which lasts for several measures. The voice is very often in unison with the piano's melodic line, but some beautiful effects are created by slight alterations (under "*chère*" the piano uses the singer's note as a harmonization; at "*chère*" the piano's G is an eighth note after the singer's). While the voice stays on A for a whole measure ("Mais à present . . .") the piano's melody continues to rise; it remains above the vocal line until they meet again at "voile."

The words for this section are:

> The voice was known and dear to you,
> But now it is veiled
> Like a desolate widow
> However like her, still proud,
> And in the long folds of her veil
> Which flutters in the autumn breeze
> Hides and reveals to an astonished heart
> The truth like a star.

At "étoile" the clear C major chord and new piano figure brighten the mood, which remains sweetly joyful almost to the end. The harmonies match this inspirational mood as do the words:

> It says, in familiar voice,
> That our life is kindness
> That of hate and envy
> Nothing remains, once death has come.

The piano interlude tenderly leads us back to the original rippling figure:

> Accept the voice that persists
> In its naive wedding song.
> Go, nothing is better for the soul
> Than to make (another) soul less sad.

As the quarter notes in the bass make the piano figure less fluid, the mood becomes more somber and tinged with sadness:

> It is in pain and transitory,
> The soul which suffers without anger,
> And as its moral is clear . . .
> Listen to the very wise song.

The long chords under "Et comme sa morale . . ." halt the flowing accompaniment for the first time, focusing attention on the message which follows. When the accompaniment begins again it is in the tonic,

E♭ major, but the unexpected flatted C in the third measure from the end injects a note of melancholy into the beautiful (VI♭+–I) final cadence.

Le Chevalier Malheur Poem by Paul Verlaine
The Knight of Unhappiness OPUS 34/2

Bon chevalier masqué qui chevauche en silence,
Le malheur a percé mon vieux coeur de sa lance.
Le sang de mon vieux coeur n'a fait qu'un jet vermeil
Puis s'est evaporé sur les fleurs au soleil.

L'ombre éteignit mes yeux, un cri vint à ma bouche,
Et mon vieux coeur est mort dans un frisson farouche.
Alors le chevalier Malheur s'est rapproché,
Il a mis pied à terre et sa main m'a touché.

Son doigt ganté de fer entra dans ma blessure
Tandis qu'il attestait sa loi d'une voix dure.
Et voici qu'au contact glacé du gant de fer
Un coeur me renaissait, tout un coeur pur et fier.

Et voici que fervent d'une candeur divine
Tout un coeur jeune et bon battit dans ma poitrine.
Or je restait tremblant ivre, incrédule un peu,
Comme un homme qui voit des visions de Dieu.

Mais le bon chevalier remonté sur sa bête,
En s'éloignant me fit un signe de la tête
Et me cria (j'entends encore cette voix):
"Au moins, prudence! Car c'est bon pour une fois."

It is obvious in this song that both Chausson and Verlaine, the composer and poet of "Le Chevalier Malheur," made conscious decisions to create a work of maximum dramatic impact. The words describe a mysterious masked knight, who silently dismounts and listens to the protagonist's woeful tale of love-gone-wrong. The text is lurid, with the poor lover's blood pouring on the flowers from his pierced heart, only to evaporate in the sun. When the knight touches the hapless lover with his armor-clad finger, the fatally wounded heart is reborn. One is doubtless meant to shudder at the glacial touch of the iron glove. At the end of the song the knight breaks his silence to warn our hero to be careful, for this miracle cure can never be repeated.

The music is replete with comparable dramatic touches. The key is C♯ minor, as the opening figure unequivocally establishes, so the D♯ in the melody at "chevauche" provides musical tension. Instead of the resolution of this tension at the tonic melodic note on "sil*ence*," a new pull is exerted by the sudden shift to an A octave in the accompaniment's bass, especially since the G♯ in the piano's right hand creates a highly dissonant effect (it is actually a suspension). Dramatic impetus is maintained, as the A♯ in the piano heralds the singer's A♯ at "Le sang" and introduces a rising chromatic line. The E minor chord at "sol*eil*" is startling, as is the accompaniment's C♯ octave which follows. The stark word "mort" receives an appropriately desolate F♮ supported by a D minor chord, and the octaves in the bass are ominous. The words thus far are:

> Good masked knight who rides in silence,
> Unhappiness has pierced my old heart with its lance.
> The blood of my old heart made only a vermilion gush
> Then it evaporated on the flowers in the sunlight.
>
> The shadow dimmed my eyes, a cry came to my lips,
> And my heart dies with a fierce shudder.

A rising figure in the piano part now breaks the music's flow to set the stage for the knight's actions ("Alors le chevalier Malheur s'est rapproché . . ."). The ominous octaves continue and there is no easing of tension. Minor, augmented, and diminished chords underscore the intensity at "Et voici qu'au contact glacé . . .". Even at the words "Un coeur me renaissait" (My heart was reborn), there are no joyous major chords to express the glad tidings, only a continuation of the diminished sound. Finally, however, at "tout un coeur pur et fier" (a heart all pure and proud), the heavy mood lifts, the dynamics drop to *mezzo piano,* and a heavenly arpeggiated E♭⁷ chord announces balm. This blissful music lasts through the words "ma poitrine":

> Then knight Unhappiness came near,
> He dismounted and his hand touched me.
>
> His finger, gloved in iron, entered my wound
> While he attested his law in a hard voice.
> And at that frigid touch of the iron glove
> A heart was reborn within me, a heart pure and proud.
>
> And so it was that fervently, with a divine candour,
> A whole heart, young and good, beat in my breast.

Although the music is still gentle at the beginning of this next section, the minor chord under "tremblant" brings back the earlier ominous feeling. Tension begins to build in the accompaniment's octaves, but to our surprise the return of the opening figure at "Mais le bon chevalier" is in the major mode, signaling that all is still right with the world. The C♯ minor tonality does reassert itself briefly at "cri*a*," but the final outcome is in the relative major, E major, so the song ends on a note of well-being.

At the risk of exposing a totally subjective appraisal, it must be said that the poem and setting seem obvious, overwrought and lacking in the sensibilities that make the bulk of this repertoire so enchanting. The poem concludes:

> Then I remained trembling, drunk, a little incredulous,
> Like a man who sees visions of God.

> But the good Knight, remounted on his beast,
> While withdrawing, nodded his head to me
> And cried to me (I still hear that voice):
> "At least, prudence! For it is good for one time."

Cantique à l'épouse
Canticle to the Wife

Poem by Albert Jounet

OPUS 36/1

> Epouse au front lumineux,
> Voici que le soir descend
> Et qu'il jette dans tes yeux
> Des rayons couleur de sang.
> Le crépuscule féerique
> T'environne d'un feu rose.
> Viens me chanter un cantique
> Beau comme une sombre rose;
> Ou plutôt ne chante pas,
> Viens te coucher sur mon coeur
> Laisse-moi baiser tes bras
> Pâles comme l'aube en fleur;
> La nuit de tes yeux m'attire,
> Nuit frémissante, mystique,
> Douce comme ton sourire
> Heureux et mélancolique.
> Et soudain la profondeur
> Du passé religieux,
> Le mystère et la grandeur
> De notre amour sérieux,
> S'ouvre au fond de nos pensées
> Comme une vallée immense
> Où des forêts délaissées
> Rêvent dans un grand silence.

Here we have a rare specimen, a love song to the poet's wife, which sings of contentment, peace, and fulfillment. As befits the words, the music is lush, warm, and calm. The mode is major, the original key is F.

The piano begins with a kind of pedal point on the tonic, but the melody soon reflects the intricate harmonic motion which begins after measure four. The return to the tonic is accomplished via a beautiful chord on D♭ at "couleur de sang." The vocal line is so harmonically conceived that it sounds almost ugly without the accompaniment.

The words begin:

Wife with luminous face,
Evening is now falling
And throws in your eyes
Rays the color of blood.

The piano interlude has a lovely melody, which breaks off for the singer's next lines:

The magical twilight
Surrounds you with red fire.
Come sing me a canticle
Beautiful as a dark rose;

Again the piano's melody bursts forth. At first it seems to settle on the tonic, but no, the harmonies continue their constant flow from one key to the next. In this song we do not feel agitation from all this harmonic motion, perhaps because the flow is so smooth, so seamless.

All motion stops briefly at "ou plutôt ne chante," which is all sung on one note over a single sustained chord. At the word "pas," which drops a half step to end the phrase, the piano's countermelody begins again, but the accompaniment is kept subdued and static.

Or rather don't sing,
Come to lie on my heart

A triplet figure in the accompaniment begins to create a sense of motion again, as the words become more impassioned:

Let me kiss your arms
Pale as the blossoming dawn;
The night of your eyes draws me.
Thrilling, mysterious night,
Sweet as your smile,
Happy and melancholy.

There are very few dynamic indications in this song, but the climactic line seems to be "Nuit frémissante, mystique." Here the singer has a high *tessitura*. (Actually the highest note in the song is found several lines back, under "Viens." This should be sung with some emphasis, but the section as a whole is gentle and quiet.) The accompanying chords have close, tension-producing intervals, the piano's rhythmic pattern is strong and angular, and the tempo has become more animated. By the next measure the accompaniment has calmed down, the melodic line is lower, and the return to the slower tempo of the opening of the song is about to begin.

After a quiet piano interlude the last section begins:

> And suddenly the profundity
> Of the religious past,
> The mystery, the grandeur
> Of our serious love,

The piano and voice have a full-fledged duet under this last line.

> Unfolds in the center of our thoughts
> Like an enormous valley
> Where abandoned forests
> Dream in a great silence.

The melody and chord progression at "au fond de nos pensées" is a repeat of the music at "Des rayons couleur de sang" (towards the beginning of the song). The piano has some embroidery at the F major chord, but the skeleton is the same. The Db–C at "ou plutôt," while harmonized completely differently, is a fragment of the same melodic material. These elements provide unity for a long song such as this, which has no real repeats.

At "Rêvent" the voice begins its climb to the dominant (C) on which the melodic line will end. The piano's melody climbs to the C with the singer and then rises further, to—and then beyond—the tonic F. The voice drops an octave to middle C while the piano returns to the tonic, but instead of coming to an end the piano continues with a beautiful, highly chromatic coda. It is as though Chausson, not wanting the piece to end, kept breathing new life into it. It is so lovely that one can hardly blame him!

Dans la forêt du charme et de l'enchantement	Poem by
In the Forest of Charm and Enchantment	Jean Moréas
	OPUS 36/2

> Sous vos sombres chevelures, petites fées,
> Vous chantâtes sur mon chemin bien doucement,
> Sous vos sombres chevelures, petites fées,
> Dans la forêt du charme et de l'enchantement.
> Dans la forêt du charme et des merveilleux rites,
> Gnomes compatissants, pendant que je dormais
> De votre main, honnêtes gnomes vous m'offrites
> Un sceptre d'or, hélas! pendant que je dormais.
> J'ai su depuis ce temps que c'est mirage et leurre

Les sceptres d'or et les chansons dans la forêt
Pourtant comme un enfant crédule, je les pleure
Et je voudrais dormir encor dans la forêt,
Qu'importe si je sais que c'est mirage et leurre.

The very first measure of this song plunges the listener deep into the "Forest of Charm (as in magic spells) and Enchantment." The piano figure suggests a magical steed flying through a silvery forest where the trees mysteriously give way, leaving an unobstructed path beneath his fleet hooves. If the verb endings sometimes seem unfamiliar, it is because they are in an infrequently used "once-upon-a-time" historical past tense.

The singer begins with a simple little scale fragment in the main key (G minor in the original):

Under your dark tresses, little fairies,
You sang very sweetly on my path

Along with the little fairies we have beautiful modulations along the way—the one to D minor under "douce*ment*" is the first to catch the ear.

Under your dark tresses, little fairies,
In the forest of charm and enchantment.

The Bb major resolution under "enchante*ment*" is another spellbinder, especially since it leads to a tinkly little countermelody in the piano part.

In the forest of charm and of magical rites,
Sympathetic gnomes, while I slept,
From your hands, good gnomes, you offered me
A gold sceptre, alas, while I slept.

The melodic line for "Dans la forêt du charme et des merveilleux rites" hews close to F, the temporary dominant. Its slightly ominous air is reinforced by the accompaniment under "rites," which sounds very scary indeed. A *crescendo* builds to a climax in the word "hélas." The accompaniment is no longer frightening—in fact the *diminuendo*, "retenu" indication, and gradual drop in register deliberately rob it of all its magic. Suddenly we are back in the real world of adulthood.

I have known since that time that it is mirage and delusion
Gold sceptres and songs in the forest
Nonetheless like a credulous child, I weep for them
And I should like to sleep again in the forest,
What does it matter if I know that it is mirage and delusion.

Fortunately, even the adult world has some beautiful moments, such as the harmonies from "chansons" to "pourtant." There is a buildup towards the big moment at "Qu'importe," with the piano re-capturing the movement if not the airborne quality of the earlier pages. These climactic measures convey an air of triumph: the poet has faced his disillusionment and refused to be daunted.

The piano, too, expresses this feeling at the end of the song, for in the coda it does return to the fleet, silvery figure of the introduction.

Henri Duparc

Chanson triste   Poem by Jean Lahor
Sad Song

Dans ton coeur dort un clair de lune,
Un doux clair de lune d'été.
Et pour fuir la vie importune
Je me noierai dans ta clarté.
J'oublierai les douleurs passées, mon amour,
Quand tu berceras mon triste coeur et mes pensées
Dans le calme aimant de tes bras!
Tu prendras ma tête malade
Oh! qualquefois sur tes genoux,
Et lui diras une ballade,
Qui semblera parler de nous,
Et dans tes yeux pleins de tristesses,
Dans tes yeux alors je boirai
Tant de baisers et de tendresses
Que, peut-être, je guérirai...

One of the cornerstones of the French art song is the little body of work by Henri Duparc. Known almost exclusively for his songs, this eccentric composer worked only from 1867 to 1885, although he lived until 1933. In each of his sixteen songs he creates a sensuous yet ethereal world, a world laden with mystery, sadness, and yearning.

"Chanson triste," or "Sad Song," has for its text a poem by Jean Lahor, a Symbolist poet whose natural pessimism led him to Oriental philosophies and the conviction that all was vanity. This poem, despite its title and the predilections of its author, does offer the hope that perhaps love can cure the suffering poet.

The song opens with arpeggios in the tonic, C major for medium voice (Eb in the original). From the second measure on, there is a little countermelody in the piano part created by the double-stemmed notes. It is difficult to bring these notes out because they are on weak beats; nevertheless they must be heard.

239

The voice begins simply with a melody that has the dominant tone (G) as its focal point. (The G under "lune d'été" is spun out for a remarkably long time.)

> In your heart sleeps a beam of moonlight,
> A sweet summer moonlight
> And to flee this troublesome life
> I would drown myself in your light.

The first of three vocal high points occurs on the E of "Je." The *crescendo* which leads to this small climax is helped by the motion of the root notes of the left hand arpeggios, which should be somewhat prominent. Again the melody returns to a G.

The bridge passage in the piano brings us to a new key, E major, but this tonality soon yields to others. The voice and piano are still strong, and there is another *crescendo*.

> I would forget past sorrows

Now there is a sudden *p*. The singer must resist the temptation to sing out on the F, because contrast is desired here:

> My love, when you rock my sad heart and my thoughts
> In the loving calm of your arms

The constantly shifting harmonies under the above lines permit no real tonal center to emerge, creating a feeling of restlessness and agitation.

The downward interval which begins the melodic line is heard now for the third time, in yet another key:

> You will take my sick head
> Oh! Now and then on your knees

A more obvious countermelody, and one that is much easier to play, appears under "tête *malade*." This time, when the high note of the phrase comes, the F♯ under "Oh!," a *forte* is not only allowed but requested. The countermelody in the piano part becomes more and more important until it finally emerges on its own (between "genoux" and "Et lui diras" and then again after "ballade").

> And recite a ballad
> A ballad which will seem to tell of us,

We have now returned to a clear C major tonality. The music is more serene, with less harmonic activity and agitation. One beautiful climax remains, at the F♮ under "Tant" (So many). This is the place which, in the first verse, required a *subito p*.

And in your eyes full of sadness
In your eyes then I shall drink
So many kisses and tendernesses
That perhaps I shall be cured . . .

The postlude continues the rocking motion and dominant-oriented melody. The inner voice, derived from the first counter-melody, lends harmonic interest and touching chromatic intervals.

Romance de Mignon
Poem by Victor Wilder
Romance of Mignon

Le connais-tu, ce radieux pays
Où brille dans les branches d'or des fruits?
Un doux zéphir
Enbaume l'air et le laurier s'unit au myrte vert.
Le connais-tu, le connais-tu?
Là-bas, là-bas, mon bien-aimé,
Courons porter nos pas.

Le connais-tu, ce merveilleux séjour
Où tout me parle encore de notre amour?
Où chaque objet me dit avec douleur:
Qui t'a ravi ta joie et ton bonheur?
Le connais-tu, le connais-tu?

Le connais-tu, ce radieux pays
Où brille dans les branches d'or des fruits?
Un doux zéphir
Enbaume l'air et le laurier s'unit au myrte vert.
Le connais-tu, le connais-tu?
Là-bas, là-bas, mon bien-aimé,
Courons porter nos pas.

Although the exact chronology of Duparc's songs is a matter of conjecture, "Chanson triste," "Sérénade," "Soupir," "Romance de Mignon," and "Galop" were published simultaneously as Opus 2. Of these five songs only "Galop" deviates from the sensuous style usually associated with this composer.

"Romance de Mignon" closely resembles another Duparc song, "L'Invitation au voyage," in its evocation of a vague, far-away place, "un radieux pays" (radiant land) where golden fruit shines in the trees and where everything speaks of love. It is also strongly reminiscent of the Goethe song "Kennst du das Land?" which may have inspired it. In "Romance," however, as we learn in the second verse, this, alas, is a lost love.

The piano begins the song with upper register tonic chords (E major in the original key) and a melancholy melody, also in treble clef, though for the left hand. The harmonic scheme is a simple I–V for the first nine measures, but the suspensions at the beginnings of the measures on the dominant lift the pattern from banality. The overall effect —due largely to the high *tessitura*—is celestial and awestruck.

The melodic line echoes this persistent I–V scheme—in fact the first two lines of verse are sung on nothing but E or B, the tonic and the dominant notes. Again, one senses a breathless wonderment in this total lack of melodic or harmonic motion.

Finally, at "Un doux zéphir" (a gentle breeze), the I–V pattern yields to new material, but there is still very little sense of motion. The piano repeats a diminished chord for five bars while the voice sings a melodic fragment, which returns to its original note after a small stepwise ascent, first with a whole step plus a half step, then with a half plus a whole. The difference is subtle enough to be overlooked unless the singer emphasizes it dynamically. At "le laurier" (the laurel tree), the voice rises (in what for this song is a wide interval) to the top of the diminished chord (F♮), obviously the climax of the first verse. The tonic pedal point, which has been heard or implied under this entire five-bar section, continues while voice and upper chords move harmonically. The chromatic step at "vert" (green) is especially telling in this context, for it moves the music—including the bass-note—away from the tonic. The section ends with a repeat of the four note phrase described above transposed to the new key. The same subtle change (whole step plus half, to half step plus whole) requires the same special attention on the part of the singer.

After the vocal part has concluded the first verse as quietly as possible, a sudden *crescendo* in the piano interlude leads to a new mood and a new key. When the singer reenters it is with an affirmative V–I* melodic interval to the high G. This momentary flurry of excitement gives the song much-needed dynamic contrast, and indeed, the whole next section is full of big *crescendos* and sudden drops to *pp*. The vocal *tessitura* is higher, there are more chromatic intervals, and more musical tension is created. Nevertheless the section ends sadly, quietly, and in the original key. The words for the first half are:

> Do you know it, this radiant land
> Where golden fruits shine in the branches?
> A soft gentle breeze
> Scents the air and the laurel is joined to the green myrtle.
> Do you know it, do you know it?
> There, there, my beloved,
> Let us hasten to bend our steps.

* In the original Flaxland edition the D♮ is inadvertently omitted.

Musically the second half of the song is an exact repeat of the first. The first hint in the text that something is amiss is the word "encore," "still" ("Où tout me parle encore de notre amour," where everything still speaks of our love). From there on the poem is explicit—love and happiness are over.

The piano postlude serves to bring the *tessitura* down to the lower register of the keyboard—gone, too, is the celestial aura of wonderment of the opening bars.

> Do you know it, this marvelous dwelling
> Where everything still speaks to me of our love?
> Where each object tells me with sadness:
> Who has snatched from you your joy and your happiness?
> Do you know it, do you know it?
>
> Do you know it, this radiant land
> Where golden fruits shine in the branches?
> A soft gentle breeze
> Scents the air and the laurel is joined to the green myrtle.
> Do you know it, do you know it?
> There, there, my beloved,
> Let us hasten to bend our steps.

Sérénade   Poem by Gabriel Marc
Serenade

> Si j'étais, ô mon amoureuse,
> La brise au souffle parfumé,
> Pour frôler ta bouche rieuse,
> Je viendrais craintif et charmé.
>
> Si j'étais l'abeille qui vole,
> Ou le papillon seducteur,
> Tu ne me verrais pas, frivole,
> Te quitter pour une autre fleur.
>
> Si j'étais la rose charmante
> Que ta main place sur ton coeur
> Si près de toi toute tremblante
> Je me fanerais de bonheur.
>
> Mais en vain je cherche à te plaire,
> J'ai beau gémir et soupirer.
> Je suis homme, et que puis-je faire? . . .
> T'aimer . . . Te le dire . . . Et pleurer!

This wistful Sérénade, with its gently rocking 6/8 rhythm, touches the heart with its simple beauty. Although the harmonic genius of its composer is apparent, it is less complex in its modulations than most of Duparc's songs, relying for long stretches on alternating broken chords (I–III–V–I for the first six bars of stanza one and the opening of stanza two) and a melodic line derived from those triads. The first real move away from the tonic, under the words "Pour frôler," takes us in orthodox fashion to the relative minor and its dominant (from G to E minor in the original key), but the last three measures of the first stanza contain the more typical chromatic, shifting tonalities which are Duparc's wont.

The structure of the song is based on that of the text, a poignant poem by Gabriel Marc in four four-line stanzas. There is a key change (to E major) between the first two stanzas, but the transition is smoothed by the use of the dominant of the new key at the end of the first section. The second stanza begins with the same material as the first, merely transposed to the new key, but instead of the switch to the relative minor at the third line, we retain the E major tonality, leaving it for a beat or two but always returning. Only in the piano interlude between stanzas three and four do we actually modulate back to the original key. This is most appropriate to the text, which is a declaration of steadfastness and fidelity:

If I were, oh my love,
The perfumed breath of the breeze,
To brush your laughing lips
I would come, fearful and charmed.

If I were the bee which flies,
Or the seductive butterfly,
You would not see me, frivolous,
Leave you for another flower.

The music for the first two lines of the third stanza duplicates that of the opening lines, save for the inclusion of an extraneous note in three of the four chords (the pattern is repeated). These unexpected notes, C, C♯, and E respectively, color the basic I, III, V chords. Increased harmonic motion and a more active melodic line with higher top notes than previously encountered underscore the rising tension in the words of the third and fourth lines:

If I were the charming rose
That your hand places on your heart
So near you, all atremble,
I would wither with happiness.

Unlike the others, the final verse eschews the song's characteristic melody, nor does the text begin "If I were," as it had in the other stanzas. Instead, Duparc gives us a melodic line full of dramatic intensity created by the insistent Ds and Es under "J'ai beau gémir et soupirer." Suddenly, after a rising arpeggio, the accompaniment breaks its flowing figure for the first time. A quiet chord sets off the despairing words (sung *quasi recitativo* according to the composer's instructions) "Je suis homme, et que puis-je faire?" After this pitiful plaint the piano's sixteenth note figure begins again. The final words, "T'aimer . . . Te le dire . . . Et pleurer!" are separated by long pauses for voice and piano. These two bars encapsulate the basic harmonic ideas of the song, after which the piano reiterates the G major tonality. The last verse reads:

> But in vain I seek to please you,
> Uselessly I lament and sigh.
> I am a man, and what can I do?
> Love you . . . Tell you . . . And cry!

Soupir   Poem by Sully-Prudhomme
Sigh

> Ne jamais la voir ni l'entendre,
> Ne jamais tout haut la nommer,
> Mais fidèle, toujours l'attendre,
> Toujours l'aimer!
> Ouvrir les bras, et, las d'attendre,
> Sur le néant les refermer!
> Mais encor, toujours les lui tendre
> Toujours l'aimer.
> Ah! ne pouvoir que les lui tendre,
> Et dans les pleurs se consumer,
> Mais ces pleurs toujours les répandre,
> Toujours l'aimer . . .
> Ne jamais la voir ni l'entendre,
> Ne jamais tout haut la nommer,
> Mais d'un amour toujours plus tendre
> Toujours l'aimer. Toujours!

This must be one of the most touching songs ever written. Each phrase in the accompaniment is a sigh, each line of the poem a cry of pain. The exquisite harmonies, be they minor, major, diminished or augmented, all seem laden with sorrow—not even the last four measures, all in the major mode, alleviate the despair.

The poet, Sully-Prudhomme (1839–1907), was a scientist as well as a poet. This unusual combination of talents produced a lucid, transparent style, free of affectation. His poetry tends to be intimate, personal and direct.

The brief piano introduction sets the mood and announces the main harmonic devices to be used throughout the song: frequent pedal points on the dominant (F♯ for medium voice), the extension of a dominant-seventh chord by added thirds, and the building of chords by adding notes one at a time.

The singer's first two lines are derived from dominant chords. Their downward curves well suit the heart-rending words:

Never to see her or hear her
Never to say her name aloud,

The accompaniment now moves to the tonic (B for medium voice, D in the original) but the melody still weaves its way around the dominant:

But faithful, always to wait for her, always to love her
To open my arms, and, weary of waiting,
To close them on emptiness,
But yet, always to offer them to her
Always to love her

There had been almost no harmonic motion under the first four lines, but under the next four there is constant modulation. Intense harmonic activity always creates a sense of excitement and tension, so a gentle climax on "Mais encor, tou*jours*" (F♮) seems appropriate.

At the cadence we have a modulation to D major (the relative major) and a temporary cessation of harmonic motion. The intensity of the vocal line, however, increases:

Ah! only to be able to offer them to her,
And then be consumed in tears,

The harmonies under "pleurs se consumer" are particularly haunting, as is the plaintive chromatic passage for piano solo which follows. The repeated E in the melody is even more morose, and the A♯ of the next "Toujours l'aimer" tears at the heart.

But these tears always flow,
Always to love her . . .

Now the words and music of the beginning of the song return, with but a slight variation in the text:

Never to see her or hear her,
Never to say her name aloud,
But with a love ever more tender
Always to love her. Always.

The last "toujours" is little more than a heart-broken whisper.

Le Galop
The Gallop

Agite, bon cheval, ta crinière fuyante,
Que l'air autour de nous se remplisse de voix,
Que j'entende craquer sous ta corne bruyante
Le gravier des ruisseaux et les débris des bois.

Aux vapeurs de tes flancs mêle ta chaude haleine,
Aux éclairs de tes pieds ton écume et ton sang.
Cours, comme on voit un aigle, en effleurant la plaine,
Fouetter l'herbe d'un vol sonore et frémissant.

Allons! Les jeunes gens, à la nage, à la nage,
Crie à ses cavaliers le vieux chef de tribu,
Et les fils du désert respirent le pillage,
Et les chevaux sont fous du grand air qu'ils ont bu.

Nage ainsi dans l'espace, ô mon cheval rapide,
Abreuve-moi d'air pur, baigne-moi dans le vent.
L'étrier bat ton ventre, et j'ai lâché la bride.
Mon corps te touche à peine, il vole en te suivant.

Brise tout, le buisson, la barrière ou la branche.
Torrents, fossés, talus, Franchis tout d'un seul bond.
Cours, cours, je rêve et sur toi, les yeux clos, je me penche,
Emporte, emporte-moi dans l'inconnu profond!

Since Duparc is best known for such exquisitely atmospheric songs as "L'Invitation au voyage," "Chanson triste," and "Soupir," this *con fuoco* (fiery) evocation of a wild ride on horseback seems quite out of character for him. Later we shall encounter Duparc in a similar mood in "Le Manoir de Rosamonde," whose tumultuous piano part also describes a galloping steed. In the song, "Le Galop," the piano's insistent chords and bravura chromatic scale fragments carry us on a headlong dash through woods, streams and plains.

The poem, written by scientist-poet Sully-Prudhomme (1839–1907) is in his usual straightforward, unaffected style. Hard, crackling sounds such as "crinière" and "craquer," and sharp double s's, as in "remplisse," "ruisseaux," and "frémissant" contribute to the relentlessly driving aura of the text. As is common among poets of the Parnassien school, Sully-Prudhomme uses a specific technical vocabulary: "l'étier" (the stirrup), "la bride" (the bridle), and the like. The last of the five four-line stanzas begins with the marvelously alliterative "Brise tout, le buisson, la barrière ou la branche." In the last line the poet allows the philosophical overtones of his words to become clear, as the rider urges his horse to carry him ever onward "into the profound unknown."

Duparc's setting begins with a four-bar introduction in which the piano states its characteristic figure: repeated chords in one hand and a descending chromatic scale fragment in the other. This somewhat obvious device creates the desired excitement and forward motion, and Duparc uses it for the first two stanzas, most of the last stanza, the introduction and the postlude.

The melody begins with an agitated rising triad from the G minor tonic chord (the opening C♯ is merely a leading tone) and continues to adhere closely to the main key (see the solid V–I under "remplisse de voix") until the modulation at the end of the stanza ("débris des bois").

> Toss your flying mane, good horse,
> Let the air around us be filled with voices,
> Let me hear crackling under your clattering hoof,
> The gravel of the streams and the debris of the woods.

In the second stanza, the melodic leaps become wilder (a ninth under "aux vapeurs") and more dramatic, as the words describe the beast becoming overheated from his exertions. The accompanying chords reflect the mounting tension with equally dramatic leaps in both hands. The dynamic peak in this generally loud section is at "Aux éclairs" after which there is a gradual *diminuendo* to a *piano* at the end of the stanza. This section is replete with modulations, ending on A minor.

> The steam from your flanks mingles with your hot breath,
> With the sparks from your feet, your foam and your blood.
> Run as one sees an eagle, skimming over the plain,
> Whipping the grass with a sonorous and trembling flight.

The third stanza begins with a sudden *fortissimo* and a change in the accompaniment. The vocal part has a dramatic octave drop, emphasized by an abrupt drop in dynamics to a *piano*. There is a rapid *crescendo* for the repeat of the *ff* Es at the second "Allons," which is now harmonized in E major instead of A minor. Once again a *crescendo* accompanies the rising melodic line under "les jeunes gens, à la nage, à la nage." Here the piano has simple chords, but at "Et les chevaux," another dynamic high point, the piano begins a dotted rhythmic figure in imitation of the horse's gallop.

> Let's go! Young men, into the water, into the water
> The old chief of the tribe cries to the horsemen,
> And the sons of the desert smell the plunder,
> And the horses are mad with the great air they have drunk.

The fourth stanza is heralded by a key change (E major) and a change in style. While still marked "passionato," the music is now more flowing, less disjointed than before, for the horse is now seen as swimming or flying through space. The rider drinks in the pure air and is bathed in the wind. Gradually the dynamics increase and the tumultuous race begins again, accompanied once more by dotted rhythms and disjointed chords. The bridge between the fourth and final stanzas brings us back to the original key and characteristic piano figure.

> Swim thus in space, oh my swift horse,
> Let me drink of the pure air, bathe me in the wind.
> The stirrup beats your belly, and I have loosened the bridle.
> My body scarcely touches you, it flies while following you.

Although based on the same tonic triad with which the vocal part begins, the melody for the final stanza is more dramatic because of its initial octave drop. This is, after all, the culminating section of this long melodrama! The *stringendo* marked at "Cours, cours" implies a headlong rush to the end, as the rider urges his horse on to greater and greater speed. The brief excursion into G major, begun at "toi, les yeux," makes the return to G minor at "profond!" an effective finale. The *diminuendo* at the end does not necessarily imply any slackening of speed, although a tiny retard at the last measure might be appropriate.

> Break everything, the brush, the barrier, the branch.
> Torrents, ditches, embankments, crossed with a single leap.
> Run, run, I dream and over you, eyes closed, I lean,
> Carry me, carry me into the profound unknown.

L'Invitation au voyage   Poem by Charles Baudelaire
Invitation to the Voyage

> Mon enfant, ma soeur,
> Songe à la douceur
> D'aller là-bas vivre ensemble,
> Aimer à loisir,
> Aimer et mourir
> Au pays qui te ressemble!
> Les soleils mouillés
> De ces ciels brouillés
> Pour mon esprit ont les charmes
> Si mystérieux
> De tes traîtres yeux,
> Brillant à travers leurs larmes.
> Là, tout n'est qu'ordre et beauté,
> Luxe, calme et volupté.

Vois sur ces canaux
Dormir ces vaisseaux
Dont l'humeur est vagabonde;
C'est pour assouvir
Ton moindre désir
Qu'ils viennent le bout du monde.
Les soleils couchants
Revêtent les champs,
Les canaux, la ville entière,
D'hyacinthe et d'or;
Le monde s'endort
Dans une chaude lumière!
Là, tout n'est qu'ordre et beauté,
Luxe, calme et volupte!

This is a song full of the mystery and allure of never-never land. Baudelaire, author of its text, was so enraptured by the sentiments he himself had expressed in the poem that he later made a second version of it, a "prose-poem." From this latter piece it would seem that Baudelaire had a specific place in mind, *les Pays-Bas* (the Lowlands, or Holland), but the music seems to describe some unearthly, unattainable paradise.

The piano opens with one of Duparc's favorite harmonic progressions—the tonic minor to a II^7 chord with a lowered fifth. These two chords alternate until measures eight and nine where we have a diminished II to a glorious tonic major. This unexpected modulation, accompanied by a rapid *crescendo,* is like the sun bursting through the haze.

The melodic line is derived from these harmonies. At first it rocks back and forth, then it soars up to its first climax at "en*sem*ble." The words to this point have been:

My child! my sister,
Think of the sweetness
Of going to live there together,

We now have a pedal point on A (the key is A minor for medium voice, C minor in the original) with harmonies shifting around this open A chord. The melody is based on the dominant (E).

To love in leisure
To love and to die
In the land which is so like you!

The predominant A and D chords yield to diminished chords on E momentarily (under "res*sem*ble"), but the pedal point A continues.

The damp suns
Of these variable skies

For my spirit have the mysterious charms
Of your treacherous eyes,
Shining through their tears.

At this point we have the same melody and accompaniment we had at the first triumphant major chord, but now the composer demands a *diminuendo* instead of a *crescendo,* and the high E is soft and distant.

The constantly moving piano figure stops abruptly and long chords accompany the refrain:

There, all is order and beauty,
Luxury, calm, and sensuality.

Each line has but one single note—the tonic first and then the dominant, and the pedal point A chord rings through all eight measures. The effect is one of frozen beauty and complete stillness.

After the *fermata,* the piece begins again with the same musical material but new words:

See on these canals
The vessels sleep
Whose nature is vagabond;

A countermelody is now added to the piano part. This is the same melody given to the singer for "Aimer à loisir, Aimer et mourir," and it makes a beautiful duet with the singer's line.

It is to fulfill your least desire
That they come from the ends of the earth.

At the *forte* under "vie*nn*ent," the ever present A pedal point finally yields to a rather unanticipated B octave, the V of the E chord which is its resolution.

A new piano figuration ripples along under a fresh melodic line:

The setting suns
Once again clothe the fields
The canals, the whole city,
In hyacinth and gold;
The world sleeps in warm light

Under this last line the old familiar melodic fragment, which announces the A major climax, has been reintroduced. This time it is marked *ff* and the *diminuendo* does not begin until the next bar. From this resplendent return we never again lose the A tonality under the piano figure, nor is there much real harmonic movement in the figure itself. The refrain is heard again, this time even more quietly than before. The piano's countermelody is now paired with these single note lines.

The composer warns against slowing down too much for the fade-out ending, because he has built in the *ritard* by increasing the value of the notes. The steady *diminuendo* from a *pp* to a *ppp* makes of the closing bars only the slightest whisper.

La Vague et la cloche   Poem by François Coppée
The Wave and the Bell

Une fois, terrassé par un puissant breuvage,
J'ai rêvé que parmi les vagues et le bruit
De la mer je voguais sans fanal dans la nuit.
Morne rameur, n'ayant plus l'espoir du rivage . . .
L'Océan me crachait ses baves sur le front,
Et le vent me glaçait d'horreur jusqu'aux entrailles,
Les vagues s'écroulaient ainsi que des murailles
Avec ce rythme lent qu'un silence interrompt . . .
Puis, tout changea . . . la mer et sa noire mêlée sombrèrent . . .
Sous mes pieds s'effondra le plancher de la barque,
Et j'étais seul dans un vieux clocher,
Chevauchant avec rage une cloche ébranlée.
J'étreignais la criarde opiniâtrement,
Convulsif et fermant dans l'effort mes paupières,
Le grondement faisait trembler les vieilles pierres
Tant j'activais sans fin le lourd balancement.
Pourquoi n'as-tu pas dit, ô rêve, où Dieu nous mène?
Pourquoi n'as-tu pas dit s'ils ne finiraient pas
L'inutile travail et l'éternel fracas
Dont est fait la vie, hélas, la vie humaine!

Since this song was originally conceived for voice and orchestra, the pianist must make the accompaniment as orchestral as possible: the surging figure in the bass must be massive and sonorous; the frequent tremolos should remind one of a string section in full vibrato; the dynamic range must be wide with full rich *fortes* and whispered *pianissimos*. The composer's instruction gives us the key word—"tumultuous."

The title of the poem contains a word, "Vague," which has two meanings in French: wave or billow, and uncertainty or vagueness. It is clear from the text that the poet is describing the waves of a wildly stormy sea, but the secondary connotation is there on a subconscious level. In fact in the last few lines, the poet does refer to the uncertainty of life itself.

The piano introduction begins with an E minor (original key) arpeggiated figure which suggests the stormy sea. The singer begins "simply and without nuance" as though telling a story:

> Once, felled by a powerful brew,
> I dreamed that midst the waves and the noise
> Of the sea

A rush of thirty-second notes in the piano leads to a section full of foreboding. One is reminded, perhaps, of Edgar Allan Poe's "The Descent into the Maelstrom" (poets and musicians of this era were much smitten with and influenced by Poe's eerie tales).

> I rowed without signal lantern in the night
> Mournful rower, having no more hope of (reaching) shore ...

Another thirty-second note run leads us back to the original piano figure, but after four measures we have new material. The piano's tremolo shimmers in a higher register for a moment, then a rapidly descending arpeggio and low register octaves bring us back into the deep. This agitated jumping from register to register exudes musical tension.

The melodic line often clashes with the ornaments in the piano part (under "*crachait*," "*sur*," "*glaçait*," "*jusqu'aux*"), but becomes consonant with the main notes. There is a strange pedal point effect on F♯—the melody is derived at first from the diminished chord on F♯ and then from an F♯ triad. Both words and music are chilling:

> The ocean spat its foam on my forehead
> And the wind froze me with horror to my entrails,

At "horreur" the harmony moves to C♯:

> The waves tumbled like walls
> With that slow rhythm that a silence interrupts ...

The rush of thirty-second notes has this time (under "Avec ce rhythm") brought the ostinato chords and melody to B, the dominant. From the tremendous *ff* climax on "ainsi," there has been a steady *diminuendo,* but the piano's sweeping scales bring us back to *ff*.

Still on the one note—B—the singer continues his remarkable tale:

> Then, everything changed ...

Soft tremolos in the bass provide the barest of accompaniments:

> The sea and its black whirl subsided

From an ominous *pp* we now have a tremendous *crescendo:*

Under my feet collapsed

"A pleine voix," the instruction to the singer, means at full voice. Obviously here the singer must use all his forces to soar over the stormy piano part and bring out the excitement of this climactic moment. After this outburst piano and voice subside, and—in declamatory style ("déclamé")—the singer intones on repeated notes, for the most part unaccompanied:

the floor of the boat...

A quick *crescendo* growling deep in the bass of the piano leads to the sudden *pp* of shimmering tremolo B and E chords.

There is a long suspenseful pause; then heavy ("lourd") chords in the bass repeat their dark pattern for 18 consecutive measures. The singer continues his story:

And I was alone in an old bell tower,
Riding furiously on a swinging bell,
I gripped the bawler (bell) stubbornly,
Convulsive and closing my eyelids in the struggle,
The roaring made the old stones tremble,
So much did I ceaselessly quicken the heavy swinging.

Throughout this entire section there has been a steady buildup of sound and musical tension. One feels the bell swinging more and more wildly and more and more out of control. Now it is Poe's "The Pit and the Pendulum" that comes to mind.

The music for the next section is even more descriptive; the heavy chords continue the rocking motion, and the left hand crosses over to give us the bell's pealing. The accompaniment becomes less noisy for the singer's plaintive question:

Why didn't you say, oh dream, where God is leading us?...
Why didn't you say if it will not end
The useless work and eternal din
Of which life is made, alas, human life.

After all the sound and fury this song ends not with a bang but with a whimper. The pedal point on the dominant, so characteristic of Duparc, lasts for fourteen measures, after which it finally yields to the ominous harmonies first found in measures 15–19. The last few bars are, of course, in the tonic, E minor.

The harmonic structure of this extended song gives it a sense of cohesiveness; through its many changes of mood we feel the logical flow of musical ideas. Even the abrupt shift in text, from straightforward narration to philosophical musing, does not disturb this overall structural unity.

Extase
Ecstasy

Poem by Jean Lahor

Sur un lys pâle mon coeur dort
D'un sommeil doux comme la mort...
Mort exquise, mort parfumée
Du souffle de la bien-aimée...
Sur ton sein pâle mon coeur dort
D'un sommeil doux comme la mort...

It is a quiet, calm sort of ecstasy depicted in this song. There are no wild, tumultuous outbursts—it is an ecstasy of repose and fulfillment.

The piano opens on the dominant, but the bass note is the V of V, which makes the harmonic progression far from obvious. In fact the whole question of tonal center is of interest here, because it is not until the last few measures of the song that any one key becomes prominent enough to warrant being called its main tonality. Most of the emphasis is on the V of V (or the II) and the V, hardly any on the I, until the piano postlude.

As in so many songs by Duparc and Chausson, there are long pedal points, which need help from the middle pedal if they are to be sustained without blurring the chords above them.

Considering the length of the song, the piano prelude, interlude and postlude are quite long. In fact the voice appears in fewer than half the measures of the piece. When the voice does enter, it is with a highly chromatic melody of very narrow range:

On a pale lilly my heart sleeps
A sleep sweet as death...

In the next measure ("*Mort ex*quise") we finally hit the tonic (D major in the original key) for the first time. Here the singer's line begins to take on more scope.

Exquisite death, death perfumed
With the breath of the beloved...

This phrase ends with an octave interval, which is an extremely wide and expressive one. The vocal line has become more ecstatic here, and the piano interlude continues this "carried away" feeling for a while, but the original quiet mood returns for the final verse. The harmony begins with a II chord instead of the V, but the melody is the same.

On your pale breast my heart sleeps
A sleep sweet as death...

The beautiful chord under "mort" (death) leads into the postlude, whose main function seems to be the belated establishment of the tonic.

Henri Duparc • 255

Lovely melodic fragments taken from the vocal line (particularly from "Mort exquise") bring the song to a close.

Sérénade florentine
Florentine Serenade

Poem by Jean Lahor

Etoile dont la beauté luit
Comme un diamant dans la nuit,
Regarde vers ma bien-aimée
Dont la paupière s'est fermée.
Et fais descendre sur ses yeux
La bénédiction des cieux.
Elle s'endort . . . Par la fenêtre
En sa chambre heureuse pénètre;
Sur sa blancheur, comme un baiser,
Viens jusqu'à l'aube te poser
Et que sa pensée, alors, rêve
D'un astre d'amour qui se lève!

This is a song of almost childlike simplicity which, in its use of uncomplicated triads in the upper registers of the piano, resembles many prayer settings. It is quite atypical of Duparc in its lack of harmonic complexity and its consistent peacefulness.

The piano begins with a melodic fragment in the left hand (Eb, D, C in the original key of F major) and tonic chords in the right. This little three-note tune crops up often in the piano part but is never given to the singer. It is particularly striking when it meets the end of the singer's phrases at "bénédiction des cieux" and "qui se lève!" The singer has arrived at the tonic in both these spots, so the piano's flatted 7th is unexpected. It should be stressed enough to make the interval clear and to allow for the *decrescendo* indicated by the composer.

The singer begins with a simple diatonic phrase:

Star whose beauty shines,
Like a diamond in the night,
Look at my beloved
Whose eyelids are closed,

The rhythm of "Regards vers ma bien-aimée/Dont la paupière s'est fermée," the last two lines quoted above, has the gentle rocking effect of a lullaby. The piano has a sweet countermelody in the left hand, which begins with its characteristic three-note phrase.

And cause to descend upon her eyes
The blessings of the skies.

The next section is a bit more sophisticated harmonically. There is a beautiful minor-major cadence under "Elle s'en d*ort*" and, at the end of that measure, an augmented chord. Nevertheless for Duparc this is simple stuff indeed!

> She sleeps ... Through the window
> Enter her happy room
> On her whiteness like a kiss,
> Come, stay there till dawn

The piano's *poco piu forte* chords, coming as they do in a relatively deep register of the piano, are somewhat startling. Perhaps it is the composer's way of reminding us that he is thinking of earthly love after all.

> And may her thoughts dream there
> Of a star of love which rises.

Le Manoir de Rosamonde   Poem by Robert de Bonnières
The Manor of Rosamonde

> De sa dent soudaine et vorace,
> Comme un chien l'amour m'a mordu ...
> En suivant mon sang répandu,
> Va, tu pourras suivre ma trace ...
> Prends un cheval de bonne race,
> Pars, et suis mon chemin ardu,
> Fondrière ou sentier perdu,
> Si la course ne te harasse!
> En passant par où j'ai passé,
> Tu verras que seul et blessé
> J'ai parcouru ce triste monde.
> Et qu'ainsi je m'en fus mourir
> Bien loin, bien loin, san découvrir
> Le bleu manoir de Rosamonde.

The cryptic title and last line of this song probably refer to legends concerning two Rosamondes. The first was the wife of a Lombard king who is said to have lived around 570 A.D. The Italian poet Alfieri (1749–1803), and the English poet Swinburne (1837–1909), both used this tale of romance and regicide as subject matter for long epic poems.

The second Rosamonde was the mistress of Henry II of England. Their romance inspired many tales, including that of a labyrinth through which King Henry had to find his way to reach her.

In Robert de Bonnières' poem, the blue manor of Rosamonde seems to symbolize someone or something which the narrator seeks but, alas, never finds.

The piano opens on the dominant with an odd, hesitant rhythm. In measure three the bass line introduces the characteristic rhythmic figure, which clearly depicts a racing horse. In retrospect the first two bars seem to have been the horse pawing at the ground, getting ready to gallop away. The voice enters in an intensely dramatic style. The words "chien" and "mordu" are given special bite.

> With its sudden and voracious teeth
> Like a dog, love has bitten me

There is a long pause after this line, set off by the piano's abrupt and dry ("sec") chord which must be shorter than the singer's last syllable. The piano interlude sets the horse in motion again and the singer reenters with a repeat of the music of the opening line:

> By following the blood I shed,
> Come, you will be able to follow my trail ...

Another long pause and piano interlude reinforce the image of the racing steed. All these abrupt pauses create tremendous, angry tension.

> Take a horse of good breed,
> Leave, and follow my arduous path,
> Bogs or lost trails,
> Let the journey not weary you!

The section quoted above contains the climax of the song. A tremendous *crescendo* leads from "Prends un cheval" to the *ff* at "Fondrière." Voice and piano remain at full *forte* through the *ritard* and the *a tempo*. Even after the *fermata* the piano reenters *ff*, but a *decrescendo* begins in the next measure and continues through the piano interlude and into the next section.

When the vocal line begins again it is soft and expressive. The rhythmic piano figure disappears and we have quietly supportive chords.

> While passing where I have passed,
> You will see that alone and wounded
> I have traveled this sad world.

A less important *crescendo* lends strength to the Gb^7 chord preceding "Et qu'ainsi." The *forte* lasts for four bars and then there is a rapid *decrescendo*. These six measures contain the most beautiful and imaginative harmonies in the song.

> And thus I have caused my own death
> Very far away, very far away,

The tempo suddenly picks up again and the galloping rhythm returns, but only for one measure. After a two bar *rallentando* we have another *a tempo,* a long pause, and then a final *a tempo.* The hushed dynamics of the last seven measures, combined with the pauses and fitful tempos, create a long-ago and far-away effect, one quite appropriate for a mysterious legend. The singer almost whispers the last line:

> without discovering
> The blue manor of Rosamonde.

Testament   Poem by Armand Silvestre

Pour que le vent te les apporte
Sur l'aile noire d'un remord,
J'écrirai sur la feuille morte
Les tortures de mon coeur mort!
Toute ma sève s'est tarie
Aux clairs midis de ta beauté,
Et comme à la feuille flétrie
Rien de vivant ne m'est resté;
Tes yeux m'ont brûlé jusqu'à l'âme,
Comme des soleils sans merci!
Feuille que le gouffre réclame,
L'autan va m'emporter aussi ...
Mais avant, pour qu'il te les porte
Sur l'aile noire d'un remord,
J'écrirai sur la feuille morte
Les tortures de mon coeur mort!

The legacy bequeathed to the loved one in this last will and testament is one of anger and pain. The stormy piano part frequently clashes head on with the vocal line, the two rhythms indicated are agitated and at odds with one another; the mode is predominantly minor (the original key is C minor) with accidentals often used for dissonance.

The piano has two distinct roles in this song: to give harmonic background (all those tremololike sixteenth notes) and to supply one or two melodic lines, for this is really a duet. When the piano is alone, its melody (the upward stemmed notes) must ring out with all the fiery passion of a soloist; when the vocal line is sung, the two are almost equal partners—"almost" because, of course, the words must be heard.

The accompaniment opens with a C minor harmony spiced by the Ab; its melody begins at the end of measure one. The singer's entrance is in the middle of a measure which immediately calls attention to the polyrhythm—3/4 for the singer, 9/8 for the pianist. Since the singer's melody rises from E♭ to F, while the piano's falls from F to E♭, we have dissonance. Most of the dissonances created in this way throughout the song can be analyzed as suspensions; they are heard as the crossing of two melodic lines.

The poem begins:

So that the wind carries them to you
On the black wings of remorse,
I shall write on the dead leaf
The tortures of my dead heart!

There has been a steady *crescendo* throughout this section, culminating for the singer in the E♭ on "de mon coeur *mort*." The piano continues the *crescendo*—its melody now in octaves—for two-and-a-half measures more and then begins the *decrescendo*. The next section is slower, less tempestuous and somewhat soothing in its predominantly major harmonies:

All my vigor has been wasted
In the clear noontime of your beauty.

The piano's melody sounds particularly lovely in the major mode at "de ta beau*té*." This aura of serenity persists a while longer:

And, as to the withered leaf
Nothing of life remains to me.

The words to the four lines quoted above are exhausted, depleted, resigned, but the music is tender and warm. This presents a problem for the interpreters. One is probably more likely to be influenced by the music than the text when performing the song. At least the two artists have the same material, for the two melodic lines have been in unison during these four lines.

At the final syllable of "reste" the C minor tonality and more rapid tempo bring back the angrier mood of the beginning:

Your eyes burned me to my soul,
Like merciless suns!

This last line is another climactic one. The vocal line is cut off abruptly for dramatic effect after "sans merci." It is in fact the same G–E♭ vocal interval we had at the high point of the first section, but the harmonic underpinnings are completely different. The vocal line and piano melody, now in octaves in the bass, are still in unison, but the piano has rising chromatic octaves between melody notes which serve to build tension. The rise to G♭ in the vocal line, accompanied as it is by rushing chromatic scales, is the climax of this section. The words have been

Leaf which the whirlpool reclaims
The wind will carry me away too . . .

After a piano interlude full of dissonance-creating suspensions, we have musical material almost identical to the beginning of the song. The words are also similar:

But first, so that it carries them to you
On the black wings of remorse,
I shall write on the dead leaf
The tortures of my dead heart!

Once again we have the tremendous vocal climax on the last word, carried even further by the piano. The last seven-and-a-half bars subdue the passionate outburst, and the song fades away. The flatted II in the third bar from the end is an important harmonic touch, which should be heard even at the *pp* decibel level.

Phidylé   Poem by Leconte de Lisle

L'herbe est molle au sommeil
Sous les frais peupliers,
Aux pentes des sources moussues,
Qui dans les prés en fleur
Germant par mille issues,
Se perdent sous les noirs halliers.
Repose, ô Phidylé!
Midi sur les feuillages
Rayonne et t'invite au sommeil.
Par le trèfle et le thym,
Seules, en plein soleil,
Chantent les abeilles volages;
Un chaud parfum circule
Au détour des sentiers,
La rouge fleur des blés s'incline,
Et les oiseaux, rasant de l'aile la colline,
Cherchent l'ombre des églantiers.
Repose, ô Phidylé!
Mais, quand l'Astre,
Incliné sur sa courbe éclatante,
Verra ses ardeurs s'apaiser,
Que ton plus beau sourire
Et ton meilleur baiser
Me recompensent de l'attente!

The words and music of this song evoke an atmosphere of ripe, languid sensuality. The heaviness one feels when the air is hot, still, and laden with flowery fragrance permeates the song. In the entire first section the singer scarcely moves from the tonic note (A♭ in the original, here analyzed in F♯, the key for medium voice)—and a relatively low note it is—and the slow quarter-note accompanying chords do nothing to disturb the sleepy tranquillity. The poem begins:

> The grass is soft for sleeping
> Under the cool poplars,
> At the slopes of the mossy springs,
> Which, in the blossoming meadows
> Sending out thousands of offshoots,
> Get lost in the black thickets.

A lovely enharmonic change (F♯–G♭) introduces the new key (E♭ major) and the next section. Although there is more motion in the piano part, which now has a nice little countermelody in whole notes, the vocal line is even more languid for the refrain:

> Rest, Oh Phidylé

In the interlude the piano introduces a new melody, which continues with the singer, eventually (under "t'invite au sommeil") resulting in a lovely duet in contrary motion.

> Noon on the leaves
> Shines and invites you to sleep.

Another key change and a change from eighth notes to triplets in the accompaniment announce the next section. Since the triplet figure immediately yields to sixteenth notes, which create the effect of increased movement, the instruction "a little faster" means that this section will sound considerably livelier than the first two. The frequent modulations found here add to the feeling of agitation.

> Amid the clover and the thyme,
> Alone in full sunlight,

Ever since Haydn's "Creation," composers have been unable to resist a glorious modulation to a full major chord at the word "light." Duparc's under "en *plein* soleil" is indeed glorious.

> The flying bees sing;

Now, for the first time in the song, we have a *crescendo* to a fairly high dynamic level. The piano has an impassioned melody, which soars higher than the vocal line:

> A warm perfume swirls around
> The curve of the paths,
> The red flower of the wheat droops,

And the birds, scraping their wings against the hillside,
Look for the shadow of the sweet-briar.

From the word "s'incline" (droops), there has been a steady *di-minuendo* to calm things down again. The rhythmic figure in the accompaniment helps by going from sixteenth notes to triplets to eighth notes. All this is necessary preparation for the gentle refrain,

Rest, Oh Phidylé,

which is now repeated in the song's original key. After a brief repetition of the piano's melody from the first interlude, the refrain is heard again. Two gorgeous harmonic changes occur under the singer's long B ("repose"); the melodic line then climbs chromatically on "Phidylé" until the dominant note (C♯) is reached. The third repeat of the refrain, which scarcely moves from the C♯, is sung *pp*—almost in a whisper. It is supported by a pedal point on C♯ in the bass, but there is also lovely chromatic filler in the accompaniment.

Whispering tremolos, which begin the next piano interlude, grow dynamically to a grand *forte* tonic chord. These few measures are much more effective in the orchestral version Duparc subsequently made of this song—perhaps he was already thinking of the orchestration when he wrote them. The voice enters "with warmth" and *forte:*

But when the Star descending
In its brilliant arc
Sees its ardors wane,

The star referred to here is, of course, the sun. These lines provide the text for an enormous climax. The melody is triumphant in its diatonic march up to F♯ (A♭ in the original key); the chords and tremolos are heavy and noble. A *diminuendo* sets in after the pianist's rising line during "éclatante."

Let your most beautiful smile
And your best kiss
Reward me, reward me for having waited!

There are several rapid dynamic swings in this last section, but the focal point is clearly the final *crescendo* to the *forte* on "l'att*ente*."

The piano postlude, all over an F♯ pedal point, is a steady *di-minuendo* to a *pp* ending.

Lamento
Lament

Poem by Théophile Gautier

Connaissez-vous la blanche tombe
Où flotte avec un son plaintif
L'ombre d'un if?
Sur l'if une pâle colombe,
Triste et seule au soleil couchant,
Chante son chant.

On dirait que l'âme éveillée
Pleure sous terre à l'unison
De la chanson.
Et du malheur d'être oubliée
Se plaint dans un roucoulement,
Bien doucement.

Ah! jamais plus près de la tombe
Je n'irai, quand descend le soir
Au manteau noir,
Ecouter la pâle colombe
Chanter, sur la branche de l'if,
Son chant plaintif!

The title of this song is its best description. From beginning to
end it is mournful, grief-stricken. Its minor mode and descending chromatic melody are heavy with sorrow, as is its beautiful text.

There are many subtle touches in the poem that should be noticed.
First, Gautier's way of evoking the visual—the tomb is white, the tree
creates a shadow, the dove is pale, the evening has a black cloak—
there is no color anywhere, only chiaroscuro. Then there is the remarkable use of sounds—the onomatopoeia of "roucoulement" ("cooing"),
with its soft vowel sounds, the inner rhymes of "tombe," "l'ombre,"
"colombe," and the deliberate repetition of sound in "Chante son
chant."

Duparc chooses relatively simple means to set off this rich text.
He also uses repetition most effectively: the melody in the opening two
bars of the piano introduction becomes the vocal line under "L'ombre
d'un if"; it subsequently appears unaltered for piano alone three more
times, and in different keys twice again in the more animated section,
and the singer has it five times in all. Since this is a short song, this
creates an almost trancelike effect.

After the piano's two-bar introduction the singer begins:

Do you know the white tomb
Where with a plaintive sound floats
The shadow of a yew-tree?

These lines are an example of what another poet of this era, Charles Baudelaire, called "Correspondances": shadows float and produce sounds because

Dans une ténébreuse et profonde unité ...
Les parfums, les couleurs et les sons se répondent.

In a secret and profound unity
Perfumes, colors, and sounds correspond to one another.

The singer's first measure is almost declamatory—he might be asking a fairly mundane question—but the falling interval on the somber word "tombe" prepares us for the increasingly emotion-charged melodic line, which culminates in the highly chromatic "L'ombre d'un if." This phrase must be set apart by a little breathing space after "plaintif."

The singer continues:

On the tree a pale dove

At the beginning of this line the piano sings a little duet with the vocalist and the mode changes to major: by the second measure, however, we are back in minor. The rise from D to E♭ in the next measure brings the first *crescendo*.

Sad and alone in the setting sun.

The modulation from the E♭ chord under "seul" to the D♭ minor, and B♭ minor chords under "couchant," are especially beautiful.

Sings its song.

The music for the above line is our oft-repeated chromatic lament.

The second verse of the song uses the same music for the continuing text:

One would say that the awakened soul
Cries under the earth in unison
With its song,
And from the sorrow of having been forgotten
Complains with a cooing sound
Very softly.

The next section is marked "a little more animated," and the piano part now has a sixteenth note figure, which always creates more movement. In a little *stretto* the piano has the chromatic figure, to which an inner voice has now been added. The syncopated melodic notes taken from the D minor arpeggio in the third measure add to the growing agitation, which gives rise to a huge *crescendo*. The singer's entrance is strong and dramatic:

Ah, never more near the tomb
Shall I go, when evening falls
In black cloak,

"Au manteau noir" is sung to the familiar chromatic melodic fragment. A big *decrescendo* has brought the dynamic level down again, but the sense of agitation remains. Throughout this section the piano has a strong countermelody, which continues until the end in a primarily downward diatonic march. The singer continues:

To listen to the pale dove
Sing on the branch of the yew,

The rising line under "branche de l'if," and the singer's long pause which follows, set up the last few sad words:

Its plaintive song!

The piano postlude ends with a repeat of the opening two bars, bringing the song full cycle.

Elégie   Poem by Thomas Moore
Elegy

Oh! ne murmurez pas son nom!
Qu'il dorme dans l'ombre,
Où froide et sans honneur repose sa dépouille.
Muettes, tristes, glacées, tombent nos larmes,
Comme la rosée de la nuit,
Qui sur sa tête humecte la gazon;
Mais la rosée de la nuit, bien qu'elle pleure,
Qu'elle pleure, en silence,
Fera briller la verdure sur sa couche
Et nos larmes, en secret répandues,
Conserveront sa mémoire fraîche et verte
Dans nos coeurs.

The text for this song is a prose translation into French of a poem (originally in English) by Thomas Moore on the death of Robert Emmet, a young Irish rebel who was hanged for treason after an abortive uprising. Moore, a friend and fellow student of Emmet, wrote this poem for Emmet's grieving sweetheart. The text here given is a re-translation of the French prose.

As one might expect from the circumstances which inspired this song, we find here a dignified, philosophical aura. Although the song is in F minor (in the original key) the ending is F major, reflecting the solace offered by the poet.

The piano begins with an oft-repeated characteristic downward half step over the F⁷ chord. Each of the piano's four introductory bars has this melodic pattern over varying harmonies, the last one preparing for the singer's entrance by giving the first note of the vocal line:

Oh, breathe not his name!
Let him sleep in the shadow,
Where cold and without honor
Rest his remains.

The vocal line has the dominant (C) as its central note, but finally sinks to the tonic on the last syllable ("dépouille"). The rise on "et sans honneur," the occasion for a *crescendo* and a *decrescendo,* is a moment of great intensity ("sans honneur" refers to the young man's ignominious death).

The vocal line now has the two-note chromatic phrase found everywhere in the piano part. These short, choppy phrases have an intensity of their own, which mounts with each word:

Silent, sad, frozen, our tears fall
Like the night's dew,

The high note under "tombent" (fall) is the climax of these measures. Calmer and sadder the voice continues:

Which moistens the grass over his head;

Triplet sixteenth notes in the accompaniment animate the tempo a little, but very little, for the next section.

But the night's dew
Though it weeps, though it weeps in silence,
Will make the green over his bed glisten

The music under these last four measures, from "en silence" to "couche," becomes quite fervent. A slight pulling back before the final *crescendo* and climax, on "*sa mémoire,*" is probably advisable.

And our tears, shed in secret
Will keep his memory fresh and green in our hearts.

The singer's last syllable ("coeurs") is on the tonic, but the accompanying chord's dissonant-sounding suspension prevents its resolution to the major tonic from being an effective final cadence. This becomes the function of the brief coda, whose final chord is indeed a satisfying end to the song.

La Vie antérieure
Life of Former Days

Poem by Charles Baudelaire

J'ai longtemps habité sous de vastes portiques
Que les soleils marins teignaient de mille feux,
Et que leurs grands piliers, droits et majestueux,
Rendaient pareils, le soir aux grottes basaltiques.
Les houles, en roulant les images des cieux,
Mêlaient d'un façon solennelle et mystique
Les tout puissants accords de leur riche musique
Aux couleurs du couchant refleté par mes yeux . . .
C'est là, c'est la que j'ai vécu dans les voluptés calmes
Au milieu de l'azur, des vagues, des splendeurs,
Et des esclaves nus tout impregnés d'odeurs,
Qui me refraîchissaient le front avec des palmes,
Et dont l'unique soin était d'approfondir
Le secret douloureux qui me faisant languir.

Like "La Vague et la cloche," this song was originally conceived and written for voice and orchestra; only later did Duparc supply a piano part. Unlike most piano reductions, however, this accompaniment is very pianistic with nary an imitation-string-section tremolo.

The piano begins with a slow, steady march in the tonic (E♭ major in the original). This single measure pattern is repeated for the entire fourteen bars of the first section. The vocal line clings to the tonic scale with only two alterations, the brief chromaticism under "les soleils marins" and the flatted VII and VI under "grands piliers." There is a prominent tonic triad ("majestueux") and a well-prepared tonic ending to the section. This simplicity is quite remarkable for the era in general and Duparc in particular. The total absence of dynamic indications in this section, coupled with the lack of melodic and harmonic complications, is ample justification for a straightforward, uninflected delivery of the words:

> I have long lived under vast porticos
> Which the sea suns tinged with a thousand fires.
> And which their grand columns, straight and majestic,
> Rendered in the evening, like basalt grottos.

Suddenly everything changes: the vocal line develops more scope and greater dynamic range; the accompaniment imitates the surging of the ocean's waves; the mode becomes minor and the whole atmosphere charged with emotion.

> The billows, churning the reflections of the skies,
> Mingled in a solemn and mystical way
> The all-powerful chords of their rich music
> With the colors of the sunset reflected by my eyes . . .

A tremendous *crescendo* has brought us to an *ff* at "mes yeux." The piano, in which a strong countermelody has developed, carries the tempestuous outburst further. The pedal point on the dominant, which began after "accords," yields to a powerful octave on the VII at "yeux." This becomes a dominant seventh which leads to the next section in a virtuosic rush of arpeggios.

One has been led to expect the emergence of G as the new key for the next section, and indeed there is a G octave in the bass, but the right hand chord and vocal line are actually in the key of C. This becomes apparent at the third bar, under "vécu." The tempo slows down considerably at the change of key; the voice remains very loud until the *diminuendo* under "les voluptés."

It is there that I lived in calm voluptuousness

At this point there is an instruction from the composer: "almost at half voice and without nuance, as in a vision." The deliberately monotonous line here is most conducive to the desired effect. The harmonies under "d'odeurs" and between "palmes" and "Et dont" are particularly beautiful. The countermelody in the piano part, under "Qui me rafraîchissaient le front avec des palmes," should be as understated and lacking in nuance as the vocal line.

The words for this trancelike section paint a picture of exotic opulence:

Amid the azure (sky), waves, splendors
And nude slaves impregnated with perfumes
Who cooled my brow with palm leaves,
And whose only care was

A dramatic chord in the accompaniment and a slight pause by the singer add to the importance of the next word, and an enigmatic word it is. Like so many words, "approfondir" can have two virtually opposite meanings: to deepen or to investigate. Which do the slaves do, for

The painful secret which made me languish.

From "approfon*dir*" to the end of the song, we are in the parallel minor. The piano postlude is doleful: three times rising arpeggios introduce falling chromatic melodic fragments, each one a little softer, a little slower, and a little sadder than the one before. Four bars before the end, the rising chromatic line in the bass with which the song began is heard again, but to quite different effect, for the prosaic major modality has been superseded by the mournful minor.

Au pays où se fait la guerre Poem by Théophile Gautier
To the Land Where War Is Waged

Au pays où se fait la guerre
Mon bel ami s'en est allé
Il semble à mon coeur désolé
Qu'il ne reste que moi sur terre.
En partant, au baiser d'adieu,
Il m'a pris mon âme à ma bouche...
Qui le tient si longtemps, Mon Dieu?
Voilà le soleil qui se couche,

Et moi toute seule en ma tour
J'attends encore son retour.

Les pigeons sur le toit roucoulent
Roucoulent amoureusement,
Avec un son triste et charmant;
Les eaux sous les grands saules coulent...
Je me sens tout près de pleurer,
Mon coeur comme un lys plein s'épanche,
Et je n'ose plus espérer,
Voici briller la lune blanche,

Et moi toute seule en ma tour
J'attends encore son retour.

Quelqu'un... monte à grands pas la rampe...
Serait-ce lui, mon doux amant?
Ce n'est pas lui, mais seulement
Mon petit page avec ma lampe...
Vents du soir, volez. Dites-lui
Qu'il est ma pensée et mon rêve,
Toute ma joie et mon ennui
Voici que l'aurore se lève,

Et moi toute seule en ma tour
J'attends encore son retour.

The text for "Au Pays où se fait la guerre" is a straightforward narrative poem by Théophile Gautier. With great dramatic flair, it describes the young woman whose lover has gone to war, her loneliness, her sadness, her short-lived hope when she hears someone mount the stairs, her desolation when she realizes it is only her page, her wish to send new thoughts to her lover on the evening breeze.

The poem consists of three stanzas, each ending with the two-line refrain:

Et moi toute seule en ma tour
J'attends encore son retour.

And I all alone in my tower
I still await his return.

The eight lines preceding the refrain have the rhyme scheme *abba cdcd,* and each line consists of eight syllables. As we might suspect from this highly structured poem, Gautier, the link between the late romantic poets and the Parnassiens, found symmetry and formal structure basic ingredients of beauty.

Duparc's setting of the poem is equally formal in concept. Each of the three stanzas is introduced by a heavy-hearted funereal figure which reminds one of a military cortège. This lends a strophic feeling to the song, even though there are some differences from one stanza to another. The overall harmonic scheme is also largely strophic, and as an additional unifying factor the introductory figure returns as a mournful postlude.

There are several places where the music is onomatopoeic, that is, imitative of extramusical sounds. Most obvious are the fluttery trills in the accompaniment where the cooing of amorous pigeons is described, and the tremolos to mark the woman's excitement when she hears someone mounting the stairs.

The song has a very wide *tessitura*. In the key for mezzo-soprano (F minor) the range is from middle C to the A♭ almost two octaves above. Alternate melody notes are given if the lower range is unmanageable, in which case E above middle C is the lowest note.

The distinctive sound of Duparc's harmonic style is heard, soon after the singer begins, in the measures "fait la guerre." This same melodic line and chord progression are repeated in each of the three refrains, although in slightly different form in the last; still another example of the emphasis put on formal structure.

On the word "guerre" the vocal line sadly echoes the introductory figure. For the next six bars we have shifting harmonies over a pedal point on the tonic, with the melody staying within the tonic scale. Unexpected use is made of F major and C major chords. At "Il semble" a recapitulation of the music of the first line begins, but at "que moi sur terre" there is a modulation to C major. This comforting major tonality suggests the woman's happy recollection of her lover's kiss. Schubert uses this device in a similar way in "Gretchen at the Spinning Wheel." An augmented chord under "bais*er*" leads to A minor, then to a diminished chord on the pedal point C. This progression is repeated, but instead of the diminished chord, a C⁷ prepares for the anguished *forte* chord which combines F minor and D♭ major (this may be analyzed as a D♭ with a major seven). The melody rises to A♭ at this climactic moment. When this chord returns softly four bars later, it is more mournful than tortured, and the melody reaches no higher than F. This leads us to the refrain. The words thus far are:

> To the land where the war is waged
> My lover has gone
> It seems to my desolate heart
> That I am alone on earth.
> In leaving at the farewell kiss,
> He took my heart from my lips . . .
> What keeps him so long, my God?
> Now the sun is setting
>
> And I, all alone in my tower,
> I still await his return.

The second stanza begins like the first, with the lugubrious introduction and rather simple melody. The accompaniment, however, now has an important countermelody. The trill figure in imitation of cooing pigeons has already been mentioned. Interestingly enough, under "Je me sens tout près de pleurer" (I feel myself close to tears), Duparc repeats the C major tonality found in the comparable place in the first stanza. This time the effect should be tender but somber. The dynamics must be very quiet, even for the Db–F minor chord and high Ab in the vocal part. The end of the stanza is slow and hushed, with a trancelike quality.

> The pigeons on the roof coo
> Coo amorously,
> With a sad and charming sound;
> The waters under the huge willows run . . .
> I feel myself close to tears,
> My heart like a blossoming lily overflows
> And I no longer dare hope,
> Now the white moon is shining,
>
> Refrain

In the interest of dramatic intensity, the third stanza begins differently from the other two, with what might be called an interlude for voice and piano. At first there are diminished tremolos and the melodic fragment from the introduction, which is also made even sadder by the diminished melodic interval. The voice, as agitated as the tremolos, sings "Quelqu'un . . ." (Someone) and then pauses dramatically. The singer's excitement mounts feverishly as she thinks it might be her lover, but the *diminuendo* in the piano part, and the return of the slow cortègelike figure from the original introduction make it clear that she will be disappointed. Even at this sad juncture Duparc reverts to C major at "page," maintaining the harmonic pattern intact.

This time the D♭–F minor chord and high A♭ in the melody at "Toute ma joie" are at full *forte,* the true climax of the song. The piano's countermelody adds to the strength of this music, which continues at a high dynamic level almost to the very end. The piano part begins to fade before the vocal part and becomes quietly mournful for the postlude. The last stanza reads:

Someone bounds up the ramp.
Could it be he, my sweet lover?
It is not he, but only
My little page with my lamp.
Evening winds, fly. Tell him
That he is my thought and my dream,
All my joy and all my pain.
Now dawn rises,

Refrain

Claude Debussy

Nuit d'étoiles   Poem by Théodore de Banville
Night of Stars

Nuit d'étoiles, sous tes voiles,
Sous ta brise et tes parfums,
Triste lyre qui soupire,
Je rêve aux amours défunts.

La sereine mélancolie
Vient éclore au fond de mon coeur,
Et j'entends l'âme de ma mie
Tresaillir dans le bois rêveur.

Je revois à notre fontaine
Tes regards bleus comme les cieux;
Cette rose, c'est ton haleine,
Et ces étoiles sont test yeux.

Although the date of this song is somewhat uncertain (probably 1876), it is surely the earliest of the fifty-five songs Debussy published over a period of almost forty years. Its charming melody is a remarkable achievement for a fourteen-year-old boy, but the naïveté of its chordal accompaniment reveals the youth of its composer.

The poem is of equal charm and youthful innocence. Its author, Théodore de Banville, like all "art for art's sake" purists, has no message to convey, no moral to expound. He simply paints a sad but lovely picture of the melancholia of lost love.

The piano introduces the Eb tonality with harplike broken chords. The tempo indication—*allegro*—warns against too languid a feeling, especially since the 6/8 rhythm can lure one into a lullaby.

The voice enters:

Starry night, under your veils
Under your breeze and your perfumes,

Until this point the chords, some plain Eb, some Eb–C minor, have all been in the upper register of the piano, obviously to create a celestial effect. Suddenly, under "tes parfums," they drop in register and become rather earthbound. Since the vocal line drops here, too, singer and pianist should try to remain delicate and avoid undue emphasis on the Bb–Eb cadence.

> Sad lyre which sighs, (in French there is a beautiful inner rhyme of *lyre* and *soupire*)
> I dream of past loves
> I dream of past loves

The second close (under the second "défunts") seems a little more effective than the first, perhaps because of the atmospheric Ab minor chord just before the Eb resolution.

> Serene melancholy
> Bursts open deep in my heart,
> And I hear my lover's soul
> Tremble in the dreaming woods

The sense of forward motion, indicated by the *poco animato* instruction at the beginning of this section, is created by the piano's rising staccato chords. A slight sense of agitation is appropriate under the last two lines quoted above and in the brief piano interlude which follows. A *ritard* brings us back to the original mood, text, and harmonic setting.

At the *animato* we have the same musical ideas but different words:

> Once again I see at our fountain
> Your eyes blue as the sky

The words continue to new melodic material

> This rose, it is your breath,
> And these stars are your eyes.

The pianist should be aware of the ostinato A octave which underlies the changing harmonies during this climactic verse, and which finally yields to a D chord under "yeux." This is the focal point of the song, and the melodic line quite naturally rises under "C'est ton haleine" for the singer's most intense moment, the G and F♯. Again we have the somewhat precipitous fall at the cadence.

When the song begins again for the third time, both performers must create a dreamy "Remembrance of Things Past" feeling. The song fades away on a final Eb chord, preceded by a strange, augmented Eb chord.

Beau soir   Poem by Paul Bourget
Beautiful Evening

Lorsque au soleil couchant les rivières sont roses,
Et qu'un tiède frisson court sur les champs de blé,
Un conseil d'être heureux semble sortir des choses
Et monter vers le coeur troublé.
Un conseil de goûter le charme d'être au monde,
Cependant qu'on est jeune et que le soir est beau,
Car nous nous en allons comme s'en va cette onde,
Elle à la mer, nous au tombeau.

This second of Debussy's published songs, written no later than two years after the first, is already the work of a master. From the very first measure one is intrigued by the rhythmic pattern—a simple triplet subdivision of the three quarter notes, but with an unexpected chord on the last triplet eighth note. The placement of this chord, recurring throughout the piece, conveys a feeling of interruption in the flow of the triplets, which matches the desolate message of the poem—life interrupted by death.

The harmonic change from measure one to measure two—from E major to D minor–B diminished—is equally masterful, as are the many changes which follow.

The constant alternation of major–diminished, major–minor, major–augmented, like the rhythmic pattern, reflects the "happiness-turned-to-sorrow" theme of the words.

The entrance of the voice on G♯, after a measure in G minor, seems the most natural thing in the world, so well has it been prepared. A few measures later the singer's D♯ flows from the D♮ of the G minor chord with the same ease and effectiveness.

The song begins

When in the sunset the streams are red,
And a warm breeze blows on the wheat fields,

At the word "blé" (wheat), the singer holds the note E, which is here the third of the augmented C chord but becomes the tonic in the next measure.

As the song continues describing the message to be happy, the original rhythmic pattern is discontinued and the triplets flow on without interruption. From "Un conseil" (advice) on, the piano has beautiful countermelodies, first in the left hand and then in the right hand octaves.

Advice to be happy seems to flow from things
And to rise towards the troubled heart

Advice to enjoy the charm of being in the world
While one is young and the evening is beautiful

Dynamically this is the high point of the song. The *animato* and *crescendo* create a feeling of excitement and exhilaration, culminating in the *forte* F♯ and the abrupt drop to G♯, which is still loud.

A short pause seems necessary before the next phrase

For we go
Like that wave

The monotone "Comme s'en va cette onde" (Like that wave goes) produces the effect of numbing despair. The accompaniment contributes to the mood by its return to the original rhythmic pattern.

The last two lines, while not quite monotones, are bleak enough.

It (the wave) to the sea,
We to the grave.

The chordal change (to an augmented G chord) under the last syllable is a wonderful way of lengthening and emphasizing the most important word of the poem, "tombeau" (grave). Like the G minor chords mentioned above, it provides a perfect leading tone back to the tonic (G–G♯) and is therefore a beautiful substitute for a V^7–I cadence.

Fleur des blés   Poem by André Girod
Wheat Flower

Le long des blés que la brise
Fait onduler puis défrise
En un désordre coquet,
J'ai trouvé de bonne prise
De t'y cueillir un bouquet.
Mets-le vite à ton corsage—
Il est fait à ton image
En même temps que pour toi . . .
Ton petit doigt, je le gage,
T'a déjà soufflé pourquoi:

Ces épis dorés, c'est l'onde
De ta chevelure blonde
Toute d'or et de soleil;
Ce coquelicot qui fronde,
C'est ta bouche au sang vermeil.
Et ces bluets, beau mystère!
Points d'azur que rien n'altère,
Ces bluets ce sont tes yeux,
Si bleus qu'on dirait, sur terre,
Deux éclats tombés des cieux.

If the opening measures of this song seem vaguely familiar to the pianist, it is probably due to the similarity they bear to the figuration, color and mood of Debussy's "Dr. Gradus ad Parnassum," written as part of the *Children's Corner* suite almost thirty years later.

Whereas the first two songs published by Debussy are really for singer with piano accompaniment, in this third song we have, as is more typical in Debussy's more mature songs, a duet for singer and pianist. Lovely effects are created as the melody in the piano rises while that of the singer falls, as though the 'cello is singing above the violin in a string quartet.

Again in typical Debussy style, the tonality of the piece is not made clear until the fourth measure. The gentle, tranquil mood is perfectly suited to the sweet little poem:

> Along the wheatfields which the breeze
> Causes to undulate and then uncurl
> In a coquettish disarray,
> I found the chance
> To gather a bouquet for you.
>
> Quickly put it on your bodice—
> It is made in your image,
> Just as it is made for you . . .

The French say "your little finger told you," whereas we would say "a little bird told you," which explains the next lines:

> Your little finger I suppose
> Whispered the reason to you

The piano's tune stops before these coy words, so that gently rolled chords can set them in relief. An extended C⁷ (dominant) chord leads back to the original music and the second verse of the poem:

> These golden stalks are the wave
> Of your blond hair
> Made of golden sunlight;
> This bouncing poppy
> Is your bloodred mouth.
>
> And these cornflowers, beautiful mystery!
> Specks of azure which nothing changes,
> These cornflowers are your eyes,
> So blue that one would call them, on earth,
> Two fragments fallen from the skies.

Once again the piano yields to the singer and provides mere accompaniment to support the last two lines. The singer's final phrase, "Deux éclats tombés des cieux" is almost the exact counterpart of the phrase "cueillir un bouquet." The slight alteration is necessary to bring the piece back to the F major tonality (the earlier phrase leaves us on the dominant). These two phrases are both points of intensity, but more attention will probably be drawn to the bridge passage "Ton petit doigt . . . pourquoi" because of the change in accompaniment. On the whole, the song is rather lacking in musical tension and calls for a limited dynamic range.

Mandoline   Poem by Paul Verlaine
Mandolin

Les donneurs de sérénades
Et les belles écouteuses
Echangent des propos fades
Sous les ramures chanteuses.
C'est Tircis et c'est Aminte,
Et c'est l'éternel Clitandre,
Et c'est Damis qui pour mainte
Cruelle fait maint vers tendre.
Leurs courtes vestes de soie,
Leurs longues robes à queues,
Leur élégance, leur joie
Et leurs molles ombres bleues,
Tourbillonnent dans l'extase
D'une lune rose et grise,
Et la mandoline jase
Parmi les frissons de brise.
La, la, la, la, la . . .

One of the first to recognize the talents of the young Debussy was Mme Mauté de Fleurville, the mother-in-law of poet Paul Verlaine. This contact with Verlaine led to a close artistic relationship— Debussy, in fact, used Verlaine's poems for eighteen of his fifty-five songs. Since Verlaine's poetry has the same fluidity of form, absence of rhetoric, and blend of the precise and the vague that we associate with Impressionism in art and music, this was a most felicitous and natural combination.

One collection of Verlaine's, *Les Fêtes galantes,* proved particularly inspiring to Debussy; from it came the songs "Pantomime," "Clair de lune," "En Sourdine," "Fantouches," "Colloque Sentimental," "Le Faune," "Les Ingénus," and "Mandoline."

"Mandoline" opens with a brightly struck G, preceded by a grace note which adds to the sonority and "ping." The sound is allowed to fade away and then the mandolinlike chords begin their sprightly introduction. Because of the discordant As and Gs, one is reminded of an instrument tuning up!

> The serenaders
> And beautiful listeners
> Exchange idle chatter
> Under the singing branches

By "Et les belles . . ." the player has gotten his instrument in tune and all is harmony thenceforth. Note the unexpected chords under the singer's chromatic descent on the second syllable of "chauteuses."

> It is Tircis and Aminte
> And the eternal Clitandre
> And Damis who makes tender verses
> For many a cruel woman

All the characters named are known literary references: Tircis and Damis are shepherds and Aminte and Clitandre are from the Italian comic opera.

The word "tendre" (tender) brings on a new mood, which is itself sweet and tender. The singer's phrases are longer, no more staccato notes and bouncy chords. Actually this little lyric section is merely a description of the characters' costumes:

> Their short silk vests,
> Their long gowns with trains,
> Their elegance, their joy
> And their soft blue shadows,

At "leurs molles ombres bleues" (their soft blue shadows), the singer and the pianist's left hand join in introducing a tune which dominates the end of the song (under all the la la la's), and which has been hinted at in the first section (under "fait maint vers tendre"). Before we reach those gay la la's, however, we have a return of the original mandolin chords and the second verse:

> Whirling in the ecstasy
> Of a red and grey moon,
> And the mandolin chatters
> In the chill of the breeze.

The chromatic line on the word "brise" can have a somewhat chilling effect, but this immediately gives way to the joyous la la la's. From here to the singer's long C, piano and singer have the melody in unison (left hand of piano). When the final note comes—just as it did at the beginning of the piece—it should be a total surprise. Be sure to observe the full five eighths of rest to best create the effect. The "toujours en allant se perdant" instruction (always getting farther away, disappearing) must be accomplished through dynamics alone, with absolutely no *ritard*.

Pantomime   Poem by Paul Verlaine

Pierrot qui n'a rien d'un Clitandre
Vide un flacon sans plus attendre
Et, pratique, entame un pâté.

Cassendre, au fond de l'avenue,
Verse une larme méconnue
Sur son neveu déshérité

Ce faquin d'Arlequin combine
L'enlèvement de Colombine
Et pirouette quatre fois

Colombine rêve, surprise
De sentir un coeur dans la brise
Et d'entendre en son coeur des voix.

Ah!

Ten years before the first of the two *Fêtes galantes* cycles appeared, Debussy had already dipped into that charming collection of poems by Paul Verlaine, setting "Mandoline," "Clair de lune," and "Pantomime" to music (there are two versions of "Clair de lune"). The poem and the music for "Pantomime" closely resemble "Fantoches" from *Fêtes galantes I* (see page 341). Both are gay and witty, and both tell incomprehensible stories about characters from the Italian comic stage. In "Fantoches" the piano begins with a melody— never given in its entirety to the singer—that is unmistakably related to the singer's opening tune in "Pantomime." Obviously these particular poems inspired the same mood in Debussy, even though a decade had elapsed between the composition of their settings.

Before analyzing the words or music of "Pantomime," we should identify the strange cast of characters. Pierrot is just an ordinary fellow and Clitandre is an amorous type, so "Pierrot qui n'a rien d'un Clitandre" is a Pierrot with no romantic sentimentality; Cassendre is an old curmudgeon—a man in this case; Arlequin is another practical man of action, and Colombine is his beloved.

The piano has an attention-getting little introduction with a perky rhythmic pattern and a jaunty trill. The voice enters with a joyous V–I (the original key is E major) but the F double sharp in the accompanying chord gives a fleeting hint of the minor mode, as does the chromaticism in the melody. Since the most effective comedy has an underlying note of sadness, this is not inappropriate. Melody and harmony continue to be highly chromatic until the words "Et pratique," which are made to stand out. However the line ends with a return to the chromatic. The words to this point are:

> Pierrot who is no Clitandre
> Empties a bottle without further ado
> And, practical, takes the first slice of a pâté.

In the original text the first stanza ends at "entame un pâté," for the poem consists of four three-line stanzas with the rhyme scheme *aab/ccb/dde/ffe*. In the song, Debussy repeats lines one and two of the first stanza and the last lines of stanzas three and four. These repeats coupled with the piano interludes and vocalized measures (all those "Ah"s) make a long song out of a short poem!

For the repeated lines Debussy has modulated to sunny C major, but there are so many key shifts that the new tonality is felt only in passing. The repeated notes of the piano interlude help the jaunty mood along.

The next section is full of chromatic scales, with an occasional whole step to keep the performers on their toes! The descending line under "Verse une larme méconnue" makes it clear that those are crocodile tears Cassandre is shedding and we needn't be distressed.

> Cassandre, at the end of the street,
> Sheds a misunderstood tear
> For his disinherited nephew.

The words of the next three lines are quickly dealt with, even though the last line is repeated. After all the harmonic shifting, the solid dominant ending on the second "quatre fois" is startling in its decisiveness.

> That rascal Arlequin plans
> The kidnapping of Colombine
> And pirouettes four times

Suddenly the mood changes to one of lyric reverie as the poet describes Colombine dreaming and listening to the voices in her heart. There is no mockery here, just beautiful harmonies and a tender melody. Under both occurrences of "en son coeur" we find lovely augmented chords, which add to the dreamy quality. The words end here but the music will continue:

> Colombine dreams, surprised
> To sense a heart in the air
> And to hear voices in her heart.

After the poem has ended we return to the original tempo for a long section vocalized on "Ah." Despite the chromatic grace notes in the accompaniment and the staccato notes in the melody, the mood never really becomes as gay as it was in the beginning, for the alternating C♯ minor and C augmented harmonies assure a wistful feeling. The great charm of the song is due in part to this variety of moods.

Clair de lune
Moonlight   Poem by Paul Verlaine

Votre âme est un paysage choisi,
Que vont charmant masques et bergamasques
Jouant du luth et dansant,
Et quasi tristes sous leurs déguisements fantasques!
Tout en chantant, sur le mode mineur,
L'amour vainqueur et la vie opportune,
Ils n'ont pas l'air de croire à leur bonheur,
Et leur chanson se mêle au clair de lune,
Au calme clair de lune, triste et beau,
Qui fait rêver les oiseaux dans les arbres,
Et sangloter d'extase les jets d'eau,
Les grands jets d'eau sveltes parmi les marbres!

A quick glance at Debussy's two versions of "Clair de lune" is sufficient to explain the fact that the first (1882–1884, given here) has virtually disappeared from the repertoire while the second (in *Fêtes galantes I,* 1892, see p. 337) has become a staple thereof. In fact, this earlier rendition is weak even in comparison with such songs as "Pantomime," "Apparition," and "Pierrot," which were composed at the same time; nor does it in any way compare with Fauré's masterful setting of the same poem (see p. 69).

The piano begins with a dominant-oriented introduction, whose most interesting feature is the use of the flatted second (G♮ since the key is F♯) as part of the harmonic scheme. The dominant chords are extended beyond the traditional 7th to include the 9th, which creates the polytonality of C♯ and G♯ minor. After this promising start, however, we have two measures of very ordinary tonic chords on which the vocal line begins.

It is interesting to compare the harmonization of the line "Tout en chantant sur le mode mineur" ("While singing in the minor mode") in the three versions of "Clair de lune": in all three cases obvious use of a minor chord at the word "mineur" has been avoided, although in both the Debussy songs the surrounding modality is minor.

The most effective melodic idea in the song—and Debussy exploits it extensively—is the use of exotic ornamental minor thirds on "*chan*son," "mêle," "de" (in both statements of the line "Et leur chanson se mêle au clair de lune"), and near the end of the song in the word "marbres" and the added sigh, "Ah." The words are:

> Your soul is a chosen landscape
> Where spell-binding masqueraders and dancers,
> Play the lute and dance,
> And are almost sad under their fantastic disguises!
> While singing, in the minor mode,
> Of love, the conqueror, and opportune life,
> They do not seem to believe in their happiness,
> And their song blends with the moonlight,
> In the calm moonlight, sad and beautiful,
> Which makes the birds dream in the trees,
> And (makes) the fountains sob with ecstasy,
> The tall, slim streams amid the statues!

Pierrot   Poem by Théodore de Banville

> Le bon Pierrot que la foule contemple
> Ayant fini les noces d'Arlequin
> Suit en songeant le boulevard du temple.
> Une fillette au souple casaquin
> En vain l'agace de son oeil coquin
> Et cependant mystérieuse et lisse
> Faisant de lui sa plus chère délice
> La blanche lune aux cornes de taureau
> Jette un regard de son oeil en coulisse
> A son ami Jean Gasparde de bureau.

This little song is a charmer which should appeal to audiences of all ages. Since the Pierrot of the title figures in the nursery tune which we know as "Au clair de la lune," Debussy uses the first eleven notes of this familiar ditty throughout the song. They appear as the basic material of the introduction, the countermelody to the vocal line, as punctuation between the singer's phrases, and, under "Et cependant mystérieuse et lisse," the principal melody.

Despite the gaiety of its associations, the song is in the minor mode and the last eleven measures have an eerie, almost ominous sound. It is interesting to see how Debussy accommodates the nursery tune, which is originally in the major mode, to the overall minor tonality. Sometimes, as in its first three appearances, the air is unaltered (in the first half of the introduction it is in C major), but its effect is changed by the surrounding chords. In other instances the ubiquitous theme is itself minor. After "les noces d'Arlequin" there is a half step between the first two notes of the tune, a further alteration.

The vocal line is bright and perky. Its range is enormous—from the E above middle C to the C two octaves above in the original key of E minor. It calls for plenty of vocal gymnastics, including a leap of a tenth ("de son oeil coquin"), but must be tossed off with gay abandon. The words are:

> The good Pierrot whom the crowd watches,
> Having finished the marriage ceremony of Arlequin
> Follows the boulevard of the temple while thinking.
> A young girl in a supple jacket
> Vainly entices him with her coquettish eye
> And, however mysterious and sleek,
> Is his dearest delight.
> The white moon like a bull's horns (crescent moon)
> Throws a glance of its eye behind the scenes
> At his friend Jean Gaspard from the office.

Apparition   Poem by Stéphane Mallarmé

> La lune s'attristait. Des séraphins en pleurs
> Rêvant l'archet aux doigts, dans le calme des fleurs
> Vaporeuses, tiraient de mourantes violes
> De blancs sanglots glissant sur l'azur des corolles.
> C'était le jour béni de ton premier baiser.
> Ma songerie, aimant à me martyriser,
> S'enivrait savamment du parfum de tristesse
> Que même sans regret et sans déboire laisse
> La cueillaison d'un rêve au coeur qui l'a cueilli.
> J'errais donc, l'oeil rivé sur le pavé vieilli,
> Quand, avec du soleil aux cheveux, dans la rue
> Et dans le soir, tu m'es en riant apparue,
> Et j'ai cru voir la fée au chapeau de clarté
> Qui jadis sur mes beaux sommeils d'enfant gâté
> Passait, laissant toujours de ses mains mal fermées
> Neiger de blancs bouquets d'étoiles parfumées.

"Apparition" is regarded as one of Mallarmé's most important poems. In it one sees at work the "demon of analogy"* with which he and the other symbolist poets seem to have been possessed. The moon is sad, flowers are calm, sighs are white, there is an odor of sadness, white bouquets are perfumed with stars. In this sense Mallarmé's poem is a direct descendant of Baudelaire's *Les Fleurs du Mal,* in which the

---

* Classiques Larousse: *Verlaine et les poetes symbolistes,* Paris: Librairie Larousse, p. 53.

earlier poet expresses his vision of the correspondence of all things—sounds, color, odors, tastes, feelings.

The structure of the poem is as rigid as its metaphors are free—eight rhymed couplets, each of the sixteen lines twelve syllables in length. There is no division into stanzas in the printed edition of the text.

The Debussy setting is suitably ambitious in length and expressivity and is the most important of his early songs. The opening section (until the first key change) is celestial, ethereal. The piano begins with a shimmering figure on the tonic triad colored by the sound of the flatted second (F natural in the key of E major); the voice enters on the dominant and dreamily intones its first six syllables on that one note. This stylistic device—a repeated melodic note surrounded by lovely harmonies—is one of Debussy's most identifiable characteristics. The complexity of the opening rhythms—3/4 in the voice against 9/8 in the accompaniment—is another Debussy trademark.

As the voice leaves the dominant note, it climbs chromatically and then undulates towards the D♮ at "Rêvant." There is a lovely augmented chord under "séraphins," which adds to the ethereal quality of the writing. This atmospheric use of chromaticism and floating chords continues until the word "corolles":

> The moon became sad. Tearful Seraphim
> Dreaming, bow in hand, in the calm of
> Hazy flowers, pulled from dying viols
> White sobs, gliding on the azure of the corollas.

For the next line,

> It was the blessed day of your first kiss

the writing becomes warm and unabashedly romantic. Full chords in the piano's middle and lower registers support the impassioned melody which begins on a high A♭.

The music reverts to its more ephemeral style as the poet describes his musings. One feels a pull towards the whole-tone scale but the fragments never last long enough to establish a true whole-tone figure. The melody is a wonderful *mélange* of repeated notes and rising lines. There is a sudden *crescendo* from the *pp* of "tristesse" to the impassioned outburst which follows immediately ("Que même . . ."). This whole section is marked by beautiful shifting harmonies which eventually lead to a new tonal center, C major. The thought carries us over the key change:

> My musings, loving to make me a martyr,
> Knowingly became drunk with the perfume of sadness

Which even without regret and without aftertaste leaves
The harvest of a dream in the heart which plucked it.

Suspense builds in the next few measures, which are the calm
before the storm. Little by little the music becomes faster, louder and
more intense. The climax of the song is at the glorious phrase beginning on high C and ending with a chromatic fall to F. Throughout this
passionate outcry the accompaniment provides the support of rich,
strong chords. Debussy's characteristic mixture of duple and triple subdivisions of the quarter note adds to the musical tension. This carries
us through the lines

I wandered then, my eye riveted on the aged pavement,
When, with the sun in your hair, in the street
And in the evening, you appeared to me, laughing,

With the next line

And I believed that I saw the fairy with the cap of light

the effusive romanticism of "It was the blessed day of your first kiss"
returns. This is the warmest music in the song, but it soon yields to the
cooler, more ethereal mood of the opening. From "Qui jadis" to the
end, we sense a hushed, awestruck feeling, the earthiness of human
passion transformed into celestial ecstasy.

The final tonality, arrived at on "Et j'ai cru . . . ," is Gb major.
Once this new key has been reached there is a steady decrease in
sound, which Debussy describes as "en allant toujours se perdant,"
always going further and further away, or "losing itself." In other
words, the song fades away with the utmost delicacy. The poem
concludes:

Who long ago passed through my sweet sleeps of a
Spoiled child, always, from her half-opened hands,
Allowing white bouquets of perfumed stars to fall like snow.

Zéphyr   Poem by Théodore de Banville

Si j'étais le Zéphyr ailé
J'irais mourir sur votre bouche.
Ces voiles, j'en aurais le clef,
Si j'étais le Zéphyr ailé.

Près des seins, pour qui je brûlais,
Je me glisserais dans la couche.
Si j'étais le Zéphyr ailé
J'irais mourir sur votre bouche.

Neither the text nor the music of this brief song distinguishes it from the hundreds of salon pieces of its type, written by lesser composers to equally innocuous words.

The introductory piano figure, which also serves as an ending, sets the key (E major) and precious mood. No harmonic surprises disturb the sweet melodic line, which pauses on the dominant on the word "bouche" while the accompaniment plays a predictable V^7–I cadence.

The middle section has some nice harmonic moments—the minor I^6 at "clef" is effective—but at no time is Debussy's true genius revealed.

The words sound more passionate in translation than in the original, which seems quite chaste. This is due to the fact that "seins" has a less erotic connotation than its English equivalent "breasts" or "bosom."

> If I were the winged Zephyr*
> I would go to die on your lips.
> To these veils** I would have the key,
> If I were the winged Zephyr.
>
> Near the bosom for which I burned,
> I would slip into the bed.
> If I were the winged Zephyr
> I would go to die on your lips.

Rondeau   Poem by Alfred de Musset

> Fut-il jamais douceur de coeur pareille
> A voir Manon, dans mes bras, sommeiller.
> Son front coquet parfume l'oreiller.
> Dans son beau sein, j'entends son coeur qui veille—
> Un songe passe et s'en vient l'égayer.
> Ainsi s'endort la fleur d'églantier
> Dans son calice enfermant une abeille.
> Moi, je la berce. Un plus charmant métier, fut-il jamais?
>
> Mais le jour vient et l'aurore vermeille
> Effeuille au vent son printemps virginal.
> Le peigne en main et la perle à l'oreille
> A son miroir, Manon va m'oublier.
> Hélas, l'amour sans lendemain ni veille—Fut-il jamais?

Like its immediate predecessor, "Rondeau" is a pleasant but somewhat insipid song. It has so little of the characteristic Debussy

* Gentle breeze
** mysteries

style that one is surprised to find that it dates from the same period as "Mandoline" and "Apparition," two early songs already aglow with individuality and mastery. *Grove's Dictionary of Music and Musicians* tells us that two other songs from this period, "Chanson d'un Fou" and "Ici-bas," originally published under Debussy's name, were later discovered to have been written by lesser known composers (the former by Emile Pessard, the latter by the brothers Hillemacher). Since so many composers wrote in the "salon" style of "Zéphyr" and "Rondeau," it is no surprise that such frauds could be carried off with some success.

The poem, written by the nineteenth-century Romantic Alfred de Musset (1810–1857) is quite lovely. Its bittersweet ending rescues it from a too saccharine aftertaste, and its language is musical and appealing. Note the skillful use of inner rhymes such as "douceur de coeur" in the first line, and the near rhymes of all the end sounds except "virginal":

pareille	l'égayer	vermeille
sommeiller	églantier	l'oreille
l'oreiller	abeille	m'oublier
qui veille	métier	veille
		jamais

Each line has ten syllables, with the phrase "Fut-il jamais" acting as a refrain after the eighth and final lines. Interestingly enough, there are thirteen lines in all, a most unusual number.

Debussy's setting is hardly in traditional rondo form—aside from the piano's introductory figure which reappears after the refrains, and the melody for the refrain itself, nothing is repeated. The melody is through composed rather than strophic. The gentle 6/8 berceuse rhythm chosen by the composer is well-suited to the mood of the text and the flowing melody enhances the words. The harmonies are pleasant, though predictable, with one mildly dissonant chord under "d'églantier." The words are:

Has there ever been such a heart-warming sweetness
As having Manon, in my arms, asleep.
Her lovely brow perfumes the pillow.
From within her beautiful breast I hear her wakeful heart—
A dream passes and comes to amuse her.
Thus sleeps the flower of the sweetbriar
Enclosing in its calyx a bee.
I rock her. Has there ever been a more charming metier?

But day comes and the crimson dawn
Sheds its virginal springtime to the wind.

Comb in hand and pearl at her ear
At her mirror, Manon is going to forget me.
Alas, love with no tomorrow and no awakening—Has it ever existed?

La Belle au bois dormant   Poem by Vincent Hypsa
Sleeping Beauty

Des trous à son pourpoint vermeil,
Un chevalier va par la brune,
Les cheveux tout pleins de soleil,
Sous un casque couleur de lune.
Dormez toujours, dormez au bois,
L'anneau, la Belle, à votre doigt.

Dans la poussière des batailles
Il a tué loyal et droit,
En frappant d'estoc et de taille,
Ainsi que frapperait un roi.
Dormez au bois où la verveine,
Fleurit avec la marjolaine.

Et par les monts et par la plaine,
Monte sur son grand destrier,
Il court, il court à perdre haleine,
Et tout droit sur ses étriers.
Dormez, la Belle au Bois, rêvez.
Qu'un prince vous épouserez.

Dans la forêt des lilas blancs,
Sous l'éperon d'or qui l'excite,
Son destrier perle de sang
Les lilas blancs, et va plus vite.
Dormez au bois, dormez, la Belle
Sous vos courtines de dentelle.

Mais il a pris l'anneau vermeil,
Le chevalier qui par la brune,
A des cheveux pleins de soleil,
Sous un casque couleur de lune.
Ne dormez plus, La Belle au Bois
L'anneau n'est plus à votre doigt.

Like so many fairy tales and legends, the Sleeping Beauty story can be found in many different cultures. Current psychoanalytic theory explains these oft-told tales as expressions of universal events, so traumatic to the individual that they must be dealt with in allegoric terms. Accordingly, the Sleeping Beauty legend represents the sexual awakening of the young girl. If in reality it will be the boy next door who awakens her, in the story it must be a handsome knight who carries her off on his prancing steed. With sexual awakening occurring younger and younger, the one hundred years of dormancy given our Beauty in the English version of the tale seems more and more excessive!

In Hypsa's evocative poem the knight is described first:

> Holes in his vermillion doublet,
> A knight goes at dusk,
> His hair full of sunlight,
> Under a moon-colored helmet.

Then comes the Refrain—always the same musical phrase and almost the same words:

> Sleep always,
> Sleep in the woods,
> The ring, Beauty, on your finger.

The introductory figure in the accompaniment gives the feeling of a galloping horse because of the hesitation at the beginning of beats one and three (first and seventh eighth notes in 12/8 time). The vocal line is ideal for storytelling with its repeated notes and limited range. The C minor–G major cadence under "par la brune" gives an antique effect suitable for relating an ancient tale. The melody develops greater range for "sous un casque" (under a helmet), and the accompaniment becomes more emphatic in its rhythmic pulse. This insistent rhythm stops for the gentle refrain and the singer has complete freedom to soften the contours with some *rubato*.

The second verse extols the brave knight:

> In the dust of battles
> He has killed loyally and justly,
> Striking with cut and thrust
> Like a king.
>
> Refrain

Third verse:

> And over mountains and plains,
> Mounted on his great steed,
> He speeds, he speeds breathlessly
> And all erect in his stirrups.
>
> Refrain

Debussy provides new music for the last two lines of the verse quoted above, music that reflects the increasing tension and pace, with its dotted rhythm and harsh discords. This time the refrain should seem even dreamier by contrast.

The fourth verse goes into new musical material right after the introductory measure. The singer has an ominous ostinato D, while the piano figuration becomes more frenzied rhythmically. The harmony, an augmented B♭ alternating with a B♭⁷ adds to the excitement.

> In the forest of white lilacs,
> Under the gold spur which rouses him,
> His steed beads with blood
> The white lilacs, and goes more quickly.

The refrains for verses three and four have slightly modified chords in the accompaniment, but the mood and melody remain the same.

The final verse says

> But he has taken the gold ring,
> The knight who goes at dusk,
> With hair full of sunshine,
> Under a moon-colored helmet.

In this long song the climax is reserved for the very end. In place of the gentle little refrain we have the triumphant

> Sleep no more, Beauty of the woods,
> The ring is no longer on your finger.

Singer and pianist are both instructed to give this happy ending all they have.

One wonders what might be the significance of the fact that, while most wedding ceremonies have the groom place a ring on his bride's finger, this one begins by removing the ring . . .

Voici que le printemps
Here Is the Spring

Poem by Paul Bourget

Voici que le printemps, ce fils léger d'avril,
Beau page en pourpoint vert brodé de roses blanches.
Paraît leste, fringant et les poings sur les hanches,
Comme un prince acclamé revient d'un long exil.

Les branches des buissons verdis rendent étroite
La route qu'il poursuit en dansant comme un fol;
Sur son épaule gauche il porte un rossignol,
Un merle s'est posé sur son épaule droite.

Et les fleurs qui dormaient sous les mousses des bois
Ouvrent leurs yeux où flotte une ombre vague et tendre;
Et sur leurs petits pieds se dressent, pour entendre
Les deux oiseaux siffler et chanter à la fois.

Car le merle sifflote et le rossignol chante;
Le merle siffle ceux qui ne sont pas aimés,
Et pour les amoureux languissants et charmés,
Le rossignol prolonge une chanson touchante.

Of the countless musical and poetic descriptions of Spring in existence, this must be one of the most charming. Simplicity, beauty, innocence, freshness—this song has them all. The poet is once again Paul Bourget (see "Beau Soir," "Paysage Sentimental," and "Romance" for other poems by Bourget used by Debussy) whose "art for art's sake" approach to poetry is perfectly suited to this topic.

The piano begins in D major—the major mode predominates throughout—with a lovely tune articulated by the left hand (double-stemmed notes). The short phrases above the long quarter notes guarantee the lightness demanded by the composer. After four bars the singer enters with the same tune, mostly in unison with the piano's left hand.

Here is spring, that airy son of April
Handsome page in green doublet embroidered with white roses
He appears, light, frisky, his hands on his hips
Like a prince welcomed home from a long exile.

The vocal quality should reflect the light, airy buoyancy which suffuses the words. This discourages any leaning into the high F♯s.

In the second verse the piano has an ostinato D chord as an anchor, but the left hand tune is even more airy, with rests between melody notes. To avoid over-pedaling, perhaps the middle pedal should be used to hold the chord.

The branches of the green thickets make narrow
The route he follows dancing like a fool;

For two measures the piano has a jaunty little solo dance, which it repeats as the singer continues

On his left shoulder he carries a nightingale,

These last six bars are an example of one of Debussy's favorite harmonic devices, the use of simple common chords under each melody note, a scheme which somehow gives the passage both a naive and an antique quality. An abrupt harmonic change occurs under the next line

A blackbird sits on his right shoulder.

This cadence, G♭–D minor with an added E♭, is almost a cliché of pop music today. Debussy repeats it three times and then resolves to B♭, which becomes the tonic for the next section.

The new key brings on a new mood—dreamier and more languid. Of course, the vocal quality should change accordingly.

> And the flowers which slept under the moss in the woods
> Open their eyes where a vague and tender shadow floats;
> And on their little feet stand to hear
> The two birds whistle and sing at the same time.

The piano part under "Et sur leurs petits pieds . . . à la fois" is very similar to a passage in "En Bateau" from Debussy's "Petite Suite" for Piano Duet, written a few years after this song.

> For the blackbird whistles—and the nightingale sings;
> The blackbird whistles at those who are not loved,

The French equate whistling with hissing or booing, so evidently those not lucky enough to be loved are to be censured rather than pitied in the poem. The music, on the other hand, sounds suitably sad.

We cannot have a melancholy ending, so it is back to D major for the last two lines:

> And for languishing and enchanted lovers,
> The nightingale prolongs his touching song.

In truth the lighthearted mood never really returns because the tempo is slower and more languid. This makes for an equally appropriate sensuous dénouement.

Paysage sentimental   Poem by Paul Bourget
Sentimental Landscape

Le ciel d'hiver, si doux, si triste, si dormant,
Où le soleil errait parmi des vapeurs blanches,
Etait pareil au doux, au profond sentiment
Qui nous rendait heureux mélancoliquement
Par cet après-midi de baisers sous les branches.
Branches mortes qu'aucun souffle ne remuait,
Branches noires avec quelque feuille fanée.
Ah! que ta bouche s'est à ma bouche donnée
Plus tendrement encore dans ce grand bois muet,
Et dans cette langueur de la mort de l'année,
La mort de tout sinon de toi que j'aime tant,
Et sinon du bonheur dont mon âme est comblée,
Bonheur qui dort au fond de cette âme isolée,
Mystérieux, paisible et frais comme l'étang
Qui pâlissait au fond de la pâle vallée.

Another poem by Paul Bourget, describing another part of the forest and a different emotional field. It is a winter landscape this time but not a bleak one, for love is still present.

The key is F major (for high voice) with many high As for the singer. The piano introduction, which is used several times in the body of the song, features an ostinato F, around which D minor, G minor and Bb minor[7] chords hover. The melody begins with a rising chromatic line harmonized by major, augmented and minor chords.

> The winter sky, so soft, so sad, so dormant,
> Where the sun wandered among the white mists,
> Was like the sweet, profound feeling
> Which made us happy—though melancholy

The word "mélancoliquement" is separated from the word "heureux" (happy). Its descending melody—actually an F scale—ends in an unexpected E♮. It is a rather wistful phrase, but the rhythmic accompaniment keeps it from being doleful.

Now the introductory passage is heard over an ostinato C. The vocal line rises to an A, expressing quiet joy.

> On that afternoon of kisses under the branches.

During the short piano interlude an even more tranquil mood emerges.

> Dead branches that no wind stirred
> Black branches with a few faded leaves

Note that while the picture painted is one of desolation, the music is merely serene. This winter scene is not used to symbolize death and decay.

> Ah! how your lips gave themselves to mine
> More tenderly still
> In this vast silent woods

The pace quickens under "Ah! que ta bouche . . ." (Ah! how your lips . . .) as erotic memory stirs the poet. The *subito pp* for piano and voice has a beautiful effect, as does the softening of the rhythmic pattern (♩. ♪ under "bouche," ♪ ♪ ♪ under "tend*rement en*cor").

> And in that languor of the death of the year,

Under this line alone does the music reflect the bleakness of the winter scene. The repeated note in the melody has a chilling effect, and the chords are somber and sometimes dissonant. Musically this is the most atmospheric line of the song.

The ascending chromatic line, with which the singer began, is now repeated to the same harmonization.

Death of everything if not of you whom I love so,
And if not of the happiness of which my heart is full,
Happiness which sleeps deep in that isolated soul
Mysterious, peaceful and cool as the pond
Which blanched in the depths of the pale valley.

The chromatic rise on the last syllable makes a lovely ending for this gentle little song.

Le Balcon   Poem by Charles Baudelaire
The Balcony

Mère des souvenirs, maîtresse des maîtresses,
O toi, tous mes plaisirs! ô toi, tous mes devoirs!
Tu te rappelleras la beauté des caresses,
La douceur du foyer et le charme des soirs,
Mère des souvenirs, maîtresse des maîtresses!

Les soirs illuminés par l'ardeur du charbon,
Et les soirs au balcon, voilés de vapeur rose.
Que ton sein m'était doux!
Que ton coeur m'était bon!
Nous avons dit souvent d'impérissables choses
Les soirs illuminés par l'ardeur du charbon.

Que les soleils sont beaux par les chaudes soirées!
Que l'espace est profond! que le coeur est puissant!
En me penchant vers toi, reine des adorées,
Je croyais respirer le parfum de ton sang.
Que les soleils sont beaux par les chaudes soirées!

La nuit s'épaississait ainsi qu'une cloison,
Et mes yeux dans le noir devinaient tes prunelles,
Et je buvais ton souffle, ô douceur, ô poison!
Et tes pieds s'endormaient dans mes mains fraternelles,
La nuit s'épaississait ainsi qu'une cloison.

Je sais l'art d'évoquer les minutes heureuses,
Et revis mon passé blotti dans tes genoux.
Car à quoi bon chercher tes beautés langoureuses
Ailleurs qu'en ton cher corps et qu'en ton coeur si doux?
Je sais l'art d'évoquer les minutes heureuses!

Ces serments, ces parfums, ces baisers infinis,
Renaîtront-ils d'un gouffre interdit à nos sondes,
Comme montent au ciel les soleils rajeunis
Après s'être lavés au fond des mers profondes?
O serments! ô parfums! ô baisers infinis!

The next five songs, which were composed during the years 1887–1889, are settings of poems by Charles Baudelaire (1821–1867). This poet created a scandal and a sensation with the publication in 1857 of his *Fleurs du Mal* (Flowers of Evil). His ideas of saintly sensuality and purification through the voluptuous earned him official condemnation by the censors and a stiff fine, but other poets and a large segment of the public recognized his serious intentions and remarkable gifts.

Baudelaire believed that the senses were so interrelated as to be interchangeable. In his poem "Correspondances" he says

Il est des parfums frais comme des chairs d'enfants,
Doux comme les hautbois, verts comme les prairies . . .

There are odors fresh as the flesh of children,
Sweet as the oboe, green as the prairies . . .

To expose the profound unity of all things, said Baudelaire, the poet must proceed by allusions, symbols, suggestions, fleeting images and oblique metaphors. It is no wonder that the next generation of poets, the so-called Symbolists, regarded Baudelaire as their spiritual father.

This particular poem, "Le Balcon," has an unusual form: the first line of each verse is repeated at the end of the verse. Debussy follows this scheme musically, only occasionally altering a final cadence for a better bridge to the next section. Hence the music under the opening line "Mère des souvenirs . . ." is repeated when those words are re‑ peated. This is true of all six verses. Since the music changes with each verse, the song has a long, meandering effect.

Verse I:

Mother of memories, mistress of mistresses,
Oh you, all my pleasures! oh you, all my duties!
You will recall the beauty of caresses,
The sweetness of home and the charm of evenings,
Mother of memories, mistress of mistresses!

The highly chromatic opening three bars of the introduction lead to a simple C major tonality for the entrance of the voice. The rich chords of the accompaniment in the next measure soon complicate matters once again. This alternation between harmonic complexity and simplicity is a recurring pattern throughout the song. The G♯ at the end of the singer's first line comes at the softest point of a *decrescendo,* but since the piano part has a little more surge here, and the vocal G♯ is a vital part of the chord—and the nicest moment in the melody—the singer will want to give it some emphasis.

The melody for the rest of this verse has great fluency and wide range. The D♯ at the end of line two (de*voirs*) deserves considerable stress, as it is melodically and harmonically beautiful.

The second verse, which begins and ends with a repeated note (D), has a much more limited vocal line. This well suits the words, which describe intimate evenings at home:

> The evenings, lit by the glow of the embers,
> And the evenings on the balcony, veiled by red mist,
> How sweet your bosom was to me! How good your heart!
> We often said everlasting things,
> The evenings lit by the glow of the embers.

The third verse resembles the first in melodic flow and harmonic color, although it is by no means an exact repeat. The key is now principally B major with the usual constant harmonic drifting. The focal dynamic point is, as it was in the first verse, at the end of the fourth line ("de ton sang").

> How beautiful was the sun on warm evenings!
> How deep is space! How powerful the heart!
> Leaning toward you, queen of the adored,
> I thought I breathed the scent of your blood.
> How beautiful was the sun on warm evenings!

The new key and relatively uncomplicated harmonies give a more open sound to the next verse. Here, as in verse two, the melodic range is more limited, but there is no line completely on one note as there was in the second verse.

> The night became as dense as a wall,
> And my eyes barely made out your pupils in the dark,
> And I drank your sigh, Oh sweetness, oh poison!
> And your feet fell asleep in my brotherly hands.
> The night became as dense as a wall.

The piano interlude between verses four and five builds musical tension, but the *ritard* in the last two bars prepares for the *dolce espressivo* of the fifth verse. This stanza has a nostalgic mood, dreamy and meandering in vocal line and piano part.

> I know the art of evoking happy moments,
> And see again my past crouched at your knees.
> For of what use is it to look for your languid beauty
> Elsewhere than in your dear body and sweet heart?
> I know the art of evoking happy moments!

The last verse is the slowest, most quiet and most ethereal.

> These vows, these perfumes, these endless kisses.
> Will they be born again from an abyss beyond our understanding,
> As the sun rises in the sky rejuvenated
> After having bathed in the depths of the sea?
> Oh vows, oh perfumes, oh endless kisses!

The only somewhat obvious spot in the music occurs under the words "montent au ciel" (rise to the sky), where the rising chords and vocal line seem a bit too inevitable. The little chromaticisms of the last three phrases in the melody are most effective, as is the final E around which the C major tonality finally regroups itself.

Harmonie du soir   Poem by Charles Baudelaire
Harmony of the Evening

Voici venir les temps où vibrant sur sa tige
Chaque fleur s'évapore ainsi qu'un encensoir;
Les sons et les parfums tournent dans l'air du soir;
Valse mélancolique et langoureux vertige!

Chaque fleur s'évapore ainsi qu'un encensoir;
Le violon frémit comme un coeur qu'on afflige;
Valse mélancolique et languoreux vertige!
Le ciel est triste et beau comme un grand reposoir.

Le violon frémit comme un coeur qu'on afflige,
Un coeur tendre, qui hait le néant vaste et noir!
Le ciel est triste et beau comme un grand reposoir;
Le soleil s'est noyé dans son sang qui se fige.

Un coeur tendre, qui hait le néant vaste et noir,
Du passé lumineux recueille tout vestige!
Le soleil s'est noyé dans son sang qui se fige!
Ton souvenir en moi luit comme un ostensoir!

This is one of Baudelaire's most famous poems. Not only does it provide the text for this beautiful song, it also inspired a *Prélude* by Debussy—"Les sons et les parfums tournent dans l'air du soir."

Although the song is in B major, Debussy begins with a C♯ minor triad. The second measure introduces a characteristic little figure, the triplet sixteenth notes, which probably represent things "turning in the air." Of the first ten notes of the melody, all but the first are at whole-tone intervals.

The words begin:

Now comes the time when, trembling on its stem
Each flower gives off scent like a censer;

For the expressive line

Sounds and scents turn in the evening air

Debussy again chooses the C♯ minor chord before the B major. The last note—the half step up to G♮—is the most beautiful, and its harmonization (G suspension over an A chord) is equally moving.

Melancholy waltz and languorous vertigo!

Under this line the piano part becomes more animated as if to suggest the dizziness of vertigo.

Each flower gives off scent like a censer;

Again it is the last note of the line that captures our attention, for the D♯ under "encen*soir*," used in the arpeggiated B chords of the previous two measures, changes enharmonically to the E♭ of the C minor chord.

The violin shudders like a wounded heart,
Melancholy waltz and languorous vertigo!

Note the structure of this poem and the use to which Debussy puts that structure:

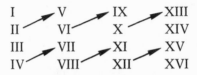

Each Roman numeral represents a line of verse; lines which are repeats of one another are connected on the chart. In the music Debussy closely follows this plan, although different keys and different endings are given, so that free harmonic flow can be maintained. For instance, when "Le violon frémit comme un coeur qu'on afflige" is sung for the second time, the voice rises at the end of the line instead of falling, as it does the first time. These differences do not affect the overall plan.

On a simple D major triad the voice continues

The sky is sad and beautiful like a great altar.
The violin shudders like a wounded heart,
A tender heart which hates the vast and black void!
The sky is sad and beautiful like a great altar.

The next line is all whole tones:

The sun has drowned itself in its congealing blood.

The music for this chilling line is serene and unaffected by the disquieting imagery.

A tender heart, which hates the vast and black void,
Gathers all the vestiges of the luminous past!
The sun has drowned itself in its congealing blood;
Your memory shines within me like a shrine!

The chromatic rise to F♯, sung as softly and serenely as possible, makes a gorgeous ending.

Three times during the poem Baudelaire has referred to objects used in the Catholic Mass: the "encensoir" (incense burner), "reposoir" (altar), and "ostensoir" (monstrance or shrine). By allusion, a mood of religious reverence is thus evoked, and one senses this in the music.

Le Jet d'eau   Poem by Charles Baudelaire
The Fountain

Tes beaux yeux sont las, pauvre amante!
Reste longtemps sans les rouvrir,
Dans cette pose nonchalante
Où t'a surprise le plaisir.

Dans la cour le jet d'eau qui jase
Et ne se tait ni nuit ni jour,
Entretient doucement l'extase
Où ce soir m'a plongé l'amour.

La gerbe d'eau qui berce
Ses mille fleurs,
Que la lune traverse
De ses pâleurs,
Tombe comme une averse
De larges pleurs.

Ainsi ton àme qu'incendie
L'éclair brûlant des voluptés,
S'élance, rapide et hardie
Vers les vastes cieux enchantés. ˋ

Puis, elle s'épanche, mourante
En un flot de triste langueur,
Qui par une invisible pente
Descend jusqu'au fond de mon coeur.

O toi, que la nuit rend si belle
Qu'il m'est doux, penché vers tes seins,
D'écouter la plainte éternelle
Qui sanglote dans les bassins!

Lune, eau sonore, nuit bénie,
Arbres qui frissonnez autour,
Votre pure mélancolie
Est le miroir de mon amour.

This highly erotic song describes the sensuous languor that comes as the aftermath of lovemaking. Some thirty-five years later Ravel, in the first of his "Chansons Madécasses" ("Nahandove"), chose to evoke a similar scene with a musical setting quite reminiscent of this song.

The piano opens with a figure meant to suggest the gentle flow of a rather quiet fountain. The voice and left hand of the piano part enter in measure two with the melody.

> Your beautiful eyes are weary, Poor lover!
> Stay for a long time without opening them,
> In this languid pose
> Where pleasure has taken you by surprise

The melody is a combination of small intervals—often chromatic —and wide skips. The right hand's fountainlike figure continues in C major, while the chromatic chords and melody float around it. The close at the end of each line brings everything back to C major.

The new rhythmic pattern in the accompaniment of the next section, two against three, creates more motion. The vocal line participates in this rhythmic pattern, which is one of Debussy's favorites.

> In the courtyard the chattering fountain
> Which is never silent, night or day,
> Sweetly sustains the ecstasy
> Into which love plunged me tonight.

A new key and a new accompanying figure change the mood to one of suppressed excitement. The thirty-second notes suggest more rapid play of water in the fountain and the rising vocal line seems to build tension. The *pp* instruction keeps things from becoming too overt—the passion is remembered, not experienced.

> The column of water which rocks
> Its thousand flowers
> Which the moon pierces with its pale beams,

Although the music is replete with augmented chords, once in a while a certain one seems particularly effective. Such a chord occurs in the measure "pâ*leurs*." In the following measure the G♯, which creates the augmentation, is retained and the rest of the chord moves to C♯—a lovely moment for the pianist and singer.

> Falls like a torrent of large tears.

A similar effect is created under "larges pleurs" with three consecutive augmented chords leading back to a C major resolution.

The *meno mosso* indication which follows might seem to suggest a containment of the incipient excitement of the previous section, but the *crescendo* leading to the only *forte* in the song (under "vastes . . . enchantés") make this the dynamic peak of the piece. The fact that the accompaniment has a more consistently rapid figure throughout this section adds to the mounting sense of excitement, and vitiates the effect of the *meno mosso*.

Thus your soul which
The burning lightning of passion sets afire,
Leaps, quick and bold,
Towards the vast enchanted skies.

Now, however, the mood does become more tranquil, and the accompaniment returns to the less active figurations of the opening section. Harmonic interest is created by the major seventh interval— D♯ in the E chord.

There it overflows, dying
In a wave of sad languor,
Which by an invisible slope
Descends to the depths of my heart.

Another rich chord to match this chromatic melodic interval under "coeur" (heart) ends this section.

The words and music for "The column of water . . . tears" come back here, and again at the end of the song. The one verse remaining between these two refrains is hushed and tranquil:

Oh you, whom the night makes so beautiful,
How sweet it is, leaning on your breast,
To listen to the eternal lament
Which sobs in the fountain!

Moon, sonorous water, blessed night,
Trees which tremble all around,
Your pure melancholy
Is the reflection of my love.

The final refrain is the softest and most evanescent of all. The return to C major is prepared a full seven measures before the end by an extended G⁷ chord, but the intervening E minor chords and the harmonization of the whole-tone melodic fragment make the ultimate return to C major totally "impressionistic."

Recueillement   Poem by Charles Baudelaire
Reflection

Sois sage, ô ma Douleur, et tiens-toi plus tranquille;
Tu réclamais le soir: il descend; le voici.
Une atmosphère obscure enveloppe la ville,
Aux uns portant la paix, aux autres le souci.

Pendant que des mortels la multitude vile,
Sous le fouet du Plaisir, ce bourreau sans merci,
Va cueillir des remords dans la fête servile,
Ma Douleur, donne moi la main; viens par ici

Loin d'eux. Vois se pencher les défuntes Années,
Sur les balcons du ciel, en robes surannées;
Surgir du fond des eaux le Regret souriant;

Le Soleil moribond s'endormir sous une arche,
Et, comme un long linceul trainant à l'Orient,
Entends, ma chère, entends la douce nuit qui marche.

The introduction to this song begins deep in the bass register of the piano. Slow and solemn, the single notes set the C♯ minor tonality and somber mood. Ascending chords, obviously influenced by the horn theme of Wagner's "Tristan und Isolde," lighten the mood a bit, but the vocal entry—virtually unaccompanied—restores sobriety.

Be wise, oh my Sadness, and be more serene.

French parents admonish their children, even little babies, to "sois sage" rather than "be good," so this opening phrase carries connotations of intimacy and affection between the poet and "his Sadness."

You craved the evening; it falls, here it is:

The vocal line for these words has been declamatory and practically without motion. It is really a second introduction.

The tempo now changes from 4/4 to 3/4, the key changes to C, and, after another darkly colored piano introduction, the body of the song begins.

A somber atmosphere envelops the city,
To some bringing peace, to others care.

The harmony in the measure "souci" is strange and haunting. Even more disturbingly dissonant are the measures "Sous le fouet du Plaisir, ce bourreau sans merci." A sense of agitation is created by the harmonic clashes and the triplet figure in the piano's left hand. The *crescendo* and *animando* help create the mounting excitement.

While the vile multitude of mortals,
Under the lash of Pleasure, that merciless tyrant,
Goes to gather remorse at the servile feast.

Gradually calm is restored as well as the original key and tempo. Once again the poet addresses his sadness with tender familiarity:

My sadness, give me your hand, come here,
Far from them.

We go back to 3/4 time, but with no change of key for the next section:

See the dead Years lean
On the balconies of the sky in wornout clothes;

For these lines the chords have risen, dissipating the dark mood of the music. The augmented chords and lovely F major resolution are gentle and sweet. Nevertheless the words continue to paint a gloomy picture.

> (See) Regret, smiling, rise from the waters' depths
> The dying sun falls asleep under an arch,

The final section returns to C major and Debussy makes a point of changing from 3/4 to 9/8 time. Although this has no actual effect, as the three quarter notes in each measure had already been sub-divided into triplets giving us nine eighth notes to a bar, the new time signature serves to emphasize the greater solemnity and weightiness desired by the composer.

> And, like a long shroud dragging to the East,
> Hear, my dear one, hear the sweet night advance.

Once again we have a strange dissonance under "En*tends*" (the F double sharp is a suspension to the G♯, which is part of the C♯ chord). Even the final resolution in the penultimate measure, rein-forced by its harmonic repetition in the last measure, seems uneasy after the three mercurial measures which precede it. The music seems less resigned, less at peace with its sadness, than the poem.

La Mort des amants   Poem by Charles Baudelaire
The Death of Lovers

> Nous aurons des lits pleins d'odeurs légères,
> Des divans profonds comme des tombeaux;
> Et d'étranges fleurs sur des étagères,
> Ecloses pour nous sous des cieux plus beaux.
> Usant à l'envi leurs chaleurs dernières;
> Nos deux coeurs seront deux vastes flambeaux,
> Qui réfléchiront leurs doubles lumières
> Dans nos deux esprits, ces miroirs jumeaux.
> Un soir fait de rose et de bleu mystique
> Nous échangerons un éclair unique,
> Comme un long sanglot, tout chargé d'adieu;
> Et plus tard un Ange, entrouvrant les portes,
> Viendra ranimer, fidèle et joyeaux,
> Les miroirs ternis et les flammes mortes.

The title of this poem would seem to presage a heart-rending account of the untimely death of two young lovers, or perhaps—alle-gorically—the tragedy of the fleeting nature of young love. To our sur-prise neither the words nor the music convey this mood; instead we have serenity and sensuality.

In his poem "La Mort des Pauvres," Baudelaire gives us what might be an explanation:

> C'est la Mort qui console, hélas! et qui fait vivre;
> C'est le but de la vie, et c'est le seul espoir
> . . .
>
> C'est un Ange qui tient dans ses doigts magnétiques
> Le sommeil et le don des rêves extatiques,
> . . .
>
> C'est le portique ouvert sur les Cieux inconnus!

> It is death which consoles, alas! and which makes us live;
> It is the aim (end) of life and its sole hope
> . . .
>
> It is an Angel which holds in its magnetic fingers
> Sleep and the gift of ecstatic dreams,
> . . .
>
> It is the gate which opens on unknown Heavens!

So death is a splendid and romantic adventure to be approached with reverence and solemnity, not fear and sorrow.

Beautiful harmonies prepare for the singer's entry:

> We shall have beds full of light fragrance,
> Couches deep as tombs

The descent of the voice to Bb on "tom*beau*" is a rather obvious musical device, but effective nonetheless.

> And strange flowers on shelves
> Bloom for us under more beautiful skies.

The use of whole-step intervals (under "Ecloses pour nous sous des" over the beautiful augmented chord) makes for a particularly lovely and ethereal moment.

> Vying with one another in their last passions,
> Our two hearts will be two vast torches,
> Which will reflect their double lights
> In our two spirits, these twin mirrors.

Despite the overall quiet dynamic range of this song, the verse quoted above is so full of allusions to fiery passion that some sense of excitement is inevitable. We have a *crescendo* marked under "vastes flambeaux" and again—with *no* intervening *decrescendo*—another dynamic rise to "lumières" and yet a third to "jumeaux." Beware the natural inclination for a *decrescendo* on the descending melodic line.

The change of key created around the enharmonic Ab–G# in the bass of the piano brings a *pp* and a more spiritual, less sensual aura:

One evening made of rose and mystical blue,
We shall exchange just one lightning streak,
Like a long sob, laden with farewells;

An interesting effect is achieved by the repeated note melodic line under "Un soir . . . bleu mystique." The little chromatic rise under "Comme un long sanglot" is lovely, too, but the most telling moment in this section is the half step fall (C#–C) at the very end ("d'adieu"). In fact, the next section grows harmonically out of this sudden modulation.

The piano interlude serves to pick up the tempo a little. Once again the voice enters on a repeated note fragment:

And later an Angel, opening the gates,
Will come to bring back to life, faithful and joyous,

The real climax of the song is on the F#–G of "joyeux." The accompaniment and vocal line have built towards it from "Et plus tard," but only in the last four measures does it really "take off."

Suddenly we have—at the key change—an Ab minor chord. This abruptly terminates the ecstatic climax and brings back a dreamy, other-worldly mood.

The tarnished mirrors and dead flames.

The brief piano postlude is a return to the harmonies and rhythmic patterns of the introduction.

Will the lovers, whose spirits are the mirrors, whose hearts are the flames, be brought back to life on Earth or is it heavenly life to which the angel leads them? Or has the whole poem been a metaphor for lovemaking? The poet only implies, suggests, alludes—we will never be certain.

Ariettes oubliées
Poems by Paul Verlaine

1. C'est l'extase
This Is Ecstasy

C'est l'extase langoureuse,
C'est la fatigue amoureuse,
C'est tous les frissons des bois
Parmi l'étreinte des brises.
C'est, vers les ramures grises,
Le chœur des petites voix.
O le frêle frais murmure,

Cela gazouille et susurre,
Cela ressemble au cri doux
Que l'herbe agitée expire.
Tu dirais, sous l'eau qui vire,
Le roulis sourd des cailloux.
Cette âme qui se lamente
En cette plainte dormante,
C'est la nôtre, n'est-ce pas?
La mienne, dis, et la tienne
Dont s'exhale l'humble antienne,
Par ce tiède soir, tout bas.

A wry story lies behind the title of this six-song collection, *Ariettes oubliées (Forgotten Airs)*. Originally published under the title *Ariettes,* in 1888, they were unnoticed by public or critics until after the success of Debussy's opera, *Pelléas et Mélisande,* some fifteen years later. Consequently, upon their republication, Debussy changed their title to *Ariettes oubliées.*

"C'est l'extase," the first song in the collection, is an unabashed description of the languorous fatigue that follows erotic passion. The composer's mood indication—"slow and caressing"—deliberately underscores the physical connotation of the words. The piano's opening chords, while played as softly as possible in light of the *decrescendo,* are heavy with sensuality (they are all based on the dominant, but the right hand begins with a suspension over the rich dominant ninth). The key for high voice is E major.

The voice enters with a slow-moving downward scale fragment. The second melodic phrase begins with an F♯ minor triad, which creates a momentary dissonance with the accompanying chord at "la." As the ascending vocal and descending harmonic lines move on, the dissonance disappears and the dominant ninth chord reasserts itself. The phrase ends with a chromatic fall to B♮ for voice, and a G♯ bass note for piano, which eventually develops into a tonic chord.

The words for these first two phrases have been slow-moving and dreamy:

This is languid ecstasy,
This is amorous fatigue.

Debussy now suggests a slightly faster pace in the music, to match the more rapidly moving syllables of the text. Conversely, the melodic line becomes almost static, with many repeated notes, and the accompaniment reflects this virtual suspension of harmonic or melodic motion.

The chords are interesting nevertheless—a major seventh over the E in the first measure and a C^9 in the second, a repeat of that pattern in the next two bars, an Eb$^7_9$ under "C'est, vers les ra . . . ," and then a totally unexpected and very lovely C major. A rather ominous D^7 changes to the familiar B^9 and the piano's original harmonies are heard again. Four lines of verse are sung in this brief section:

This is all the trembling of the woods
In the embrace of the breezes
This is, through the gray branches,
The chorus of little voices.

By changing the last chord in the piano's descending figure, Debussy introduces a new tonality, this one based on C♯. Again we have lush 7 and 9 chords, some with major thirds, some with minor. Vocal line and accompaniment again clash intermittently in the contrary motion chromatic phrases (from "cela ressemble au cri doux" through "expire"). The words are still quite rapidly dealt with in this section:

Oh the frail and fresh murmur
It twitters and whispers
It resembles the soft cry
That the ruffled grass exhales.

The accompaniment continues to be highly chromatic. (In the International Edition for high voice, there is a misprint in the measure under "Tu dirais": the left hand chord in the piano part should read F♯, D♮, as it does two bars later.) The melody here is based on an F♯ minor triad, but the harmonies shift in a rather vague way until all come together on a D major chord under "cailloux." The words are a strangely evocative metaphor:

One would call it, under the swirling water,
The muted rolling of pebbles!

D^7 and B^7 chords alternate at the beginning of the next section. Suddenly a G^9 is heard (under "C'est la nôtre"); this is the signal for a brief but intense flurry of excitement in tempo and dynamics. The chord in the next measure gives an almost ominous sound; but the real climax is obviously on the highest note of the phrase ("la tienne"). The piano carries the *crescendo* beyond this point, but the descending vocal line quickly brings us back to a languid, almost motionless mood.

The melody concludes on the tonic note, but the actual E major tonality is not reached until the third measure of the piano's postlude. The final lines of the poem are:

This soul which laments
In this quiet plaint
It is ours, is it not?
Mine, tell me, and yours,

Which exhales the humble anthem,
On this mild evening so quietly.

N.B. See p. 87 for an analysis of Fauré's setting of this poem.

2. Il pleure dans mon coeur
My Heart Cries

Il pleure dans mon coeur
Comme il pleut sur la ville.
Quelle est cette langueur
Qui pénètre mon coeur?
O bruit doux de la pluie,
Par terre et sur les toits!
Pour un coeur qui s'ennuie,
O le bruit de la pluie!
Il pleure sans raison
Dans ce coeur qui s'écoeure.
Quoi! nulle trahison?
Ce deuil est sans raison.
C'est bien la pire peine,
De ne savoir pourquoi,
Sans amour et sans haine,
Mon coeur a tant de peine.

Of all the poems of Paul Verlaine, this is probably the best known. Its marvelous opening lines are based on the similarity of the words "pleuvoir," to rain, and "pleurer," to cry. In the third person singular these words sound almost alike: "Il pleure" (it is crying) and "il pleut" (it is raining). In a way, the entire poem is a restatement of a famous line of the seventeenth-century philosopher Pascal, who said "Le coeur a ses raisons que la raison ne connaît point" (The heart has reasons the reason knoweth not). For Fauré's setting, see page 75.

When considering a poem with a great and familiar text, the first question that comes to mind is "does the music really enhance the words?" In this case one must answer with an unqualified "yes," for the mood set by the composer—vague, misty, melancholy—provides the perfect aura for the poem. The simple piano figure is the gentle rain —this is no raging tempestuous storm—and the intentionally monotonous vocal line reflects the poet's sad ennui. The equally bland melodic line in the piano's left hand, based first on the whole tone scale and then on the chromatic scale, contributes appreciably to the feeling of vagueness and melancholy. The chromatic drop in the vocal line under "ville" is an unexpected end to this opening section:

It weeps in my heart
As it rains in the city.

Despite the vagueness created by the use of whole tones and chromatic passages, one senses the G# minor tonality (for high voice) in the first section; for the next two lines of verse Debussy moves to A major. The vocal line develops much greater range, leading the singer from middle C# to the G# one and a half octaves higher and back down again almost as far. Once again a chromatic fall on the last syllable ends one section and leads to the next. The strongly arched vocal line is well-suited to the questioning, perhaps even querulous, words:

> What is this languor
> That pervades my heart?

A piano interlude, in the original key and based on the introductory measures, leads to the next section, in which the voice echoes the piano's whole-tone melodic line. This time the last syllable is part of an accented diminished chord, which seems very strong after the gentle G# minor scale fragment which precedes it. The text for this section is:

> Oh soft sound of the rain
> On the ground and on the roofs!

The brief piano interlude which follows repeats the diminished chord, then gives an even stronger sound, the dissonance of C# and D♮ in the two measures before the reentry of the voice. This dissonance is beautifully resolved to F# for the next part of the vocal line. Twice Debussy interrupts the lovely harmony with a dark dissonance, first under "Oh *le* bruit" and then under "de *la* pluie." The words here are:

> For a heart that grows weary
> Oh the sound of the rain!

Now comes the core of the poem's meaning:

> It cries without reason
> In this disheartened heart.

Two beautiful transitions make these lines unforgettable: the false cadence (B[7]–G major) under "raison," and the addition of the E♭ to the A minor[7] chord at "s'*écoeure*." Once again the melodic line drops one half step at the end to accommodate the new harmony, a D[7], but this time the transitional chord leads to a dead stop on a B♭ chord. This sudden cessation of the piano figure makes the next words stand out in bold relief:

> What! No treachery?
> This mourning is without cause?

The first of these two lines is declaimed with *recitativo*-like rhythmic freedom. The octave leap at "Ce deuil" is all the more gripping

because of the near monotone which preceded it. The last four syllables
—again all on one note—are hushed as though in dazed bewilderment.

At the last syllable the piano resumes its figuration and gradually
reintroduces the G♯ minor tonality and the whole tone melody. Very
effective use is made of the chromatic rise and fall under "*De ne savoir*,"
which was not part of the earlier material but which leads back into the
original vocal phrase. After the chromatic fall at the end of the phrase
we once again move to A major as we did in the first part, but the
melody rises only one octave to a C♯, where it is held over the accompaniment's C♯°⁷ chords and single note F double sharp. This F double
sharp becomes part of a dominant seventh chord as the melody falls to
the dominant note, D♯, to allow the piano postlude to begin in the
original key. This is a most imaginative recapitulation, precisely because it is not an exact repeat. The final lines of the poem are the most
poignant of all:

> It is by far the worst pain
> Not to know why,
> Without love and without hate
> My heart has so much pain.

The postlude surprises us with a new harmonic idea—the B major
resolutions in the second, fourth, and fifth bars. Debussy finally supplies the closing cadence to G♯ (there is no median note, so it is neither
major nor minor) by way of the C♯ minor⁷ chord in the fifth measure
from the end.

Debussy's instructions at the beginning of the song read "sad and
monotonous." In keeping with this overall melancholy there are relatively few dynamic fluctuations and the range is from a whispered *pp*
to a subdued *mp*.

3. L'Ombre des arbres
The Shadow of the Trees

> L'ombre des arbres dans la rivière embrumée
> Meurt comme de la fumée,
> Tandis qu'en l'air, parmi les ramures réelles,
> Se plaignent les tourterelles.
> Combien, ô voyageur, ce paysage blême
> Te mira blême toi-même,
> Et que tristes pleuraient dans les hautes feuillées
> Tes esperances noyées.

The brief poem which is the text of this song was inspired by
a description of a nightingale who, seeing his reflection in the water

beneath the tree in which he is perched, thinks that he has fallen into the river and is afraid that he will drown.

Debussy makes no attempt to extend Verlaine's few lines of verse with expansive piano interludes or long held notes. Instead, he creates an atmosphere so distinctive and effective, in the thirty-one measures of music, that the listener senses completeness and is satisfied.

The piano begins with a device used often by Debussy as an opener—a suspension. This gives a certain vagueness to the tonality (C♯ major for high voice), which is furthered in the next measure by the resolution to G major. This two-bar pattern is heard four times in the song, accounting for twenty-five percent of the accompaniment. Similar patterns occur in four other instances, giving the song remarkable coherence and reinforcing the gloomy mood.

The singer enters with a repeated note intoning the first six syllables. The melody then rises in an exotic, Eastern succession of intervals, but the next line returns to a deliberately monotonous series of repeated notes. The octave rise at "Tandis" lifts us suddenly "en-l'air" (in the air), while the accompaniment has a vaguely Oriental-sounding figure. Once again the melody rises in an unusual pattern, settling on the B♮, which leads to the next phrase with its leap to F♯ and its descent of an octave. This completes the first section:

> The reflection of the trees in the mist-covered river
> Fades away like smoke,
> While in the air, amid the real branches
> Turtledoves lament.

The music of the opening measures returns, but with fewer repeated notes and less motion in the melodic line in the first phrase. In the singer's second phrase, only the first two measures are taken from the earlier section, for Debussy uses the rise to and fall from "même" as preparation for the highest note of the song, the A♯ on "Et." Lest the singer be tempted to belt out this note, the composer puts a *p* alongside the accent. This is true of the other climactic high note, the G♮ at "noyées." It is obvious that the dynamics are to be subdued and muted throughout the song. Nevertheless the *crescendo* and *stringendo* instructions leading to the high A♯ suggest mounting tension and excitement, satisfied by the piano's *sforzando* chord, and then enhanced by the singer's soft high note floating above the accompaniment. Of the two climactic moments, "noyées" is the stronger, because the high note is held and the harmonies—suspensions over diminished chords—rivet the attention. This is also the most dramatic word in the text, which reads:

How much, Oh traveller, this colorless landscape
Reflected you, yourself pale,
And how sadly among the high foliage cried
Your drowned hopes.

The postlude focuses on E♯, the median note of the tonic triad, as a way back to the final C♯ chord. It is a strange, vague return, absolutely appropriate for the mood of the song.

4. Chevaux de bois
Wooden Horses

Tournez, tournez, bons chevaux de bois,
Tournez cent tours, tournez mille tours.
Tournez souvent et tournez toujours,
Tournez, tournez au son des hautbois.

L'enfant tout rouge et la mère blanche,
Le gars en noir et la fille en rose,
L'une à la chose et l'autre à la pose,
Chacun se paie un sou de dimanche.

Tournez, tournez, chevaux de leur coeur,
Tandis qu'autour de tous vos tournois
Clignote l'oeil du filou sournois.
Tournez au son du piston vainqueur!

C'est étonnant comme ça vous soûle,
D'aller ainsi dans ce cirque bête:
Rien dans le ventre et mal dans la tête,
Du mal en masse et du bien en foule;

Tournez dadas, sans qu'il soit besoin
D'user jamais de nuls éperons
Pour commander à vos galops ronds.
Tournez, tournez sans espoir de foin.

Et dépêchez, chevaux de leur âme,
Déjà voici que sonne à la soupe
La nuit qui tombe et chasse la troupe
De gais buveurs, que leur soif affame.

Tournez, tournez! Le ciel en velours
D'astres en or se vêt lentement,
L'Eglise tinte un glas tristement.
Tournez an son joyeux des tambours, tournez.

Every so often, amid the gentle, vaguely melancholy songs of Debussy, one finds an outgoing and vigorous romp like this one. One might compare it to "Golliwog's Cake-Walk" in the body of Debussy's piano compositions—full of characteristic touches, but different in mood and temperament from the vast majority of pieces.

The poem's insistent rhythms and sounds make it absolutely perfect as the text for a song. In the first verse the repetition of the syllable "tour" masterfully suggests the merry-go-round's endless mechanical turning. Line three is particularly effective in its use of the "ou" vowel sound ("*Tournez souvent et tournez toujours*").

There are many differences between the text of the poem as given in Classiques Larousse's *Verlaine et les Poètes Symbolistes* (page twenty-five) and the words of the song as published by the International Music Co. In Larousse, for example, the second verse reads

> Le gros soldat, la plus grosse bonne
> Sont sur vos dos comme dans leur chambre;
> Car en ce jour, au bois de la Cambre
> Les maîtres sont tous deux en personne.

> The fat soldier, the fatter maid
> Are on your backs as (at ease) as in their room;
> For today, in the woods of la Cambre (an amusement park)
> Both their masters are there.

instead of "L'Enfant tout rouge et la mère blanche" etc. This changes the complexion of the poem considerably, the former version being far less childlike and innocent. In the sixth stanza only the first line is the same in both versions. Larousse has

> Et dépêchez, chevaux de leur âme,
> Déjà, voici que la nuit qui tombe
> Va réunir pigeon et colombe,
> Loin de la foire et loin de madame.

> And hurry, horses of their soul,
> Already the night which is falling
> Is going to reunite pigeon and dove
> Far from the fair and far from madame.

The last two lines of the poem are also changed: Larousse has

> Voici venir l'amante et l'amant.
> Tournez au son joyeux des tambours.

> Here come the lovers.
> Turn to the joyous sound of the drums.

In the former version the whole poem can be interpreted quite cynically, from the pickpocket ("filou") in the third verse to the pigeon and dove hiding from their mistress in the sixth. Particularly subject to this sardonic interpretation is the fourth stanza, which could well be a metaphor for the futility of life. Here there is one tiny but enormously important difference in texts: Larousse has "*Bien dans le ventre*" while the song has "*Rien dans le ventre*" (feeling fine in the stomach *versus* with nothing in the stomach). In the song the note of cynicism can be detected only in the fourth stanza; the rest is joyous and straightforward.

The music begins with a strong trill and a heavily accented rhythmic figure. The subdivision—a triplet in beat one and plain eighth notes in beat two—is a favorite pattern of this composer. As soon as the voice enters, we hear another characteristic Debussy device, the harmonization of each important melody note with its own triad. The strong dynamics of the opening words must yield immediately to a *p,* so that the series of *crescendos* can be effected. The little chromatic rises under "Tournez cent tours, tournez mille tours" add to the overall mood of excitement and motion. The words for verse one are:

> Turn, turn, good wooden horses
> Turn one hundred turns, turn one thousand turns
> Turn often and turn always
> Turn, turn to the sound of the oboes.

After all the excitement of the first verse with its tremendous *crescendi* to *ff,* there is a sudden drop to *pp.* The melody changes from its wild ride to a subdued, almost static stance, but all the while one senses the suppressed excitement, which breaks out again in another enormous *crescendo* to "dimanche." This verse reads

> The child all red and the white mother
> The boy in black and the girl in rose
> One at one thing, one at another,
> Each one paying his Sunday penny

The strange and abrupt modulation at "dimanche" hurls us into a recapitulation of the music of the opening stanza, but in a different key. After the two chromatic phrases, there is an unexpected *pp* and an augmented chord (under "*cl*ignote"). Debussy advises "discretion" at this point but perhaps "guile" would have been a better word, for the singer is describing the pickpocket who is slyly looking the crowd over! Once again a chromatic line builds excitement, and this stanza ends *ff,* too.

> Turn, turn, horses of their hearts,
> While around your turnings
> Winks the eye of the sly pickpocket.
> Turn to the sound of the triumphant trumpet.

At "vanqu*eur*" a new piano figure begins, as vigorous and cheerful as the first. We have once again modulated to a new key, which adds to the excitement created by the trills and rhythmic figure. Suddenly the mood darkens—the piano drops to relatively low chords and the trill sounds more ominous than gay. There is still suppressed excitement in the chromatic melody; but now it seems anxiety-ridden. The words are far from childlike:

It is astonishing how it intoxicates one
To go thus in this stupid circus:
Empty stomach and aching head,
Feeling bad in general and good in the crowd.

Once again the last syllable of one verse thrusts us into the music of the next section. This overlapping is part of the general excitement and continuous sense of forward motion. After the piano interlude, which is based on an augmented chord, the original music and mood of joyous vigor return in yet another key. The augmented chord under "Pour" has no real effect on the harmonic line, although of itself it is a bit of a surprise.

Turn hobby horses with no need
Ever to use any spurs
To command your gallop
Turn, turn, with no hope of hay.

After all the galloping motion of the first five verses, suddenly the harmonies stand still, the dynamic level begins to diminish and the tempo starts its long *ritard*. Neither the melody nor the rhythm reflects the merry-go-round in this rather languid section. Since the right hand figure is harmonically static, even its thirty-second notes do not really suggest speed. The augmented chord under "soupe" provides a lovely harmonic moment.

And hurry, horses of their soul
Already the dinner bell is ringing.
The night which falls and chases the crowd
Of gay drinkers whose thirst makes them hungry.

The *ritard* continues through the piano interlude, which consists of a beautiful B^7 chord with a flatted fifth, which becomes a regular B^7 chord. Since the original key is E major (for high voice) this B^7 is the dominant and should reintroduce the tonic. The melody does indeed enter with the expected V–I, but the harmonies are an unexpected A and G♯ minor, leading finally to a gorgeous D♯ minor under "*lentement*."

At the *a tempo* the vocal line is exactly half as fast as it originally was because Debussy has doubled each melody note's time value. The *pp* indication, added to the slower melodic movement, suggests that the ride is long over and is now just a memory.

Turn, turn! The velvet sky
Slowly clothes itself with golden stars.
The church sadly tolls the knell.

Suddenly there is a real *a tempo* for the last line of the poem:

Turn to the joyous sound of the drums, turn.

but this flurry of excitement is short-lived and is not reflected in the
dynamics, which remain soft. The piano's trills become lower and
lower until they finally melt into an E major chord, unprepared by
any suggestion of the dominant. The pianist will probably have better
control of the sonorities at the end if he plays the chord in the third
measure before the last with right and crosses the left hand over for the
three top notes.

5. Green (Aquarelles I)
Water-colors I

Voici des fruits, des fleurs, des feuilles et des branches,
Et puis voici mon coeur qui ne bat que pour vous.
Ne le déchirez pas avec vos deux mains blanches,
Et qu'à vos yeux si beaux l'humble présent soit doux.
J'arrive tout couvert encore de rosée,
Que le vent du matin vient glacer à mon front,
Souffrez que ma fatigue à vos pieds reposée,
Rêve des chers instants qui la délasseront.
Sur votre jeune sein, laissez rouler ma tête,
Toute sonore encore de vos derniers baisers;
Laissez-la s'apaiser de la bonne tempête,
Et que je dorme un peu puisque vous reposez.

For no known reason Verlaine chose to give English titles to several of his poems: "Spleen" follows "Green," and "Nevermore," not
set to music, also comes to mind. Under "Green" and "Spleen" we
find the subtitle "Aquarelles" ("Water-colors"), which is worthy of
discussion since Verlaine usually saw his poems in terms of music
rather than painting. In "Art Poétique," his key statement on poetry,
we find the following lines:

De la musique avant toute chose,
Pas la Couleur, rien que la Nuance!
Prends l'éloquence et tords-lui le cou!
De la musique encore et toujours!

Music before all else,
No Color, nothing but Nuance!
Take eloquence and wring its neck!
Music still and always!

The gist of these and other statements in the poem is that poetry should avoid the precise images of painting and literature in favor of the vague nuances of music. A glance at the text of "Green" suggests that, despite the title and subtitle, we have very few precise images and some extremely musical effects in the words themselves (the rich vowel sounds of "Toute sonore encore," the alliterative f's of "fruits," "fleurs" and "feuilles" in the first line, etc.).

Lest the performers mistake this song for yet another languid bit of melancholia, Debussy gives the indication "joyously animated" at the beginning. Even at a fairly brisk tempo, however, the minor chords of the piano introduction do not give the song a very gay send-off, and even the beautifully arched opening melodic line carries the typical *minore* touch of sadness. The Db^9 chord (the key is Gb for high voice) before "Et puis" dispels the minor feeling for the singer's second line and, in fact, for the rest of the section; when the introductory piano figure returns at the end of the section it, too, is in the major mode. There is a misprint in the International Music Edition for high voice— the chord under "*blan*ches" should have a G♮, as it does two measures earlier. The first verse reads:

Here are fruits, flowers, leaves and branches,
And then here is my heart, which beats only for you.
Do not tear it to bits with your two white hands,
And in your eyes so beautiful may the humble present be sweet.

There is a change of key for the middle section of this essentially ABA song. The melody for "encore de rosée" is based on the whole tone scale, as are the pianist's accompanying scales here and three bars later. The piano's left hand chords are diatonic, which somewhat obscures the whole-tone effect.

Midway through this section, Debussy begins to hold back the tempo ("un peu retenu"). The music becomes slower and slower to the very end, in musical imitation of the protagonist who, having spent all his energies on the journey and initial greeting to his beloved, is now content to lie at her feet and rest. Throughout the song Debussy, as he so often does, has alternated duple and triple subdivisions of the half measure in both vocal line and accompaniment. Since the line preceding the *un peu retenu* has been all 6/8, the basically 2/4 rhythm at "Souffrez que ma fatigue" will seem even slower in comparison. This is, of course, intentional. The relatively low notes at the ends of the last three phrases (under "fat*igue*," "repos*ée*, and "délass*eront*") also contribute to the increasing lassitude. The last line must be slow, free, and tender.

I arrive still all covered with dew
Which the morning wind has just frozen on my brow.

Allow my fatigue, placed at your feet,
To dream of the dear moments which will refresh it.

For the final verse Debussy reintroduces the music of the opening section, but this time it is slower and "caressing." The vocal phrase for the second line rises instead of falling, as it does in the beginning, thus preparing the new music of the ending. This high note is the softest note of the *decrescendo* which ranges from *p* to *pp*. The *ritard* still continues and the dynamics become more and more hushed. From the *plus lent,* the vocal line scarcely moves, and the last six syllables are intoned all on one low note. The last verse reads:

On your young breast, let my head rock
All ringing still from your last kisses.
Let it be appeased after the good storm,
And let me sleep a little while you rest.

It is clear from the composer's dynamic markings that the point of this song is the projection of a gentle, warm, tender mood. Nowhere is there room for virtuosic display of any kind.

Since both Debussy and Fauré have set this poem to music, comparisons are interesting and instructive. For a description of the Fauré song see page 83.

6. Spleen (Aquarelles II)
Water-colors II

Les roses étaient toutes rouges,
Et les lierres étaient tout noirs.
Chère, pour peu que tu te bouges,
Renaissent tous mes désespoirs.
Le ciel était trop bleu, trop tendre,
La mer trop verte et l'air trop doux;
Je crains toujours, ce qu'est d'attendre,
Quelque fuite atroce de vous!
Du houx à la feuille vernie,
Et du luisant buis je suis las,
Et de la campagne infinie,
Et de tout, hors de vous, Hélas!

Dictionary definitions of the word "spleen" range from ill temper and melancholia to hatred, animosity, and bile. Actually these are figurative descriptions of moods, once thought to be caused by an internal organ known as the spleen.

The protagonist in this poem is indeed in a black frame of mind.

He fears that his beloved will flee from him and, alas, he is weary of everything but her.

Like the preceding song ("Green") "Spleen" has a subtitle, "Aquarelle," or water-color. While the text is full of references to color —red roses, black ivy, blue sky, green sea, green-leaved holly—the mood is too bleak to suggest the delicate palette of most water colors.

The piano begins with a four-bar solo, which introduces one of the main melodic ideas of the song. Although this theme is present in one form or another throughout the accompaniment, it is never used in the vocal line. The singer enters with a stark *recitativo* on a single note. The octave leap to "Chère" is most effective after all the repeated notes, but the descending scale quickly brings us back to the original note. The mood is subdued until the word "bouges," after which the rhythm in the accompaniment begins to create a sense of anxiety and nervous tension. This is abetted by the little chromatic thirty-second note figures, the increase in dynamics and the *poco stringendo* (small *accelerando*). The words for the first section are:

> The roses were all red,
> And the ivy was all black.
> Dear one, when you become a little restless
> All my despair is reborn.

At the change of key the mood reverts to a dreamier, less anxious one; nevertheless, the pulsating accompanying chords continue. Are they heart beats, little gasps? Meanwhile the piano's original melody with its dotted eighth-note figure is also heard. Fortunately, the rhythm in the vocal line is quite straightforward and the piano's upper voice has steady quarter notes to keep the complicated subdivisions in check. The music and two lines of text in these four measures suggest the recalling of happier times:

> The sky was too blue, too tender,
> The sea was too green and the air too soft.

Reminiscences over, the anxiety-ridden mood and original key now return. The singer once again begins with a repeated note and the piano reiterates its plaintive melody. After two measures the tremendous buildup, which will eventually culminate in the *ff* climax at "tout, hors de vous" begins (marked *stringendo* and *crescendo*). The piano's rushing thirty-second notes and dotted eighth-note rhythm, coupled with rising intervals, lead to an interim high point at "houx." Here the pulsating chords begin again, and the melody drops an octave to prepare for yet another ascent. The tempo accelerates with each rising melodic figure until we reach the powerful B♭ high note at "tout." At this moment of intensity the tempo pulls back to the *lento* of the beginning and a *decrescendo* begins. The piano makes the most of the *diminuendo* and *rallentando* by itself and one might think the vocal part over, but no, the singer has one last poignant word—"Hélas." This must be wrung from the tortured soul of the poet and quietly supported by the low, lugubrious chords in the accompaniment. The text concludes:

> I always fear what may happen!
> Some atrocious flight of yours.
> Of the green-leaved holly
> And of the shining boxwood I am weary,
> And of the endless countryside
> And of everything, but you . . . Alas!

Deux Romances
Poems by Paul Bourget

1. Romance

> L'âme evaporée et souffrante,
> L'âme douce, l'âme odorante
> Des lis divins que j'ai cueillis
> Dans le jardin de ta pensée,
> Où donc les vents l'ont-ils chassée,
> Cette âme adorable des lis?
> N'est-il plus un parfum qui reste
> De la suavité céleste
> Des jours où tu m'enveloppais
> D'une vapeur surnaturelle,
> Faite d'espoir, d'amour fidèle,
> De béatitude et de paix?

This wisp of a song is one of Debussy's briefest efforts, but in its twenty-eight short measures it creates an atmosphere and mood as distinctive and effective as many a full-length aria. In his novel, *Doctor Faustus*, Thomas Mann says that there is more drama in Chopin's "C♯ minor Nocturne" (Opus 27), which lasts a mere five minutes, than in a five-act opera by Wagner. While one would make no such claims for this ephemeral song, its economy of means is remarkable indeed.

As is the case in so many of Debussy's songs, the piano has its own melody, which first serves as an introduction and is thereafter heard repeatedly throughout the song. Towards the end of the piece, at "Faite d'espoir, d'amour fidèle," the singer uses this material, too. This is really a perfect duet for the two performers, with particularly rich effects when there is an overlapping of the two separate lines. One such moment occurs at "pensée," where the piano's tune begins on the high F♯ while the singer's phrase ends on the G♯ below (analyzed in D major, the key for high voice).

The vocal line begins with a series of repeated notes on a broken E minor triad. These declamatory opening syllables create a more melancholy mood that the amiable piano introduction has led one to expect. The silence in the accompaniment increases the impact of the measure. The A♯, in melody and accompaniment at "odorante," moves the harmony to B minor, creating in the process a rather exotic effect. Special attention should be paid to the descending E major scale fragment created by the half notes in the bass.

As the vocal line rises to "cueillis," a *crescendo* begins which culminates on the G♯ at "pensée." The melody twists and turns unpredictably to suit the text, which is equally full of surprises: one learns that the soul referred to is that of lilies, and that the poet has gathered these flowers in the thoughts of his beloved. The first four lines of verse are:

> The fleeting and suffering soul,
> The sweet soul, the scented soul,
> Of the heavenly lilies that I have gathered
> In the garden of your thought,

The piano makes a rapid *decrescendo* to permit the singer to enter quietly again. This time the accompanying A_7^9 chords make it apparent that Debussy was thinking not of E minor, but of A^9 chords when he began his melody. The four measures of music for these two lines of verse serve as a bridge to the next section:

> Where then have the winds chased
> This adorable soul of the lilies?

For the next eight bars, the accompaniment abandons its own melody to provide a rich wash of color for the vocal line. The tempo becomes slower and freer. For five syllables, the singer lingers on one note; when the melody first rises from that F♯ it is immediately pulled back to it. Finally, the melody soars from the F♯ and its freedom and fluidity are reestablished. This entire section is soft and dreamy. The words are:

> Is there no longer any fragrance left
> Of the celestial sweetness
> Of the days when you enveloped me
> In a supernatural haze

At the return of the original tempo, piano and voice join for the first time in the original piano melody. The dynamic level rises temporarily, but a *decrescendo* sets in almost immediately. If one insists on finding a climactic moment in this essentially quiet, wistful song, it would be at the top of the rise under "De béati*tude*." From this point the fade-out ending begins. The closing lines of the poem are:

> Made of hope, of faithful love,
> Of blessedness and of peace?

2. Les Cloches
The Bells

> Les feuilles s'ouvraient sur le bord des branches,
> Délicatement.
> Les cloches tintaient, légères et franches,
> Dans le ciel clément.
> Rythmique et fervent comme une antienne,
> Ce lointain appel
> Me remémorait la blancheur chrétienne
> Des fleurs de l'autel.
> Ces cloches parlaient d'heureuses années,
> Et, dans le grand bois,
> Semblaient reverdir les feuilles fanées,
> Des jours d'autrefois.

"Les Cloches," the second of the *Two Romances,* is another delicate wisp of a song. There are no startling events in words or music, just the projection of a fleeting, nostalgic, wistful mood.

Throughout the piece the piano accompaniment suggests the sound of bells. The chord under "*clément*" is particularly effective in so doing, as are the momentary clashes between the vocal line and the accompaniment in such places as "dé*li*catement," "*clé*ment," "loin-*tain*," etc.

Debussy's favorite rhythmic device, the subdivision of a half measure into triplet quarter notes in the voice over regular eighth notes in the accompaniment, is frequently in evidence. Far more noteworthy is the fact that the three-note melodic fragment, introduced in the very first measure by the piano's left hand (the tune of the bells), continues to be heard in all but eight measures of the song. It is somewhat obscured by the underlying chords from "Les cloches tintaient" to "une antienne"; it moves to the right hand at "Ce lointain," and it is augmented rhythmically at the "un peu plus lent" piano interlude, but it is almost always present. Since it is such a marvelous structural device, and since it represents the song of the bells, the listener should be aware of its existence from start to finish.

The singer enters with a melodic line firmly rooted to the sub-dominant note (A in the high voice key of E major). There is a deliberate monotony to this phrase, and indeed to the melodic lines in the entire first section. An almost hypnotic effect seems to be desired. Even the phrase "Me remémorait la blancheur chrétienne," which climbs to the highest note in the first half of the song, is brought back to the note on which it started. The dynamics are severely limited, with but one small surge allowed in the second line. The mood conveyed by music and text is one of pleasant, spiritual nostalgia:

> Leaves opened on the edge of the branches,
> Delicately,
> The bells clanged, light and clear,
> In the mild sky.
> Rhythmic and fervent as a hymn,
> This distant call
> Reminded me of the Christian whiteness
> Of the flowers of the altar.

By the end of this section we have modulated to the relative minor. The piano interlude which bridges the song's two parts is rich in detail: on top there is the rhythmically augmented three-note theme of the bells previously described; just under this are chords on weak beats; the left hand has broken chords on top and long ringing notes below, which must be held for their full time value. Fortunately, the notes themselves are quite simple, so the pianist should be able to control all these elements.

The closing portion of the song contains one of those magic moments that give pleasure even after countless hearings—the unexpected G♮ at "fanées" (faded). This G♮ is repeated for five long syllables, after which it finally yields to a G♯ to form the tonic major chord.

The first line of this section, like so many of the phrases in the first part, is limited in range and begins and ends on the same note. In the next line, however, we have a real sweep up to the high G♯ under "semblait" and a matching, albeit moderate, *crescendo*. While the melodic line descends from its high note, the accompaniment continues the *crescendo* with a rising arpeggio. Obviously the voice must remain strong through this measure, but a *decrescendo* would seem appropriate during "*les feuilles fanées*" so that the G♮ can be sung softly. The words for this section are:

> These bells spoke of happy years,
> And in the great woods
> Seemed to make the faded leaves green again
> As in days gone by.

The piano postlude reminds the listener twice again of the three-note melodic fragment—the sound of the bells.

Les Angélus
The Angelus

Poem by G. LeRoy

Cloches chrétiennes pour les matines,
Sonnant au coeur d'espérer encore!
Angélus angelisés d'aurore!
Las! Où sont vos prières câlines?

Vous étiez de si douces folies!
Et chanterelles d'amours prochaines!
Aujourd'hui souveraine est ma peine,
Et toutes matines abolies.

Je ne vis plus que d'ombre et de soir;
Les las angélus pleurent la sort,
Et là, dans mon coeur résigné, dort
La seule veuve de tout espoir.

Perhaps it is mere coincidence that "Les Angélus" immediately follows "Les Cloches" (see page 324), or perhaps Debussy's musical imagination was not yet ready to leave the challenge of incorporating the sound of ringing bells in a song. In any case, we have in this second song a completely different, and even more effective, piano figure to imitate the "tintinnabulation of the bells, bells, bells."

The composer describes the mood he wants as "a sad sweetness," and the music he provides is suitably gentle and melancholy. The strongest lines of verse, "Aujourd'hui souveraine est ma peine, Et toutes matines abolies" ("Today my sorrow is sovereign, And all Matins are abolished"), receive the most dramatic treatment in vocal line and accompaniment, with a buildup to "peine" and a strong *diminuendo* for the descending melodic phrase of the second line. There are other small *crescendos* and *decrescendos,* but by and large the dynamics are kept within a very narrow range—from *pp* to *mf* at most.

The piano begins with its bell-like figuration, which it maintains —with the exception of the two bars under "Et toutes matines abolies" —until the end. The singer enters with a favorite Debussy device, the use of a single repeated note for several syllables. In the first section only, the first phrase has this static quality—the others have considerable sweep and flow. The first verse reads:

Christian bells for Matins (morning Church service)
Telling the heart still to hope!

Angelus (bell rung to signal early morning service) made angelic by the dawn!
Alas! where are your beguiling prayers?

It is obvious that the word "Las!" (Alas) must be separated from what follows as well as from the preceding phrase. Although there is no rest after the half note, the dot above it indicates a shortening of the time value to create a small space.

After the brief piano interlude we have another vocal line featuring repeated notes, a device which always creates a feeling of suspended motion. The second line has some movement at the end, but the most powerful lines—already described above—are the last two:

You were of such sweet madness!
And harbingers of love!
Today my sorrow is sovereign,
And all Matins are abolished.

The final section of the song is even more gentle than the first two. There is only one small *crescendo* in the otherwise *p* vocal part, and the piano's dynamics range from *pp* to *ppp*. The tempo, moderate to begin with and "retenu" (held back) at the end of section one, is marked "slower" at the second line and "still slower" for the last phrase. Under this "encore plus lent" the bells toll slowly indeed, and the piano figure changes from eighth notes to quarter notes in imitation.

"Résigné" (resigned) is the key word to the mood of music and text for this last stanza. Only the third line really frees itself from the repeated note melodic format, although in the last line we have alternating neighboring notes as a variant. The fact that the melody falls to the low tonic note (the key for high voice is C♯ minor) adds to the feeling of sad resignation. The poem concludes:

I no longer see anything but shadow and evening;
The weary Angelus mourns death,
And there, in my resigned heart, sleeps
The lonely widow of all hope.

Dans le jardin   Poem by Paul Gravelot
In the Garden

Je regardais dans le jardin,
Furtif au travers de la haie;
Je t'ai vue, enfant! et soudain,
Mon coeur tressaillit; je t'aimais!
Je m'égratignais aux épines,
Mes doigts saignaient avec les mures,
Et ma souffrance était divine:

Je voyais ton front de gamine,
Tes cheveux d'or et ton front pur!
Grandette et pourtant puérile,
Coquette d'instinct seulement,
Les yeux bleus ombrés de longs cils,
Qui regardent tout gentiment,
Un corps un peu frêle et charmant,
Une voix de mai, des gestes d'avril!
Je regardais dans le jardin,
Furtif, au travers de la haie;
Je t'ai vue, enfant! et soudain
Mon coeur tressaillit: je t'aimais!

This is a charming song, full of the wondrous rapture of young love. Debussy says its mood is to be "gay and light" and provides a sparkling piano introduction to set the stage. His choice of scale and harmonies for this introduction creates an almost mythical effect, as though we were about to hear a fairy tale rather than a slice-of-life narrative. This is due to the fact that the scale figures in the first two bars can be heard as being in the Dorian mode (the medieval church mode formed by the intervals of the white notes from D to D') more easily than as the minor scales of F♯ or C♯, the other two choices (analyzed in the key for high voice). The overall key for the song is quite ambiguous as Debussy vacillates between the relative major and minor, i.e., C♯ minor and E major in the key for high voice.

When the singer enters, the pace seems to slacken because Debussy switches from triplet sixteenth notes to regular sixteenth notes in the moving line, and the accompaniment has a long chord. Note that the word "furtif," in the first line, is separated from the word which follows by a breathing mark given by the composer himself. The piano returns to its triplet figure at the end of the singer's first line, and from the second line on, throughout the song, we have the duple rhythm in the vocal part pitted against the triple rhythm in the accompaniment. This is Debussy's most often-used rhythmic device.

The whole first section should be sung with breathless, awestruck amazement. The only long phrases are "Mon coeur tressaillit," which calls for a *crescendo* in the vocal line to match the one marked for the piano, and "Je t'aimais!" which is sung quietly. The first verse reads:

I looked in the garden
Furtively, over the hedge;
I saw you, child! and suddenly
My heart trembled: I loved you!

As the singer lingers over the last syllable the piano scampers gayly up the keyboard, still with a slightly antique sound. The melody becomes a *recitativo* for the next two lines, and most of the motion is in the piano part. At the "retenu" (held back) the mood becomes dreamy and languid:

I scratched myself on the thorns,
My fingers bled from the brambles,
And my suffering was divine:

The tempo picks up again briefly at the change of key, while the poet begins to describe his beloved; but the dreamy mood overtakes him again:

I saw your saucy face
Your golden hair and your pure brow!
Grownup yet childlike,
Coquettish only by instinct,

We now return to the original key signature, but Debussy wants the mood to remain "sweet and caressing" for a while longer, and only gradually to become gay and light as before. The piano figure consequently shifts to regular sixteenth notes, with the triplet figure held in abeyance. The entire section is one buildup in tempo and dynamics, until the ecstatic high note is reached by the singer at "d'avril."

The blue eyes shadowed by long lashes
Which look so gently,
A body somewhat frail and charming,
A voice of May, gestures of April!

The piano carries the *crescendo* to completion after the last syllable has been sung, and one is suitably prepared for the recapitulation, but two surprises await the listener: first is the *subito pp* which is effective in itself, but more interesting is the straightforward harmonization which makes of our initial complicated Dorian mode a simple descending E major scale! Now we have the kind of sound more commonly associated with light-hearted gaiety. Of course, this harmonic simplicity does not last long—we have fragments of whole-tone scales under "haie" and "Je t'ai vue," a beautiful A chord with a major seventh under "sou*dain*," etc.

After the *a tempo* we have a steady *ritardando* to the end of the vocal part. The piano postlude begins with a forward spurt, but becomes very slow again within three measures. Debussy maintains the tonal ambivalence to the end, writing half the postlude in C# minor and half in E, the relative major.

The final lines of verse repeat the first stanza, but the original breathless quality is replaced by a dreamier, more tranquil mood:

I looked in the garden
Furtively, over the hedge
I saw you, child! and suddenly
My heart trembled: I loved you!

La Mer est plus belle   Poem by Paul Verlaine
The Sea Is More Beautiful

La mer est plus belle
Que les cathédrales;
Nourrice fidèle,
Berceuse de râles;
La mer sur qui prie
La Vièrge Marie!

Elle a tous les dons,
Terribles et doux.
J'entends ses pardons,
Gronder ses courroux;
Cette immensité
N'a rien d'entêté.

Oh! Si patiente,
Même quand méchante!
Un souffle ami hante
La vague, en nous chante:
"Vous, sans espérance,
Mourez sans souffrance!"

Et puis, sous les cieux
Qui s'y rient, plus clairs,
Elle a des airs bleus,
Roses, gris et verts . . .
Plus belle que tous,
Meilleure que nous!

Throughout this song surging arpeggios evoke the restless energy
of the sea. Even in the slow middle section we feel the sea's power,
sometimes benign, sometimes threatening, but always there.

The piano introduction is *forte,* as is the opening melodic line.
The piano's arpeggios in the first three bars, and the singer's initial four
notes, are all part of the dominant D major chord (the key for high
voice is G minor); the unexpected modulation at "belle" to F minor
produces a moment of great beauty. There is a rapid *decrescendo* in
the measure for solo piano after "cathédrales," and the next line is
gentle and caressing. An equally rapid *crescendo* brings us back to full
forte for the last line of the stanza:

The sea is more beautiful than the cathedrals,
Faithful nurse,
Cradle of death rattles,
The sea over which the Virgin Mary prays!

The imagery in the third line ("râles" or death rattles) is rather startling, but the word "berceuse"—which may mean cradle, or woman who rocks the cradle, or lullaby—suggests that the sea gives solace to the dying. Certainly the music for the second line is gentle and soothing; the modulation to B♭ under "râles" is fervent and glowing, with no touch of the sinister or ominous. The *crescendo* at "La mer" provides a triumphant climax within this B♭ tonality, which continues unabated through the next measure and is reinforced by the accompaniment's return to the original D major arpeggios under "Marie!" A change of key under a repeated note in the melody is always an effective device; in this case it gives a very strong ending to the first stanza.

The *molto diminuendo* of the brief piano interlude prepares us for the next section. Here we do have an ominous sound, which builds from the soft first measure to a crashing climax at "immensité," only to subside again. The dynamics of this song are unusually extreme for Debussy, but then the sea he is describing in the earlier sections of the song is a turbulent one:

It (the sea) has all qualities,
Terrible and gentle;
I hear its forgiveness,
Its scolding fury;
This immensity brooks no stubbornness.

A big *ritard* in the piano figuration brings the tempo down for the "calm and sweet" middle section. Temporarily the roaring ocean becomes a gentle pond and the piano figure seems to describe splashing fountains rather than crashing waves. The melodic line has many repeated notes—a very effective setting for the words "Si patiente"— a favorite ploy of Debussy's. At the end of the second line, appropriately enough under the word "méchante" (evil) an ominous sound is heard in the accompaniment. The *crescendo* to and the *decrescendo* from a *p* must be eerie and threatening. At "hante" there is an abrupt change of mood, accomplished by a lovely modulation to G major. The tempo becomes even more relaxed and the dynamic level still more quiet, as the key changes once again to E♭ for the last two lines of the section:

Oh! So patient
Even when evil!

A friendly breeze haunts
The waves, and sings to us:
"You, without hope
Die without suffering!"

Debussy has interpreted these last two lines, as he did the line
which deals with death rattles, in the most benign way. There is no
irony, no bitterness in the music; he is grateful to the sea for its willing-
ness to engulf the sufferer and end his pain.

As is so often the case, the piano interlude serves to change the
tempo, this time bringing us back to *tempo I°*. The flamboyant mood of
the beginning does not, however, return, for the music remains soft and
gentle. The tempo soon begins to yield to the dreamier mood and there
is a gradual *ritard* to the end. The last melodic phrase makes a very
strange and vague ending, and the harmonies for the last three bars
are equally unusual: the vocal line clashes with the piano's upper voice
on both notes of "meil*leure*"; the D^7 immediately following is dis-
placed by B minor under "que"; the final syllable, sung on the dominant, is supported by a chord which combines G^7 and D; and the final
resolution to G seems unprepared despite all that preceded it. Stranger
still is the overall choice of key signature, for nowhere in the song do
we find a G minor chord—every reference to G is in the major mode.
One would like to be able to ask Debussy "Why?" The last stanza
reads:

And then under the skies
Which smile more brightly,
It seems blue,
Red, grey and green . . .
More beautiful than all,
Better than we!

Le Son du cor s'afflige   Poem by Paul Verlaine
The Sound of the Horn

Le son du cor s'afflige vers les bois,
D'une douleur on veut croire orpheline
Qui vient mourir au bas de la colline,
Parmi la bise errant en courts abois.

L'âme du loup pleure dans cette voix,
Qui monte avec le soleil, qui décline
D'une agonie on veut croire câline,
Et qui ravit et qui navre à la fois.

Pour faire mieux cette plainte assoupie,
La neige tombe à longs traits de charpie

A travers le couchant sanguinolent,
Et l'air a l'air d'être un soupir d'automne,
Tant il fait doux par ce soir monotone,
Où se dorlote un paysage lent.

The words and music of this song are so laden with gloom that it is hard to bear in mind that they describe nothing more than the sound of a horn! Of course, to poets like Baudelaire and Verlaine the sound of a horn, or any musical sound for that matter, could convey a mood more powerfully than words, for there is as much nuance in a sound as there is in a sentiment. Verlaine felt that if one must use words, as one must in a poem, one should be vague, for the more precise words try to be, the more they obscure feelings. In this song the text and the setting are both deliberately evocative and imprecise—the quintessence of symbolist-Impressionist writing.

The piano introduction begins with an open fifth, which un-doubtedly represents the sound of horns. The rhythmic marking in this measure deliberately obscures the 9/8 meter, as do the double-stemmed notes in the next measure, the tied note in the following bar, and the repetition of the rhythmic pattern of the first measure in bar four. The modulation to A major (analyzed in F minor, key for high voice) just before the singer's entry is as beautiful as it is unexpected.

Although the accompaniment has 9/8 for its time signature, the vocal line is written in 3/4 time. This allows Debussy to pit regular eighth notes against triplet eighth notes, his favorite rhythmic device, with great ease. The immediate effect when the singer enters is one of slowing down, especially since the accompaniment's held chord does not remind the listener of the original triple meter. This effect is all the more striking because there is neither harmonic nor melodic move-ment—the first nine syllables are sung on one note. This is also quite typical of Debussy. When the melodic line finally ascends a half step at "bois," the A major chord becomes an augmented chord. No one could mistake this style of writing for anything but French Impres-sionist!

The vocal line develops more rhythmic and melodic motion in the next phrase, but it is brought back to its single note monotone for the third line of verse. The accompaniment does provide some sense of motion here with its rich augmented chords. The dynamics are in-teresting—the singer is told to murmur very softly while the piano strikes the first and third chords with considerable strength. Very sen-sitive pedaling is necessary to create the desired *fp* effect in these two measures. The stanza ends with an unprepared modulation to C major.

The words require more than mere translation for their effect to be maximized. The word "s'afflige" in the first line, for instance, actually means "is afflicted" or "grieves"; in the second line we have not just any orphan but a female orphan; "la bise" is the cold and dry north wind; and "abois," while literally the barking of a dog is figuratively used to mean desperate straits. Now, a workable translation:

> The sound of the horn goes grieving towards the woods,
> With a grief that makes one think of an orphan
> Who comes to die at the foot of the hill,
> Mid the wandering Northwind's howling gusts.

The next section is marked "un peu animé," a little livelier; the triplet eighth notes in the melody and the throbbing chords in the accompaniment help create the desired sense of motion. This is not matched by harmonic motion, for one chord suffices for the two measures of line one, and another for the two bars of line two. There is more harmonic activity for lines three and four and we end the section where we started it, in C major. The pulsating accompanying chords and flowing melodic line create a sense of excitement which builds to a *forte* at "ravit," whose second syllable gets an accent. The chromatic rise from E♭ to E at "D'une" is an exciting moment and the chord there is powerful in its dissonance. The words are full of paradoxes: the sound of the horn, now compared to the cry of a wolf, rises with the sun, but the sun is setting; it has an agony that fondles or cajoles; it is ravishing and yet heart-rending:

> The soul of the wolf cries in that voice
> Which rises with the sun which sets
> With an agony one would think cajoling
> And which ravishes as it tears the heart.

The more languid feeling of the first section now returns and the song becomes slower and dreamier as it draws to a close. There is little feeling of motion in the first four bars of accompaniment, but the melodic line does have an upward flow. The descending chords under the falling melodic line of "La neige tombe à longs traits de charpie" have a strong sense of direction, because each is the major triad of the melody note it harmonizes. This is a favorite device of Debussy. The song becomes almost motionless as the melody continues on one note and the accompanying chords change ever so slowly. The instructions say "dying out" and the words speak of a hushed lament:

> To improve this hushed lament
> The snow falls in long strokes of lint
> Across the sunset tinged with blood.

The chords in the piano interlude sound muffled and distant, like footsteps in the snow. The play on words in the next line, "l'air a l'air," stems from the idiom "avoir l'air," which means to resemble or seem like. After the Northwind and snowfall, one is somewhat surprised that the air is like a breath of autumn, but why quarrel with a poet's vision? For the two measures of "Tant il fait doux par ce soir mono-tone" the rhythmic roles are reversed, the accompaniment having two against the singer's three. The melodic phrase for these two bars provides some welcome motion before the very quiet ending. Once again the final resolution is unexpected and unprepared. Nowhere, except at the very end, does F minor assert itself as a tonal center and, were the last two chords erased, one would be much more likely to guess Db as the principal key. The poem ends:

> And the air seems like a breath of autumn
> So gentle it is on this monotonous evening
> In which a languid countryside indulges.

L'Echelonnement des haies
The Slope of the Hedges

Poem by Paul Verlaine

L'échelonnement des haies
Moutonne à l'infini, mer
Claire dans le brouillard clair,
Qui sent bon les jeunes baies.

Des arbres et des moulins
Sont légers sur le vert tendre,
Où vient s'ébattre et s'étendre
L'agilités des poulains.

Dans ce vague d'un Dimanche,
Voici se jouer aussi,
De grandes brébis, aussi
Douces que leur laine blanche.

Tout à l'heure déferlait
L'onde roulée en volutes
De cloches comme des flûtes
Dans le ciel comme du lait.

The text of this song describes a pastoral scene of great charm and beauty. Mankind is subtly insinuated into this landscape by references to Sunday—a human time division—and bells like flutes—a human invention for the creation of sound.

There are many interesting details to note in the poem: the inner rhyme of "mer/Claire" at the end of line one and the beginning of line two (note that this warrants a *crescendo* and *sforzando* in the musical setting); the repetition of Claire/clair (same meaning, same pronunciation) in the second line; and the repeated sounds "tendre" and "s'*étendre*," "aussi" and "aussi," "défer*lait*" and "lait" as rhymed endings.

Read without musical background, the poem can seem gentle and languid, but Debussy's setting creates a brisk, bouncy mood of joyous exhilaration which carries the words along at a merry pace for most of the piece. Throughout the song the piano frequently features the somewhat unusual subdivision of five sixteenth notes to a quarter note; this contributes considerably to the liveliness. The accented double-stemmed notes at the beginning of each beat should sound like guitar pluckings or violin pizzicati. They, too, keep things bouncy and gay.

The voice enters with a light-hearted, airy melody which is echoed by the piano's double-stemmed notes. Even the almost motionless final line of the stanza fails to subdue the general high spirits, especially since there is a wonderful modulation under the repeated notes of "jeunes baies." The first stanza reads:

> The graduated slope of hedges
> Undulates towards infinity, a sea
> Clear in the clear mist,
> Which the young bayberries scent.

After the piano interlude the accompaniment becomes less pointed, more like a wash of color. In this stanza the fourth line is all on one note, and the accompaniment makes no startling modulations to disturb the gentle and open sound of the C major arpeggios (here analyzed in C♯ minor, the key for high voice). The words are:

> The trees and windmills,
> Are light on the tender green,
> Where to frolic and romp come
> The agile colts.

The next section is calmer and less active, the five sixteenth-note figure changing to the slower-moving, normal four sixteenth notes per quarter note after the first measure. There are no longer any accents on the initial notes of each beat in the accompaniment, and the *legato* phrases become longer. The second line in the vocal part is still marked *staccato,* but the last two lines are in long *legato* phrases. The final line calls for a *ritard.*

> In this Sunday haze
> Here also play
> Large sheep as
> Soft as their white wool.

The original tempo returns at the new time signature, but since we still have regular sixteenth notes the music seems a little less lively than it did at the very beginning. With the exception of the piano introduction and the first piano interlude, the dynamics of the entire song have been quite subdued. The small *crescendo* and *sforzando,* at "mer/Claire" in the first stanza, are the only indications other than *p* given to the singer. This last stanza is even softer and more gentle for both performers than the first three. The singer has sustained notes at "cloches," "flûtes," "ciel," and of course the final syllable, "lait." Everything is *legato* and breaths are quickly stolen between phrases.

There is a lovely harmonic contrast created by the B♯ in the phrase "Dans le ciel" and the B♮ in the following phrase, "comme du lait." The clash between melody and harmony on the singer's last syllable (caused by a suspension) and its resolution on the next chord are also noteworthy effects. The last lines are:

> Suddenly unfurled,
> The wave rolled in spirals of
> Bells like flutes
> In the sky like milk.

The paucity of verbs in this last stanza makes the picture all the more vague, as befits a scene viewed from the distance and through the haze!

Fêtes galantes I
Poems by Paul Verlaine

1. En sourdine
Muted

> Calmes dans le demi-jour
> Que les branches hautes font,
> Pénétrons bien notre amour
> De ce silence profond.
>
> Fondons nos âmes, nos coeurs,
> Et nos sens extasiés,
> Parmi les vagues langueurs
> Des pins et des arbousiers.
>
> Ferme tes yeux à demi,
> Croise tes bras sur ton sein,
> Et de ton coeur endormi
> Chasse à jamais tout dessein.
>
> Laissons-nous persuader
> Au souffle berceur et doux

Qui vient à tes pieds rider
Les ondes de gazon roux.

Et quand solennel, le soir
Des chênes noirs tombera,
Voix de notre désespoir,
Le rossignol chantera.

In 1869 Paul Verlaine published a collection of poems called
Les Fêtes galantes. These poems, many of which were set to music by
both Debussy and Fauré, were inspired by an exhibition of the courtly,
graceful, opulent paintings of Watteau, with their flirtatious, be-
ribboned, rosy-cheeked demoiselles and their gallant, chivalrous
courtiers.

Although "Clair de lune" is the first poem in Verlaine's collection, Debussy begins his cycle *Fêtes galantes I* with "En sourdine."
Fauré uses this poem in his Opus 58, which is a five-song cycle also
based entirely on Verlaine's poetry.

The enigmatic quality of the poem and the music is immediately
expressed by the opening chord, a diminished chord with a major
third added. The resolution in the second measure is to B major (for
high voice) which seems to be the tonic. The voice enters quietly,
singing "Calmes dans le demi-jour" (calm in the half-light) all on one
note. In fact, the melodic line hovers around that one note for six
long measures, creating a still, mysterious mood. The words are
equally mystic:

Calm in the half-light
Created by the high branches
Let us steep our love well
In this deep silence

The melody is based largely on the black note pentatonic scale
(except for the two E♯s) which creates a somewhat Oriental effect,
especially where the harmony moves to D♯ minor (under "*amour*").

A new and beautiful harmony—a richly extended B chord containing the 7, 9, and 13—introduces the next section, which finally
settles on a polyphonic chord, B major and G♯. There is no third in the
G♯ chord, another Oriental effect. Here the accompaniment has its
own repeated note. The melodic line begins more freely and with
greater scope, only to be pulled back for the words "vagues langueurs
Des pins et des arbousiers." This section may be translated

Let us base our souls, our hearts
And our ecstasy-filled senses,
In the vague weariness
Of the pine and arbutus trees.

The singer continues

> Close your eyes half way,
> Cross your arms on your breast,
> And from your sleeping heart
> Chase all design forever.

The triplet figure in the accompaniment creates a sense of motion hitherto lacking, and Debussy's advice ("en animant un peu"—getting a little livelier) emphasizes this forward surge. The singer and pianist must take pains to assure the exact placement of the vocal eighth notes against the accompanying triplets. This is not a good place for too much *rubato!*

The accompanist now has two whole measures of a simple broken D chord. The singer reenters with an ostinato D, and again the melody is tightly held in rein until it soars under the words "de gazon roux." The words in this section are full of soft sounds—nous, souffle, doux, roux, pers*ua*der, berc*eur*, gaz*on:*

> Let us be persuaded
> By the gentle and rocking breeze
> Which comes to your feet to ruffle
> The waves of the reddish lawn.

The accompaniment, with its triplet chords, imitates the ripples of breeze-swept grass, but we are once again becalmed:

> And when solemnly, the evening
> Falls, from the black oak trees
> Voice of our despair,
> The nightingale will sing.

The fade-out ending brings back the pentatonic black-note melody, and the final chord unites B major and G♯ once again.

2. Clair de lune
Moonlight

> Votre âme est un paysage choisi
> Que vont charmants masques et bergamasques,
> Jouant du luth et dansant, et quasi
> Tristes sous leurs déguisements fantasques,
>
> Tout en chantant sur le mode mineur
> L'amour vainqueur et la vie opportune.
> Ils n'ont pas l'air de croire à leur bonheur,
> Et leur chanson se mêle au clair de lune,

Au calme clair de lune triste et beau,
Qui fait rêver les oiseaux dans les arbres,
Et sangloter d'extase les jets d'eau,
Les grands jets d'eau sveltes parmi les marbres.

Verlaine's poem "Clair de lune" inspired two settings by Debussy and one by Fauré. For discussions of the earlier work by Debussy and that of Fauré see pages 283 and 69.

Debussy's first "Clair de lune" is a rather immature effort, but this later setting is comparable in inspiration and execution to the masterpiece of Fauré. In many respects the two songs are quite similar. Like the Fauré song, Debussy's begins with an independent piano prelude, but instead of the flowing lines given us by Fauré, we have a figuration based on the black-note pentatonic scale which seems to suggest the sound of a gentle fountain. It is not until the fifth measure, the measure in which the singer enters, that the real key of the piece (G♯ minor for high voice) is established.

It is no accident that the main rhythmic stress of the first line is placed on "pay*sage*" by both composers—this stress is natural and inevitable. In fact, one finds almost total agreement on rhythmic emphasis throughout.

There are many exquisite harmonic changes in the Debussy song. The first of these occurs between measures 7 and 8, under "berga-masques," where the pianist arrives at a B♭⁷ chord from a diminished chord based on A♯ (the sound of the held G♯ adds a major third to the diminished chord). The effect is one of being lifted harmonically while the singer's melodic line falls. The next measure has another totally unprepared and absolutely glorious harmonic lift to an augmented chord. Here the vocal line is an insistent repeated note, while the underlying chords change once again. The constantly soaring accompaniment leaps again in measure 11, but in bar 12, at "déguise-*mente*," singer and accompaniment meet on a D♯ (the dominant) chord so the song can return to its G♯ minor tonality.

Although the accompaniment now seems to be going into a second verse similar to the first, the vocal line immediately leads to new material. From "Au calme claire de lune" to the end of the song, the singer has a ravishing, serenely ethereal line to sing. The *p* indication at "au calme claire de lune" (*pp* for the piano) must be taken very seriously indeed. The *crescendo* over "d'extase les jets" should lead at least to a *mezzo forte* so that another *subito piano* can be made on "d'eau." The pianist may have to push the tempo a little under the singer's long "marbres," but can compensate with a *ritard* at the exquisite fade-out ending.

From "sangloter" until the end of the song, the accompaniment climbs in unadulterated major or minor triads. Only a faint echo of the figure of the opening measure disturbs the gossamer purity of the harmonies, giving cyclic structural unity.

Your soul is an elect landscape
Where spell-binding masqueraders and dancers,
Play the lute and dance,
And are almost sad under their fantastic disguises!

While singing in the minor mode
Love, the conqueror, and opportune life,
They don't seem to believe in their happiness,
And their song blends with the moonlight.

In the calm moonlight, sad and beautiful,
Which makes the birds dream in the trees,
And (makes) the fountains sob with ecstasy,
The tall, slim streams amid the statues!

3. Fantoches
Puppets

Scaramouche et Pulcinella,
Qu'un mauvais dessein rassembla,
Gesticulent noirs sous la lune,
Cependant l'excellent docteur Bolonais
Cueille avec lenteur des simples
Parmi l'herbe brune.
Lors sa fille, piquant minois,
Sous la charmille, en tapinois,
Se glisse demi-nue,
En quête de son beau pirate espagnol,
Dont un amoureux rossignol
Clame la détresse à tue-tête.

This final song of the *Fêtes galantes I* is in marked contrast to the other two. Whereas "En sourdine" and "Clair de lune" are dreamy and hushed, "Fantoches" is gay and irreverent. Its musical wit is some-what mordant and defiant, spiced by the Spanish flavor of the guitar-like plucked repeated notes of the accompaniment.

The poem makes little sense unless one knows that Scaramouche and Pulcinella are characters from the Italian comic theatre. Since they can be traced back to early Spanish literature, the guitar references have validity. Scaramouche was always a braggadocio buffoon, orig-inally dressed entirely in black. The good Doctor from Bologna and his pretty daughter complete the strange cast of characters in this little plotless skit.

The highly chromatic accompaniment begins with an A major (for high voice) chord which drops to A♭ for the singer's fanfare entry. The sudden shift to A minor (under "Qu'un mauvais") underlines the comic menace in the word "mauvais" (evil, bad). The poem says

> Scaramouche and Pulcinella,
> Brought together by a mischievous plot,
> Gesture black under the moon,
> La, la . . .

After the repeated notes we have the A major tonality and chromatic figure of the opening bars, but this time we stay in A and the vocal line is also chromatic.

> However the good doctor from Bologna
> Slowly gathers medicinal herbs
> Among the brown grass

Through modulations and chromatic progressions we arrive at innocent C major for the description of the doctor's daughter:

> While his saucily pretty daughter,
> Under the arbour slyly
> Glides half-nude,
> La la la . . .
> In search of her handsome Spanish pirate
> Whose distress an amourous nightingale
> Declares at the top of its lungs

A marvelous *glissando* brings back the original A major tonality, which dominates the piano postlude, the singer adding two cheery "la la's" along the way.

This song must be tossed off with dash and insouciance. Since nothing makes much sense, let's have fun!

Proses lyriques
Poems by Claude Debussy

1. De Rêve
From a Dream

> La nuit a des douceurs de femme,
> Et les vieux arbres, sous la lune d'or,
> Songent! à Celle qui vient de passer,
> La tête emperlée.
> Maintenant navrée, à jamais navrée,
> Ils n'ont pas su lui faire signe . . .
> Toutes! Elles ont passé:

Les Frêles, les Folles,
Semant leur rire au gazon grêle,
Aux brises frôleuses la caresse charmeuse des hanches fleurissantes.
Hélas! de tout ceci, plus rien qu'un blanc frisson . . .
Les vieux arbres sous la lune d'or
Pleurent leurs belles feuilles d'or!
Nul ne leur dédiera
Plus la fierté des casques d'or,
Maintenant ternis, à jamais ternis:
Les chevaliers sont morts
Sur le chemin du Grâal!
La nuit a des douceurs de femme,
Des mains semblent frôler les âmes,
Mains si folles, si frêles,
Au temps où les épées chantaient pour Elles!
D'étranges soupirs s'élèvent sous les arbres:
Mon âme c'est du rêve ancien qui t'étreint!

"De Rêve" is the first of four songs for which Debussy wrote the words as well as the setting. Since this composer's critical essays on music are highly regarded for their style as well as their content, it is not too great a surprise to find that these four *Proses lyriques* (lyrical prose pieces), as he calls them, are very fine indeed. The very first line of "De Rêve" has exquisite elegance and grace. The subtle repetitions and variations in the text (line one repeated as line nineteen; line eight: "Les Frêles, les Folles"; line twenty-one: "Mains si folles, si frêles"; line five: "Maintenant navrée, à jamais navrée"; line sixteen: "Maintenant ternis, à jamais ternis") provide structural unity in this long poem which, written in free verse, has no rhyme scheme. The imagery is striking: "La tête emperlée" (the head covered with pearls); "des hanches fleurissantes" (blossoming or flowering hips); trees which "Pleurent leur belles feuilles d'or" (shed like tears their beautiful golden leaves) and so forth. The way in which Debussy gradually makes us aware of the subject of his dream, from the earliest suggestion of ancient mode of dress ("la tête emperlée") to the precise picture of knights seeking the Holy Grail, makes the poem effective reading, even from a narrative point of view.

As soon as one hears the opening bars of the song, it is clear that Debussy has written the ideal text for his own characteristic style of composition. The piano begins with an arpeggiated augmented chord, and there are suggestions of whole-tone orientation despite the diatonic alternating arpeggios. The opening vocal line is also characteristic Debussy, with little motion and repeated notes.

Throughout the song one finds long pauses in the vocal line, pauses filled with beautifully atmospheric piano interludes. The first of these breaks occurs after the word "Songent" (think), and in the song the word is followed by an exclamation mark. This punctuation is, not found in the text and really makes no sense, for the line reads "Songent à Celle . . ." ("think of Her"). It is quite impossible for the singer to convey this continuity because the piano's music makes a fresh beginning in the middle of the interlude. This is an unexplained contretemps between Debussy the poet and Debussy the composer!

At the *andantino* Debussy introduces his favorite rhythmic device, regular eighth notes against triplet eighth notes. The melody becomes highly chromatic under "Maintenant navrée, à jamais navrée" and then soars to the highest note of the section (under "Ils n'ont pas su") only to descend again. The words for this section are:

> The night has the tenderness of a woman
> And the old trees, under the golden moon,
> Think of Her who just passed by,
> Her head covered with pearls,
> Now broken-hearted, forever broken-hearted,
> They did not know how to call to her . . .

The piano interlude introduces a new figuration and a new rhythmic pattern—four sixteenth notes against three triplet eighth notes. This, added to the "un peu animé" (a little livelier) indication, gives a sense of quickened pace appropriate to the description of all the women who have passed by under these old trees:

> All! They have gone:
> The frail, the mad,
> Scattering their laughter on the pitted lawn,
> In the lightly grazing breeze the charming caress
>   of their blossoming hips.

At "aux brises frôleuses" (In the lightly grazing breeze) and "la caresse charmeuses" (the charming caress), we have whole-tone scales for voice and piano. Because of the two-against-three rhythm, the singer seems to follow the piano in the first half of the measure. This not-quite-synchronized duet does come together in the next measure.

The tempo is pulled back again, and the singer intones one sad line:

> Alas! of all that, nothing more than a pale chill . . .

The piano now returns to the music of the opening bars, enriched by full chords and with all the arpeggios augmented. The second line of verse is repeated to its original music, but there is no break in the vocal line after "Pleurent" comparable to the one after "Songent." Debussy's instructions say "little by little become faster and louder"; the singer must make a *crescendo* on her high note (at "d'or") and the accompaniment must continue this *crescendo* until both reach a *forte* at "Nul." The tempo is now like the beginning, but "more pointed." The chords are sonorous and weighty, the melodic line firm and vigorous to the climactic high note at "fierté." The *diminuendo* does not begin until the word "ternis," but is then quite rapid so that the low notes of "à jamais ternis" are full of pathos.

At the *plus lent* the key suddenly changes to C major (analyzed for high voice). Here this generally sunny tonality produces a funereal effect, like a cortege perhaps. The melodic line is severely restricted, an intoned message of gloom. The words for this section are:

> The old trees under the golden moon
> Shed like tears their beautiful golden leaves!
> Nothing will dedicate to them
> Any longer the pride of golden helmets
> Now tarnished, forever tarnished:
> The knights have died
> On the way to the Holy Grail!

Once again the music of the opening bars is reiterated, this time with the same text and exactly the same notes. This recapitulation lasts but two measures and then an even dreamier, wispier mood sets in. At the pause in the vocal line after "si frêles," there is a final surge in tempo and dynamics, which leads to the highest note and most intense climax of the song (at "chantaient pour Elles!"). From this point we have a steady *diminuendo* and a fade-out ending. The ultimate modulation in this song-of-many-keys is to F♯. The vocal line ends with four long C♯s, the dominant note in this new tonality, but the D♯ in the piano's upper chord under the final syllable, and again two bars later in the postlude, keeps the harmonies suitably hazy. The poem ends:

> The night has the tenderness of a woman,
> Hands which seem lightly to graze our souls,
> In the days when swords sang for Them!
> Strange sighs rise under the trees.
> My soul is from an ancient dream which embraces you!

2. De Grève
Of the Shore

> Sur la mer les crépuscules tombent,
> Soie blanche effilée.
> Les vagues comme de petites folles,
> Jasent, petites filles sortant de l'école,
> Parmi les froufrous de leur robe,
> Soie verte irisée!

Les nuages, graves voyageurs,
Se concertent sur le prochain orage,
Et c'est un fond vraiment trop grave
A cette anglaise aquarelle.
Les vagues, les petites vagues,
Ne savent plus où se mettre,
Car voici la méchante averse,
Froufrous de jupes envolées,
Soie vert affolée.
Mais la lune, compatissante à tous,
Vient apaiser ce gris conflit,
Et caresse lentement ses petites amies,
Qui s'offrent, comme lèvres aimantes,
A ce tiède et blanc baiser.
Puis, plus rien . . .
Plus que les cloches attardées des flottantes églises,
Angélus des vagues
Soie blanche apaisée!

Since Debussy is once again his own lyricist in this song, it behooves us to scrutinize the text as well as the music. Like the three other *Proses lyriques* (lyrical prose pieces), "De Grève" is written in unrhymed lines. Its poetic qualities are found in its imagery—(clouds seen as "grave voyagers," waves "chattering like school girls" and "offering themselves like loving lips to the moon's caress")—and in the rhythmic flow of its words. As he had done in the preceding song, "De Rêve," Debussy uses repetition as a unifying structural device. In this case one metaphor for the sea, silk ("soie"), in used in four different lines at irregular intervals (lines two, six, fifteen, and twenty-four, the last line). At first the silk is white and unravelled; when next described it is green and iridescent; it is then green but bewitched, and finally white and appeased.

It is interesting that Debussy felt impelled to write this song about the sea in 1892, just one year after having composed the setting for Verlaine's poem "La Mer est plus belle" (see page 330). His major orchestral work, *La Mer,* was composed over a decade later, from 1903 to 1905.

Like most musical evocations of the sea, the piano part to this song is a busy one, full of rapid tremolo figures, surging arpeggios, ponderous chords, and rushing scales. Most of the more frenzied activity occurs in the first half of the piece, for we start with a turbulent sea, encounter a storm, and then witness the gradual becalming of the waters. Very often in the song the stormy figurations in the accompaniment are balanced by single-note, or almost single-note melodic lines ("Soie blanche effilée," "Soie verte irisée," "Mais la lune, . . . ce gris conflit," "Plus que les cloches attardées," "Angélus des vagues," and "Soie blanche apaisée"). This is characteristic of Debussy's style. Another characteristic device, found frequently in this song, is the two against three rhythmic pattern ("Soie blanche effilée," ". . . petites filles sortant," etc.).

The piano has a long, rumbling introduction, in which the ostinato tonic chord (D major for high voice) clearly establishes the tonality. The D major tonality is easily identifiable at the end as well, making "De Grève" unusually tonal compared to the several preceding songs. In the third measure of the introduction a strange dissonance is heard, which carries over to the next bar, but then the D major chord is reestablished. The mood is one of suppressed excitement; the instructions read "very even and very muffled."

The voice enters with a severely restricted melodic line, which is echoed in the piano's double-stemmed notes. The singer then intones a line all on one note, while the piano plays its somewhat ominous and dissonant countermelody. The third line has a little more melodic scope and the triad in the fourth line (under "filles sortant") seems finally to release the vocal line from its restraints. The next line, marked *scherzando,* uses the frivolous word "frou-frous" (rustling), and the sixteenth notes in the accompaniment's triplet figure give a light-hearted relief after the constant rumbling of the thirty-second notes. The next line, which brings the first section to a close, takes the melody back to its almost monotone structure, but the accompaniment is still gay and dancing. The words to this point are:

On the sea dusk falls,
Silk white, unravelled.
The waves like little foolish ones
Chatter, little girls leaving school,
Mid the rustling of their dresses,
Silk green, iridescent!

The first section has drawn to a close on the tonic, but now there is an abrupt change of key and mood. Suddenly the music is ominous, with heavy chords and an eerie chromatic melody. This threatening aura lasts but three measures, after which words and music seem to be gayly mocking the serious mood of the previous moment. The melody jauntily rises at "aquarelle" (water-color), and the accompaniment has augmented chords.

Trills in the piano part now herald the big storm that is about to begin. The vocal line becomes somewhat frenzied, aided by the downward cascade of notes under "ne savent *plus.*" Insistent chords and repeated notes in the accompaniment add to the excitement, as do the rushing whole-tone scales. The rising intervals under "envolées" and "affolée" are all the more effective for coming after repeated notes, and are the climactic moments of the song. Despite the strong dynamics and enormous rhythmic energy of this section, the fact that the accompaniment is all in the treble clef robs it of the kind of power one sometimes finds in descriptions of storms at sea. The words for this section are:

> The clouds, grave voyagers,
> Gather for the coming storm,
> And it is truly too grave a background
> For this English water-color.
> The waves, the little waves,
> No longer know where to go,
> For here is the wicked downpour,
> Rustling of billowing skirts,
> Silk green, maddened.

The remainder of the poem is spent gradually calming the waters. The whole tone piano interlude seems very quiet, in contrast to the busy thirty-second notes of the previous sections, and the voice enters with a very calm monotone phrase. Even the thirty-second notes under "compatissante" fail to disturb the tranquillity, because they serve merely as a wash of color. There is little harmonic motion, and the melody notes seem very long and sustained in the measures containing half notes and quarter notes. Even the eighth notes are slow-moving as the tempo gets slower and slower.

Towards the end Debussy introduces a new idea, the sound of church bells tolling the Angelus. In his poem "La Mer est plus belle" Verlaine compares the sea to a cathedral; here Debussy speaks of "floating churches." Is the "Angelus of the Waves" a figment of Debussy's imagination, or is it perhaps the sound of bells from warning buoys, or passing ships? Whatever the real reference, in the music we hear a single note—the supertonic—first in the measure before "Plus que les cloches" and then in four consecutive measures beginning with "Angélus des vagues." These notes, which never fit into the given harmony, undoubtedly represent the bells.

From "Plus que les cloches" until the end, the vocal line scarcely moves. Unlike comparable places in the beginning, however, this stillness in the vocal part is matched by the monotonous, almost hypnotic figures in the accompaniment. Just as one can become mesmerized from watching the sea, one is bemused listening to this musical evocation. To accomplish Debussy's aims in the last two measures, the pianist must hold the right hand chord without pedal while repeating the two final left hand notes. The words for the final section are:

> But the moon, sympathetic to all
> Comes to appease this grey battle

And slowly caress her little friends
Who offer themselves for loving lips
To this warm and white kiss.
Then, nothing more . . .
Nothing but the tardy bells of the floating churches,
Angelus of the waves,
Silk white, appeased!

Note: There is a misprint in measure twenty-six of the International Edition for High Voice: the second chord for the right hand should read D♮, B♭, F♯, as it does in measure twenty-four.

3. De Fleurs
Of Flowers

Dans l'ennui si désolement vert
De la serre de douleur,
Les fleurs enlacent mon coeur
De leurs tiges méchantes.
Ah! quand reviendront autour de ma tête
Les chères mains si tendrement désenlaceuses?
Les grands Iris violets
Violèrent méchamment tes yeux
En semblant les refléter,
Eux, qui furent l'eau du songe
Où plongèrent mes rêves si doucement,
Enclos en leur couleur;
Et les lys, blancs jets d'eau de pistils embaumés,
Ont perdu leur grâce blanche,
Et ne sont plus que pauvres malades sans soleil!
Soleil! ami des fleurs mauvaises,
Tueur de rêves! Tueur d'illusions,
Ce pain béni des âmes misérables!
Venez! Venez! Les mains salvatrices!
Brisez les vitres de mensonge,
Brisez les vitres de maléfice,
Mon âme meurt de trop de soleil!
Mirages! Plus ne refleurira la joie de mes yeux,
Et mes mains sont lasses de prier,
Mes yeux sont las de pleurer!
Eternellement ce bruit fou
Des pétales noirs de l'ennui,
Tombant goutte à goutte sur ma tête,
Dans le vert de la serre de douleur!

This third *Prose lyrique*, "De Fleurs," written by Debussy between 1892 and 1893, harks back for its inspiration to the collection of poetry by Baudelaire, *Les Fleurs du Mal*, which shocked the literary world at its appearance in 1857. Once again Debussy's imagery is powerful and enigmatic: boredom is desolately verdant—it is the greenhouse of sorrow. The flowers in the greenhouse are evil and menacing: they twist themselves around the poet's heart; they maliciously violate the beloved's eyes by seeming to reflect them. The lilies are sick from lack of sun (*Les Fleurs du Mal* can also be translated as "The Flowers of Sickness" since *mal* can mean ill as well as evil) for the sun is the friend of evil flowers, not of the pure lily. Perhaps the most striking metaphor is that of the senseless noise of the black petals of boredom falling, drop by drop, on the poet's head. Sibelius has written a song called "Black Roses," and Saul Bellow has referred to boredom as "the shriek" of unused capacities, but Debussy's strange combination of the aural and the visual is *sui generis*.

Obviously, in view of the text we expect no *scherzando* setting! The opening chords are indeed slow and sad with that special mournful quality also found in some of Duparc's songs. When the singer enters we realize that the chords have anticipated the vocal line, with each chord harmonizing in a triad one melody note. The piano continues its chordal pattern while the melody retreats to a single-note line. After a few rising notes the vocal line again settles on one note for eight long syllables. The harmonic background has meanwhile moved from the tonic major (C in the key for high voice) to the relative minor. There is a heavy, oppressive monotony to the chords and melody under "Ah! quand reviendront . . . tête." The sudden rise under "si tendrement" is unexpected; the rapid fall from this peak is gently buffered by the rising chords in the accompaniment. The original funereal chords and single-note melodic line return to end the section musically, but the last line of verse properly belongs to the next part of the text:

> In the boredom so desolately verdant
> Of the greenhouse of sorrow,
> Flowers twist around my heart
> Their evil stems.
> Ah! when will there be again around my head
> The dear hands so tenderly soothing?
> The large violet Iris
> Violated maliciously your eyes

Note the word play of "violets" and "violèrent" (violet and violated). In the French texts these words immediately follow one another; in the song they are separated by a one bar piano interlude.

A change of key and a change of piano figuration herald the new section. The instructions say to accelerate progressively, and the new activity in the accompaniment adds to the feeling of increased forward motion. A modest *crescendo* begins to build at "Eux qui furent" and peaks at "mes rêves," after which tempo and dynamics are subdued to match the opening bars. Since the piano figuration does not cease, however, we do not reach the deep gloom of the original chords. Towards the end of the section a more powerful *crescendo* results in a real *forte* at "sans soleil," with the high note making a tremendous impact. The words in this section are very strange and ambiguous. To understand them a little better we repeat the last two lines quoted above:

> The large violet Iris
> Violated maliciously your eyes,
> In seeming to reflect them,
> They that were the water in the dream
> In which my reveries so gently plunged,
> Enveloped in their color;
> And the lilies, white fountains of fragrant pistils,
> Have lost their pure grace,
> And are only poor sick ones without sun!

Once again the key changes at this climactic moment. The piano figure continues in triplets, but the many intervals of a second, and the increasingly animated tempo, bring a feeling of agitation and unrest. The word "soleil" is repeated an octave lower than its first impassioned expression, and the melodic line again becomes very limited in scope. Another key change brings a further increase in tempo and a big *crescendo* to the tremendous *forte* on "Venez." The key changes again at this new peak, as does the piano figure, which now consists of the chordal pattern of the opening, transposed from C to B, made more turbulent by the rushing scale patterns between the chords. The word "Venez" is also repeated, as the poet passionately calls for the hands of salvation. The key shifts to the original tonic, as the chords and cascading scales continue under the anguished frenzy of the singer's words and melody. Tremolos replace these figures as the dramatic outburst draws to a close. Here, too, the words are strange and highly symbolic:

> Sun! friend of evil flowers,
> Murderer of dreams! Murderer of illusions,
> That consecrated wafer of miserable souls!
> Come! Come! Hands of salvation!
> Break the glass panes of lies,
> Break the glass panes of sorcery,
> My soul is dying of too much sunshine!

A rapid *diminuendo* brings the dynamic level down to a *piano* and the accompanying figures become gentle. The entire final section is one of *diminuendo* and *ritardando*. Aside from the flowing melodic line at "Mes yeux sont las de pleurer!" the singer has heavy, colorless mono-

tone or severely limited phrases to intone. There is an air of hopeless-
ness, despair. The chords of the opening bars are brought back most
effectively six measures before the end. They make an eerie backdrop
for the single-note phrase "goutte sur ma tête." The last lines of
verse read:

> Mirages! No more will joy flower again in my eyes,
> And my hands are weary of praying,
> My eyes are weary of crying!
> Eternally this senseless noise
> Of the black petals of boredom,
> Falling drop by drop on my head,
> In the verdure of the greenhouse of sorrow!

4. De Soir
Of Evening

> Dimanche sur les villes,
> Dimanche dans les coeurs!
> Dimanche chez les petites filles,
> Chantant d'une voix informée,
> Des rondes obstinées,
> Ou de bonnes tours
> N'en ont plus que pour quelques jours!
> Dimanche, les gares sont folles!
> Tout le monde appareille
> Pour des banlieues d'aventure,
> En se disant adieu
> Avec des gestes éperdus!
> Dimanche les trains vont vite,
> Dévorés par d'insatiables tunnels;
> Et les bons signaux des routes
> Echangent d'un oeil unique,
> Des impressions toutes mécaniques.
> Dimanche, dans le bleu de mes rêves,
> Où mes pensées tristes
> De feux d'artifices manqués
> Ne veulent plus quitter
> Le deuil de vieux Dimanches trépassés.
> Et la nuit, à pas de velours,
> Vient endormir le beau ciel fatigué,
> Et c'est Dimanche dans les avenues d'étoiles;
> La Vierge or sur argent
> Laisse tomber les fleurs de sommeil!
> Vite, les petits anges,
> Dépassez les hirondelles
> Afin de vous coucher
> Forts d'absolution!
> Prenez pitié des villes,

Prenez pitié des coeurs,
Vous, la Vierge or sur argent!

Its title notwithstanding, the subject of this poem is obviously Sunday (Dimanche), rather than Evening (Soir). Perhaps Debussy chose to call the song "De Soir" to keep the titles of the four *Proses lyriques* symmetrical, for as they stand each has a two syllable name: "De Rêve, "De Grève," "De Fleurs," and "De Soir."

Even without the text, the music immediately conveys the aura of the Sabbath, with its church bell piano figuration in the first six bars and its church music cadence under "Dimanche chez les petites filles." Frequent repetition of the word *Dimanche* holds the rambling poem together as do to a lesser degree the other repeated phrases, "Prenez pitié des" and "La Vierge or sur argent." Although this text, like the other *Proses lyriques,* is in free verse, there are a few rhymed endings ("tours" and "jours," "unique" and "mécaniques," "manqués" and "trépassés," and so forth). "Villes" and "filles" are visual but not aural rhymes, since the double *l* in *villes* is pronounced almost as it would be in English (this is an exception to the rule), whereas the double *l* in *filles* is pronounced like a *y* as it almost always is in French.

This is one of the few songs of this era in which modern mechanization, which certainly had already begun, is acknowledged. The imagery of trains devoured by insatiable tunnels is disturbing, but the anthropomorphism of the "good train signals," which exchange their mechanical impressions with their single eyes, can be seen as a comforting humanistic touch. Although the language of the poem is much clearer and less difficult to interpret than that of the previous two, the quicksilver moods tantalize. We veer from the gaiety of young girls' voices singing on Sunday to the chilling observation that their days are few; pleasure-seeking crowds in the railroad stations call forth the nightmare of tunnels devouring trains; the poet's Sabbath reveries are of celebrations missed and bygone Sundays. The final image is most subject to differing interpretations: is a Virgin made of gold on silver to be adored or is it a vulgarization of the religious symbolism? If we seek the answer in the music, we must conclude that the religious spirit is sincere and reverent.

The piano opens with the church bell figure. The singer enters with a joyous melody featuring two exuberant intervals of a fifth, both on the word "Dimanche." The first important modulation also takes place at the word "Dimanche," on its third occurrence in the first three lines. The initial burst of enthusiasm gradually yields to a much more quiet mood, and the sad words "plus que pour quelques jours" are intoned all on one note. The words for this section are:

Sunday in the cities,
Sunday in the hearts!
Sunday in the home of little girls
Singing with unformed voices
Obstinate rounds or good turns.
They have no more than a few days left!

The original exuberant mood now returns with the buoyant interval of a fifth under the word "Dimanche," and the church bells, much reinforced by octaves and filler notes, in the accompaniment. After the section's *forte* beginning there is a *subito piano,* a *crescendo* to a *forte* at "éperdus," another *subito piano* and consequent *crescendo* to a tremendous *ff* on "Dimanche," and yet another *p* and final *crescendo.* The section ends its roller coaster dynamics with a *diminuendo.* In the middle of the section the word "Dimanche" is again sung to a triumphant interval of a fifth. This time its bell figure accompaniment has been altered to resemble the clanging sound of trains. The accompanying figure then is simplified to describe the mechanized signals; it becomes a steady march of quarter notes subdivided into sixteenth notes. The words for this section are:

Sunday, the stations are mad!
Everyone leaves for unknown suburbs
Saying goodbye to one another
With bewildered gestures!
Sunday, the trains go quickly,
Devoured by insatiable tunnels;
And the good signals of the routes
Exchange with a single eye
Totally mechanical impressions.

The *diminuendo,* which had begun to calm the dynamics at the end of the previous section, is continued by the piano interlude until a dreamy, gentle *piano* is reached. The melodic interval under "Dimanche" is reduced to a fourth, and the rest of the line is sung on one note. The piano figure is gradually reduced from sixteenth notes to triplet eighth notes, and then to a mixture of eighth notes and quarter notes. The dynamics grow softer and the tempo becomes slower. The next "Dimanche" is part of an almost static melodic line and actually moves down a whole step. Bell sounds are still part of the accompaniment, but either they are muffled, as under "Et la nuit," or heard from afar, as under "laisse tomber les fleurs de sommeil." The words are:

Sunday, in the blue of my dreams,
When my sad thoughts of missed fireworks
No longer wish to leave the funereal mourning
For old bygone Sundays.

And the night with steps of velvet
Comes to put the beautiful, tired sky to sleep,
And it is Sunday in the pathway of stars;
The Virgin of gold on silver
Lets fall the flowers of sleep!

The pace quickens momentarily, as gentle tremolos support the intoned single-note melodic line. For one two-bar phrase, the melody develops some motion again, only to be pulled back to a solemn single note for the words "Forts d'absolution." The accompanying tremolos and muffled chords fade away as the tempo slows down again. The accompaniment then ceases, so that the singer may deliver the "Prenez pitié" lines *à la recitative*. The wispy postlude ends with the ringing of distant bells. The final lines are:

Quickly, little angels,
Outstrip the swallows
Before going to sleep
Strengthened by absolution!
Take pity on the cities,
Take pity on the hearts,
Thou, the Virgin of gold on silver!

Chansons de Bilitis
Poems by Pierre Louÿs

1. La Flûte de Pan
Pan's Flute

Pour le jour des Hyacinthes,
Il m'a donné une syrinx faite
De roseaux bien taillés,
Unis avec la blanche cire
Qui est douce à mes lèvres comme le miel.
Il m'apprend à jouer, assise sur ses genoux;
Mais je suis un peu tremblante.
Il en joue après moi, si doucement
Que je l'entends à peine.
Nous n'avons rien à nous dire,
Tant nous sommes près l'un de l'autre;
Mais nos chansons veulent se répondre,
Et tour à tour nos bouches
S'unissent sur la flûte.
Il est tard;
Voici le chant des grenouilles vertes
Qui commence avec la nuit.
Ma mère ne croira jamais

Que je suis restée si longtemps
A chercher ma ceinture perdue.

The three *Songs of Bilitis,* of which "La Flûte de Pan" is the first, are the result of a literary hoax. Pierre Louÿs, the actual author of the texts, claimed to have discovered and translated these poems which, according to him, were written by an unknown female Greek poet. Like original forgeries in paintings (as opposed to copies of existing works) the merits of these hybrids are always debatable; in this case the musical response they inspired in Debussy has earned them a permanent place in the legitimate repertoire.

In the article on Debussy in the fifth edition of *Groves Dictionary of Music and Musicians,* "La flûte de Pan" and "La Chevelure," the second song of the imaginary Greek poetess Bilitis, are referred to as "the most individual of [Debussy's] love songs," with the former cited as the more sensitive, and the latter as the more passionate. While other listeners might find other contenders for the title "most individual," these two songs assuredly are characteristic of Debussy in a way that makes them easily distinguishable from even such close contemporaries as Chausson and Ravel. The not quite whole-tone scale, introduced in the first measure of "La Flûte de Pan," the long melodic phrases on one note, duple versus triple rhythms, antique-sounding chord progressions—these are Debussy's stylistic stock-in-trade.

Monsieur Louÿs, claiming that he could not do justice to the Greek originals in French verse, offered his "translations" in prose. Unlike the unrhymed texts of *Proses lyriques* (discussed on pp. 342–355), however, the words of "La Flûte de Pan" are genuine, albeit very elegant, prose. The sentence structure is simple and natural—the last three lines could be spoken by any teenage girl! Of course there are references to antiquity such as the "day of Hyacinthus" and the "syrinx" (the Greek word for pipe or tube from which we derive "syringe"), but these are delivered naturally, as they would be by someone alive at the time.

The music is a brilliant combination of late nineteenth-century Impressionism (the song was written in 1897) and Renaissance-like chord progressions. Since we really cannot reconstruct the sound of Greek music with any certainty, the spirit of the Renaissance, when all the arts sought inspiration from the ancient Greeks, is evoked instead. Both of these elements are heard in the two-bar introduction.

The scale figure is, of course, the flute. The three-note pattern first heard at "unis avec," which is repeated in the vocal line and then taken up by the accompaniment, might be the novice flutist practicing her first lesson. The voice sinks tremulously for the words "je suis un peu tremblante" (I tremble a little) and again for "je l'entends à peine" (I scarcely hear him). The melodic line becomes highly chromatic under "mais nos chansons veulent se répondre" (but our songs want to correspond), and the equally chromatic rise under "nos bouches s'unissent sur la flûte" (our lips are united on the flute) provides a sense of climax despite the *ritard* and *pp* dynamics. The words to this point are:

> For the day of Hyacinthus
> He gave me a syrinx made
> Of well-trimmed reeds,
> Held together with the white wax
> Which is as sweet as honey to my lips.
> He teaches me to play, seated on his knees,
> But I tremble a little.
> He plays after me, so softly
> That I can scarcely hear him.
> We have nothing to say,
> So close are we to one another;
> But our songs want to correspond,
> And little by little our lips
> Are united on the flute.

At this last word we suddenly hear two flutes at play, one darting over and under the other, but the voice reenters with a repeated note warning: "Il est tard"—it is late. The two flutes (or are they the two reeds of the double-aulos?) cannot ignore her—after two more measures they yield to light chords and a grace-note figure that may be the sound of the frogs. Again the voice has a repeated note line, which is sung "almost without voice" and at increased speed, for she really must hurry. The postlude is played as though from afar, as the young girl goes off with her flute. The final chords once again remind us that this all happened long, long ago. The last lines are:

> It is late:
> Here is the song of the green frogs
> That starts the night.
> My mother will never believe
> That I stayed so long
> Looking for my lost belt.

2. La Chevelure
Tresses

> Il m'a dit: "Cette nuit, j'ai rêvé.
> J'avais ta chevelure autour de mon cou.
> J'avais tes cheveux comme un collier noir

Autour de ma nuque et sur ma poitrine."
"Je les caressais, et c'étaient les miens;
Et nous étions liés pour toujours ainsi,
Par la même chevelure, la bouche sur la bouche,
Ainsi que deux lauriers n'ont souvent qu'une racine."
"Et peu à peu, il m'a semblé,
Tant nos membres étaient confondus,
Que je devenais toi-même,
Ou que tu entrais en moi comme mon songe."
Quand il eut achevé,
Il mit doucement ses mains sur mes épaules,
Et il me regarda d'un regard si tendre,
Que je bassai les yeux avec un frisson.

This second prose "translation" of a nonexistent poem by an imaginary Greek poetess (see previous song for complete explanation) is more than just an exquisitely erotic statement, for it expresses the union of two souls as well as two bodies. The last line is perhaps the most telling; in it the young woman lowers her eyes and trembles at her lover's great passion and tenderness.

The language of this second *Song of Bilitis* is a little more deliberately "poetic" than that of the first: there is repetition (J'avais ta chevelure" . . . "J'avais tes cheveux"), simile (". . . tes cheveux comme un collier noir"—your locks like a black collar), and a more rhythmic flow of the words. The central image of the two lovers intertwined like two laurels with a single root is evocative indeed.

The music begins gently and slowly. A somewhat mysterious aura is created by the introductory chords, so that when the voice enters somberly with "Il m'a dit:" (he said to me) we are prepared to hear an extraordinary tale. The voice pauses as the piano introduces a different chord pattern at a slightly faster pace. When the singer actually begins her story (this song must be sung by a woman for the text to make sense) the melodic line is still sombre and low in pitch and dynamics, but the composer's instructions say "very expressive and passionately concentrated." There is a small *crescendo* (under "autour de mon cou") which continues to grow in volume and intensity through the word "poitrine," the first climactic point. The words to this point are:

He said to me:
This night, I dreamed.
I had your hair around my neck.
I had your locks like a black collar
Around my neck and on my breast.

From the last words quoted above, "sur ma poitrine," until the change of key signature after "toujours ainsi," melody and harmony are based entirely on one whole-tone scale. The melody is, in fact, a descending whole-tone scale and all the accompanying chords are combinations of the notes found in that scale. This is one of the most subtle examples of whole-tone writing to be found in all of Debussy's songs.

At "Je les caressais" the dynamics drop suddenly to *piano,* but an even stronger *crescendo* soon begins. This *crescendo* sweeps us into the next section, where we find an ecstatic rising melodic line which culminates in the passionate "la bouche sur la bouche." The accompaniment has a soaring arpeggio under "par la même," and then strong descending chords. The words are:

> I caressed them, and they were mine;
> And we were joined thus for ever,
> By the same hair, mouth upon mouth,

A sudden *piano,* a return to the slow tempo of the beginning, and a subdued melodic line give a special flavor to the next line, the central image of the text:

> As two laurels often have but one root.

The voice pauses for a moment while the accompaniment resumes its measured chords. As the narrative continues, the pace quickens and another *crescendo* develops. This buildup reaches its peak—the real climax of the song—at the word "songe." Interestingly enough, this tremendous double *forte* (*ff*) is not sung on a high note; the highest note of the phrase occurs on the word "moi." The singer must be careful not to allow the high note to eclipse the real climax, especially since the piano has a very full, very rich chord under "songe." Here the words are:

> And little by little, it seemed to me,
> So much were our limbs intermingled,
> That I became you,
> Or that you entered into me like my dream.

Here the dream ends. The last measure is a bridge between the passionate music of the previous section and the slow, gentle music of the opening bars, which are now repeated. The singer enters again with the notes of her first line. The accompaniment becomes more static, echoing the vocal line, as it did under "j'avais tes cheveux" in the first section. The harmonies for "il me regarda d'un regard si tendre" are beautiful, first the tonic plus a ninth (G♭ for high voice) and then the flatted seven plus a ninth (F♭ in this key). The harmonies move more quickly under the last line, settling on a dominant 7–9 chord. The postlude is an echo of the original chords plus a final tonic chord.

The entire last section is sung in a mood of dazed tenderness which is immensely poignant and touching:

When he had finished,
He gently placed his hands on my shoulders,
And he looked at me with a look so tender
That I lowered my eyes and trembled.

3. Le Tombeau des naïades
The Tomb of the Naiads

Le long du bois couvert de givre, je marchais;
Mes cheveux devant ma bouche
Se fleurissaient de petits glaçons,
Et mes sandales étaient lourdes
De neige fangeuse et tassée.
Il me dit: "Que cherches-tu?"
Je suis la trace du satyre.
Ses petits pas fourchus alternent
Comme des trous dans un manteau blanc.
Il me dit: "Les satyres sont morts.
Les satyres et les nymphes aussi.
Depuis trente ans, il n'a pas fait un hiver aussi terrible.
La trace que tu vois est celle d'un bouc.
Mais restons ici, où est leur tombeau."
Et avec le fer de sa houe il cassa la glace
De la source où jadis riaient les naïades.
Il prenait de grands morceaux froids,
Et les soulevant vers le ciel pâle,
Il regardait au travers.

"Le Tombeau des naïades," the last of the three *Chansons de Bilitis* (see p. 356 for a discussion of the unusual history of this group of songs), is completely different in mood and subject matter from the other two: whereas "La Flûte de Pan" and "La Chevelure" are intimate love poems, this last is a rather impersonal narrative. The only characteristic the three pieces have in common is their references to early Greece, in this case to the mythological satyrs (demigods of the forest who were part man, part goat), nymphs (goddesses of woods, mountains, waters), and naiads (specifically water nymphs).

The piano part to this song is exceptionally interesting. The first bar introduces a sixteenth note figure which is "walking music"—we are not surprised when the singer announces that she has been walking along the frost-covered woods. Although their pattern changes, steady sixteenth notes go on inexorably throughout the piece, from start to finish. Whenever the words speak of satyrs or nymphs, the sixteenth notes are combined with octaves in a way that makes them express frolicsome gaiety. The first example of this is under "Je suis la trace du satyre" (I follow the satyr's tracks). In the piano interludes before "Il me dit" and after "Les satyres sont morts," the combined octaves and sixteenth notes sound bleak and full of despair. All these changing moods are conveyed more strongly in the piano part than in the vocal line.

The words are somewhat puzzling, in that they seem to build up to an anticlimactic ending. In the first few lines the language is quite poetic, despite the fact that this was supposed to be a prose translation of a Greek poem. The placement of the subject and verb, "je marchais," at the end of line one is a poetic or at least rhetorical device; the imagery of little icicles ("petits glaçons") blossoming ("se fleurissaient") on the windblown hair is certainly effective, as is the simile of the buck's tracks like holes in a white cloak ("Comme des trous dans un manteau blanc").

After the phrase quoted above, which is about midway through the text, the language becomes quite matter-of-fact until the last four lines, where once again one feels poetic inspiration at work. The last line however seems an unsatisfactory and inconclusive ending.

The melodic line is typical of Debussy in its quasi-*recitativo* style. The singer's first seven syllables are intoned on one note, and after a rise, to the major third above, the melody sinks back to the original note. Debussy's mood indication is "gentle and weary." There is much more freedom and scope in the next melodic phrases, but at the first pause we again return to the original tone. Vocal line and accompaniment have been bleak and chill to this point, and the somber mood is intensified through "Que cherches-tu?" The words thus far are:

Along the woods covered with frost, I walked;
My hair blown in front of my mouth
Blossomed with little icicles
And my sandals were heavy
With muddy and thick snow.
He said to me: "What are you looking for?"

Suddenly the mood brightens; the accompaniment becomes light and playful—the half-step interval between the two top notes of so many of the rolled chords creates a tinkling, bell-like sound—and the melody trips gayly along in sixteenth notes. While the accompaniment is still frolicsome, the vocal line changes abruptly to suit the mood of the stark words "Les satyres sont morts." (The satyrs are dead.) The accompaniment catches this mood in the next measure and the chords become weighty and oppressive. The left hand octaves echo the vocal line at "Les satyres et les nymphes aussi" and "La trace que tu vois est celle d'un . . . ." Although there have been small *crescendos* and *decrescendos* in the preceding phrases, the first real climax is at the word *bouc* ("buck"), which is, of course, preceded by a dynamic rise. The words for this portion are:

> I am following the satyr's tracks.
> His little forked footprints alternate
> Like holes in a white cloak.
> He said to me: "The satyrs are dead.
> The satyrs and nymphs too.
> For thirty years we have not had such a terrible winter.
> The tracks you see are those of a buck."

The chords under "bouc" are very full and sonorous, but the next measure brings the dynamic level down to a "very gentle" piano. In the last section, which now follows, words and music sometimes seem at odds with one another. The melody for "Mais restons ici, où est leur tombeau" (but let's stay here at their tomb) is suitably somber, but the accompaniment rises optimistically. The whole-tone melodic line under "Et avec le fer de sa" builds to a moderate climax at "houe," and to a far stronger peak at "les naïades," and the music for these lines has become gay and frolicsome again. This gaiety and the triumphant climax at "les naïades" come at a rather grim point in the narrative. They are however completely appropriate to the musical structure of the piece, and might be interpreted as the laughter of the naiades echoing from the past.

A *diminuendo* sets in immediately after the high note of "naiades," but there is one final dynamic surge at the last syllable of text. This, too, seems based completely on musical rather than textual considerations, which may be attributable to the weakness of this last line.

The piano part remains interesting to the very end. The grace notes in the postlude are reminiscent of the bell-like sounds given to the satyrs; the four short bars of this piano solo are remarkably full of dynamic contrast, and the last measure combines the tonic chord, F♯ major, with its relative minor, D♯ minor (in the key for high voice). The last lines of text are:

> But let us stay here at their tomb."
> And with the iron of his hoe he broke the ice
> Of the spring where naiads formerly laughed.
> He took large cold pieces,
> And raising them to the pale sky,
> He looked through them.

Fêtes galantes II
Poems by Paul Verlaine

1. Les Ingénus
The Innocents

Les hauts talons luttaient avec les longues jupes,
En sorte que, selon le terrain et le vent,
Parfois luisaient des bas de jambes,
Trop souvent interceptés!
Et nous aimions ce jeu de dupes.
Parfois aussi le dard d'un insecte jaloux
Inquiétait le col des belles sous les branches,
Et c'étaient des éclairs soudains des nuques blanches,
Et ce regal comblait nos jeunes yeux de fous.
Le soir tombait, un soir équivoque d'automne:
Les belles, se pendant rêveuses à nos bras,
Dirent alors des mots si spécieux, tout bas,
Que notre âme depuis ce temps tremble et s'étonne.

Debussy composed his second set of songs based on poems from Verlaine's collection *Les Fêtes galantes* in 1904, twelve years after the first group chosen from these poems appeared. As one can see, his friendship and admiration for Verlaine, Mallarmé, and Baudelaire remained strong influences throughout his creative life.

Like the first set, *Fêtes galantes II* consists of three nonrelated songs, "Les Ingénus" (The Innocents), "Le Faune" (The Faun), and "Colloque Sentimental" (Sentimental Colloquy). The first, "Les Ingénus," expresses the breathless wonder with which unsophisticated young men of the mid-nineteenth century (the poems were published in 1869) viewed their equally naive female companions. As Cole Porter said, "In olden days a glimpse of stocking/Was looked on as something shocking"; in our permissive era when "Anything Goes" it is hard to imagine the reverent awe for the female, the erotic thrill of the sight of a white throat or a bare calf, the mysterious nature of young girls' chatter. For every gain there is a loss!

The piano begins with a delicate, somewhat exotic figure which continues for fifteen measures. This highly chromatic background seems to float, free from any tonal moorings, until the last two bars "trop souvent interceptés!" (too often intercepted), where it settles into A major (analyzed in the key for high voice). The key signature indicates E♭ major, but there is much tonal ambiguity throughout the song. The unusual combination of A♮ and A♭ is in evidence in several passages in the song, including the strangely beautiful ending, where the A♮ chords are in the minor mode, which makes the juxtaposition all the more poignant.

The singer should enter with an awestruck, tremulous feeling. Like the majority of Debussy's melodic lines, the opening phrase contains a series of repeated notes. The suppressed excitement, with which the entire song is suffused, breaks out a little in the *crescendo* under "Parfois luisaient des bas," but the crucial words "de jambes" (of legs) are once again very soft—one did not say such intimate words too loudly! The words for the first section are:

> The high heels battle the long skirts,
> So that, depending on the terrain and the wind,
> Sometimes gleamed the calves of legs,
> Too often intercepted!

A new figure in the accompaniment, this one securely anchored to E♭, ostensibly the tonic, albeit in augmented form, introduces the next section. The right hand's inner voice should be heard throughout the next eleven bars, the duration of this figure. The vocal line is derived from the whole-tone scale, which includes the E♭, until the B♭ under "était." The accompanying harmony changes here, too, as we are led into the next section. The grace note pattern darting above and below the right hand's repeated figure lends a spirit of playfulness to the music, but delicacy and grace remain the paramount effects. The words here are:

> And we loved this game of trickery.
> Sometimes, too, the sting of a jealous insect
> Bothered the neck of the beauties under the branches,

The key shifts to A major, the tempo begins to quicken, and the dynamics are allowed to increase from *mezzo forte* to *forte* for this one excited line:

> And there were sudden flashes of white necks,

The tempo continues to increase but the dynamic level is pulled back to *piano* again. The key now hovers around A♭ minor, which gradually yields to C♭. In these few measures all the pent-up excitement is allowed to burst forth in a wonderful climax at "nos jeunes yeux de fous":

> And this delight filled our young, foolish eyes.

The rest of the song is gentle, tender and *misterioso*. The young men are puzzled and bemused as evening falls and the girls whisper strange sweet nothings. The piano figure reflects the sense of mystery in its augmented and highly chromatic chords. The key signature has returned to E♭, but this tonal center is not yet heard in the music. The singer reenters with an exotic, quasi-Oriental melodic line, and then continues (under "Les belles") with the notes of an augmented E♭ chord. One can see how this relates structurally to the first two sections of the song. After "tout bas" the accompaniment comes to a halt, to allow the singer freedom to set up the marvelous sound combination (an A♭ melody note over an A minor chord) at "âme" (soul). This throbbing harmony underlies this whole measure and the following two bars, and it would seem, from the emphasis on the chord, that the piece should end in the key of A minor. Debussy had other plans, however, and with a truly inspired sense of the dramatic, he ends the song on an augmented A♭ chord. These last five bars are unforgettable. The final lines of verse are:

> Evening fell, an enigmatic autumnal evening:
> The beauties leaning dreamily on our arms,
> Then whisper such deceptive words,
> That our soul since then trembles and is astounded.

2. Le Faune
The Faun

> Un vieux faune de terre cuite
> Rit au centre des boulingrins,
> Présageant sans doute une suite
> Mauvaise à ces instants sereins,
> Qui m'ont conduit et t'ont conduite,
> Mélancoliques pèlerins,
> Jusqu'à cette heure dont la fuite
> Tournoie au son des tambourins.

In Debussy's setting for Verlaine's brief poem "Le Faune," the words are preceded by a long, exotic piano prelude in which the three major musical elements of the song are introduced: the flutelike cadenzas, the open fifth rhythmic figure in the bass, and the augmented chords which float above this insistent drumlike beat. There is a strong Oriental flavor to this hypnotic music, which weaves its spell by rhythmic repetition, vague harmonies, and sinuous lines.

As in so many of Debussy's songs, the tonality is quite ambiguous: the never-changing bass figure suggests B♭ as the tonic, but the key signature (four flats in the key for high voice) and the final right hand chords describe A♭, albeit an augmented A♭. The chord before the singer's entry is F minor and the vocal line seems to begin in that key. However, despite other references to F minor this key never really becomes a strong tonal center.

The poem is a model of tight, succinct writing. Its eight lines have but two end sounds—"uite" and "ins." In its few words it suggests the age old story of the fleeting nature of love, and the heartless laughter of the cruel world, which gleefully predicts a bad dénouement for all melancholy pilgrims who try to snatch a few moments of serene pleasure.

The prelude begins with a sparkling flutelike flourish. French composers have always had a special feeling for the flute, and Debussy's love for the instrument is manifest in his songs (see "La Flûte de Pan"), his orchestral works, as in "L'Apres Midi d'une Faune," and pieces for solo flute such as "Syrinx." After the opening cadenza the left hand's rhythmic figure begins. Debussy says this is to be played as though from far away, without nuance, but very rhythmically. Chords rise from this bass, then the sinuous melodic fragment is heard. The dynamics are very low and "sourde," or muffled. Augmented A♭ chords then float above the bass notes and an F minor chord prepares for the vocal entry.

The singer's first phrase is distinguished by its final note, the E♮ on "cuite," which provides the desired exotic flavor. The C♭, first heard in the rolled chord in the following piano interlude, is the "color" note for the next several measures; it becomes even more striking when combined with the G at "Mauvaise," which means "bad." The harmonic tension eases appropriately for "instants sereins," "serene moments," and for the "walking-music" of the next line—"Qui m'ont conduit et t'ont conduite" (which led me and led you). The words thus far are:

An old faun of terra-cotta
Laughs in the middle of the bowling green,
Predicting no doubt a bad
Outcome to these serene moments,
Which led me and led you,

The music becomes more and more exotic, as strange chord combinations and the weaving melodic fragment reassert themselves in the accompaniment. The flute reappears and becomes the focal element in the postlude. The voice fades away on the last line, a line of only two notes for ten syllables.

Nowhere in the song do the singer's dynamics rise above a *piano* —the little *crescendos* and *decrescendos* are merely gentle undulations. The piano part has one *sforzando* in the interlude between "boulingrins" and "Présageant," but this, too, should be within the context of the overall piano range. The essence of the song is understatement. The final lines are:

Melancholy pilgrims,
To this hour whose flight
Whirls around in the sound of the tambourines.

3. Colloque sentimental
Sentimental Colloquy

Dans le vieux parc solitaire et glacé
Deux formes ont tout à l'heure passé.
Leurs yeux sont morts et leur lèvres sont molles,
Et l'on entend à peine leurs paroles.
Dans le vieux parc solitaire et glacé
Deux spectres ont évoqué leur passé.

—Te souvient-il de notre extase ancienne?
—Pourquoi voulez-vous donc qu'il m'en souvienne?

—Ton coeur bât-il toujours à mon seul nom?
    Toujours vois-tu mon âme en rêve? —Non.

—Oh! Les beaux jours de bonheur indicible
    Où nous joignions non bouches! —C'est possible.

—Qu'il était bleu, le ciel, et grand l'espoir!
—L'espoir a fui, vaincu, vers le ciel noir.

Tels ils marchaient dans les avoines folles,
Et la nuit seule entendit leurs paroles.

"Colloque sentimental" is the last song by Debussy to be based on a poem of Verlaine, and a more disturbing text is hard to imagine. While it is true that many poets seem obsessed by the ephemeral nature of erotic love, few poems treat this subject in as stark and grim a fashion as this "Sentimental Colloquy." The title is, of course, meant to be ironic, for the principal protagonist in this dialogue is totally unable to arouse a sentimental or even nostalgic response from her former lover. When one realizes that this poem was part of the collection *Les Fêtes galantes*, inspired by the charming and frivolous paintings of Watteau, and that other poems from this group are as light-hearted as "Les Ingénus," "Fantoches," "Clair de lune," and "Mandoline," one is all the more struck by the macabre quality of these lines.

To convey the meaning of the song, the singer must make vocal distinctions between the two speakers. This is quite difficult, because at one point, lines nine and ten, the first person asks two questions before receiving the one word answer—"No"; whereas, in the other exchanges, there is an alternating question and response pattern. The first question elicits another question as the response, which further complicates interpretative matters for the vocalist. In general the melodic phrases for the answers are much shorter and more static than the questions, but this is less obvious in the first and last exchanges.

The song opens with a brief piano introduction based for three of its four measures on a whole-tone scale. The chill and lonely mood is established immediately by the emptiness of the single notes in the first bar. The whole-tone scheme is broken in the fourth measure by the low note (A in the key for high voice) and the harmony finally settles on an A major chord at the singer's entry.

The feeling of chilling emptiness is sustained by the first unaccompanied vocal line, and the repeated G (on which nine of the next ten syllables are intoned) does nothing to lighten the gloom. With the exception of the reiteration of the words and music for "Dans le vieux parc solitaire et glacé," the remaining lines of the introductory narrative are all confined to few if any changes of pitch. The accompaniment reverts to whole-tone patterns, with the exception of the D♯ under "morts" and the chords under "le vieux parc . . . glacé." At the word "spectres" a C♮ is heard in the piano part; this becomes a very significant note for the body of the song. The words of the introduction are:

> In the old park, lonely and chilled
> Two shapes have just passed by.
> Their eyes are dead and their lips are slack,
> And one scarcely hears their words.
> In the old park, lonely and chilled
> Two spectres have evoked the past.

The C♮ now begins to reveal its importance: it is present in every measure of the central section of the song (the entire dialogue) and is almost always used as a syncopated rhythmic figure (the measures where the C is merely held are under ". . . tu mon âme en rêve?" and the last syllable of "indicible"). Sometimes this insistent note is played alone and sometimes it is buried in chords, but wherever possible it should be heard. The significance of the note in the context of the words is subject to discussion: Is it a bell tolling inexorably the passing hours? Is it the beating of their hearts? Is it rain falling on the sad scene? Neither Debussy nor Verlaine tells us.

A melancholy, expressive chord played as though from afar starts the next section. After the two-bar piano solo the first voice enters with a reasonably flowing melodic line. The sixteenth notes give considerable movement, especially since a slight increase in tempo is suggested at the beginning of the section. When the second voice responds, the tempo is held back again, which emphasizes the slower-moving eighth notes and more restricted intervals of this line. The first lines of dialogue are:

Do you remember our bygone ecstasy?
Why then do you want me to remember it?

The tempo moves ahead again for the two questions asked by the first voice, whose increased agitation can be assumed from the *crescendo* and rising melodic line under "toujours à mon seul nom?" There is a *subito piano* in the piano part under the high note at "nom," but the singer should not make the drop in dynamics until the octave drop in pitch. The answer to these questions comes on one chilling syllable—"Non." These two lines are:

Does your heart still beat merely at my name?
Do you always see my soul in your dreams?—No.

The agitation and excitement continue to mount as the music becomes faster and louder. The accompanying chords grow fuller as singer and pianist reach their peak at the extended word "indicible," the highest note in the song. Now the *subito piano* is a hush of ecstasy as the first voice relives the erotic past, but the tempo increases as the second voice answers impatiently, "C'est possible."

Ah! the beautiful days of indescribable happiness
When our lips were joined!—It's possible.

The music remains quiet and subdued for the final exchange, she remembering with nostalgia, he recalling only the bitter ending:

How blue the sky was, and how great was hope!
Hope has flown, vanquished, towards the dark sky.

There is an epilogue to the brief drama. The original key signature is reintroduced (four sharps in the key for high voice) and the repeated C♮ is heard no more. Short chords barely support the *quasi-recitativo* melody, and then the accompaniment stops while the voice solemnly intones "Et la nuit" on one note. The characteristic piano figure used so often during the dialogue section returns, but much more quietly and slowly than before. At this point the tonal center, C♯ minor, begins to assert itself. The fade-out ending reminds one of Schumann's instructions at the end of "Carnaval," where he tells the pianist first to play as fast as possible and then to play a little faster. Here it is as soft as possible, and then still softer or "plus rien" (literally "more nothing"), as Debussy puts it. The final C♯ octave should be short and muffled—it merely reminds the listener of the tonality. The words for the epilogue are:

Thus they walked in the wild oats,
And only the night heard their words.

Trois chansons de France

1. Le Temps a laissié son manteau   Charles d'Orléans
The Season Has Shed Its Cloak

Le temps a laissié son manteau
De vent de froidure et de pluye
Et s'est vestu de broderye,
De soleil raiant, cler et beau.
Il n'y a beste ni oisieau
Qui en son jargon ne chante ou crye.

Le temps a laissié son manteau,
Rivière, fontaine et ruisseau
Portent en livrée jolye
Goultes d'argent d'orfaverie
Chascun s'abille de nouveau,
Le temps a laissié son manteau.

Since the majority of poems set to music by Debussy are the works of nineteenth-century French poets, it is a refreshing contrast to find these three *Chansons de France,* whose texts were written so much earlier. The first and third are the works of the great "seigneur poète,"* Charles d'Orléans (1394–1465); Tristan l'Hermite (1601–1655) is the author of the second.

Charles, duc d'Orléans, lived through one of the most turbulent eras of French history, a time of civil wars and wars with England. The great heroine of the age was, of course, Joan of Arc, the Maid of Orleans. Charles was an active participant in these upheavals—he was at one time a prisoner of war†—but this did not deter him from becoming a poet of distinction.

The language of the fifteenth century differs considerably from present-day French in spelling and usage, but pronunciation has actually changed very little. For example, in the text one finds the letter *y* where *i* is now used in *pluye, broderye, crye,* and *joye;* instead of the modern *ê* we have *es* in *vestu* and *beste:* in both instances modern pronunciation approximates that of the fifteenth century. Similarly the ancient spellings for the words *clair* (*cler*), *goutte* (*goulte*), and *chacun* (*chascun*) have little or no effect on their pronunciation. There is, however, one audible difference: in the past participle *laissié,* the extra *i* is pronounced (the modern form is *laissé*).

The poem itself is a delightful salute to Spring. Its rhyme scheme is an intricate interlacing of but two end sounds, *eau* and *ye* (*ie* in modern French). The imagery of the winter season abandoning its cloak of

* Encyclopédie Larousse
† Encyclopedia Britannica

wind, cold, and rain to bedeck itself in the embroidery of sunlight has been oft repeated since the fifteenth century, and was probably part of the accepted poetic vocabulary even then. Nevertheless, the poem retains its freshness and open-hearted sincerity.

The music echoes the youthful exuberance of the text—*Grove's Dictionary of Music and Musicians* calls it the "freshest and most open-air music Debussy ever wrote." The piano begins with a "joyous and animated" passage, which gradually tapers off to a strange, anticipatory rolled chord. The melody rises above the accompanying chords in a cheerful, positive declaration. The first archaic touch in the music is in the chord progression from E minor to A major under "laiss*ié son manteau de vent.*" The original piano figure returns under this lively melodic line, and at the crucial word "soleil" (sunshine) the accompaniment bursts into triumphant chords which continue after the last syllable of the verse. Here, too, melody and accompanying chords provide an antique effect. The words thus far are:

> The season has abandoned its cloak
> Of wind, of cold and of rain,
> And has clothed itself in embroidery,
> In radiant sunshine, bright and beautiful.

The ensuing piano interlude is delicate and somewhat *sostenuto;* its half note octaves ring out like bells above the marching eighth notes. These ringing octaves continue to be heard over the eighth notes throughout the section. The vocal line retains its vibrant vitality. The words are:

> There is no beast or bird
> Who, in his jargon, neither sings nor cries.
> The season has abandoned its cloak,

The archaic-sounding chord pattern (begun under the last line quoted above) grows in importance until it reaches a *forte* in the piano interlude. Then the dynamics drop suddenly in preparation for the continuation of the vocal line, which begins softly and builds steadily to the glorious climactic ending. The accompaniment contributes mightily to this joyous *crescendo* and its last chords are rich, full and bright. Once again the key signature (two sharps for high voice) is somewhat of a mystery, as the song ends on an unequivocal E major chord. There are several places in which B minor predominates, notably under "De soleil raiant, cler et beau," but E major still seems the more logical choice. The final lines of verse are:

> River, fountain and brook
> Wear in pretty livery

Drops of silver jewelry.
Each one adorns himself anew.
The season has abandoned its cloak.

2. La Grotte   Tristan l'Hermite
The Grotto

Auprès de cette grotte sombre
Où l'on respire air si doux,
L'onde lutte avec les cailloux
Et la lumière avecque l'ombre.

Ces flots, lassés de l'exercise
Qu'ils ont fait dessus de gravier,
Se reposent dans ce rivier
Où mourût autrefois Narcisse...

L'ombre de cette fleur vermeille
Et celle de ces joncs pendants
Paraissent estre là dedans
Les songes de l'eau qui sommeille.

Tristan l'Hermite, the author of the poem "La Grotte," lived in the first half of the seventeenth century (1601–1655), the beginning of the great age of Classicism in France. First Louis XIII and then Louis XIV, the "Sun King," reigned over the nation, increasing its power and wealth. A trio of titans, Corneille, Molière, and a little later Racine, brought French literature to unprecedented glory. For the first time the artistic center of Europe shifted from the Italian cities of Rome, Florence, and Venice to Paris.

To a large extent the aesthetics of this Classic Era in France (not to be confused with the eighteenth-century age of Classicism in music, which was largely a German development) were extensions of Renaissance ideals: a return to the graceful and symmetrical structure of Greek and Roman art, a preoccupation with form and style, a desire to be noble and universal. The plight of the common man was seen as proper subject matter for comedy but not tragedy, where the tragic flaw in the noble hero was the principal theme. Comedy and tragedy were two separate forms, never to be mingled. Delicacy and correctness of language were of the utmost importance, and rules for poetry were strict as to meter, rhyme and content. One of the favorite subjects for short poems was the beauty of nature, exemplified by the poem "La Grotte."

As one can see, two remnants of old-French spelling remain in this poem: *avecque* for *avec* and *estre* for *être*. Evidently both spellings were in use for *avec* at that time—Tristan used *avecque* when he needed the extra syllable and *avec* when he did not. (Each line of the poem has eight syllables; the final "feminine" *e* is not pronounced or counted as a syllable in spoken poetry, although it is when the poem is set to music; hence lines one, four, five, eight, nine, and twelve have nine syllables when sung, eight when spoken.) The *s* is not pronounced in *estre*—the word sounds just like its modern counterpart, *être*. The rhyme scheme is regular: *abba/cdde/effe*, and there is a typical reference to Greek mythology, the story of Narcissus, who, falling in love with his own image reflected in a pool of water, fell into the water and drowned. The imagery is delicate and evocative, with no trace of sentimentality.

The music begins with a B minor chord (the key signature for high voice is two sharps), but a G♯ which reverberates above the chord is sounded immediately after. The same G♯ is heard above a D⁷ chord in the second measure of the introduction, after which it moves down an octave to become the principal bass note at the vocal entry. This G♯ in the harmony and melody remains a constant throughout the song, actually putting the piece in the ancient church mode called the Dorian, whose scale can be heard by playing the white notes on the piano from D to D′. The rhythmic figure—the thirty-second note is just a little longer than an on-the-beat grace note—is also repeated throughout the song.

The melodic lines for the first two stanzas flow freely and smoothly. The triadlike rise under "L'onde lutte" is very pretty, as is the descent which follows. There is a rather strong *crescendo* under the rising line of "Se reposent dans ce rivier," although considering the generally tranquil nature of the song a *mezzo forte* top would probably be sufficient. The first two stanzas are:

> Near this dark grotto
> Where one breathes such sweet air,
> The waves struggle with the pebbles
> And the light with the shadow.
>
> These currents, weary of the exertion
> They have made beneath the gravel,
> Rest in this stream
> Where long ago Narcissus died . . .

The music for the final verse has some strictly Impressionist touches, which fit admirably with the archaic sounds of so many of the chords: a whole-tone scale begins on the first beat of the measure in which we find "L'ombre de cette," and continues through "fleur"; it is set off by the single-note melodic line, a favorite stylistic device of

Debussy. There is a faint echo of this whole-tone pattern for the words "ces joncs pendants." One finds almost no dynamic contrast in this last section—the range is from p to pp. The last two measures of the vocal part and the entire postlude emphasize again the original sound combination—B minor with G♯ or the Dorian mode. The last stanza reads:

> The shadow of that vermilion flower
> And that of the hanging jonquils
> Seem to be there within
> The dreams of the sleeping water.

3. Pour ce que Plaisance est morte   Charles d'Orléans
Because Plaisance Is Dead

Pour ce que Plaisance est morte
Ce may, suis vestu de noir;
C'est grand pitié de véoir
Mon coeur qui s'en désconforte.
Je m'abille de la sorte
Que doy, pour faire devoir,
Pour ce que Plaisance est morte,
Ce may, suis vestu de noir.
Le temps ces nouvelles porte
Qui ne veut déduit avoir;
Mais par force du plouvoir
Fuit des champs clore la porte
Pour ce que Plaisance est morte.

For this third *Chanson de France,* Debussy returns to the poetry of the fifteenth-century "seigneur poète," Charles, duc d'Orléans. Inevitably this means that the text has many spellings no longer in current usage—the very title contains the archaic *Pour ce que* instead of the contemporary *parce que* (because). In addition we have *may* for *mai* ("May"), *vestu* for *vêtu* ("dressed"), *véoir* for *voir* ("to see"), *désconforte* for *déconforte* ("grieve"), *doy* for *deuil* ("mourning"), and *plouvoir* for *pleuvoir* ("to rain"). With all these changes in spelling, only *pour ce que, véoir,* and *plouvoir* have pronunciations appreciably different from their twentieth-century counterparts. One structural difference may be noted: there is no personal pronoun before "suis," which in this case means "I am." The reason for this is that in the fifteenth century all verb endings were sounded; the listener knew from the form which personal pronoun was implied.

Like the other poem by this author set to music by Debussy, "Le Temps a laissé son manteau" (see page 370), "Pour ce que Plaisance est Morte" has a complex rhyme scheme based on only two end sounds: "orte" and "oir." The pattern is *abba/abab/ab/baa*. There are thirteen lines instead of the usual twelve; the first line is repeated once midway and once at the end. The words are very sad, describing the poet's sorrow and his refusal to be comforted by the pleasures brought by the month of May. The dramatic contrast between the bright Spring season and the speaker's black mourning attire—the central image of the poem—is forcefully expressed.

The setting is a surprisingly impressionistic interpretation of the poem, with very few references to music of antiquity. The piano's introductory bars express a gentle melancholia. The strongest chord occurs on the second beat of the third bar, just before the singer enters. This dissonance is repeated under the singer's second syllable, where its sounds quite mournful. Each time the words "Plaisance est morte" are sung, they are accompanied by a whole-tone scale which has an otherworldly effect. The words are themselves part of the same whole-tone scale. After the scale, the melodic line becomes more expansive, and a variation of the original piano figure is heard.

From the beginning there has been insistence on the note F in the piano figure and the piece ends firmly in F minor, which for once is in agreement with the key signature (analyzed in key for high voice), but we have not as yet heard a single F minor chord. The last line of the first stanza is highly chromatic, but faint echoes of the whole-tone sections creep in between the half-step intervals. F as a tonal center is temporarily forgotten.

Although the stanza ends, the music continues, including the next three lines of verse before the section ends. "Je m'abille" is sung to a harmonic minor scale ending, and the end of "pour faire devoir" is chromatic, but, with the repetition of the line "Pour ce que Plaisance est morte," whole-tone music is heard again. The words thus far are:

> Because Plaisance is dead
> This May, I am dressed in black;
> It is a great pity to see
> My heart which is so distressed by this.
> I am dressed in a kind
> Of mourning, to do homage,
> Because Plaisance is dead.

The next line is a repeat in both words and music of the second line of the song. For the next two lines of verse Debussy wants a much slower, more mournful tempo. There is a *crescendo* to a *forte* at "Mais par force du plouvoir," and the pace quickens for the measure; at "porte" the dynamics are still strong, but the tempo is again held back. The final *diminuendo* begins as the sad words "Pour ce que Plaisance est morte," with their accompanying whole-tone music, are heard for the last time. The postlude is gentle in its sorrow—no angry passion here. The F minor tonality is finally established by way of a lovely rolled chord (the lower G and A♭ in the treble clef should be played with the left hand). The second half of the poem reads:

> This May I am dressed in black.
> The season brings its message
> (To) him who wishes no pleasure;
> But by the strength of his weeping
> Flees the fields, shuts the door,
> Because Plaisance is dead.

Le Promenoir des deux amants
Poems by Tristan l'Hermite

1. Auprès de cette grotte sombre
Near This Dark Grotto

This song was originally published (1904) as the second of the *Trois Chansons de France*. In that group it is entitled "La Grotte." For a discussion of the song, see page 372.

2. Crois mon conseil chère Climène
Believe My Advice, Dear Climène

> Crois mon conseil chère Climène
> Pour laisser arriver le soir,
> Je te prie, allons nous asseoir
> Sur le bord de cette fontaine.
>
> N'ouis-tu pas soupirer Zéphire,
> De merveille et d'amour atteint,
> Voyant des roses sur ton teint
> Qui ne sont pas de son empire?
>
> Sa bouche d'odeur toute pleine
> A soufflé sur notre chemin,
> Mélant un esprit de jasmin
> A l'ambre de ta douce haleine.

Having established a mysterious atmosphere of murmuring sounds and shadowy visions the poet and composer now introduce us to "Les deux amants" (the two lovers). "Crois mon conseil chère Climène" is a charming little love song in which an unidentified suitor subtly flatters his beloved. The first stanza of the brief poem serves as a prologue to the other two. In it the protagonist advises Climène to sit at the edge of the fountain with him and allow evening to come. These opening four lines are treated as a recitative by Debussy.

After a lovely three-measure introduction, in which the piano states its characteristic theme, the singer enters with a declamatory phrase on a whole-tone fragment, during which the accompaniment holds a rather unexpected C major chord (the key is B major). When the singer has finished the rest of the *recitativo* (after "fontaine") the main body of the song begins. Once again the piano states its characteristic phrase, this time accompanied by lovely diminished and regular seventh chords. A triplet figure in the piano's upper register provides motion and lightness while the voice intones on one low note "N'ouis-tu pas soupirer." The vocal line rises a bit on "Zéphire," a reference to the Greek personification of the west wind, the mildest and most gentle of all the woodland gods.

The new piano figure, first heard before "De merveille," adds to the tender but lighthearted quality of the accompaniment, while the voice continues to be somewhat more somber. At "Qui ne sont pas de son empire?," the vocal line rises in a whole-tone scale fragment to a D$\sharp$. The piano's *tessitura* is still much higher than the singer's, and continues to be so to the very end. The slow trill begun under "empire" is heard until the final arpeggios, while under this figure the piano's characteristic theme is repeated.

The vocal line becomes much freer and more melodic in the third stanza. It climbs to an F$\sharp$ at "d'odeur toute pleine" and eventually works its way back to the F$\sharp$ an octave below for the last syllable. The piano's rustling arpeggios end the song with gentle charm. The words are:

Believe my advice dear Climene
To allow the evening to come,
I beg you, come let us sit
On the edge of that fountain.

Don't you hear Zephyr sigh,
For wonder and love attained,
Seeing roses on your complexion
Which are not from his realm?

His mouth full of scent
Has breathed on our path,
Mingling an essence of jasmine
With the amber of your sweet breath.

3. Je tremble voyant ton visage
I Tremble Seeing Your Face

Je tremble voyant ton visage
Flotter avecque mes désires,
Tant j'ai de peur que mes soupirs
Ne lui fassent faire naufrage.

De crainte de cette aventure
Ne commets pas si librement
A cet infidèle element
Tous les trésors de la Nature.

Veux-tu, par un doux privilège,
Me mettre audessus des humains?
Fais-moi boire au creux de tes mains
Si l'eau n'en dissout point la neige.

Debussy's setting for this final song of *Le Promenoir des deux amants* has the most contemporary, most "Debussyan" flavor of the three. It is full of stylistic trademarks—whole-tone scale fragments, pentatonic (all the black notes) chords, harmonies including the sixth as well as the triad.

In the first measure we hear a keyboard figure which becomes a unifying factor in the song, for fragments of it are used in the first verse and it reappears significantly in the final stanza (under "privilège," after "humains," and from "l'eau" to the end). As the voice enters, the piano begins a syncopated bass which creates a rhythmic counterpoint to the straightforward melodic line. The chord under "Flotter," a Db minor triad with the sixth added, provides an exotic harmonic effect.

Under "de peur que mes soupirs," there is a chromatic rise in the melody accompanied by a rather strong *crescendo*, the focal point of the first stanza. The words for these lines are:

I tremble seeing your face
Adrift with my desires,
So much do I fear my sighs
Will cause it to be shipwrecked.

The accompaniment becomes soft and dreamy before the next stanza begins, with atmospheric chords (reminiscent of the sounds in Debussy's piano piece "Clair de lune") replacing the syncopated bass figure. In this second stanza the poet carries forward his original metaphor of the beloved's countenance being the vessel in which all his desires are held. The "faithless element" is, of course, the sea.

For fear that this adventure
Will commit so freely

To that faithless element
All the treasures of Nature.

There are two striking harmonic moments in the final stanza—the all-black-note chord before "Veux-tu," and the dissonance (Cb in the bass, Bb in the piano's upper voice, and Db in the melody) under "humains." From the word "privilège," we have a return of the original piano figure which seems to evoke the ripples of water, furthering in the music the underlying symbol of the song. The last stanza reads:

Do you wish, by a sweet privilege,
To place me above human beings?
Let me drink from the hollow of your hands,
If the water doesn't melt the snow from them.

Trois Ballades de François Villon
Poems by François Villon

1. Ballade de Villon à s'amye
Ballade from Villon to His Love

Faulse beauté, qui tant me couste cher,
Rude en effect, hypocrite doulceur,
Amour dure, plus que fer, à mascher;
Nommer te puis de ma deffaçon soeur.

Charme felon, la mort d'ung povre cueur,
Orgueil mussé, qui gens met au mourir,
Yeulx sans pitié! ne veult droict de rigueur,
Sans empirer, ung povre secourir?

Mieulx m'eust valu avoir esté crier
Ailleurs secours, c'eust esté mon bonheur:
Rien ne m'eust sceu de ce fait arracher;
Trotter m'en fault en fuyte à deshonneur.

Haro, haro, le grand et le mineur!
Et qu'est cecy? mourray sans coup férir,
Ou pitié peult, selon ceste teneur,
Sans empirer, ung povre secourir.

Ung temps viendra, qui fera desseicher,
Jaulnir, flestrir, vostre espanie fleur:
J'en risse lors, se tant peusse marcher,
Mais las! nenny: Ce seroit donc foleur,
Vieil je seray: vous, laide et sans couleur.

Or, beuvez fort, tant que ru peult courir.
Ne donnez pas à tous ceste douleur
Sans empirer ung povre secourir.

Prince amoureux, des amans le greigneur,
Vostre mal gré ne vouldroye encourir;
Mais toute franc cueur doit, par Nostre Seigneur,
Sans empirer, ung povre secourir.

These three songs, based on sections of "Le Testament," the major work by the fifteenth-century writer François Villon (1431–1463) are manifestations of Debussy's continuing preoccupation with ancient texts. From 1904 to 1910, the year in which these songs appeared, Debussy set to music two texts by Villon's contemporary Charles d'Orléans and four by the early seventeenth-century poet Tristan l'Hermite, as well as the three by Villon. We have already dealt with the problems of changes in language, particularly in regard to spelling, in the discussions of the songs by Charles and Tristan (see pages 370 and 372). In general the pronunciation approximates the contemporary sound despite differences in spelling (*faulse* is pronounced like *fausse, couste* like *coûte,* etc.). Any change that affects the sound or meaning of a word will be discussed as it appears in the text.

François Villon is one of the most colorful figures in the history of French literature. He was immensely popular among the poor people of Paris with whom he drank, joked, and brawled. Despite the elegance and polish of some of his poetry, he loved the lusty street language of the day, and was able to evoke medieval Paris with absolute realism. His life and works are a series of contradictions: this author of the devoutly religious "Ballade que Villon feit à la requeste de sa mère pour prier Nostre-Dame" (the second of the three Ballades) robbed a chapel of 500 gold crowns and was thought to be the ringleader of a band of roving thieves; this writer of the most delicate love poetry was constantly being thrown into prison for involvement in street fights violent enough to have resulted in at least one death.

The first poem, "Ballade de Villon à s'amye" (from Villon to his love), is a bitter tirade against a cruel beloved. It is included in his last will and testament (the literary device which is the basis of "Le Testament") as his legacy to his faithless lover, whom he refers to as a dirty tramp! It is an extremely complex poem, with every line ending in an *r* and the initial letters of the first fourteen lines an acrostic spelling FRANÇOIS MARTHE, probably the lady's name coupled with his. Like all ballades it has a refrain: "Sans empirer, ung povre secourir" (Don't worsen matters, help a poor soul). Each line has ten syllables, and the rhyme scheme is an intricate interlacing of three end sounds: *abab//bcbc//abab//bcbc//* etc. There are six stanzas of four lines, every other one ending with the refrain.

The music is heavy with sorrow and bitterness. The characteristic falling piano figure, with which the song begins and which is heard throughout the piece, expresses the despair felt by the poet. A strong accent on the first of the two chords heightens this effect. The sharp dissonances under appropriate words such as "rude" (harsh) lift the music far from the realm of sentimentality—we are dealing with raw feelings. In each of the first three stanzas, the melody begins with a mournful minor third interval. This pattern is broken when the poet warns his love that time will rob her of her beauty, but that happens much later in the song. The music is not unrelenting in its sorrow—there are comforting major chords under "Amour dure . . . soeur," but the words retain their bitterness:

> False beauty, who costs me so dear,
> Harsh in reality, hypocritical tenderness,
> Grinding love, harder than iron!
> I can name you, my own ruin certain.

In this last sentence we have an example of archaic syntax very different from contemporary usage.

The next four lines bring even harsher dissonances, especially under "Yeulx sans pitié! ne veult droict de rigueur," and an increase in dynamics. The poet's sorrow is tinged with anger.

> Thieving charm, the death of a poor heart,
> Hidden pride which leads men to death,
> Eyes without pity! lacking not in severity,
> Don't worsen matters, help a poor soul!

The third stanza begins tranquilly in much the same manner as the first two, but the anguished cries ("Haro, haro") at the beginning of the fourth stanza reach a new level of intensity, as though the poet can bear no more:

> I should have done better to cry
> Elsewhere for help, that is where my happiness is:
> Nothing would have known how to snatch me from this fate;
> I must run in flight and dishonor.
>
> Help me, help me, the great and the small!
> And what is this? Shall I die without striking a blow,
> Or may you take pity, just to this degree,
> Don't worsen matters, help a poor soul!

At this point the music changes considerably. The lugubrious falling figure and melancholy minor melodic interval are dropped, and the mood becomes ominous rather than tortured. Strange dissonances and odd melodic intervals heighten the impact of the words:

> A time will come, which will dry,
> Yellow, wither the flower of your bloom:

Debussy's instructions now say "ironically and lightly"; the thirty-second-note figure in the accompaniment undoubtedly represents the laughter mentioned in the words:

> Then I shall laugh, if I can open my mouth that wide,

The accompaniment ceases, better to dramatize the cries of the voice:

> But alas, fool, that would be madness

In this line we find two archaic pronunciations: *seroit* (serwa) for *serait* and *foleur* for *folie*.

> I shall be old; you, ugly and colorless.

The sound of laughter now introduces the next section, which delivers the "Gather your rosebuds while ye may" message:

> Then drink well, while the stream runs.

The original piano figure returns now, but as the tempo is brighter the effect is not as dismal as in earlier verses. The melody has an upward-moving line which, though still in the minor mode, is not quite as sad as the minor third usually heard with this figure. The refrain is enlivened by the staccato chords that rise under it, and the *subito forte* rolled chord at the end of the phrase is triumphant. The poet now makes his final appeal to the God of Love. The music here is quite modern in feeling compared to the rest of the composition, especially the augmented chord under "encourir." After four bars of this, the original piano figure brings back a quieter, more wistful mood as the poet is told that he will never really be free of his passion. When the refrain is heard for the last time, the accompaniment plays a series of three rising major chords, which bring back the archaic atmosphere of the music. The last lines are:

> Don't add to all this woe,
> Don't worsen matters, help a poor soul.
> Amorous prince, king of lovers,
> Your disfavor I've no wish to incur.
> But in all frankness, by Our Lord,
> Don't worsen matters, help a poor soul.

2. Ballade que Villon feit à la requeste de sa mère pour prier Nostre-Dame
Ballade that Villon Made at the Request of His Mother to Pray to Our Lady

> Dame du ciel, régente terrienne,
> Emperiere des infernaulx palux,

Recevez-moy, vostre humble chrestienne,
Que comprinse soy entre vos esleuz,
Ce non obstant qu'oncques riens ne valuz.

Les biens de vous, ma dame et ma maistresse,
Sont trop plus grans que ne suys pecheresse,
Sans lesquelz bien ame ne peult merir
N'avoir les cieulx, je n'en suis menteresse.
En ceste foy je vueil vivre et mourir.

A vostre Filz dictes que je suys sienne;
De luy soyent mes pechez aboluz:
Pardonnez-moy comme à l'Égyptienne,
Ou comme il feit au clerc Theophilus,
Lequel par vous fut quitte et absoluz,

Combien qu'il eust au diable faict promesse
Preservez-moy que je n'accomplisse ce!
Vierge portant sans rompure encourir
Le sacrement qu'on celebre a la messe.
En ceste foy je vueil vivre et mourir.

Femme je suis povrette et ancienne,
Qui riens ne sçay, oncques lettre ne leuz;
Au moustier voy dont suis paroissienne,
Paradis painct où sont harpes et luz,
Et ung enfer ou damnez sont boulluz:

L'ung me faict paour, l'aultre joye et liesse.
La joye avoir fais-moy, haulte Deesse,
A qui percheurs doivent tous recourir,
Comblez de foy, sans faincte ne paresse.
En ceste foy je vueil vivre et mourir.

This Ballade is probably the most convincing religious statement to be found among Debussy's songs. The simplicity of Villon's words obviously inspired Debussy's unaffected setting, which is transfigured by the depth of its feeling into a universal expression of piety.

As the title states, Villon wrote the Ballade at his mother's request, for her to use as a prayer. It is his legacy to her in "Le Testament" in remorse for having caused her much grief. The special feeling that women had when praying to the Virgin Mary, and their desire for her to intercede on their behalf with her Son, are beautifully conveyed. The sense of unworthiness and guilt, the hope for forgiveness, the tears of the contrite—all this is expressed so poignantly by the roguish Villon that we feel the prayer is as much for himself as for his mother (see p. 380 for a description of his short, dissolute life).

To qualify as a ballade, a poem must have a refrain which is repeated at the end of every other stanza. In this case each of the three two-stanza sections contains ten ten-syllable lines with the following rhyme scheme: *ababb/ccdcd/*.The refrain, which serves as a unifying structural device in the music as well as in the poem, is "En ceste foy je veuil vivre et mourir" (In this faith I wish to live and die). In this one sentence we have three examples of old French spellings (*ceste* for *cette*, *foy* for *foi*, *veuil* for *veux*) which result in pronunciations approximately equivalent to the modern words. For a more complete discussion of old French see pages 370 and 372.

Debussy begins the song with a simple unaccompanied melodic line. The chords which follow are solemn and archaic-sounding, perhaps as bells, with a strange discord in the third bar (F♯–G). The tonal center for melodic line and accompaniment is A minor until the last syllable of "chrestienne," where an unexpected F♮ appears harmonized with an F major chord. This leads to the C major chord in the next measure. The melody for "Recevez-moy, vostre humble chrestienne" is chantlike and reminiscent of a church service. The chords which support this fragment are heavy and dolorous; they are a repeat of the third bar of introduction and, like it, contain the dissonance. After the C major chord, the accompaniment seems to evoke church bells while the melody becomes more *recitativo*-like. The repeated Cs under "Ce non obstant . . . rien" presage the music for the refrain. The words for this stanza are:

> Lady of Heaven, Regent of Earth,
> Empress of infernal swamps,
> Receive me, your humble Christian,
> That I may be among your chosen ones,
> Without this nothing has value.

On the second syllable of "valuz" Debussy modulates to E major and the church bells continue in the new key. At "Sont trop plus grans," a series of chords composed of parallel fifths and octaves begin to support the melodic line. This device, which continues to the refrain, strongly evokes medieval church music. There is an abrupt modulation to C major one measure before the refrain—the singer intones the seven syllables of this measure on middle C—after which a somber A minor chord introduces the refrain, which also ends on C. The first and second time we hear the refrain, the final C is harmonized by an F major chord, forcing the music on; the last time it ends with finality on a C major chord. The words for the second stanza are:

> Your goodness, my Lady and my Mistress,
> Are greater than my sins,
> Without Your good soul no one can merit
> Your skies, I do not deceive myself.
> In this faith I wish to live and die.

The third stanza begins like the first, but after five measures we have new music: instead of the church bells there is a continuation of the somber chords. Discords abound in the bar mentioning the devil ("le diable"), and when the bells do reappear (from "messe" to "encourir") they are agitated and threatening. The calm of the C major chord and the repeated-note vocal line under "Le sacrement" once again prepare us for the refrain. This section reads:

> To Your Son, say that I am His;
> May my sins be absolved by Him.
> Pardon me as was the Egyptian woman,
> Or as He did for the clerk Theophilus
> Who was freed and absolved through You,
>
> Even though he had made a promise to the Devil.
> Save me from doing thus!
> Virgin without blemish, who bore
> The sacrament one celebrates at Mass.
> In this faith I wish to live and die.

The final section begins even more simply and humbly than the first two. Gone is the arresting opening interval—now the melodic line moves only by modest steps. The chords under the chantlike "Recevez-moy . . ." and "Pardonnez-moy . . ." (in stanzas one and three) have been replaced by single notes in unison with the voice for "Au moustier . . . paroissienne," their counterpart in this last section. The resolution at the end of "paroissienne" is a beautifully soothing D major chord; this, and the other rolled chords which follow, imitate the harps ("harpes") the suppliant envisions as part of heaven. Even though she speaks of Hell and damnation in the next line, her mood continues to be one of hope and exaltation. Debussy uses the word "extatique" (ecstatic) to describe the desired feeling, but it is a quiet ecstasy, tranquil and serene. The A minor chord before the refrain is the last gloomy sound we hear, as the piece concludes in C major. The final stanzas read:

> I am a poor old woman,
> Who knows nothing, I neither write nor read;
> In the monastery of my parish,
> Paradise is painted, where there are harps and light,
> And a Hell where the damned are boiled;
>
> One frightens me, the other fills me with joy and merriment.
> Let me have the joy, Exalted mother of God,
> To whom all sinners must hasten back,
> Full of joy, without idleness or sloth.
> In this faith I wish to live and die.

3. Ballade des femmes de Paris
Ballade of the Women of Paris

Quoy qu'on tient belles langagières
Florentines, Veniciennes,
Assez pour estre messaigières,
Et mesmement les anciennes;

Mais, soient Lombardes, Romaines,
Genevoises, à mes perils,
Piemontoises, Savoysiennes,
Il n'est bon bec que de Paris.

De beau parler tiennent chayères,
Ce dit-on Napolitaines,
Et que sont bonnes cacquetières
Allemandes et bruciennes;

Soient Grecques, Egyptiennes,
De Hongrie ou d'aultre païs,
Espaignolles ou Castellannes,
Il n'est bon bec que de Paris.

Brettes, Suysses, n'y sçavent guères,
Ne Gasconnes et Tholouzaines;
Du Petit Pont deux harangères
Les concluront, et les Lorraines,

Anglesches ou Callaisiennes,
(Ay-je beaucoup de lieux compris?)
Picardes, de Valenciennes...
Il n'est bon bec que de Paris.

Prince, aux dames parisiennes,
De bien parler donnez le prix;
Quoy qu'on die d'Italiennes,
Il n'est bon bec que de Paris.

A greater contrast can hardly be imagined between this light-hearted, witty tribute to the ladies of Paris and the poignant prayer which precedes it in this group of *Three Ballades by François Villon*. Debussy certainly chose wisely among the poems of Villon in terms of program-building! If he deliberately set out to illustrate the contradictory nature of the poet he has succeeded admirably, for we see bitterness, insouciance, piety, and puckish humor emphasized in turn in the cycle.

"Ballade des femmes de Paris" follows the general formula for all ballades: a refrain repeated after every other stanza. In this poem each stanza is composed of four eight-syllable lines; the rhyme scheme is *abab/bcbc/* and there are three-and-a-half complete sections.

The piano begins with a gay sprinkling of repeated staccato notes and chords. The melody bounces along on one note for most of the first line. As previously explained, the line has one syllable more when sung than when spoken, because final feminine e's are silent when spoken but pronounced when sung. Melody and accompaniment are in contrary motion for a while in the second line, and the stanza ends with a perky downward scale. The words thus far are:

> However beautifully spoken are
> Florentines, Venetians,
> Good enough to be messengers,
> Even the ancient ones;

Staccato repeated notes comprise the brief interlude between stanzas, after which a jaunty almost jazzlike figure is heard in the accompaniment. The melody is equally modern in feeling—one might mistake it for a Gershwin tune! An abrupt C major chord sets off the refrain—a series of exuberant melodic intervals and accompanying chords which culminate triumphantly in E major, the tonic. This stanza reads:

> But, whether Lombards, Romans,
> Genevese, I'll give you odds,
> Piedmontese, Savoysiens,
> Only Parisians have "le bon bec."

It is impossible to convey in a translation of the refrain, the last line quoted above, the *double entendres* contained in the original. "Bec" literally means beak or bill; its figurative slang meaning is "mouth" (as in, to have a big mouth, to be a big talker) or, by extension, face. Its secondary figurative meaning is kiss, as in bill and coo, so in one word Villon is saying that only in Paris can one find pretty faces, well-spoken women, and good kissing! Since we know that sexual innuendo is a constant theme throughout "Le Testament," of which this ballade is a part, more lascivious translations can easily be imagined!

The interlude is a sort of "vamp 'til ready" for three measures, after which the repeated-note figure returns. By the second line of the stanza we have the sound of the lightweight popular music hall song. Other French composers of this era, in particular Ibert, Milhaud, Satie, and Poulenc, shared the opinion that classical music needed a dash of spice from the popular idiom in the form of jazz rhythms and music hall irreverence. This little section is actually more characteristic of Satie or Ibert than Debussy. The style and mood continue through the next stanza right to the refrain, which is always sung to the same melody:

For speaking well professorial chairs are held,
They say, by Neapolitan women,
And good chatterboxes are
Germans and Prussians;

Whether Greek or Egyptian,
Hungarian or from other lands,
Spanish or Castilian,
Only Parisians have "le bon bec."

The pace seems to accelerate, as the poet names more and more places whose women are inferior to the Ladies of Paris. Suddenly, at the key change before "Du Petit Pont" the music becomes, in Debussy's words, "expressive and mocking." There is an air of ironic seriousness, of tongue-in-cheek romantic posturing, which lasts for six bars, after which the music-hall jauntiness returns. The accompaniment halts as the poet asks roguishly, "Ay-je beaucoup de lieux compris?" and then the bouncy repeated notes lead to the refrain.

Bretons, Swiss, scarcely know anything,
Nor the Gascons and Toulousians.
From the Petit Pont* two fish-wives
Would finish them all, plus the Lorrainers,

English or Callaisians.
Have I included many places?
Picardians, Valencians,
Only Parisians have "le bon bec."

The last section begins with mock solemnity, the marching octaves and *legato* phrasing in marked contrast to the skittering repeated notes of the other interludes. The vocal line is stentorian and self-important. At the next interlude the carefree feeling returns, but for the first time in the song the chords have an archaic sound. A big *crescendo* leads to the marvelous chords at the beginning of the refrain and the piece ends with a glorious *glissando*. Of all Debussy's songs, this one is the most fun! The last lines are:

Prince, to the Parisian ladies
For speaking well, give them the prize;
Whatever one says of Italians,
Only Parisians have "le bon bec."

* Paris landmark—a bridge over the river Seine.

Trois Chansons de Mallarmé, 1913
Poems by Stéphane Mallarmé

1. Soupir
Sigh

Mon âme vers ton front où rêve, ô calme soeur
Un automne jonché de taches de rousseur
Et vers le ciel errant de ton oeil angélique
Monte, comme dans un jardin mélancolique,
Fidèle, un blanc jet d'eau soupire vers l'Azur!
—Vers l'Azur attendri d'Octobre pâle et pur
Qui mire aux grands bassins sa langueur infinie
Et laisse, sur l'eau morte où la fauve agonie
Des feuilles erre au vent et creuse un froid sillon,
Se trainer le soleil jaune d'un long rayon.

Throughout his adult life Debussy had been acquainted with and preoccupied by the works of Verlaine, Baudelaire, Mallarmé, and other contemporary poets. His deep affinity for their poetry led him to seek their friendship, and he spent far more time in their company than with other musicians. He was particularly close to Verlaine, who had a strong influence on his early life, and Mallarmé (1842–1898), whose literary salon he attended regularly. Interestingly enough, although he chose sixteen texts by Verlaine for his songs, he set only four poems by Mallarmé: "Apparition," the most ambitious of his early songs (1882), and this penultimate trio, "Soupir," "Placet futile," and "Eventail" (1913). Only "Noël des enfants qui n'ont plus de maisons" follows in Debussy's song output (1915) and for that song he wrote his own text. Of course, it was a piece by Mallarmé that inspired Debussy's "Prélude à l'après-midi d'un faune," one of his greatest orchestral works (1892–94).

"Soupir," the first of the trilogy, is a hauntingly beautiful miniature. From the opening measure we sense a tonal ambiguity that contributes to the wispy quality of the music, for the tonic Ab chord is never stated without the 6th, the F, which might suggest the relative minor. Then, too, Debussy uses rhythm to convey vagueness—in the fourth bar of the introduction the rhythm subtly shifts so that one arrives at the high note of the figure before the last beat. The Eb octave, at the beginning of that measure, must be held by the middle pedal so that the quarter note rest before the Ab in bar five can be honored. The lack of strength on the first beat of bar five, and the fourth beats of bars four and five, create an ephemeral airborne quality akin to the sigh the music is supposed to suggest.

After this evocative introduction the voice enters *a cappella*. The dreamy melodic line contains triplet quarter notes which soften the rhythmic outline. Slowly the voice rises, and at its high note the piano offers a beautiful arpeggiated supporting chord. This chord contains an E♮ and an E♭, while the following chord has a D♮ and a D♭, but the effect is far from discordant. The piano falls silent again after two measures and the voice continues alone. The melody is vaguely antique, its rhythm totally dependent on syllabification (hence the extra beat in the 5/4 measure), as in the music of the early Greeks. When the piano reenters, the voice drops to a low D♭ which is repeated for nine of the next eleven syllables. The accompaniment traces a delicate pattern on E♮ with the right hand, while the left hand plays chords containing two sets of seconds and single notes from the tonic chord. Despite the veritable tone cluster of D♭, E♭ and E♮ there is no harshness to the sound. Under "fidèle" a new harmonic progression is heard—C major to A♭ combined with A♭ augmented. The melody for the next phrase, "un blanc jet d'eau soupire vers l'Azur!" is quite Oriental in effect, especially since it is heard over the augmented A♭. The words thus far are:

> My soul towards your brow where dreams, oh calm sister
> An autumn sprinkled with touches of russet
> And towards the roving sky of your angelic eyes,
> Rises, as in a melancholy garden,
> Faithful, a white jet of water sighs towards the Blue!

The tempo becomes a little livelier and the accompaniment a little fuller for the next five measures, but with the words "sur l'eau morte" (on the still water) the original dreamy mood returns, and the song begins its long fade-out ending. Closely spaced chords featuring seconds continue to characterize the accompaniment, while the rhythm abounds in two-against-three subdivisions of the quarter note. A repeat of the introductory piano figure ends the song with the ever-ambiguous A♭ chord. The closing lines are:

> Towards the Blue made tender by pale and pure October
> Which reflects its infinite languor in the large basins
> And allows, on the still water where the wild agony
> Of the leaves drifts in the wind and hollows a cold furrow,
> The yellow sunlight to draw itself out in a long ray.

2. Placet futile
Futile Petition

Princesse! à jalouser le destin d'une Hébé
Qui poind sur cette tasse au baiser de vos lèvres,

J'use mes feux mais n'ai rang discret que d'abbé
Et ne figurerai même nu sur le Sèvres.
Comme je ne suis pas ton bichon embarbé,
Ni la pastille, ni du rouge, ni jeux mièvres
Et que sur moi je sais ton regard clos tombé,
Blonde dont les coiffeurs divins sont des orfèvres!
Nommez nous . . . toi de qui tant de ris framboisés
Se joignent et troupeaux d'agneaux apprivoisés
Chez tous broutant les voeux et bêlant aux délires,
Nommez nous . . . pour qu'Amour ailé d'un Eventail
M'y peigne flûte aux doigts endormant ce bercail,
Princesse, nommez nous berger de vos sourires.

The language of this poem is so flowery and involuted that it is easy to lose track of the general idea! An Abbé is uselessly petitioning ("Placet futile" means "Futile petition") a beautiful blond princess. He envies the Greek goddess painted on her china cup, her lap dog, her makeup—anything that comes into contact with her lips or her body. Resigned to his lowly station, resigned to her indifference, he asks only to be "the shepherd of her smiles."

The poem is so exaggerated one can only assume that it is not meant to be taken seriously. This makes it quite different from the "Fêtes galantes" of Verlaine to which it has been compared,* for the Verlaine poems are an observer's sober descriptions of madcap scenes, while "Placet futile" comes right from the heart of the zany protagonist.

This raises the all-important question . . . is the music also intended as a parody? From the gentle introductory measures one receives no hint of such intention. The descending thirds are sweet and graceful (the composer's indication reads *doux et gracieux*) and the harmonies are typical of Debussy. The parallel fifths underlying "à jalouser . . . d'une Hébé" lend an antique effect to the music, as does the IV–I progression under "au baiser de vos lèvres." This is reminiscent of a courtly seventeenth-century minuet (the tempo indication reads "Dans le mouvement d'un Menuet lent"). The descending figure of the first measure is now repeated in the next two bars, from "lèvres" to "d'abbé," where it terminates in an unexpected Bb (the relative major) chord. The next few syllables are accompanied by parallel octaves, followed by a temporary V^7–I on C^7–F. To this point the music seems serious despite the bizarre words:

Princess! to envy the fate of the Hebe (the Greek goddess of youth)
Who springs to life on that cup at the kiss of your lips,

* *Trois chansons de Mallarmé*, Edition Peters #9243: Introduction by Reiner Zimmerman (Leipzig, 1971).

I waste my suffering but have only the modest rank of an Abbe
And shall not figure even nude on the Sèvres cup.

At last, beginning with the piano figure under "Sèvres," the music begins to reflect the roguish quality of the text. Certainly the 64th-note figure, and eighth-note chords under "la pastille, ni du rouge" have a comic effect. Although, with the exception of the last downward 64th-note figure in the penultimate bar, this is the only place where the music is deliberately parodistic. The rest of the song is colored by the knowledge—now clear in music as well as words—that we are not to take this song too seriously. The descending figure from the introduction, which returns after "Nommez nous . . . toi de qui," after "nommez nous . . . pour qu'Amour," and before "Princesse," now sounds—or can be made to sound—pompous. In fact the words "Nommez nous," sung while the piano is silent, can be projected with exaggerated intensity to emphasize the ridiculous nature of the Abbe's petition. Nevertheless, so much of the music is genuinely tender and lovely—the chords under "mièvres . . . tombé," the melody of "m'y peigne . . . bercail," which is accompanied by flutelike trills—that the parodistic aspect of the song seems secondary. This is never true of the words, which conclude:

> Since I am not your long-haired lap dog,
> Nor the pastille, nor the rouge, nor roguish games
> And since I know that on me your glance falls unaware,
> Blond whose divine coiffeurs are made by goldsmiths!
> Name us . . . you from whom so many raspberry-flavored smiles*
> Join one another like a group of tamed sheep,
> Everywhere nibbling vows and bleating with delight,
> Name us . . . so that Love winged with a fan
> May paint me there, flute in my fingers, lulling this sheepfold to sleep,
> Princess, name us the shepherd of your smiles.

3. Eventail
The Fan

> O rêveuse, pour que je plonge
> Au pur délice sans chemin,
> Sache, par un subtil mensonge,
> Garder mon aile dans ta main.
>
> Une fraicheur de crépuscule
> Te vient à chaque battement
> Dont le coup prisonnier recule
> L'horizon délicatement.

* The word "ris" actually also means sweetbreads!

Vertige! voici que frissonne
L'espace comme un grand baiser
Qui, fou de naître pour personne,
Ne peut jaillir ni s'apaiser.

Sens-tu le paradis farouche
Ainsi qu'un rire enseveli
Se couler du coin de ta bouche
Au fond de l'unanime pli!

Le sceptre des rivages roses
Stagnants sur les soirs d'or, ce l'est,
Ce blanc vol fermé que tu poses
Contre le feu d'un bracelet.

In "Eventail" we see language cut loose from the moorings of
syntax and logic, and music lifted out of the framework of tonality.
The result is an ambiguity that can prove most unsettling to the listener
who expects narrative or descriptive rationality in the text or identifiable tonal centers in the music. Instead of these accustomed guidelines, in the score we have extreme chromaticism, melodic intervals
based on augmented chords which by definition have no specific roots,
pentatonic (hence equally rootless) or polytonal accompanying figures,
and an ending which drifts off in a harmonic haze suggestive of E
minor.

The words are obviously chosen more for their sound and rhythm
than for their specific meaning. This makes any translation painfully
inadequate, but we provide one nevertheless. The poet seems to be
begging his dreamy loved one to keep him from flying away by "subtle
lies." She holds his wings in her hands. By the second verse—and with
a hint from the title (The Fan)—we surmise that "he" is a fan, making
space tremble like a kiss born for no one. This is pushing the idea of
universal analogy beyond the imagination of the literal-minded—either
one is able to succumb to the imagery or one is not! Certainly the
sounds are captivating: "Une fraicheur de crépuscule" has an inner
rhythmic rightness; the vowel-consonant combination of "l'unanime
pli" pleases the ear; "Le sceptre des rivages roses" combines long and
short syllables with mastery, and subtly carries the alliterative *r* sound
through the line; "stagnants sur les soirs d'or" is elegant and sonorous.

The music opens with an ornamental pentatonic figure and settles on a C octave. The polytonality of the C and the Gb⁷ chord which
follows is similar to Stravinsky's harmonic patterns. The key note in
the brief piano prelude is the F♯ in the bass which is intoned for four
measures, before the singer's entrance and under the first three vocal
phrases. The opening melody consists of short chromatic phrases, each
a little longer than the one preceding. At "sache" the bass note moves

up to G♯ and the melody has its first nonchromatic interval, a major third. Another chromatic line leads to a repetition of that interval under "men*songe*." There is a disjointed stop-and-start quality to the vocal line until the somewhat extended rise to the high F♯ at "main," which is held for a whole measure. This completes the first stanza:

> Oh dreamer, that I may plunge
> In pure delight without a path,
> Know, by a subtle lie,
> How to keep my wing in your hand.

The piano's introduction is now repeated, but instead of the chromatic vocal phrases of the initial melodic line we have a monotonous alternation between two notes. This is accompanied by a similar chordal pattern. After some movement under "vient à chaque battement dont le" we hear five long syllables on a repeated low D. After a one measure departure from the D, we return to that note, which then becomes the beginning of a strange climb of major third–major third–minor third. This takes us through the next four lines:

> A coolness of twilight
> Comes to you at each beat
> From whose imprisoned flutter
> The horizon delicately recoils.

A partially chromatic, partially diatonic triplet sixteenth note figure, played at a more rapid pace than the preceding music, sets off the exclamation of "Vertige!" (Vertigo). The highly chromatic figure in the next nine measures of the accompaniment is an aural expression of "que frissonne l'espace," as the beating of the fan makes the air seem to tremble. The melody is also very chromatic, despite some dramatic wide intervals at "comme un," "bai*ser* qui," and "personne." The section ends with a climb to a D♯ at "s'apai*ser*," which is accompanied by a strikingly dissonant chord containing C⁷ and C minor. This is the most striking stanza of the poem:

> Vertigo! Here trembles
> Space like a great kiss
> Which, frenzied at having been born for no one,
> Can neither burst forth nor be appeased.

The next stanza begins with a continuation of the dissonant chords and a partially declamatory melodic line. For the words "ainsi qu'un rire . . . bouche" Debussy gives us an Oriental-sounding melodic line over a tremolo accompaniment. Perhaps we are to envision a Chinese or Japanese beauty hiding her smile behind her fan. The dissonant chords return for the two-note melodic phrase "au fond de l'unanime pli."

> Do you feel the wild paradise
> Like a stifled laugh
> Run from the corner of your mouth
> Deep into the even folds!

The introductory pentatonic figure and C–Gb polytonality return once again to herald the last stanza, the most obscure of all. The piano figure under "roses" is extremely dissonant and the melodic line is mysterious. Under the word "d'or" a B⁷ chord seems to emerge as a possible dominant, paving the way for the E minor ending. This is deliberately complicated by the C♯s in the piano part before the last vocal entrance, and by the C major chords and reference to B major in the last five measures. The singer intones the presumed tonic (E) throughout these harmonic excursions, reinforcing the idea of a final tonality. None of these concessions to tonality diminishes the aura of mystery and vagueness generated by this lovely ending. The final stanza reads:

> The sceptre of red river banks
> Stagnating on golden evenings, it is that,
> This white closed flight that you place
> Against the fire of a bracelet.

Noël des enfants qui n'ont plus de maisons
Poem by Claude Debussy
Christmas Carol for Homeless Children

Nous n'avons plus de maisons!
Les ennemis ont tout pris, tout pris, tout pris, jusqu'à notre petit lit!
Ils ont brûlé l'école et notre maître aussi.
Ils ont brûlé l'église et monsieur Jésus-Christ
Et le vieux pauvre qui n'a pas pu s'en aller!
Nous n'avons plus de maisons.
Les ennemis ont tout pris, tout pris, tout pris, jusqu'à notre petit lit!
Bien sur! papa est à la guerre,
Pauvre maman est morte!
Avant d'avoir vu tout ça.
Qu'est-ce que l'on va faire?
Noël! petit Noël! n'allez pas chez eux, n'allez jamais chez eux,
Punissez-les!
Vengez les enfants de France!
Les petits Belges, les petits Serbes, et les petits Polonais aussi!
Si nous en oublions, pardonnez-nous Noël!
Noël! surtout, pas de joujoux,

Tachez de nous redonner le pain quotidien.
Nous n'avons plus de maisons!
Les ennemis ont tout pris, tout pris, tout pris, jusqu'à notre petit lit!
Ils ont brûlé l'école et notre maître aussi.
Ils ont brûlé l'église et monsieur Jésus-Christ
Et le vieux pauvre qui n'a pas pu s'en aller!
Noël! écoutez-nous, nous n'avons plus de petits sabots:
Mais donnez la victoire aux enfants de France!

Two tragic events—one private and one shared by most of Europe
—dominated the last few years of Debussy's life: his painful and lingering illness (cancer) and the devastation wrought by World War I. No
specific reference to his own personal agony can be found in the songs,
but his last song, "Noël des enfants . . . ," for which he wrote the words
and the music, is a poignant expression of his grief over the sufferings
caused by the war.

France was the principal battlefield of the four-and-a-half year
struggle that introduced modern warfare to a shocked world. The
dreadful combination of hand-to-hand combat in the trenches and the
first massive use of modern armaments meant heavy losses among
civilian as well as military personnel. As the warring armies fought
endlessly over the same terrain, food and shelter became scarce. 1916,
the year in which this song was published, was a particularly bleak
one, for the entry of the United States had not as yet eased the burden
of the weary Europeans.

Debussy makes us see the stark picture from the point of view of
children whose homes have been destroyed. It is Christmas and the
children pray, not for toys, but for their daily bread. Anger breaks
through their plaintive prayers as they ask that Noël, or Santa Claus,
punish the enemy by denying them Christmas. The mournful litany of
their losses—even their little beds were taken from them and they no
longer have shoes—is broken at the end by a defiant demand for
victory.

The power of this song lies in its simplicity and sincerity. There is
no attempt to make the ends of lines rhyme—it is as though such an arti-
ficial conceit would cheapen the sentiment. It is true that the refrain,
"Les ennemis ont tout pris, tout pris, tout pris, jusqu'à notre petit lit!"
("The enemies have taken everything, everything, everything, even our
little beds!") contains the inner rhymes "pris," "petit," and "lit," but
the rhythmic asymmetry prevents the rhymes from detracting from the
strength of the line. The structure of the sentences is absolutely
straightforward and might really have come from the mouth of a child.

The setting is equally genuine and devoid of artifice. Unadorned
A minor triads in a simple 12/8 meter introduce the sad little tune. Bass

notes on the IV, first in minor then in major, vary the harmony before "Les ennemis . . . ," and the repeated words "tout pris" are emphasized by their widening melodic interval. The modulation to C major at "lit" underscores the childlike innocence of the music. As the story becomes grimmer ("Ils ont brûle l'école . . ."), musical tension mounts, culminating in an ugly dissonance at "s'en all*er*." The words to this point are:

> We have no homes anymore!
> The enemies have taken everything, everything, everything, even our
> little beds!
> They have burned the school and our teacher too,
> They have burned the church and the Lord Jesus Christ
> And the old beggar who couldn't get away!

A lugubrious piano interlude now repeats the dissonant sound and prepares the way for a repeat of the opening lines:

> We have no homes anymore!
> The enemies have taken everything, everything, everything, even our
> little beds!

The key now changes to A major, lightening the mood of the music, but not the gloom of the woeful story:

> Of course! papa is at the war!
> Poor mama is dead!
> Before having seen all this.
> What are we to do?

As the child demands that the spirit of Christmas punish the enemy, the music becomes more excited. A strong *crescendo* leads to the loud cry "Punissez-les!" The repeated E♭s in the accompaniment bring a militant sound to "Vengez les enfants de France," as the melodic line again excitedly climbs to high F. As the child names the other victims of war, little Belgians, Serbs, Poles, an *accelerando* begins. An even more tempestuous *crescendo* begins to build under "Si nous en oublions," culminating in the anguished "Noël! Noël!" The words to this climactic point are:

> Noël, little Noël! don't go to them, never again go to them,
> Punish them!
> Avenge the children of France!
> The little Belgians, the little Serbs and the little Poles too!
> If we forget some, forgive us, Noël! Noël!

A sudden break in the dynamics brings us to the quiet, wistful little lines "surtout, pas de joujoux/Tachez de nous redonner le pain quotidien":

Above all, no toys,
Try to bring us back our daily bread.

The piano interlude fades away into lower and lower registers of the bass, eventually bringing back the tempo, words and music of the first section. Instead of the dissonance at "s'en all*er*," however, we have repeated Es gravely intoned at a slower tempo. The next line is murmured on but two notes, C and E, as the piano accompanies the *recitativo* with C and F chords:

Noël! listen to us, we no longer have our little wooden shoes:

From the close of this phrase to the last measure of the song, we have a steady buildup in the original tempo, ending with the defiant words

But give victory to the children of France!

which are supported by vigorous, full chords. The last sound is a proud A major chord with the E as the melody note, an unexpectedly "upbeat" ending to this poignant song. Note that the word "Noël," whose literal meaning includes Christmas and Christmas carol, is used to mean "Santa Claus," the spirit of Christmas, in the child's prayer.

BIBLIOGRAPHY

Aronson, Theo. *The Fall of the Third Napoleon.* Indianapolis: Bobbs-Merrill Co., 1970.

Barricelli, Jean-Pierre, and Weinstein, Leo. *Ernest Chausson.* Norman: University of Oklahoma Press, 1955.

Canaday, John. *Mainstreams of Modern Art: David to Picasso.* New York: Simon and Schuster, 1959.

Cate, Curtis. *George Sand.* New York: Avon Books, 1975.

Classiques Larousse, 9th ed. Paris: Librairie Larousse. *Théophile Gautier, Charles Baudelaire,* and *Verlaine et les poétes symbolistes.*

Cohn, Robert Greer. *The Writer's Way in France.* Philadelphia: University of Pennsylvania Press, 1960.

Encyclopedia Britannica, 1952. "French History" and "French Language."

Flaubert, Gustave. *Madame Bovary.* New York: Scribner's 1930.

Grove's Dictionary of Music and Musicians, 5th ed. New York: St. Martin's Press, 1954. "Chausson," "Debussy," "Duparc," and "Fauré."

Hugo, Victor. *Poésies Choisies.* New York: Brentano's, n.d.

Kinnell, Galway. *The Poems of François Villon.* Boston: Houghton Mifflin Co., 1965.

Maurois, André. *Olympio ou la vie de Victor Hugo.* Ottawa: Librairie Hachette, 1954.

Mellers, Wilfred. *Man and His Music,* Part 4: *Romanticism and the Twentieth Century.* New York: Schocken Books, 1969.

Myers, Rollo. *Emmanuel Chabrier and His Circle.* London: J. M. Dent and Sons Ltd., 1969.

Proust, Marcel. *Remembrance of Things Past (Swann's Way).* New York: Random House, 1970.

Vallas, Leon. *Claude Debussy.* New York: Dover Publications, 1973.

Vuillemin, Louis. *Gabriel Fauré et son oeuvre.* Paris: Durand, 1914.

Zuckerkandl, Victor. *The Sense of Music.* Princeton: Princeton University Press, 1959.

INDEX OF FIRST LINES

Fauré

A la très chère, à la très belle, 27
Alors qu'en tes mains de lumière, 149
L'âme d'une flûte soupire, 111
A mes pas le plus doux chemin, 126
A quoi, dans ce matin d'Avril, 156
L'aube blanche dit à mon rêve, 140
Automne au ciel brumeux, aux
  horizons navrants, 39
Avant que tu ne t'en ailles, pâle
  étoile de matin, 101
Avec son chant doux et plaintif, 127
Avril est de retour, 21
Avril, et c'est le point du jour, 152
Bientôt nous plongerons dans les
  froides ténèbres, 14
Calmes dans le demi-jour, 81
Ce soir, à travers le bonheur, 146
C'est le premier matin du monde, 132
C'est l'extase langoureuse, 87
Le ciel est, par dessus le toit, 113
Comme Dieu rayonne aujourd'hui, 138
Comme elle chante dans ma voix, 135
Comme tout meurt vite, la rose, 44
Dans un baiser l'onde au rivage, 7
Dans un parfum de roses blanches, 145
Dans un sommeil que charmait ton
  image, 25
Des jardins de la nuit s'envolent les
  étoiles, 55
Diane, Séléné lune de beau métal, 174
Donc, ce sera par un clair
  jour d'été, 103
Emporte ma folie, 57
Les donneurs de sérénades, 79
Etendue au seuil du bassin, 162
Gondolier du Rialto, 29
Heureux qui meurt ici, 72
L'homme a, pour payer sa rançon, 32
L'Hiver a cessé, la lumière est tiède, 106
Ici-bas tous les lilas meurent, 34
Il était une Fée, 53
Il m'est cher, Amour, le bandeau, 157

Il pleure dans mon coeur comme il
  pleut sur la ville, 75
J'aime tes yeux, j'aime ton front, 51
J'ai presque peur, en vérité, 99
J'allais par des chemins perfides, 96
Je dirai la Rose aux plis gracieux, 77
Je languis nuit et jour et ma peine est
  extrême, 108
Je me poserai sur ton coeur, 154
Je me suis embarqué sur un vaisseau
  qui danse, 173
Je mettrai mes deux mains sur ma
  bouche, pour taire, 129
J'étais triste et pensif, 41
Je veux que le matin l'ignore, 49
Le long du Quai, les grands vaisseaux, 45
La lune blanche luit dans les bois, 94
Lydia sur tes roses joues, 12
Ma belle amie est morte, 10
Ma pensée est un cygne harmonieux
  et sage, 160
La mer est infinie et mes rêves sont
  fous, 171
Mystiques barcarolles, 85
N'est-ce pas? nous irons, gais et lents,
  dans la voie, 104
Nocturne jardin tout rempli de
  silence, 166
Notre amour est chose légère, 47
La nuit descend du haut des cieux, 64
La nuit, sur le grand mystère, 66
L'oiseau dans le buisson, 20
O mort, poussière d'étoiles, 148
O toi que berce un rêve enchanteur, 8
La pauvre fleur disait au papillon
  céleste, 1
Pendant qu'ils étaient partis pour la
  guerre, 169
Pleurons nos chagrins, chacun le
  nôtre, 70
Puisque l'aube grandit, puique voici
  l'aurore, 93

Puisque Mai tout en fleurs dans les
  prés nous réclame, 2
Quand la fleur du soleil, la rose
  de Lahor, 109
Quand tu plonge tes yeux dans mes
  yeux, 151
Que me fait toute la terre, 130
Que tu es simple et claire, 141
Quoique tes yeux la voient pas, 155
Ramure aux rumeurs amollies, 117
Roses ardentes, 137
Les roses d'Ispahan, 62
Une Sainte en son auréole, 91
S'asseoir tous deux au bord du flot
  qui passe, 30
Sentiers où l'herbe se balance, 18
Seuls, tous deux, ravis, chantant,
  comme on s'aime, 4
Si la voix d'un enfant peut monter
  jusqu'à vous, 89
S'il est un charmant gazon, 15

Si tu demandes quelque soir, 67
Si tu veux savoir ma belle, 23
Soeur des Soeurs tisseuses de
  violettes, 168
Sur la mer voilée, 120
Sur l'eau bleue et profonde, 5
Ta rose de pourpre à ton clair soleil, 35
Toute, avec sa robe et ses fleurs, 159
Tremble argenté, tilleul, bouleau, 123
Vaisseaux, nous vous aurons aimés en
  pure perte, 176
Veilles-tu, ma senteur de soleil, 142
Veux-tu qu'au beau pays des rêves, 59
Voici des fruits, des fleurs, des feuilles
  et des branches, 83
Voici que les jardins de la nuit vont
  fleurir, 116
Votre âme est un paysage choisi, 69
Vous me demandez de me taire, 42
Voyageur, où vas-tu, marchant dans
  l'or vibrant de la poussière? 37

Chausson

Bois chère aux ramiers, pleurez doux
  feuillages, 178
Bon chevalier masqué qui chevauche
  en silence, 232
La caravane humaine, au Sahara
  du monde, 202
C'est la fillette aux yeux cernés, 223
Dans la forêt chauve et rouillée, 182
Ecoutez la chanson bien douce, 230
Epouse au front lumineux, 234
Fuis mon âme, fuis! 225
Il est mort ayant bien souffert,
  Madame, 229
Ils ne savent plus où se poser ces
  baisers, 213
J'ai perdu la forêt, la plaine, 198
Loin de moi, loin de moi ces lèvres
  que j'adore, 228
La lune blanche luit dans les bois, 194
Mon amour d'antan, vous souvenez-
  vous? 189
Ne crois pas que les morts soient
  morts! 204

Nos sentiers aimés s'en vont
  refleurir, 190
Nos souvenirs, toutes ces choses, 192
La nuit était pensive et ténébreuse, 188
O cet ennui bleu dans le coeur! 211
O Cigale, née avec les beaux jours, 200
O les passions en allées, 215
O serre au milieu des forêts! 208
Les pâles heures, sous la lune, 219
Les papillons couleur de neige, 180
Partons en barque sur la mer, 183
Quand les anges se sont perdus, 220
Quand ton sourire me surprit, 179
Sous vos sombres chevelures, petites
  fées, 236
Le temps des lilas et le temps des
  roses, 206
Tes grands yeux doux semblent des
  îles, 196
Le vert colibri, le roi des collines, 186
Vous voyez, Seigneur, ma misère! 217
Les yeux baissés, rougissante et
  candide, 184

Duparc

Agite, bon cheval, ta crinière
  fuyante, 247
Au pays où se fait la guerre, 270
Connaissez-vous la blanche tombe, 264
Dans ton coeur dort un clair de lune, 239
De sa dent soudaine et vorace, 257
Etoile dont la beauté luit, 256
Une fois, terrassé par un puissant
  breuvage, 252
Le connais-tu, ce radieux pays, 241

L'herbe est molle au sommeil, 261
J'ai longtemps habité sous de vastes
  portiques, 268
Mon enfant, ma soeur, 249
Ne jamais la voir ni l'entendre, 245
Oh! ne murmurez pas son nom! 266
Pour que le vent te les apporte, 259
Si j'étais, ô mon amoureuse, 243
Sur un lys pâle mon coeur dort, 255

L'âme évaporée et souffrante, 322
Auprès de cette grotte sombre, 372, 376
Le bon Pierrot que la foule contemple, 284
Calmes dans le demi-jour, 337
C'est l'extase langoureuse, 307
Le ciel d'hiver, si doux, si triste, si dormant, 294
Cloches chrétiennes pour les matines, 326
Crois mon conseil chère Climène, 376
Dame du ciel, régente terrienne, 382
Dans l'ennui si désolement vert, 349
Dans le vieux parc solitaire et glacé, 367
Des trous à son pourpoint vermeil, 290
Dimanche sur les villes, 352
Les donneurs de sérénades, 279
L'échelonnement des haies, 335
Faulse beauté, qui tant me couste cher, 379
Les feuilles s'ouvraient sur le bord des branches, 324
Fut-il jamais douceur de coeur pareille, 288
Les hauts talons luttaient avec les longues jupes, 363
Il m'a dit: "Cette nuit, j'ai rêvé, 357
Il pleure dans mon coeur, 310
Je regardais dans le jardin, 327
Je tremble voyant ton visage, 378
Le long des blés que la brise, 277
Le long du bois couvert de givre, je marchais, 360
Lorsque au soleil couchant les rivières sont roses, 276
La lune s'attristait. Des séraphins en pleurs, 285
Mère des souvenirs, maîtresse des maîtresses, 296

La mer est plus belle, 330
Mon âme vers ton front où rêve, ô calme soeur, 389
Nous aurons des lits pleins d'odeurs légères, 305
Nous n'avons plus de maisons! 395
La nuit a des douceurs de femme, 342
Nuit d'étoiles, sous tes voiles, 274
L'ombre des arbes dans la rivière embrumée, 312
O rêveuse, pour que je plonge, 392
Pierrot qui n'a rien d'un Clitandre, 281
Pour ce que Plaisance est morte, 374
Pour le jour des Hyacinthes, 355
Princesse! à jalouser le destin d'une Hébé, 390
Quoy qu'on tient belles langagières, 386
Les roses étaient toutes rouges, 320
Scaramouche et Pulcinella, 341
Si j'étais le Zéphyr ailé, 287
Sois sage, ô ma Douleur, et tiens-toi plus tranquille, 303
Le son du cor s'afflige vers les bois, 332
Sur la mer les crépuscules tombent, 345
Le temps a laissié son manteau, 370
Tes beaux yeux sont las, pauvre amante! 301
Tournez, tournez, bons chevaux de bois, 314
Un vieux faune de terre cuite, 365
Voici des fruits, des fleurs, des feuilles et des branches, 318
Voici que le printemps, ce fils léger d'avril, 292
Voici venir les temps où vibrant sur sa tige, 299
Votre âme est un paysage choisi, 283, 339